PERIMETERS OF DEMOCRACY

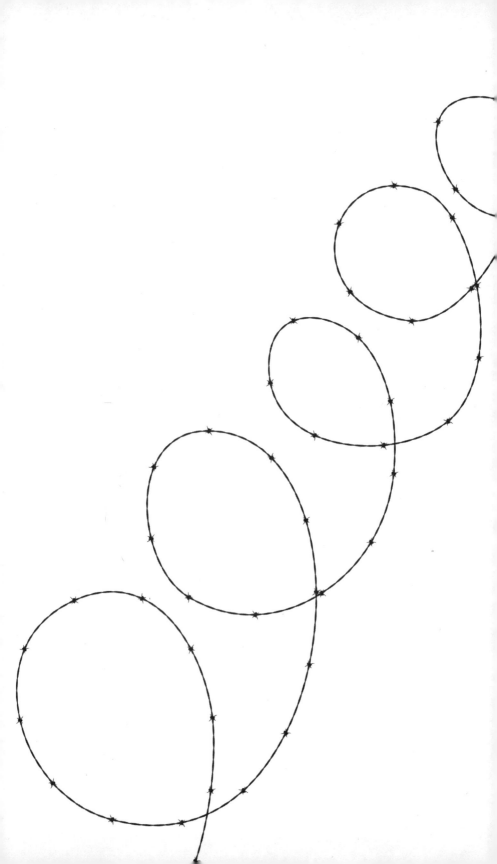

PERIMETERS
OF
DEMOCRACY

INVERSE UTOPIAS AND THE
WARTIME SOCIAL LANDSCAPE
IN THE AMERICAN WEST

HEATHER FRYER

University of Nebraska Press | Lincoln and London

Library of Congress Cataloging-
in-Publication Data
Fryer, Heather.
Perimeters of democracy : inverse utopias and the wartime social landscape in
the American West / Heather Fryer.
p. cm.
Includes bibliographical references and
index.
ISBN 978-0-8032-2033-1 (cloth : alk.
paper)
1. Government-controlled communities—United States. 2. World War,
1939–1945—United States. 3. Internal
security—United States—History—20th
century. 4. Klamath Indian Reservation
(Or.)—Social conditions—20th century.
5. Los Alamos (N.M.)—Social conditions—20th century. 6. Topaz (Utah)—
Social conditions—20th century.
7. Vanport (Or.)—Social conditions—
20th century. 8. West (U.S.)—Social
conditions—20th century. I. Title.
D769.8.G68F79 2010
307.770978'09044—dc22
2009047713

Set in Quadraat by Kim Essman.
Designed by Nathan Putens.

Contents

Illustrations

Acknowledgments

This book got its start in a graduate seminar in urban history taught in 1997 by Marilynn Johnson, whose book *The Second Gold Rush: Oakland and the East Bay during World War II* lit up my historical imagination. War mobilization and the complicated social geography of the American West became instant fascinations. So too did the commonalities between Oakland and the lost city of Vanport, Oregon, which resided in a hazy place in the historical memories of Pacific Northwesterners.

This fascination quickly became a dissertation topic under Lynn's direction. When she gently suggested a comparative study of Vanport and another community (probably meaning *one*), I proposed comparing five before narrowing it down to four. If my insistence on studying a bunch of places I knew next to nothing about made Lynn doubt my common sense, she never showed it. Always generous with her knowledge, wisdom, and time, she helped me build the foundation for *Perimeters of Democracy* and for my practice as a historian more generally. Cynthia Lynn Lyerly and Kevin Kenny, as members of my dissertation committee, pressed me to bring real precision to this comparative analysis. The History Department at Boston College also lent its support through a dissertation fellowship that funded the greater part of the research for *Perimeters of Democracy*, along with an Albert J. Beveridge Grant from the American Historical Association.

The Creighton University College of Arts and Sciences and my colleagues in the History Department provided everything from release time to reorganize the manuscript to the moral support necessary for seeing a long project through. Julie Fox saved the day before a deadline more than once, helping me get overwhelming piles of paper into the mail on time. I am tremendously grateful to the Reinert Alumni Library staff, which did a thousand favors and worked a few miracles to keep my research going.

Sustained research can be a rough road, so I was fortunate to find so many brilliant librarians and archivists across the country to help smooth the way. The staff of the Los Alamos Historical Museum and Archives was helpful and hospitable, as were the professionals at the Bancroft Library who went out of their way to help me locate documents and illustrations. Todd Kepple and Lynn Jeche at the Klamath County Museum located Klamath Reservation photographs and made them available to me in Omaha, and the National Archives Pacific Coast branch in Seattle helped me navigate Record Group 75, even in the immediate aftermath of the 6.0 earthquake that brought my first research day to an unsettling halt. The Truman Presidential Library, and Dennis Bilger in particular, took extraordinary time and care in locating valuable material on all four communities. I also relied heavily on the resources of the Multnomah County Public Library in Portland, Oregon, especially the beautiful Sterling Room for Writers, where much of the first draft was written.

The Oregon Historical Society (OHS) deserves special mention, not only for giving me a start as a volunteer researcher from 1992–95 but also for allowing me to use their reading room as my home base for two years. Not only did they act as real partners in my research, bringing to light sources I would never know to look for, they were wonderful people to spend time with.

OHS is also where I met Sieglinde Smith, librarian and treasured friend to many historians, who gave me my first lessons in archival research. I am also indebted to Franklin Brummett and Barbara Alatorre, who after agreeing to sit for just a single interview with me became long-term consultants on Vanport and the Klamath Reservation, respectively. They offered valuable perspectives as independent historians and former residents of both communities.

My interviews with Regina Flowers, Jim and Fumi Onchi, Vern Marshall, Diane Norstrand, Ramona Rank, George Saslow, and June Schumann, while brief, helped me see the connections between the four inverse utopias. Where most people would ignore an inquiry about their lives from a stranger, they were tremendously generous in sharing their time and their recollections.

I am deeply grateful to my editor at the University of Nebraska Press, Heather Lundine, who has seen this project through its transformation from four discrete case studies to its current thematic form (which, frankly, is so much better). She, Bridget Barry, and Joeth Zucco led the exciting transformation from manuscript to book, making the publishing process a truly rewarding experience. Christopher Steinke's keen and insightful copyediting brought great clarity to the final version of the text. I also want to thank the anonymous readers whose comments and critiques helped immensely in the conceptual and narrative development of the manuscript. The final product is far richer for your generous input.

I could not have completed this project without the love and support of my family and friends, who at times probably felt like this project had taken over their lives as well as mine. Tracy Leavelle, my partner in all things, was ever ready with an editor's pencil, a cup of tea, or a minute to talk through a fuzzy idea. Amy Bográn shared half of a studio apartment when I had just a pocket full of fellowship money and two years of research ahead of me. My father passed away in 2004, but his love of history has made its mark on this volume. My mother, who probably thought she would be done shuttling kids from place to place years ago, was still dropping her thirty-something daughter off at the library during my visits to her home in Oregon. Visits home never turned all work and no play: my sisters, Holly and Stephanie, reminded me to take much-needed down time, and my nephew and nieces—Patrick, Sophie, and Olivia—were always right there with the comic relief, reminding their occasionally frazzled auntie why searching the past to chart new possibilities for the future is well worth the labor.

PERIMETERS OF DEMOCRACY

INTRODUCTION

Discovering the Inverse-Utopian West

Hard as it is to believe, there is a ghost town in the center of the Portland International Raceway. The foundations are vaguely discernible at the center of the track, and the stories are etched into the collective memory of lifelong Portlanders. For most, the details are vague: Vanport City (later shortened to "Vanport") was one of the many miracles of war production in 1942, built on 648 acres to house about 40,000 shipyard workers on a twenty-four-hour production schedule. It was rumored among Portlanders during the war that this motley crew of "Americans all" led a wild life in their out-of-the-way enclave on the floodplain: they drank, danced, plotted revolution, and even encouraged whites and blacks to mingle. But just as quickly as the "miracle city" rose to keep the rabble in the shipyards and away from Portland, it vanished under surging floodwaters in 1948. Now, the roar of engines and cheers of racing fans make it hard to envision rows of government-issue apartments clustered around government-run stores, theaters, day-care centers, schools, patrols, bus routes, and all the other small-town amenities. It is even harder to imagine that seven to fifteen people (some say more) drowned in this place while awaiting an evacuation order that never came. Perhaps the hardest thing of all to comprehend, however, is that the federal government could make the extraordinary effort to build such an elaborate planned community in 1943, only to abandon it—and its thousands of residents—in 1948.

Until recently, Vanport lived on in the reminiscences of former residents and their Portland neighbors, who watched the government's "miracle" from a safe distance. In addition to being Oregon's second largest city in 1943, Vanport was also home to the state's largest African American community, making this government outpost an enduring landmark in the local history of regional race relations. Depending on the critic, Vanport was a textbook example of the excesses of the New Deal welfare state, a miraculous technology for labor efficiency, or a measure of how thoroughly the government converted the home front for war. Still others saw the founding of Vanport as a protective measure to prevent Portland from being overrun by a wave of newcomers and "undesirables." Vanporters kept to themselves until the flood washed them into Portland, expanding the black community several times over. No matter how one tells the story of Vanport, the government's hand in shaping the social landscape by creating this tightly controlled space is always the driving theme.

In Japanese American communities in Portland, San Francisco, and elsewhere, people tell a different story about life inside remote, government-run wartime communities. In 1942–43, as Vanport materialized on the Columbia River flood plain, the War Relocation Authority (WRA) threw up ten "relocation centers"—or concentration camps—in desolate areas of the West.[1] They, like Vanport, would be fully self-sustaining enclaves whose populations would rival those of the region's largest cities. Millard County, Utah, for instance, became the temporary home to the state's fifth largest city, the Central Utah Relocation Center. The Center, better known as "Topaz," was placed on 640 acres of scrub desert, where roughly 8,100 internees lived in neatly lined barracks poised lightly on the land. In addition to unit after unit of cramped housing, the government equipped Topaz with hospitals, schools, a newspaper office, and mess halls that served as churches, movie houses, and community meeting spaces. While they were built for very different purposes, Topaz and Vanport shared more than their size or amenities. Their built environments both displayed a government-issue uniformity that projected regimentation rather than the mad chaos of building stemming from the easy money, unfettered optimism, and fervent individualism that generated the great western boomtowns.

The carefully arranged, demountable units at both Vanport and Topaz appeared ever ready to be whisked away upon orders from Washington, along with the people the government brought to live there. The barbed wire and armed guards encircling the all-Japanese desert city signaled that security, surveillance, and social control were the raisons d'être for this self-sustaining town. At first glance, the barbed wire, "yellow-peril" rhetoric, and desolation of the internment camps make any similarity to Vanport seem unlikely. But the government's decision to solve its wartime problems by building "cities" instead of urban housing projects and prisons was an intriguing common thread. Placing Vanport into this broad but vaguely defined context raised the possibility that, despite its five-year history, the city was part of a larger historical picture that included open spaces, national security, the welfare state, demographic management, and the construction of "American communities" — both concretely and in the abstract. Thin as this thread might appear to be, it is clearly woven into a larger history of people, place, the federal presence, and the widely divergent experiences of being "American" in the wartime West.

Setting the two communities within a collective biography failed to reveal the full range of connections between them. A rigid comparative analysis missed some of the particularities of both places and did not help explain how their idiosyncrasies fit into larger narratives — and counternarratives — of "the American experience." As strikingly similar as Vanport and Topaz were, there were also significant differences between them. It serves no purpose to warp the historical record by suggesting that the residents' experiences were fundamentally the same, just as it is not useful to make totalizing statements about "the" social history of the West or advance conspiratorial notions that the federal government hatched a hundred-year plot to suppress minorities on the far side of the Rockies.

Writing two separate histories of Vanport and Topaz is certainly not necessary, as scholars from a range of disciplines have developed a rich body of literature on the particular communities, ethnic groups affected by them, and local conflicts and their manifestations as individual grievances with Washington. Instead of flattening these political, economic, and social histories to fit a rigid analytical construct, they are set within a single constellation that captures the broad context of this collective history, offers a fuller assessment of the significance of security towns to the West as a whole, and accounts for the uniqueness of each separate place while articulating the commonalities between them. The constellatory scheme, which is gaining renewed currency within the field of cultural studies, has its origins in Theodor Adorno's assertion that placing objects categorized separately into a single frame "illuminates the specific side of the object, the side which to a classifying procedure is either a matter of indifference or a burden." Far from presenting an incoherent mash-up of people, plywood, and government agencies, this constellatory comparative approach highlights "the historical dynamic hidden within objects" whose various properties "[exceed] the classifications imposed upon them." In other words, the constellation lends complexity, not simplicity, to the individual and collective histories of federally run wartime communities.[2]

Vanport and Topaz were obvious selections for such a constellation with their noted similarities and because of what they might reveal about race, class, geography, and the differential restrictions on civil liberties during World War II. But race was only part of the story. The secret laboratories of the Manhattan Project required fully developed townsites for reasons of both efficiency and security. Its processing plants at Hanford, Washington, and Oak Ridge, Tennessee, resembled Vanport's labor-efficiency system. Its third facility, hidden in the desert at Los Alamos, was a high-security installation where several hundred world-class scientists disappeared in the race against Germany to develop the world's first atomic bomb. The government put most residents in housing units that were dead ringers for Vanport apartments. Los Alamos also included a post exchange (PX), a community center, a hospital, and space for a school that the scientists' wives had to run themselves. These amenities were the only ones available because residents were not allowed to enter and leave the community freely. The top-secret town sat upon fifty-four thousand acres of land as desolate as the alkali desert at Topaz and bound just as tightly by armed guards and barbed wire.

In addition to widening the geographic sweep of federal community building, Los Alamos was one of the few civilian enclaves populated with white elites (though many were émigrés from Axis nations and Jewish Americans). Although the reasons for the secrecy and security surrounding the bomb project were abundantly clear, it is curious that a group of renowned scientists and their families lived within the same stark surroundings as the war workers and internees. Topaz provided evidence enough that racial anxiety was central to federal demographic management—the process by which federal agencies gathered data on individuals, aggregated them into groups, marked them as potentially dangerous, and situated them physically in carefully demarcated spaces in calculated proximity to the general population. The purpose behind such careful management had less to do with known security concerns (individuals who engaged in criminal acts that compromised national security were, like most criminals, identified, arrested, charged, tried, and sentenced) than with creating the illusion that the government had internal dangers under control. It also was part of the larger, more practical picture of demographic management, which sought to move available workers to areas with clear, concrete labor shortages. Reservations, internment camps, and public housing were always near and porous enough that resident labor could be deployed at the pleasure of the supervising government agency.

In most cases, "race" was the marker for "danger," but the presence of Los Alamos suggested that less obvious concerns, such as the tendency toward eccentricity, pacifism, and radical politics on university campuses, might also be at play. Franklin D. Roosevelt's expansion of the welfare state as well as his appointment of Jews to numerous prominent federal offices led Americans to rank Jews as the third greatest menace to the nation in February 1942; they were "less menacing" than the Japanese (ranked highest) and Germans, but considerably "more menacing" than blacks. When the townsite was under construction, in 1942, most Americans saw the Jewish population as eternally foreign, with 15 percent favoring their expulsion as a means of curbing their "excessive power" in the United States.[3] In the unknown city of Los Alamos, public opinion had little bearing on the surveillance and security structures. Still, Commanding General Leslie Groves and FBI Commissioner J. Edgar Hoover maintained longstanding suspicions of "reds" and "godless longhairs" that made intrusive surveillance structures as natural a part of project planning as laboratory equipment and housing provisions. The degree to which restrictions on personal liberties stemmed from concrete security concerns or reflected other anxieties about the national, ethnic, and political profiles of the most powerful Los Alamosans is not immediately apparent. In light of the histories of the other three communities, however, this question clearly demands answers. This demand gained urgency with the espionage charges against Los Alamos scientist Wen Ho Lee in 1999, which revealed the intersections between racial anxiety, national security, and civil liberties. Although there was some indication that Lee, a naturalized Taiwanese American, mishandled some computer tapes, the evidence of espionage was slim, and the rush to place him in pretrial solitary confinement was tragically swift. Ultimately, the judge in the Lee case apologized for the botched legal proceedings, but the remedy came too late, as it did at Topaz, Vanport, and dozens of communities like them. Yellow-peril rhetoric swirled through the press, along with revelations that the Lee case accelerated the departure of talented scientists of color already angered by the persistence of institutional racism at the Los Alamos National Laboratory. Despite the apology, Lee sustained irreparable damage: he could not regain the lost time with his family and at his job, his reputation, or his full capacity to live and work as he had before his arrest. The continued tension between security, profiling, and fidelity to the principles of American freedom from the mid-twentieth century into the twenty-first makes the history of Los Alamos a critical component of this larger constellation of federally managed wartime communities.[4]

The Klamath Indian Reservation in southern Oregon extends this history in the other direction by drawing the chronology to the nineteenth-century origins of federal community building in the West. Tempting as it was to limit this study to World War II, it was impossible to ignore century-old federal settlements from the "Indian wars" that sit alongside their twentieth-century counterparts. (Los Alamos and some of the WRA relocation centers bordered or were built within the boundaries of Indian reservations.) Until Pearl Harbor, the "Indian wars" had been the last time Americans feared a military invasion of "their" West. Clashes between settlers pursuing America's "manifest destiny" and southern Oregon tribes defending their homelands from white invaders brought escalating bloodshed in the 1840s and 1850s. While it was well understood in Washington that American settlers provoked most of these incidents, federal officials received compelling pleas from U.S. citizens for protection. A settler named "Rogue River Citizen" complained in 1855 that "we must tamely endure the presence and almost daily visits of the most cold-blooded murderers and midnight assassins that our country has ever been cursed with," and that the government appeared to be more interested in protecting the Indians than fulfilling its constitutional obligation to provide for the common defense of its own citizens.[5]

Like many Oregon settlers, Rogue River Citizen called for the government to use the newly established reservations to incarcerate the Native populations and worry less about their protection than their neutralization. Laying down the gauntlet, Rogue River concluded cynically, "Perhaps it is wrong to expect Uncle Sam's men to fight, for it would be a loss to government should they get killed."[6] In less than a decade, nearly all the southern Oregon tribes were confined to reservations where, as an alternative to extinction, they would be trained to live as American citizens. If all went according to plan, the U.S. government would transform Indian "hostiles" into docile, loyal Americans.[7]

Despite its common origin in the wartime West, it is important to note that the Klamath Indian Reservation has a remarkably different history than Topaz, Vanport, and Los Alamos. First and foremost, the Office of Indian Affairs (known colloquially as the Indian Bureau) established the reservation as a permanent homeland for the Klamaths, Modocs, and Yahooskin Snake Paiutes in a treaty ratified by Congress in 1866. In exchange for ceding approximately twenty million acres of their ancestral lands and "acknowledg[ing] their dependence upon the Government of the United States," the three tribes would share 2.2 million acres and an array of government goods and services, from food, clothing, and tools to saw mills, schools, and medical care—all administered by the Indian Bureau. Army units stationed at nearby Fort Klamath would keep whites from encroaching on Klamath lands and prevent Indians from crossing the reservation boundary.

Within this stable, segregatory perimeter, however, the Klamath reservation looks remarkably similar to its twentieth-century counterparts. Officials from the Indian bureau believed they created a replica of an American small town, where democratic institutions, structured work routines, controlled development of tribal assets, and the habits of Christian living would transform tribal members from "hostile Indians" into "good Americans." It was a great show of faith in the power of America's institutions to instill the values of individual freedom, democracy, free enterprise, and Christian morality in even the most resistant subjects, Americanizing the frontier one person at a time.[8]

The most significant event in postwar Klamath history, however, came in 1954, when the reservation was dissolved under the Klamath Termination Act. Termination, which sought to accelerate the process of assimilation through rapid detribalization, had been on the agendas of the War Relocation Authority, the Federal Public Housing Authority, and the Atomic Energy Commission for several years. Although the federal government built the four communities at different times and with different purposes in mind, it sought to rid itself of all four at the conclusion of World War II. The War Relocation Authority resolved to close Topaz and the other nine camps as soon as possible, starting in 1943. Vanport's future had been hotly debated since its dedication day, and the issues remained unresolved when the flood hit in 1948. For many, the disaster settled the question of how to encourage residents to reestablish their lives outside the project. Only Los Alamos was slated to remain, but the Atomic Energy Commission insisted upon a slow but steady conversion from a "communistic" colony to a more open society of independent individuals. This constellation measures the significance of both Topaz, Vanport, and Los Alamos's common starting point and the government's near-simultaneous termination of all four communities between 1943 and 1953, when even the Klamath Reservation was erased from the map.

After assembling this four-community constellation, situated within a 120-year span in the history of the American West, I spent two years traveling the West, poring over archival material, visiting whatever remained of the four communities, and interviewing former residents along the way. From the multitude of facts, figures, anecdotes, rumors, reminiscences, and questions come a set of persistent, if disparate themes: fear, suspicion, and stereotyping; displacement, protective custody, and isolation; thin walls, lost privacy, cold nights, and bad food; regimentation, surveillance, ritualized citizenship, and limited economic horizons; powerlessness, anger, dependency, and stigmatization. It was evident that relationships of some sort existed between the four communities, but the nature and substance of these relationships, their meaning, and their larger significance was far less apparent.

The unique histories of Klamath, Topaz, Vanport, and Los Alamos are central to the story of the changing social landscape of the mid-century West, and while the order in which they were founded is somewhat telling, a straight chronology does not reach the most penetrating historical questions. Instead of recounting four histories and connecting them in the conclusion, this study is organized thematically, according to the phases of a consistent, if occasionally imperfect, pattern that shaped the histories of these government-run, high-security enclaves.[9] In keeping with Adorno's concept of constellatory analysis, the chapters focus on the creation of these controlled spaces as security structures, the chasm between the American values the government promoted in these reformative communities and the authoritarian measures it practiced, the shrill dissonances of living as government wards in a region characterized by its independent spirit, and the long-term consequences of inverse-utopian lives on residents' experiences as American citizens. In addition to revealing numerous points of comparison, this constellation illuminates a consistent (if occasionally imperfect) pattern within the life spans of all four communities.

The pattern connecting these four places began in the anxious aftermath of an attack on the home front, with citizens feeling powerless against an intangible enemy and the government feeling pressure to make a *visible* defensive act. In response to public pressure and well-founded concerns about the handful of likely saboteurs on the home front, the executive branch hastily constructed a profile of the "internal enemy." Instead of singling out dangerous individuals, it cast a wide net over Americans with perceived ethnic or ideological ties to foreign threats, thus creating thousands of "enemies" with faces, bodies, and profiles that enabled officials to watch, detain, discipline, or reform them. Government agencies rationalized subsequent measures to criminalize, isolate, and detain "enemies" and deny them fundamental rights as a preventative security measure, in which the government invades privacy, restricts movement, or confines individuals first and asks questions later. In the great American tradition of self-correction, questions of ethics and constitutional law were revisited when the danger had passed and such self-reflection became "safe" again. But the correction did not come before long-term damage was done to affected individuals, and Americans, coming to their senses, were faced with a shameful blot on the historical record. Yet Americans have been quick to forget these historical lessons in the face of renewed threats from "barbarians," in the form of vaguely identified tyrants, savages, hostiles, saboteurs, Communists, terrorists, or, to use President George W. Bush's early-twenty-first-century terminology, "evildoers." Psychologists Robert Reber and Robert Kelley, in their cross-cultural study of enmification (the psychological term for developing a profile of "the enemy"), contend that the creation of an identifiable, visible, and manageable enemy is not confined to aggressor nations. They argue instead that "the dangerous reality is that enmification can and does get loose in human affairs and, once it does, it impinges on the peace-loving no less than on the warlike."[10]

The Historical Backdrop

This historical pattern of attack, enmification, confinement, Americanization, disposal, and discontent emerges against the backdrop of the history of westward expansion and Thomas Jefferson's call to build an "Empire for Liberty" that would be a beacon to the world, fulfilling America's historic destiny as the agent of individual liberty. The open spaces along the western frontier became the postrevolutionary proving ground for the nation's claims as the leading agent of global progress and human freedom. Jefferson inspired the new nation to build "such an empire for liberty as [the earth] has never surveyed since the creation" by transforming the "empty" region into the terrain of the independent, wholly self-sufficient yeoman farmer.[11] Journalist John O'Sullivan's admonition to go "onward to the fulfillment of our mission — to the entire development of the principle of our organization — freedom of conscience, freedom of person, freedom of trade and business pursuits, universality of freedom and equality" was, and still is, readily accepted as America's "high destiny," "future history," and "blessed mission to the nations of the world."[12]

The confluence of American nationalism, the demands of growing capital markets, and the rise of physical anthropology and racial pseudoscience provided the conceptual pieces for an intricate logic of national unity and racial difference that put white supremacy in the service of shared prosperity and human liberty. One of the most influential tracts on race and human capability was Samuel Morton's *Crania Americana* (1839), a work of physical anthropology that forwarded a racialized social hierarchy based on the relative size of white, black, Native, and Asian skulls. As president of the Academy of Natural Sciences and professor of medicine at the University of Pennsylvania, Morton influenced a generation of social scientists who believed in the evolutionary potential of the "darker races" to become more like — if not fully equal — to whites. To scientists and the general public, the numbers described more than brain size; they indicated the potential for various non-white peoples to become fully self-determining individuals and contributing members of society. The most significant measure, however, was the degree of "fitness for self-government" attainable for each race. Caucasians, with "large and oval" skulls boasting "full and elevated" anterior portions, had heads outfitted to "attain the highest intellectual endowments." In addition to giving humanity its "fairest inhabitants," Caucasians had the ingenuity to settle across the earth, bringing the benefits of their highly evolved intelligence to the smaller-headed, darker races.[13] Physical anthropologists debated the finer points of taxonomy and the evolutionary process, but Caucasians' place at the top of the racial hierarchy was considered an incontrovertible scientific fact. This understanding of "race" permeated public discourse as well, remaining in the popular imagination long after scientists questioned the validity of craniology's pseudoscientific methods.

Morton's measurements placed Asians next on the hierarchy as "olive-skinned" people whose intellect was "ingenious, imitative, and highly susceptible to cultivation."[14] In the evolutionist terms of the day, this meant that Asians could learn to be "civilized" by imitating their white superiors, whose influence would spur their evolution.[15] Morton noted, however, that when compared to the "monkey race," Asians were similarly unable to pay attention to any one thing long enough to carry it through effectively—like industrial innovation or democratic self-governance.[16] Although the "less civilized" races could unleash amoral bloodlust without provocation, Asian ingenuity and susceptibility to cultivation posed a threat of a different kind. Unlike people of African or indigenous American ancestry, Asians were savage and intelligent enough to imitate American technologies to use against them. This anxiety became a common trope in turn-of-the-century popular fiction and a persistent stereotype of the Japanese in the wake of their stunning naval victory in the Russo-Japanese War.[17]

Native Americans differed from Asians in more than their "brown" hue. Their smaller skulls made them "averse to cultivation" and placed them in a "continued childhood" from infancy to old age.[18] These child-like people were, on the flipside, "restless, revengeful, and fond of war," with a "demoniac love of slaughter."[19] Like Asians, Indians were "crafty," but they were "incapable of a continued process of reasoning on abstract subjects" and ate foods that were "disgusting" and "unclean."[20] These "eternal children" needed protection and discipline, lest their violent tendencies get out of control, or lower-order whites lead them toward corruption instead of civilization. Africans, the smallest-skulled population and at the lowest tier of Morton's racial hierarchy, were also "fond of warlike enterprises," and their social institutions tended toward "superstition and cruelty."[21] They were intellectually unsuited to invention, but good at imitating "the mechanic arts."[22] This, combined with their ease in adapting to different circumstances and "yield[ing] to their destiny," made them well suited for slave labor.[23] Despite being cast as childlike, they were only conditionally "innocent"; they were also uncontrollably violent and without moral restraint, threatening social chaos and a tyranny of savagery and bloodshed.

This social order, combined with the notion of divine providence, made American colonization of Native lands, exploitation and social rejection of immigrants, and forcible expansion into Asian markets consonant with the liberating mission of civilization, Christianization, and expanding "free trade." Those who took their proper place in society and complied with the tenets of American civilization would be included in the American body politic to the extent they were considered capable. Those who were incapable of self-government remained eternal children, of sorts, who were reasonably placed under the restrictive protection of their "civilized betters" so they were not crushed under the wheels of progress and, more importantly, did not impede its course. This elevated level of civilization, from which peace, prosperity, and God's continued favor would follow, lay at the heart of the utopian vision of westward expansion.

Even after the reservation system put Indians at a safe distance from white settlements, westerners and Washington insiders remained anxious about real and imagined threats to the newly established social order along the American frontier. For all the utopian rhetoric of the West as the providentially bestowed "magnificent domain of space and time," where the "noblest temple ever dedicated to the worship of . . . the Sacred and the True" would bring the nation of nations under the rule of "God's natural and moral law of equality" and the "law of brotherhood," white Americans held nightmarish visions of racial disorder that brought an end to liberty and civilization.[24] In them, the "uncivilized races" used their powers of imitation to fashion American weapons and unleash their warlike characteristics against white Americans. In these scenarios, the Empire for Liberty was overrun by barbarian tyranny. Americans perceived this open, distant, freshly civilized region to be vulnerable to "Japanification" through trans-Pacific migration, enemy infiltration through Mexico, and domination by such "foreign" political movements as the American Communist Party.

Popular fiction about Asian fifth columnists destroying western civilization appeared as early as 1879, and more would follow in the 1890s with the closing of the western frontier and the acquisition of Hawaii and the Philippines.[25] Japan's real attack on the Pacific fleet at Pearl Harbor hit close to home, unleashing well-developed images of a Japanese apocalypse into American public life. As the facts of the attack melded with images from paperback novels of Japanese with super-weapons laying waste to California, Idaho, and Montana, the exotic charm of Japantowns gave way to perceptions of busy swarms of "Japanese spies and saboteurs, firmly entrenched through their Black Dragon Leagues and other Tokyo-controlled organizations in Japanese American communities on the West Coast." The FBI found no evidence to support claims of Japanese disloyalty, but that fact did little to alter the public's impression that Japanese immigrants and their citizen children had paved the way for an invasion of the California coast. So while the American West has been synonymous with power and freedom in the popular imagination, the military was regularly concerned that the region could be lost and that America's manifest destiny, in which American civilization marched west, would remain unfulfilled. Yielding to domination from the East was as unthinkable as surrendering Oregon Territory to the Indians.[26]

President Franklin D. Roosevelt responded to Japan's infamous attack by declaring war on December 8, 1941. With Executive Order 9066, issued on February 19, 1942, the government barred all persons of Japanese descent from the Western Defense Command, which encompassed much of Arizona, California, Oregon, and Washington. As with the Indians, all "known hostiles" on the FBI's Custodial Detention Index (the secret listing of individuals slated for immediate arrest in the event of a national emergency) were summarily detained, while the remaining 120,000 members of the Japanese American community, having committed neither crimes nor acts of disloyalty, were removed to isolated reservations operated by the Department of the Interior—the agency in charge of the Office of Indian Affairs.

These actions repeated the pattern within the federal government of palliating wartime anxieties by fashioning profiles of the "enemy" based on shared, immutable characteristics. Frequently, the characteristic was "race," a biological and cultural fiction that whites rewrote and represented to accord with every new threat. Religion, political affiliation, and being a social outlier of some sort were less visible, malleable, and highly charged than "race," but they still figured prominently in drawing "visible" profiles of "the enemy." Attaching threatening connotations to the outward appearance of a "dangerous" group allowed a panicky nation to "see" its attackers and take comfort as the military and law enforcement agencies collected them in a wide net, took them a safe distance away, and even isolated them in confined spaces for supervision at all times. This supposedly dangerous population was subject to discipline and punishment if they attempted to inflict any harm on America. For the majority whose containment was purely preventative, government-run communities would aid their evolution toward true Americanism. Placed within a *tableau vivant* of middle-class Americanism, and through the temporal elaboration of the act(s) of "civilized" Anglo-American life (to borrow Michel Foucault's description of modern disciplinary ritual), Indians could evolve to the point of assimilation, softening into the melting pot where they would no longer pose a threat. In any case, the government's Japanese reservations demonstrated to the American public that the West was again secure, the status quo restored, and the nation's powers of self-mastery fully intact.[27]

As World War II progressed, however, different threats—imminent and imagined—emerged before wary westerners. Bloody race riots swept through urban defense centers during World War I, and they would break out again in Detroit, New York, and Beaumont, Texas, in 1943. In cities crowded with newly arrived war workers, the riots brought forth Reconstruction-era nightmares of African Americans seizing a vulnerable America to overturn the racial order. This fear was especially acute in Pacific states like Oregon, where black populations had historically been very small. Early security concerns that settlers of African descent, enslaved or free, might ally with disaffected Northwestern tribes against American settlers prompted the passage of exclusion laws that prohibited blacks from settling in Oregon Territory. These laws were folded into the first state constitution, and fear of a black apocalypse was woven into the local culture. As far as Oregon was from the South, Portland audiences "applauded . . . cheered . . . and stood up in the intensity of their emotions as they saw the great mounted army of the Ku Klux Klan sweeping down the road" at the crowded premiere of D. W. Griffith's *Birth of a Nation* in 1915.[28] Even when the exclusion laws were lifted, black peril mythologies permeated the local culture, making it an inhospitable place for African Americans to live.[29]

When Portlanders stood firm against a plan to build public housing within the city limits, the Federal Public Housing Authority approved the construction of Vanport as a separate city. Residents moved to Vanport voluntarily and indeed quite happily in the wake of the Great Depression. They were not held in preventative detention, but their reservation was nonetheless bounded by its geographic and social isolation from Portland proper. FBI agents and internal police officers patrolled Vanport continuously, watching the black section of town and monitoring the activities of African American residents and their white friends who fit the profile of dangerous labor radicals. Vanport not only made it easy for shipyard workers to remain productive; it also made it easy to spot any "hostiles"—fascist sympathizers, Communists, or race rioters—before they could do any damage.

The government's concerns about Communist infiltration were not confined to the "usual suspects" among ethnic minorities and the working class. When scientists sounded the alarm in Washington that the Germans might be developing an atomic bomb, Roosevelt approved the Manhattan Project, a top-secret military-civilian collaboration to develop this weapon of mass destruction before Hitler could use one on the United States. The impressive assemblage of foreign and American scientists at the research facility at Los Alamos was enough to assure even the most nervous insiders that the Allies would have a fighting chance. What disconcerted them, however, was the number of great lights whose "political tendencies" matched those of the FBI's two enemy profiles: foreign fascists and homegrown Communists. Both groups were well represented on the Bureau's Custodial Detention Index, which, along with Japanese American community leaders, included high-profile Axis nationals like Enrico Fermi and Emilio Segrè as well as American-born activists and intellectuals like J. Robert Oppenheimer.[30]

The longstanding conflation of Jewish immigration with revolutionary activity in the United States influenced the planning of the Manhattan Project. Classified by Samuel Morton as Caucasians, Jews were considered civilized, though they fell between the northern Europeans at the top of the Caucasian hierarchy and the Aryan "Hindoos" at the bottom.[31] To most Americans, it was not cranial size, skin tone, or religion that made Jews suspect Americans, but the perpetual myth of a worldwide Jewish conspiracy to put the rest of the world under their economic and political control. One of the most visible watchdogs of the "international super-capitalist government" held together across the Jewish diaspora by a bond of "blood, faith, and suffering" was Henry Ford, whose articles for the *Dearborn Independent* in 1920 were in the mainstream of American political discourse.[32] He warned that Jews, like Asians, segregated themselves in ghettos to consolidate their power within the United States and refused to assimilate because they were a communal people, financed with old money from Europe to gain power for the race "wherever there is power to get or use."[33] Ford described the world's Jews as "the world's enigma": they were small in numbers and rejected by much of the world, yet in the United States alone they were members of the most powerful circles, from the Supreme Court and the inner circle of the White House to the center of international finance.[34] Holding themselves out as a "superior race," Jews had no reason to assimilate, having amassed an "undue and unsafe degree of power" by maintaining "the adhesiveness of an intense raciality."[35] Ford's final warning admonished Americans to be alert to the number of Jews involved in the Russian Revolution and to note that "[Jewish] Students of that Red School are coming back to the United States" having refined revolutionary activity to "a science."[36] Their ultimate vision was a United States inhabited only by "'slavs, Negroes, and Jews, wherein the Jews will occupy a position of economic leadership.'"[37]

Ford enumerated several characteristics of Jews that put them at odds with the independent yeoman farmer. Jews were communal and connected to powers apart from and outside the United States. They were clannish and tyrannical in their determination to "[fasten] a yoke on society." They excelled in every enterprise but farming, because they were "not men of the land" like the American frontiersman. Like hostile

Indians, Japanese Americans, and multiethnic labor radicals, Jews were conspiratorial and deceptive; Ford cited the practice of using Gentile banks and trust companies to create a "front" that allowed them to hide Jewish influence. Worst of all, the presumed conspiracy to control the world's people and resources could thwart the American project for individual liberty.[38]

The many foreign and domestic Jewish scientists—and their close associates—were perceived as having dangerous, disloyal tendencies that, like those pinned to Indians, Japanese Americans, and multiethnic laborers, threatened the future of freedom and the progress of manifest destiny with Jewish conspiracy or Communist revolution. Jewish scientists like Leo Szilard, who persuaded the Roosevelt administration to initiate the bomb project, came under additional scrutiny by agents who noted how often they ate lunch in a deli, had their hair cut by Jewish barbers, or spent time with Jewish friends. Ultimately, Szilard was considered too great a risk to be housed at Los Alamos. Although there is no record of overt anti-Semitism on the Manhattan Project, one scholar of the period identified centuries-old "Jewish peril" fantasies in which Jews across the diaspora used their wealth, talent, or intellectual abilities to enter the halls of power and stealthily create a Jewish-dominated world. His wartime polling data led him to conclude that "Jews were considered nonconforming strangers with a self-centered morality [that] permitted them to undercut the patriotism of the larger society."[39]

After screening out active Communists and determining that the net "brain gain" from Hitler's Europe was worth the risk of sheltering scientists from the Axis nations, the American government placed the remaining scientists, worrisome political tendencies and all, behind barbed wire and armed guards to work for the duration of the project—and hopefully for the American cause. To ensure the loyalty of the scientists, censors read their mail, military intelligence listened to their conversations, guards prevented anyone from entering or leaving, and the bodyguards hired to "protect" them did double-duty as informants. If all went according to plan, the fortified community at Los Alamos would protect America from both the terrifying threat of Hitler's nuclear ambitions and the slightly less worrying danger of enemy infiltration.

After the government identified the enemy within — or the people who looked or thought like them — its next step was to create a space to contain and neutralize these enemy bodies. By 1943 nearly 674,000 Americans and resident aliens were removed from the mainstream and placed in government-run political, social welfare, and national security structures.[40] The government's bounded communities included 1,500 people at the Klamath Indian Reservation, 8,100 at Topaz, and 40,000 at Vanport. Los Alamos jumped from about 300 to nearly 1,500 residents between the first scientists' arrival in 1943 and the day of Japan's surrender in 1945. Preventative detention, from its starkest form at Topaz to the softer variation at Vanport City, may have quelled mainstream America's wartime anxieties, but it posed an ideological, if not an ethical dilemma. The true strength of the "land of the free" lies in its ideals, not its exercise of overwhelming state power. The very freedom the United States worked to cultivate in the West and to restore to victims of fascist tyranny required a commitment to due process for all, creating the conditions for social equality and economic opportunity. With these ideals in mind, the government sought to nurture and strengthen residents' patriotic feelings by providing them with scaled-down, highly mediated "American small towns" to replace the home communities from which they were removed.

Guarded little communities seemed like the way to address everyone's wartime concerns. Rehabilitative spaces had, after all, been part of the American social landscape for generations, ranging from religious communes, asylums, and company towns to the Farm Security Administration's subsistence homestead projects for displaced workers. In the wartime communities, the enmified were taken a safe distance from the western home fronts so they could build temporary lives or even improve them through supervised work routines and the daily rituals of American small town life.

It was no coincidence, then, that the federal government transferred several members of its staff from the Office of Indian Affairs to the War Relocation Authority when the time came to design the relocation centers. Nor was it a coincidence that Indians in defense industries, Japanese American internees being relocated to Portland at the end of the war, and the occasional Hanford worker were placed at Vanport, where they would still be in undoubtedly very familiar, government-supervised surroundings. The federal government's system of highly controlled communities was far from a random collection of odd little enclaves. It promoted them as utopian settlements where, for instance, internees would "reclaim the desert" and scientists would find their "ideal city." As individuals who had committed no crimes or acts of disloyalty, the residents were not cast as "detainees" but as pioneers of a sort, whose plywood settlements contained the stuff of which their own American dreams would be made.

The pattern continued as federal officials crafted quasi-democratic institutions to suit their "all-American" authoritarian communities. Community councils, modeled loosely on the nation's legislative bodies, were considered de rigueur among Washington planners, if not the residents themselves. The composition and procedures differed somewhat in each of the four communities, but they all afforded the residents the opportunity to pass resolutions that government project directors could veto (or simply disregard) at their discretion. One War Relocation Authority employee, observing the community affairs at another relocation center, described the internees' project of supervised self-government as the creation of a "cultural structure of realistic democracy."[41] Awkward as it is, the phrase captures the dissonance between the WRA's desire to promote democratic practices and its regime of confinement and social control. In cases where elected officials proved "disruptive," WRA project directors could appoint "appropriate" representatives in their place. A certain amount of disagreement was tolerable, but antigovernment protests were taken as a sign of greater subversive intentions. In a true democracy, every participant exercised an equal measure of power. In the government's small towns, every resident, from elected officials to children, was equally powerless against the rule of the federal government. Residents at Topaz and Los Alamos recalled their near-identical experience of serving on the student councils in high school with a bit of irritation. If the government failed to persuade its charges, it took advantage of the residents' isolation and dependency to encourage conformity. Agents leveraged access to resources, placed troublemakers under surveillance, and used intimidation, threats, and incarceration in ways that would be suspect constitutionally in the more visible corners of society.

Although free enterprise and economic self-sufficiency were the cornerstones of American citizenship (at least ideally), free market capitalism was a world away from America's bounded communities. Government agencies controlled supply and demand, set wages in many communities, and provided little opportunity for free enterprise, for managing assets to build wealth, or for receiving the benefits of full banking services. Hard work was viewed as an indicator of loyalty and cooperativeness, not personal ambition, wage-worthiness, and the all-American drive to "do better" for oneself and one's children. With the exceptions of Vanport, where people earned and saved (though many lost their savings in the flood), and the Tech Area at Los Alamos (where scientific careers flourished), federal agencies created low-paying jobs to keep people busy, to supplement depleted labor pools outside the community, and to offset the cost to the government of running total communities.

Despite the challenges of living in federally run towns, residents worked cooperatively to build truly functional American societies. Klamath Indians created public parks, Topazians played baseball, Vanporters formed religious congregations, and Los Alamosans ran their own little theater—not because they were trying to "look American," but because they *were* Americans who strived to live according to the values of community, independence, participation, and freedom from excessive government control. The isolated enclaves were staging areas for America's tragic ironies in which innocent individuals were denied the promises of American life and the ideals that supported the promise were undermined.

The irony deepened to hypocrisy in 1945 when the political landscape shifted from beating back fascism to stamping out the Red menace. Hitler had no bomb, and the fear of race riots (and certainly Indian raids) paled in comparison to the specter of global Communism. As the hot war turned cold, government enclaves were cast as collectivist dystopias, and Washington called for all of them—including the Indian reservations—to be dismantled. Finding themselves suspect yet again, Topazians and Vanporters faced being uprooted from the places that had sustained them (however marginally) and thrown back into the mainstream to sink or swim. Los Alamos, too critical to the Cold War to be discarded, could not continue to exist as a government-run collective. Its transition to a "real American town" involved reconfiguring openness and security into a scientific fortress for the postwar age.

This final part of the pattern emerged fully when the rush to dismantle all things collective led Congress back to the reservation system, which produced the original federally run communities. Termination bills abounded, voiding most treaty obligations and dissolving tribal land bases. The vast majority of these bills terminated the tribal status of small bands on fairly small land bases, which proved devastating to the individuals in these communities. Klamath was one of three targeted reservations with a sizable population and land base, making its termination a milestone in Congress's push for radical individualism and free market democracy. The Klamath Termination Act of 1954 liquidated the reservation and re-categorized detribalized Klamaths as "legal non-Indians," suggesting that even after the reservation era they would be both insiders and outsiders in America. Removing the geographic borders did little to bridge the wide gap between those who lived inside and outside the government's bounded communities, and many Klamaths fell into the breach. Generations of powerless politics, gainless economics, and education for second-class citizenship left most Klamaths unprepared for the postwar consumer age. One tribal member lamented in the 1980s that after termination, "we were just a bunch of people with nothing."[42]

In isolating and confining people to federally controlled towns, the government pursued the incompatible goals of protective custody and preemptive incarceration. In other words, the government awkwardly attempted to protect its enmified populations while curbing their rights and freedoms without cause. Government agents' initial optimism about its Americanization programs gave way as a "detention psychology" took hold among the residents, manifesting itself in a loss of initiative, a sense of alienation, and increased dependency.[43] The prescribed rituals of self-governance, the work routines, and the opportunities to demonstrate one's Americanness were undermined by the isolation and forced dependency of people who had previously been socially engaged and economically self-sufficient. The government's conclusion that life in the internment camps "loomed only as a blank interlude in what had been up to then a purposeful life" held true at other government communities as well.[44] Federal officials' claims to having provided arenas of self-empowerment were soon met with the reality that government-run communities made dependents of formerly independent people, making the benefits of full citizenship elusive in the years and even decades after the communities had disappeared.

Each part of this pattern is elaborated in the chapters that follow. Chapter one examines the process by which Indians, Japanese Americans, a multi-racial labor force, and atomic scientists were cast as having dangerously disloyal tendencies based on race, ethnicity, and political affiliation. Chapter two centers on the communities themselves and the government's attempt to build structures to restrict freedom and promote democracy simultaneously. Chapter three considers the economic impact of the artificial economies of federally run enclaves, and how this frustrated residents' pursuit of the American ideal of the self-made individual. Chapter four focuses on how the slippages between democratic rhetoric and life as government wards affected residents' experiences as loyal Americans. Chapters five and six trace the process behind the rapid disposal of the four enclaves and its surprisingly traumatic impacts, particularly on the Klamath Tribes, whose extensive, years-long termination process requires a chapter of its own to fully recount this complicated history. The final chapter assesses the long-term effects of these communities on the residents, the surrounding communities, and the American nation. Although the individual stories vary considerably, they all underscore the failure of these communities to project the American values they purported to enshrine. The fact that they made more skeptics than believers of their residents make them not American's utopias but its *inverse* utopias.

Inverse Utopias in the West: Americanism in Reverse

The idea of the federal government building utopian communities at all is an odd one because spiritual seekers and political dissidents have been the main architects of America's utopian experiments. From New Harmony to Onieda to the Hog Farm, Americans voluntarily opted out of the mainstream to escape the moral corruption of Washington, Wall Street, and popular culture in the hope of recapturing lost values and reestablishing them in American life. Utopia is, generally speaking, a longed-for place to which one either journeys or hopes to return. The government's utopian communities, by contrast, were built for conformity to the status quo and to reform individuals, not society as a whole. Federal agencies populated their utopias with suspects to manage, not seekers following their hearts.

There is a hidden logic to the government's invocation of "utopia," but it ties these four communities to the utopian vision of the West, not to the tradition of smaller utopian communities. Jefferson's vision of westward expansion rests on the literal definition of "utopia" given in the *Oxford English Dictionary*: the "imaginary, indefinitely-remote region" and a "place, state, or condition ideally perfect in respect of politics, laws, customs, and conditions." His Empire for Liberty populated by independent yeoman farmers formed what historian Henry Nash Smith describes as "an agrarian utopia in the West" where land, liberty, and freedom were linked symbiotically.[45]

America's utopia is not an isolated place like Thomas More's fictional island that emblazoned the idea of "the best place" (which was also "no place") in the western imagination. All the world is America's utopia, subject to transformation by independent Americans bringing liberty, individual freedom, and the capacity for self-government to the uncivilized reaches of the continent, leading all humanity toward the full enjoyment of their natural rights. Morton's racial hierarchy coupled with the Jeffersonian ideal of educating for democracy served as an organizing structure that harmonized white supremacy and social equality in a single ideological frame. Utopia, then, would produce self-governing, self-determining, self-made individuals, starting with white European-

American settlers, and bringing Natives, immigrants, blacks, and other "inferior" races up the evolutionary scale toward greater civilization, if not fitness for full citizenship. Monarchy, Communism, barbarism and other forms of tyranny would find no fertile soil in the West, and, in time, the American beacon would shine into the dark corners of the world, lighting the way to freedom of all.

In all eras, America's expansive Empire for Liberty has been held out as a "high example" to the world that would "smite unto death the tyranny of kings, hierarchs, and oligarchs." Successfully defending the West from foreign invaders, hostile Indians, predatory Japanese, and Communist traitors was not a mere matter of national security; it was proof that the American experiment had succeeded, and that the United States would continue to fill its manifest destiny as "the great nation of futurity" under whose direction civilization would evolve to its highest levels. Although the built environment in the utopian Empire for Liberty is less prominent than in other utopian experiments, its social and political architecture served much the same function as its more materially based urban counterparts.[46]

The federal government's reservations and security towns were built with certain utopian ideals in mind. To the outside world, they were structures that contained potential dangers at a moment when the promise of American freedom was vulnerable. With a mixed population of the mostly innocent and a handful of true hostiles, they gave assurances that those who were disloyal to the cause of American freedom were contained and under watch. The loyal people who were caught in the government's dragnet, either by virtue of having been swept up and moved or having moved voluntarily into a zone of heavy surveillance and control, would have the opportunity to become better Americans by developing those abilities in scaled-down political, economic, and social institutions that were ultimately controlled by federal agencies. Government agents and security structures created perfect little Americas where, theoretically, nothing bad could happen. No one would be without food and shelter, and everyone would have something productive to do. The wheels of democracy would never turn too fast to make sweeping changes, and dissent would never reach disruptive levels. The schools would teach children to value freedom and social equality in the classroom, without making too much of their own segregation from the rest of the nation. Scaled small and tightly enclosed, these enclaves offered a refuge from the complexities of real life in America, in favor of life stripped to its fundamentals. It was, in a sense, Americanism with training wheels for people who needed them as well as those who did not.

Ordinarily, these time-honored institutions ensured that every citizen participated in self-governance and enhanced prosperity through self-directed economic activity. In Topaz, Vanport, Los Alamos, and Klamath, however, these scaled-down institutions actually worked in inverse fashion. Political participation was an exercise in powerlessness, the government-controlled economies forged bonds of dependency in otherwise self-sufficient people, and the public schools left many students behind their mainstream peers in the postwar era. The political limitations, government-controlled economies, and confusing educational programs bred isolation and dependency, not participation and self-sufficiency. While far from utopias, the four communities were not quite dystopian; they were, after all, free of the extreme repressive violence and exterminationist mission of concentration camps in Europe. Rather, they were *inverse* utopias, built to both limit and promote freedom. They removed people from the even playing field of American opportunity and instilled skepticism and dissent in otherwise cooperative individuals who, in large part, were doing what the government asked of them to help realize the future of American freedom.

But these controlled, miniaturized Americas did not capture every spy or saboteur; in fact, the illusion of containment drew attention away from individuals who ultimately harmed the nation because they did not fit the government's profile of the enmified. And instead of nurturing freedom, inverse utopian life cut people off from the political process, ended lives of economic independence, and made thousands of patriotic individuals question the sincerity of America's fundamental beliefs. These would-be utopias were bound in space and closed off by geographic or social distance, secrecy and silence, or barbed wire and armed guards. The utopian ideals of freedom remained the lingua franca of these enclosed spaces, defending democracy was their central concern, and the spirit of reform for racial and political outsiders stayed firmly in place. But instead of freedom flourishing, invasive government agencies fell into tyrannical practices. Far from shining a beacon for the world, the inverse utopias became fodder for Axis propagandists, who beamed stories about them to "prove" that American freedom was a fantasy spun from empty rhetoric. Instead of uniting America's diverse peoples in a structure of ever-evolving freedom, the inverse utopia drove wedges along lines of race, class, region, privilege, and politics. Intended as neither havens nor prisons, Klamath, Topaz, Vanport, and Los Alamos were inverse utopias that "proceed[ed] in the reverse direction" (part of the OED's definition of "inverse") — not rejecting American ideals, but turning them inside out to make them formless and hollow.

What began as a history of weird American places became a history of how the government has arrayed people, space, power, and conceptions of American identity in wartime, and the hazards of mistaking the government's inversion of American ideals for its protection of them. Americans' deep faith in their supposedly divinely ordained mission has always been accompanied by an equally strong apocalyptic fear that foreign interlopers, evil savages, or greedy tyrants would destroy the nation's experiment as a free and open society, twisting freedom of speech into weapons of propaganda and using freedom of assembly to unleash violent internal chaos. It appeared to some that the great American melting pot could become a boiling cauldron of subversion. Fearful citizens turned to the state to control suspect peoples, guarantee security at any cost, and preserve American dreams of progress and perfection.

The government's small inverse utopias were intended to protect the utopian Empire for Liberty envisioned for postrevolutionary America by Jefferson and enacted through westward expansion. Pitting ideals of freedom against realities of profiling and social control brought the opposite of what the government had intended. They may have calmed the uncertainty of a nation under attack, but in the long term these communities undermined the bedrock principles of independence, fidelity to due process, and a brotherhood of self-determining individuals under the banner of freedom and civilization in the Empire for Liberty.

As the dystopian vision of losing the West to savagery and tyranny took hold, and as enmification and profiling eclipsed fidelity to the Constitution, Klamaths, Topazians, Vanporters, and Los Alamosans—and thousands of others who lived in communities like theirs—came to question the government's dedication to the values it proclaimed to protect. John O'Sullivan's utopian brotherhood under equality gave way to a Mortonian world of categorization and control in which Americans less capable of democratic self-government had to be contained, cultivated, and deemed loyal and capable of taking part in society. These tensions have contributed to the complicated history of American freedom and how its ideals evolved in the "untrodden lands" of the American West and fed back into the national discourses of peacetime inclusiveness and wartime segregation.

This history fills in a portion of the long and tumultuous story of the federal presence in the West and addresses the significance of western developments to the nation as a whole. Historians of the West, like westerners themselves, have grappled with the complicated relationship between freedom and restriction in the West and the significance of this dynamic to the American experiment as a whole. Frederick Jackson Turner, in addition to affirming Jefferson's vision and O'Sullivan's call, argued that the region's function as America's safety valve was essential to the nation's political stability. Ultimately, Turner's westerners became exemplary Americans, showing easterners the true meaning of independence, non-whites a model of civilization, and Americans everywhere a clear sense of identity. While historians like Earl Pomeroy challenged Turner's "frontier" construct by shifting focus to urban centers and institutions, the Turnerian West remained historical orthodoxy until the 1980s. All at once, a "gang" of four New Western historians rode onto the scene for a showdown with Turner's adherents and, to a lesser extent, with one another. Patricia Nelson Limerick and Richard White rejected Turner's safety-valve image, but their descriptions of the West's relationship to the nation differed dramatically. Where Limerick described the region as the nation's "potential dumping ground, a remote place to which to transplant people whose presence annoyed, angered, or obstructed the majority," White cast it as the "kindergarten of the state" from which newly formed social ideas flow back to the nation as innovations, rather than refuse.[47]

In the West's inverse utopias, Turner's, Limerick's, and White's assertions hold true (which is perhaps a good measure of just how strange these communities were). Their inhabitants, branded "undesirables" by the federal government, were removed to remote locales, where neither their presence nor their problems would disturb national unity. Each project was, in its way, an experiment in social engineering and demographic distribution situated precariously within the American democratic tradition. Klamath, Topaz, Vanport, and to a lesser degree Los Alamos served as kindergartens of a sort, where residents received training in the fundamentals of Americanism. The region, in turn, became the government's laboratory for an experimental synthesis of authoritarianism and democracy that would defend the nation from unknown internal enemies in times of war. The federal government thus built its western empire, but whether it served the cause of liberty for all, as Jefferson imagined, remains an open question.

For instance, generations of freedom-seekers have piled into wagons, train cars, and Volkswagen vans and headed west to escape the many constraints of the East, from the rigid dictates of civilized society to the overbearing institutions of a federal government that is too near. While the myth of radical freedom remains embedded in America's vision of the West, residents and scholars of the region know well that the thousands of miles between Washington and its western frontier did little to ameliorate government influence. Historians remind us that the federal government distributed the land that drew settlers west, secured the terrain with forts and military bases, invested in massive infrastructure projects from dams to nuclear power plants, and continues to manage its 760-million-acre holdings across eleven western states.[48]

Yet the sheer concentration of inverse utopias in the West made them a powerful influence on the region's political and social landscape. While southerners struggled with Jim Crow, westerners grappled with the consequences of the federal government's wartime demographic management scheme (or, as President Roosevelt put it in 1942, "hav[ing] the right numbers of the right people in the right places at the right time").[49]

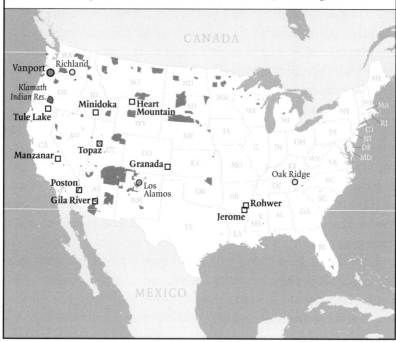

Inverse Utopias in the United States, 1943

This new manifestation of the federal presence went beyond pitting newcomers against established western communities to hardening the government's grip on western land and regional policy, fueling the hostility of many westerners toward their leaders in Washington. Contrary to the individualism and egalitarianism that characterized American freedom, the federal government categorized, marked, and segregated specific populations and restricted rights that were inalienable to all the other loyal, law-abiding people in America. The tensions never fully eased, and westerners continue to struggle over power, place, and who among the old-timers and newcomers, Natives and scientists, European Jews and Japanese immigrants, African Americans and staunch political progressives truly belongs in the region. Federal demographic management contributed significantly to the course of race relations in the West, and it is an element that distinguishes this history from the trajectories of slavery and European immigration that shape the national narratives of race, citizenship, and American nationhood.

Finally, all four cases underscore the fact that inverse utopias deprived loyal Americans of fundamental freedoms based on grave miscalculations about the treacherous tendencies of ethnic minorities, industrial workers, and perceived radicals. Their histories serve as reminders that the balance between maintaining a sense of national security and preserving the integrity of the principles of American freedom is a delicate matter, requiring thoughtful policy instead of impulsive initiatives. It should come as no surprise, then, that Americans who spent time in inverse utopias gave a great deal of thought to questions of civil liberties and national security. In the decades that followed the war, they marched at civil rights demonstrations, presented testimony to Congress, led campaigns for redress, ran for office, and served as the conscience of the nation by committing their views to print. This activist engagement took its most visible form when Japanese American civil rights organizations mobilized in defense of Arab and Muslim Americans who were subject to preventative detention following the al-Qaeda attacks on New York City and Washington DC in 2001. In a completely unintended way, the inverse utopias did make their residents into exemplary American citizens; as self-appointed guardians of civil liberties, it is they who keep watch on the government and resist every sign of tyranny, the ultimate un-American activity.

This is some of the history that lies beneath the bleachers at the Portland International Raceway and within the eroded foundations that form the last trace of Topaz. It is a history that ties the bustling science town of Los Alamos, in which Colonel Sanders looks out upon one of the few cities in America where the federal government owns more property than corporate America, to the tranquil paths of the Winema National Forest, which was part of the Klamath Reservation until termination acts wrested it from the Indians in the 1950s. In the Klamath Basin, it brings together

Oregon's Nikkei and Native communities on the Japanese American Day of Remembrance.[50] Gordon Bettles, steward of the Klamath Longhouse, was taught by his parents to view the abandoned site of the Tule Lake Relocation Center as part of his own social geography. Bettles recounted his parents' history lesson in an interview in 2006. They began with the story of the internment itself, adding that the Japanese Americans were "treated like animals; they said this is exactly what happened to the Modoc tribe when they were forced off their cultural property and placed on the Klamath reservation. If you think about it, the reservation they kept us in was like internment. We couldn't leave unless we had passes, we couldn't communicate with other tribes." The article features another community member, Hiroto Zakoji, a former internee at Tule Lake who was hired by the Klamath Tribes to serve as general manager and director of the Klamath Adult Indian Education and Training Program.

These ties are becoming more widely recognized and memorialized; the Confederated Tribes of the Grande Ronde, for instance, are major donors to the Japanese American Art Memorial in Eugene, Oregon, in recognition of their shared histories of "hardship, government betrayal, denial of civil liberties and racism, but also (and some would say more importantly) of community, cultural preservation, and perseverance."[51]

There have been great erasures in these histories, making the connections between them all but invisible until now. This is due in part to the longstanding perception that each community's "unusual history" made residents' struggles solely their own. The cloak of wartime secrecy that surrounded every inverse utopia dampened voices very early, and the federal government has had little reason to say much about places that, in its view, no longer exist (or no longer exist in federal-utopian form). Former residents have understandably engaged in a great deal of self-censorship for decades. Some chose to focus on the future, while others tried to deemphasize the strangeness of their wartime experiences. Still others avoided discussing the poorly understood circumstances of their lives in inverse utopias for fear of re-stigmatizing their experiences.

Although there were vast differences between the experiences of the four populations, they all shared the marginalization, repression, displacement, and disillusionment with federal government that flourished within the confined spaces of America's inverse utopias. Most importantly, their experiences are not theirs alone; they are part of a patterned, national wartime dynamic that makes certain citizens of the Empire for Liberty into enemies while the government fights to extend the blessings of American freedom to every corner of the globe.

CHAPTER ONE

BEWARE OF CRAFTY BANDITS

Enmification in the Empire for Liberty

In his first fireside chat after the bombing of Pearl Harbor, President Franklin D. Roosevelt prepared Americans to "face a long war against crafty and powerful bandits" because "the attack at Pearl Harbor can be repeated at any one of many points in both oceans and along both our coast lines and against all the rest of the Hemisphere." America's territory, interests, and people were in "grave danger," but the president pledged that the nation would defend itself "to the uttermost" to ensure that Japan's "form of treachery shall never endanger [Americans] again." Nothing less than absolute victory would suffice, as the very "life and safety of [the] nation" were at stake. Reports had already arrived that Japan's "crafty bandits" had torpedoed U.S. ships between San Francisco and Honolulu, raising longstanding fears that a West Coast invasion was in the works. It was well understood that, if victorious, the Japanese "war lords" and their Nazi allies would bring a quick end to American republicanism so that fascism might ring. The stakes in this conflict extended far beyond territorial supremacy: it was a struggle to defend the very principles of American freedom.[1]

World War II was unlike any previous war in its scale, its totality, and its implications for the future of human liberty. Given this, comparisons to the Oregon crisis of the early nineteenth century do not readily spring to mind, yet the pattern of enmification and containment of presumed internal enemies is discernible in both events. Despite the differences in era and circumstance, the historical record reveals remarkable parallels in popular perceptions, public discourse, federal policy, and relationships between citizens and the government that form part of the larger pattern of inverse-utopian development. In both conflicts, Americans feared that foreign tyrants and their barbarous allies would destroy the Empire for Liberty by conquering the west shore. Nineteenth-century observers feared that the British sought the aid of indigenous communities in securing the Oregon country for the crown and making subjects of American citizens. Much like the perception of the German-Japanese alliance, Americans saw a crafty European power joining forces with a "savage," war-making race. So while Roosevelt's warnings were most urgent, they were not unprecedented.

The Oregon conflict wore on for decades longer than World War II, and the public perception of the threat ebbed and flowed depending, in part, on the degree to which Indians appeared willing to form alliances with the British. Even at moments when Americans seemed ambivalent about their nation's ties to Oregon, the specter of submission to English tyrants or Native savages did such violence to the vision of the West as the province of liberty-loving Americans that settlers and senators rallied to defend it from foreign control (never mind that, from an indigenous perspective, the English and Americans were the foreign invaders).

The War of 1812 brought an abrupt pause to the march of progress in Oregon, the greatest humiliation coming with the sale of the port city of Astoria to Britain for fifty thousand dollars. When the HMS *Raccoon* landed at Astoria, the captain staged a ceremony of possession in which he renamed the town "Fort George"—emblazoning the king's name upon a center of American enterprise. Although the ceremony was intended to make Astoria "doubly British" (and to deliver a round slap to the face of the Americans), its implication that Britain held the land by right of occupation, not purchase, meant that the victorious power would claim the fort at the conclusion of hostilities. In 1817 President James Monroe sent Captain James Biddle and the USS *Ontario* to reestablish American control over Astoria. The deed was done when Secretary of State James

Prevost personally replaced the Union Jack with the Stars and Stripes. The guns had been silent for three years by this time, but each country's struggle to fulfill its national purpose perpetuated a war of words that persisted almost thirty years.[2]

To keep the peace, officials in London and Washington established a joint occupancy agreement in 1818 that allowed both countries to settle and trade in the area from the 42nd parallel (California's current northern border) to 54 degrees, 40 minutes north (now the Alaska–British Columbia border). The arrangement made good sense to diplomats but not to Americans in and outside of Oregon. They argued that, if the eighteenth century taught the Atlantic World anything, it was that "subjects" and "citizens" could not coexist. The Monroe Doctrine made joint occupancy all the more problematic by encouraging a wave of European decolonization that swept Spanish America. The doctrine stated that the United States would not interfere with political affairs on the European continent and that Europeans — whether retreating Spaniards or encroaching Englishmen — would not exert political influence in the Americas. Monroe made no specific mention of Oregon, but Thomas Hart Benton, a renowned Anglophobe, aided the cause of enmification in this statement before Congress in 1825: "[T]he greatest of all advantages to be derived from the occupation of this country, is in the exclusion of foreign powers from it. . . . England now has her iron grasp upon it, and it will require a vigorous effort of policy, and perhaps of arms, to break her hold to it, that no part of this continent is open to European colonization."[3]

One strategy, interestingly, was to fight colonization with colonization, asserting a right of rule by placing more American citizens than British subjects in the disputed territory. Although most eastern settlers braved the overland trail for personal reasons, boosters and government officials knew that Washington's hold on the territory became firmer with every new American occupant in it. The increased settlement heightened political tensions in 1827, when the number of British and American settlers became conspicuous.[4] The strategy became more deliberate in 1840, when Jason Lee led the "Great Reinforcement" of Christian missionaries, farmers, and laborers to establish settlements, heighten the U.S. presence in the territory, and Christianize the Indians (although Lee himself was concerned less with manifest destiny or the Oregon question and more with bringing the most industrious, law-abiding settlers to the territory and affording the Indians their best opportunity for reform).[5]

The British did not interfere with American settlement over this fifteen-year period, but local Indian tribes did. Increasingly, indigenous communities resorted to violence to defend their shrinking homelands, waning resources, and diminishing powers of self-determination. Hall Kelley of the American Society for Encouraging the Settlement of the Oregon Territory sounded the alarm about England's tyrannical designs on America's promised land while making a call for immediate settlement. He argued that hardy individualists could contribute to more than just the numbers game with the British. Such exemplary Americans would also be best suited to "enlighten the minds" of potential Native allies. The civilizing mission would not merely "dignify the nature of this unfortunate race" but prevent "their unjust and unequal alliances with *another* nation" and ensure that "their friendship be secured to *this*."[6] The navy was less hopeful: a report to Washington warned that the British at Fort Vancouver had convinced the local tribes that they held supremacy over the Americans and were arming these Indians for the common defense.[7] This alliance of British strategists and Native warriors was, to the Americans, an unholy marriage of European brilliance at political calculation and non-Europeans' unmitigated bloodlust—a pairing much like that of the "treacherous" Germans with the "savage" Japanese in the Second World War.

The enmification of the British and the Indians had a marked influence on immigration rates. Unfortunately for Oregon boosters, the dramatic renderings of the conflicts in eastern newspapers caused prospective settlers to think twice before venturing into the conflict zone. After enrolling four thousand families for emigration to Oregon, Hall Kelley could persuade only five hundred to make the journey. He called on Congress in 1831 to take bold, effective, and observable action on behalf of "a large number of the citizens of the United States" by sending "troops, artillery, military arms, and munitions of war, for the defence and security of the contemplated settlement." American settlers had sacrificed the comforts of "civilized life" to fulfill the nation's historic destiny: they were "pledged to one another, to their children, to their friends, and to mankind, to sustain by all just and possible means, the interests of their country" but demanded the "protection and fostering care of Congress."[8] Senators David Rice Atchison and Lewis F. Linn, both of Missouri, brought "Oregon bills" before Congress in 1842 to compel the president to erect forts, increase troop levels, make vast grants of land to settlers who would occupy it (in a sort of proto-Homestead Act), and appoint more Indian agents to "superintend the interests of the United States." To them, crowding out the British and subduing the Indians were two parts of a single mission of bringing Oregon into the union and making the territory safe for republicanism.[9]

On June 11, 1846—four days before the signing of the Oregon Treaty—President James Polk warned that the security situation in Oregon remained dire not because of the British but because of the Indians. Polk shared excerpts of an angry letter from Oregon settlers, who charged the army with failing to "inspire the Indians with sufficient fear of Americans" to deter them from threatening their property and personal safety. The president was spared no wrath; the settlers demanded he fulfill the essential duties of his office by bringing Indians under full military control. Polk told Congress that the poorly represented settlers, while "strong in their allegiance and ardent in their attachment to the U. States," had been "cast to their own resources," which had tested their faith in a government they feared had abandoned them.[10]

Although it appeared to many that Britain and her Native allies might plot a Pearl Harbor–like sneak attack (before there was such a thing) on Americans in the territory, British officials, for their part, were far less eager to engage the United States than the Japanese and Germans would later prove to be. Government officials were reluctant to go to war over a distant territory they had no interest in settling, but they could not tolerate the loss of national honor to a people enthralled with "nonsense about flying eagles and never-setting stars" and "fourth of July harangues," smug in their "infinite superiority of the Yankee over all mankind, past, present, and to come."[11] Political cartoonists depicted such a retreat in the form of a sensible father looking down at a diminutive young bumpkin as he puts up his fist, the caption reading, "What? You Young Yankee Doodle, Strike Your Own Father!"[12] In popular discourse, questions of land and title were eclipsed by the mostly ideological, perceptibly oedipal conflict between the preservation of old-world civilization and the progress of republican freedom. As *Blackwood's Edinburgh Magazine* pointed out, childish Americanism threatened much more than institutionalized foolishness: it would place government — and, by extension, all of civilization — "at the mercy of the multitude."[13] If the region were to fall to chaos, Britain would have no choice but to impose order, in keeping with its historic mission of bringing true "civilization" to all corners of the world.

Despite their impassioned pleas for a comprehensive Oregon settlement, most Americans hoped to avoid war with Britain, especially as hostilities with Mexico escalated and sectional conflict threatened internal security. Yet a vocal minority shouting "fifty-four forty or fight!" called for war before territorial compromise with Britain. A Philadelphia group printed its firm resolution that "to yield any portion of a claim thus made and sustained, to a threat or fear of war, would be to yield more than the land. It would be to suffer a Republican Government to bow its head to the arrogant and insolent command of the power of kings and aristocrats and their miserable minions. Such proceedings would be a shame in our government and a disgrace to our country." It further admonished Congress and the president that "the interests and honor of the nation equally impel the government to prefer war in maintaining our rights, to the slightest taint of dishonor in even a supposed abandonment of them."[14]

Diplomats managed to avert war with the somewhat anticlimactic signing of the Oregon Treaty of 1846, which resolved the "doubt and uncertainty which has hitherto prevailed respecting the sovereignty and government of the territory on the northwest coast of America" by establishing the border at the forty-ninth parallel. Britain could continue to develop trade in the north with the aid of shared access to the Columbia River, and the United States secured the contiguous (and limited) territory necessary to realize its republican vision (which included its own robust trade opportunities). The settlement was a great diplomatic achievement; not only did it prevent war between England and the United States, it allowed Britain to save face and pursue its national interests as the Americans continued their providential mission of republican expansion.

The Oregon question was settled with the British but not the Indians. The treaty did not resolve the remaining territorial disputes with the local tribal communities, and it did not confer territorial status on the Oregon country, making the ties between the settlers and their government palpable but weak. Settlers called on Washington to complete the victory against Britain by granting Oregon territorial status and protecting citizen-settlers from the Indians who interfered with development. They exerted their greatest pressure upon President Polk in the wake of the Whitman Massacre of 1847, in which fourteen missionaries were killed, including Dr. Marcus Whitman and his wife Narcissa. The Whitman mission had served as an important stop for new emigrants on the overland trail and had attracted several Native followers until a deadly outbreak of measles led the Cayuses to believe that Dr. Whitman was a sort of malevolent shaman with murderous intentions.[15] Joseph Meek, a territorial legislator, former sheriff, and vocal proponent of territorial incorporation with the United States, hastily mustered the Oregon Volunteers to subdue the Cayuses. He then led a delegation to Washington to demand that Polk grant Oregon territorial status—which he did in 1848. At long last, Oregon was fully claimed and on the path to Americanization, with its settlers assured of their full rights and protections as citizens.[16]

The new legislation had just as much impact on Indians because it set the stage for the local reservation system. Polk made the territorial governor ex officio superintendent of Indian affairs and gave him two opposing charges: to defend the limited rights of Native people and to protect the interests of American citizens. Then Washington reaffirmed the right of the federal government to pass, implement, and alter laws governing Indian affairs, which were generally crafted with settlers' interests—and not Native rights—in mind. Shortly upon taking office, Governor Joseph Lane surveyed the condition of Indians across the territory. He reported his observations in an early speech to the territorial legislature, tempering statements about the glorious bounty of the Oregon country with warnings that American prosperity came at the expense of Native resources, and that local tribes were increasingly driven to "poverty, want, and crime." Asserting that "the cause of humanity calls loudly for their removal from causes and influences so fatal to their existence," Lane persuaded the legislators to issue a memorial to Congress in July 1849 calling for the purchase of Indian lands and the means to move them into isolated spaces.[17]

In southern Oregon, the "Indian problem" (meaning white settlers' problems with the Indians, and not vice versa) gained urgency after the discovery of gold in northern California, which increased the number of violent encounters between eastern fortune hunters and indigenous Californians. Indian agents in Oregon readily acknowledged that whites had provoked most of the so-called "Indian outbreaks" and that Indians had acted in self-defense. Samuel L. Culver, reporting to Washington in the wake of the Rogue River conflict of 1854, described how hostilities had unfolded throughout the territory's short history. Settlers seeking their fortunes, most "without a wish to sow the seeds of future discord," grew hostile toward Natives who destroyed their property, stole their hard-won gains, or murdered their fellow settlers. In less than ten years, most settlers displayed a "feeling of hostility" that was "almost impossible to realize, except from personal observation." Yet what they failed to recognize, Culver noted, was that "Indians complained that the white people had come into their country, taken their homes, destroyed their means of subsistence, and shot down their people, until, with the uncertainty of food and of life which surrounded them, and the agonies of continual mourning, life had become almost a burden."[18] These stories of violence and vulnerability became the rhetorical foundation for the reservation system. Conceived as temporary structures of preventative detention and protective custody, these enclosed worlds seemed to offer a tidy solution to the complexities of race and place in the region.

There was never a Klamath "outbreak" on the scale of the Whitman Massacre or the Rogue River conflict, yet Klamaths were enmified in print as fierce hostiles, which prompted demands from settlers that the government take control of the tribe as a matter of national security. Methodist missionary Joseph Wilkinson Hines recalled his fear of Klamaths as he made his first journey to California: "In passing over the northern part of the district, it was impossible to reach the appoints without passing through the territory occupied by the Klamath tribe of Indians, who were considered among the most treacherous in all the northern part of the State, and the most dreaded by the whites."[19] Such encounters with Klamaths grew increasingly rare as the tribe became subject to greater military control and missionization and, in 1864, confinement to a reservation. The hope was that this new arrangement would protect the Klamath Basin tribes from clashes with whites, so they might live in peace with the ever-expanding population of Americans.

The creation of the Klamath Indian Reservation—considered by many in Washington to be exemplary—illustrates how the combination of national security objectives and social progress made it harder, instead of easier, for Indians to be peaceful and loyal to the United States. The government rewarded Klamath attempts to assimilate and participate in American society with continued isolation and further dispossession. Although the reservation system should have seemed an obvious flaw in the fabric of American democracy, it became a template for future contain- ment measures during World War II. Forged in conflict, the development of the reservation system shaped the organization and administration of federal communities in wartime. Thus, the Klamath experience with the government is an appropriate starting point for understanding the intricacies of efforts to control potentially dangerous minorities in the World War II era.

The story of the Klamath Indian Reservation, however, begins with the arrival of the first families of settlers in the Klamath region. Perhaps the most formative, sustained Native-settler relationships in Klamath country were those established between the tribes and the family of trailblazers headed by Lindsay Applegate, who came to the region to open a southern route to the California gold fields. Like most settlers, the Applegates had heard the stories of "Indian treachery" and ventured forth "in fear of ambush" with overwhelming firepower at their disposal. Yet despite their wariness, the Applegates resolved to engage solely in defensive warfare. They would rely on their extensive knowledge of indigenous languages and customs to engage with the Indians and to stem the escalation of hostilities. "Native warriors" watched the Applegate party all along the way, but "not once did they show any sign of attack." Applegate recalled later that even if their dialogues had gone awry, the Indians would have had no opportunity to attack before they "at once exposed themselves to our fire."[20]

Arriving safely at their Klamath Basin homestead in 1843, Applegate and his sons Elisha, Jesse, Ivan, Lucian, and young Oliver Cromwell made their living by farming and developing transportation routes to connect local growers to markets in the gold fields. Their early successes positioned all the Applegate men to be leading citizens of the Oregon Territory. Jesse, a prominent politician, sat for several terms on the provisional and territorial legislatures, and Lindsay and Oliver served in the Oregon Volunteers. As they ascended the ranks of the territorial elite, the Applegates retained their interest in the Indians among them and hoped to use their influence to ensure the welfare of the Klamath Basin's first peoples.

Their humanitarian aims quickly ran afoul of the realities of life in a conflict zone. The War Department mobilized military units across the western expanse to assure the safety of prospective emigrants and to prevent new arrivals from purposely antagonizing the Indians. With as much as 90 percent of the army stationed in the western territories, areas like the Klamath Basin, with routes to the gold fields, became military zones. The Modoc, Klamath, and Paiute tribes mounted fierce resistance to the invasion. Most protests involved cattle theft or burning down newly built structures, but on occasion Klamath Basin Indians killed encroaching settlers in an attempt to stop the invasion. Modocs attacked emigrant trains as they approached their lands; one notorious spot was named "Bloody Point."[21]

Klamaths also gained a reputation for savage violence, but theirs stemmed from a case of careless misidentification in May 1846. It began with a nighttime ambush on John Frémont and Kit Carson's scouting party that left three men dead, including scouts from the Delaware tribe. Frémont, who had traveled the region with a cannon in tow three years earlier, was aware that wary Indians had been following him for days (as they had the Applegates), yet he still sought immediate retaliation for the "surprise" attack. Not knowing where the attackers actually came from, Frémont and his men sought revenge in the first Native village they found. They settled the score by slaughtering an estimated 175 Indians (including a chief) and burning the small fishing village to the ground, never knowing if these people had any relationship to the men who had launched the ambush. Reflecting upon the incident, Frémont concluded, "[I]t will be a story for them to tell while there are any Tlamaths [sic] on their lake." In identifying his attackers as "Klamaths," Frémont implicated all area tribes in the attack. His failure to acknowledge the assault as an act of resistance only reinforced the notion that every indigenous southern Oregonian made a sport of slaughtering Americans without provocation, and that every effort to contain the threats such "savagery" posed to the region's nascent civilization was more than justified.[22]

Polk favored using well-placed civilians like the Applegates to manage the "Indian problem," which was widely understood to originate with reckless, racist whites. Equally important, in light of the clash between Frémont and the "Klamath," was for the federal government to "cultivate amicable relations with the Indian tribes of the territory" by establishing agencies in the far West. Polk continued to send troops to secure the Oregon Territory, but he began sending more civilian agents to manage conflicts between settlers and Indians and do anything necessary to discourage grand alliances of the Oregon tribes against the United States.[23]

The government formally demilitarized Indian relations by transferring Indian affairs from the War Department to the Department of the Interior in 1849, even as deadly clashes continued across Oregon through the 1850s. In 1852 a band of Modocs killed sixty-five settlers, including men, women, and children, at Bloody Point. The violence was reported as being unspeakably horrific, so much so that a history of the incident published in 1953 simply says "they outdid themselves in fiendishness and tortures of unprintable character." Ben Wright, a leading citizen in Yreka, California, who historians have alternately described as "head of a rescue party" and "Indian hunter," sought to crush the Modoc resistance by killing fifty-two men, women, and children, a figure that constituted 10 percent of the Modoc population. Some reports stated that Wright lured Modocs to the peace table and poisoned them, others that his men fired on forty men and killed them all (as well as several bystanders). When all was said and done, two facts were abundantly clear: Modocs sustained a devastating loss, and Washington had branded them a security risk that required the strictest possible state controls.[24]

In addition, southern Oregon saw two wars between the Oregon Volunteers and the Rogue River Indians (whose plight Samuel Culver described) that began when miners in Jacksonville launched their own extermination campaign by murdering Indians without provocation. Because the military presence in the region had been reduced, Oregon Volunteers did much of the fighting and sustained most of the losses. Outraged at the loss of as many as twenty-five men in a single engagement, Oregonians demanded federal intervention and permanent removal of the "savages" among them. The Rogue River wars were subdued by 1856 but not forgotten in 1859, when Oregon was admitted to statehood. The legislature pressured Washington to ensure internal security in its war-torn southern region, making pointed requests to establish control over Klamaths and "the troublesome Modocs and [Yahooskin] Snakes" before Yahooskins, too, could make themselves a threat to the developing area.[25]

The federal government responded in 1863 with the announcement that the Klamaths, Modocs, and Yahooskin band of the Snake Paiutes were slated for confinement to a reservation and that the army was preparing to build Fort Klamath, where approximately fifty soldiers would be stationed. This scheme allowed for civilian management and military control over the reservation, which was both in keeping with Washington's stated desire to foster "amicable relations" and a show of responsiveness to southern Oregonians' insistence upon strict security. The task of removing and resettling approximately two thousand members of the three tribes fell to J. W. Perit Huntington, superintendent of Indian affairs in Oregon. Huntington began by marking out a parcel of arable land large enough to "support all the Indians which are ever likely to be placed upon it." The tract was "not likely to be traversed by any important line of transportation," minimizing the possibility of subsequent removals to accommodate rail lines, as often happened on the plains. Although there were portions that whites would covet for settlement, Huntington deliberately located the reservation so that the Indians' "separation from whites would be nearly as complete as possible," making it an ideal location for a new Indian homeland. Even if the land proved less than ideal, the Klamaths would be prohibited from leaving the reservation without authorization and supervision, and violators would be arrested and imprisoned at Fort Klamath.[26]

Furthering Washington's assimilationist vision, Huntington emphasized that the new reservation was well suited for "supporting a colony of Indians by industrial pursuits." Reservation life would thus enable the Klamath Tribes to learn American work routines, develop marketable skills, and become more self-sufficient. Most important, however, was the belief that living like an American would, in the best of circumstances, not simply make Indians loyal but Americanize them beyond the point of being "Indian" at all. If the reservation failed to generate solutions to the "Indian question," it could make the question disappear by spurring Native people to "evolve" beyond Indianness.

Knowing that day would not arrive for some time, the Indian Bureau left sixteen thousand pounds of flour at Fort Klamath to feed the tribes through the winter and "have the effect to quiet them and convince them of the good faith of the government."[27] Superintendent Huntington appointed Lindsay Applegate, now a twenty-year resident of the Klamath Basin, as agent for the Klamath Basin tribes. The Applegate family had gained a reputation for understanding the Indians and having cordial relationships with them. No one objected when Applegate hired his sons Ivan, Elisha, and Lucien as assistants.[28] Oliver's facility with Chinook jargon (a Pacific Northwest trade language) garnered him the job of interpreter, which prepared him to assume his father's position as Indian agent several years later.[29]

Superintendent Applegate's first duty was to negotiate a treaty with Klamaths, Modocs, and Yahooskins that would place them into a single community for the first time in their long histories. The Treaty of 1864, which reduced the Klamaths' land from approximately twenty-two million acres to 2.2 million, set the terms of the relationship between Klamaths and the Applegates. The Indians gave up land and access to vital natural resources, and in exchange, the U.S. government would provide subsistence in the form of food, clothing, and farm supplies to be disbursed at the discretion of Agent Applegate. In order to build infrastructure without perpetuating dependency, the government promised to operate a sawmill, flourmill, vocational schools, and health services on the reservation for a period of twenty years. The final articles established the power dynamic between the government and the Indians. Indian signatories acknowledged their dependence on the government of the United States and pledged to treat white settlers as neighbors, to cease intertribal warfare, and to never manufacture, sell, or consume alcohol. Additionally, the tribes promised not to "communicate with or assist any persons or nation hostile to the United States," whether Native or European.[30]

The treaty appeared straightforward, but it contained contradictory provisions that made the Klamaths' path to regaining self-sufficiency far from clear. Article 1, for instance, guaranteed the Klamaths a permanent homeland, while Article 9 gave federal officials overriding authority to make any land-use policy it wanted. The articles promising provisions and infrastructure for twenty years implied that the federal government would only be a temporary presence, yet it had no intention of dismissing agents before tribal members became loyal Americans. The conflicting provisions created enormously complex legal and management problems in the long run, but at the time it was drafted, the treaty offered something to everyone with an interest in the Klamath Basin's "Indian problem."[31]

The process of Americanizing the Klamath Tribes met resistance before the treaty could reach Congress for ratification. Washington's commitment to assimilation came at a moment of increased doubt about Indians' fitness for citizenship. Still reeling from the betrayal of southern tribes who allied with the Confederacy in the Civil War, Congress began chipping away at Chief Justice Roger B. Taney's argument in *Dred Scott v. Sanford* that Indians, like other foreign immigrants, could become naturalized citizens. The distinction between Indian citizenship and that of freedmen was debated again during ratification of the Fourteenth

Amendment, with some legislators arguing this time that African Americans had no foreign ties and were naturally American citizens. Indians, however, had unbreakable bonds to their foreign tribal entities, which made them incapable of developing an exclusive loyalty to the United States.[32] So Native people were expected to demonstrate a loyalty that, according to the U.S. Supreme Court, could never be achieved. Moreover, they were to do this by living "as Americans" in a wholly un-American environment. The tenets of American freedom held, in their case, that as individuals they were to fulfill their own destinies. But as *Indian* individuals, they were to fulfill government-approved destinies according to the dictates of federal agencies. For the reservation's new residents, the path to regaining their self-sufficiency and self-determination was far from clear. But neighboring whites at the farthest edge of the Empire for Liberty took comfort in knowing that the government would protect them from the people they perceived as the great looming threat to their life, liberty, and pursuit of happiness.

Inscrutable Traitors on the Pacific Coast

By the 1940s Native communities were all but invisible to the American mainstream, apart from pueblos and villages visited by ethno-tourists who flocked to view "real Indians" in their "native habitat." Otherwise, Indians disappeared behind reservation boundaries drawn in the popular imagination, if not inscribed on the landscape itself. In the end, boundaries real and imagined cast the illusion that the hard-won West was, indeed, white Americans' inalienable promised land. In the 1890s, when the United States set its sights on China's vast markets after laying claim to Hawaii and the Philippines, America's manifest destiny seemed to move ever westward, continuing to bring land into productive use and "savage" peoples into the fold of civilization.[33] The government believed that Asians, like indigenous Americans, could be civilized but were deadly dangerous if left in their "natural, warlike state."

So when the news hit the Pacific Coast that Japanese forces had struck the U.S. Naval base at Pearl Harbor, a rhetorical firestorm blew across the region. The American frontier had been ambushed by an "inferior race" that resorted predictably to the imitation of western weapons, tactics, and diplomatic customs to gain the upper hand. President Roosevelt underscored this fact in his declaration of war on December 8, 1941, in which he broadcast to the world, "[T]he distance of Hawaii from Japan makes it obvious that the attack was deliberately planned many days or even weeks ago. During the intervening time the Japanese Government has deliberately sought to deceive the United States by false statements and expressions of hope for continued peace." It was the first sneak attack since the Indian wars. And, according to the president, "[T]he news has been all bad. We have suffered a serious setback in Hawaii. Our forces in the Philippines, which include the brave people of that Commonwealth, are taking punishment, but are defending themselves vigorously. The reports from Guam and Wake and Midway Islands are still confused, but we must be prepared for the announcement that all these three outposts have been seized." These losses on the Pacific frontier were the beginning of what the president promised would "not only be a long war, it will be a hard war."[34]

This revelation outraged Americans in the interior states, where mountains, deserts, and a vast ocean separated them from their foreign enemy. Roosevelt's words won over even the most ardent anti-New Dealers. Among them was Tom K. Ritchie, a Tucson attorney whose sole post-bombing beef with the president was an administration official's reference to the Japanese as "rattlesnakes":

> "rattlesnakes . . . have too much of the gentlemen in them. They should be referred to as copperheads, crawl on their belly, camouflage, and carrying a deadly poison that is silent and strikes without any warning whatever. . . . They should be crushed [with] ruthless force without any squeamishness and without any feeling that we are doing other than killing snakes. And when we clean out a nest of snakes we not only kill the father snake, we kill the mother snake and we break their eggs. And that, I think, is what should be done here, that they should be utterly wiped out."[35]

For Americans like Ritchie, the Pearl Harbor bombing was not the moment they came to fear the Japanese; it was the moment when a long-anticipated invasion had arrived. Popular fiction about Asian fifth columnists destroying western civilization appeared as early as 1879, with more to follow in the 1890s upon the closing of the western frontier and the acquisition of Hawaii and the Philippines. As Chinese markets became the new arena for American manifest destiny, Japan became a problem; its victory against a European power in the Russo-Japanese War gave it significant influence in the region. So much so, in fact, that Theodore Roosevelt, whose political persona was steeped in frontier culture, determined China was not worth a challenge to Japanese hegemony. That Japan could develop western weapons to beat a western power only amplified concerns about the future military surprises that might be in store.[36]

Jack London gave shape to these fears with "The Unparalleled Invasion," written in 1906 and published in *McClure's* in 1910. In it, Japan takes control of China, industrializes it, and mobilizes the Chinese to conquer the civilized world. Ernest H. Fitzpatrick's *The Coming Conflict of Nations: Or the Japanese American War* envisions a heroic British-American alliance against Japanese invaders—aided by Japanese fifth columnists—who made an apocalyptic ruin of Montana and Idaho. *The Vanishing Fleets*, by Roy Norton, centers on the American loss of Hawaii and the Philippines in the wake of a Japanese sneak attack. Its success was due, in part, to fifth column activity by American Communists. The president, invoking sweeping powers to create a superweapon, ultimately restores civilization by deploying a deadly technology. John Ulrich Geisy's *All for His Country*, published in 1915, describes a Japanese attack on Hawaii that proceeds to California, where immigrants leave their Japantown storefronts and farms to join the Japanese invasion force after its attack on San Francisco.[37] The Office of War Information (OWI) drew on these familiar images in its informational film *Our Enemy: The Japanese*, which describes them as "primitive, murderous, and fanatical." Echoing Samuel Morton, the film asserts that the Japanese mind was impossible to understand, but "their weapons are modern, their thinking two thousand years out of date." "Never a creative or inventive people," they had imitated western military technologies, and their daily newspapers "aped" those of "the great American dailies." In an inverse version of Jefferson's Empire for

Liberty, the narrator warns that "[t]hey believe it is the right and destiny of Japan's emperors to rule the world" and that Japan would bring about its divinely ordained destiny by destroying nations that stand in its way, without benefit of a moral code."[38] The OWI's warning of a dystopian reversal of America's manifest destiny sealed its easy process of enmification, which required nothing more than stirring fears that were embedded in the popular imagination and deeply rooted in the American psyche.[39]

Farther west, rage at fantastical Nipponese was eclipsed by fear of the real Japanese among them. In large coastal cities like San Francisco, proximity to Japan was most evident in the presence of vibrant Japanese communities, or Nihonmachi. When the president stated plainly that "[h]ostilities exist. There is no blinking at the fact that our people, our territory and our interests are in grave danger," and that "American ships have been reported torpedoed on the high seas between San Francisco and Honolulu," Bay Area residents sprang into action. Air raid drills, blackouts, and Red Cross operations began in earnest on December 8. The combination of the Japanese American presence, generations of yellow-peril stories, and the sudden intrusion of civil defense operations in the day-to-day life of westerners took its toll very quickly. One government report noted that "in the early weeks of the war the West Coast population suffered hypertension, living in constant expectation of attack from the air or the sea."[40]

Within a week of the bombing, San Franciscans heard military officials refer to California as part of the Western Defense Command, denoting the region's transformation into a military zone. President Roosevelt stated in two proclamations that according to sections 21–24 of Title 50 of the U.S. Code, "all natives, citizens, denizens, or subjects of [Axis nations] being of age fourteen and upward, who shall be in the United States and not actually naturalized, shall be liable to be apprehended, restrained, secured, and removed as alien enemies." Approximately one million people across the United States were subject to this section of the code, including 91,858 Japanese who became the most conspicuous segment of this seemingly vast "enemy within."[41] Military officials noted that Japanese people lived near "sensitive military targets" such as water supplies, shipyards, railroad tracks, and even power lines. While it was clear that not every Japanese American was a saboteur (Japanese Hawaiians, whose labor was vital to the sugar economy, would not be subject to mass incarceration), government officials presumed, as they had with Indian tribes, that the threat posed by even a handful of "hostiles" was too great to leave any Japanese outside the reach of tight security controls. General John DeWitt, a direct descendant of a celebrated veteran of the U.S. military campaign against Utes, warned the Tolan Commission that "we must worry about the Japanese all the time until he is wiped off the map."[42]

San Franciscans' growing sense that their hometown was becoming a danger zone widened preexisting racial fault lines and augmented longstanding racism to the point of racial hysteria. Suddenly, Japanese Americans' stereotypical politeness, industriousness, and compliance were eclipsed by looming visions of treachery, deception, and a devotion to the Japanese emperor that was so strong, not even the blessings of American citizenship could break it. Political cartoonists depicted the Japanese enemy as insects and apes, and articles increasingly made reference to the "White Man's War."[43] General DeWitt did not distinguish between the subjects of the Japanese Empire and law-abiding Americans. In an oft-quoted memo, DeWitt explained, "[R]acial affinities are not severed by migration. The Japanese race is an enemy race, and while many second and third generation Japanese born on United States soil, possessed of United States citizenship, have become 'Americanized,' the racial strains are undiluted."[44] Rumors that Japanese Americans in Hawaii helped execute the Pearl Harbor bombing gave rise to speculation that the San Francisco Nihonmachi was also filled with Japanese agents poised to deliver the city to the emperor like the characters in the Geisy novel *All for His Country*, in which Japanese immigrants emerge from their San Francisco enclave to join a Japanese invasion force. The U.S. government paid greater attention to rural Californians' decades-old complaints that Japanese agriculturists used their wily ways to cultivate bad land and corner the regional produce market. Through this lens, contemporary events appeared illustrative of Japan's desire to expand its hold on California.[45]

Although the Nikkei became "hostiles" in public discourse after Pearl Harbor, the Office of Naval Intelligence (ONI) first placed them under surveillance in 1935. Four years later, J. Edgar Hoover ordered FBI field offices to compile lists of foreign nationals and American radicals to be interned automatically upon American entry into the war. Many Nikkei discovered they were "dangerous" when FBI agents burst into the homes of prominent men, scouring every corner from cellar to attic, tearing into closets, desks, and ladies' underwear drawers. When frustrated agents found neither bombs nor invasion plans, they confiscated firecrackers, road atlases, high school report cards, Japanese books, and English books with Japanese marginalia (thought to be a way of developing code.) Instead of abandoning the raids, the FBI confiscated "a preponderance of knives, flashlights, and other potentially dangerous weapons," which became a basis for removing every individual of Japanese ancestry from the West.[46]

Suddenly, heads of Japanese community groups, businesses, and families disappeared as the FBI and Department of Justice arrested scores of targeted individuals without benefit of due process or even search warrants. Agents did not inform family members of loved ones' whereabouts, trusting that a letter or a bit of hearsay would let them know where he was being held. While most detainees were released after a short period, hundreds remained with no explanation of the charges against them. The process strained constitutional limits, but segregating the "hostile" first-generation Issei also created a power vacuum in the community that made the West Coast Japanese more susceptible to federal control. In a virtual replay of the early days of the Indian reservation system, government agents declared the hereditary chiefs incompetent, imposed agency rule through themselves or their proxies, and left little opportunity for new indigenous leaders or leadership structures to develop from within the community.[47] As the Klamath Tribes could have told their Japanese neighbors, once ties to leaders are severed, immediate resistance is almost impossible to organize.

Initially, San Franciscans of all races were concerned about both enemy infiltration and what many recognized as the persecution of a racial group whose members had yet to commit a crime, let alone an act of treachery. Proclaiming that the "Question of Loyalty is Personal," the *San Francisco Chronicle* asserted that Japan's claim on the Nisei as imperial subjects meant nothing because they were native-born Americans living on American soil and entitled to every constitutional protection. This message might have been more potent had the *Chronicle* been mindful of its anxiety-laden coverage of the fall of Singapore, where complacent British residents had continued to drink tea and play cricket while Japan made threatening advances. The paper's report on Britain's stunning loss included projections that Japan would use Singapore as a stepping-stone to the Dutch East Indies, which would be an ideal launching point for an invasion of Australia and perhaps even San Francisco. White Californians' fear that they lived among "hostiles" became increasingly pronounced as they wondered if they, like the British, had settled into dangerous complacency.[48]

San Francisco News editorials from Arthur Caylor and Westbrook Pegler localized these fears by suggesting that African American neighborhoods were close enough to Nihonmachi for the Japanese to spread the most dangerous Axis racial propaganda. Caylor warned that the propaganda would not be "the ridiculous Nazi kind" that made preposterous claims that black Americans were black Aryans, but the Nihonmachi tract "points out subtly that . . . there is less difference between brown and black than black and white." The Singapore story and the Nihonmachi race war predictions triggered fears in different San Francisco constituencies. Even the Communist Party became wary of the "enemy race" within its ranks. The party suspended Japanese memberships for reasons of "unity" and "national security," fearing Japanese agents could operate easily in the multiethnic party ranks. Ernest Iiyama, who as a member of the Young Democrats joined Congress of Industrial Nations picket lines in the 1930s, was deeply disappointed when no one protested his dismissal from his job as a county clerk solely for being Japanese. Elaine Yoneda, a leader of the San Francisco Communist Party, was horrified at her ejection from the party; she knew that once radical civil libertarians had caved to racial fears, there would be no one to defend the Japanese. Yoneda had good reason to be fearful. Even though she was born to a Russian-Jewish family, she ended up spending much of the war in the

Manzanar Relocation Center with her husband Karl, who was active in the Japanese American community and the local Communist party.[49]

Japanese Americans closer to the mainstream looked to the federal government for protection but were disappointed by its reluctance to distinguish them from the Pearl Harbor bombers. Dozens of young men like graduate student Charles Kikuchi ran to military recruiting stations to protect the country from Japanese aggression and eagerly awaited the call to serve their country. They received it in February 1942, but not as GIs. President Roosevelt shocked the Nisei by issuing Executive Order 9066, which authorized the army to remove and detain all Japanese nationals ("non-citizen enemy aliens") and American citizens of Japanese ancestry, who, by the government's logic, were something like non-alien enemy citizens. Agonized that "the German system could happen in America," one young man struck against it with the only power he had: resistance to standards of American middle-class respectability. His back-talking, petty criminal behavior, and defiance of authority were considered so shocking that sociologists studied him after the war to determine how a *Japanese* could act so squarely against racial expectations.[50]

Germans and Italians fell subject to restrictions as well. They had to register at civil control stations and abide by strict curfews and travel restrictions. Several individuals were arrested and detained for subversive activity, but the entire German or Italian population was never slated for mass detention, and targeting the American-born citizen population was out of the question. As one congressman noted, such an order would require the evacuation of the mayors of both Los Angeles and San Francisco as well as Joe DiMaggio's father, who lived in Oakland. There is no question that German and Italian internees suffered miserably in jail cells and Department of Justice detention centers, but the key difference between their ordeal and that of the Japanese was that the Germans and Italians were treated as individuals. California attorney general Earl Warren asserted that the loyalty of Euro-Americans, but not the "particularly inscrutable" Japanese, was "testable." The evidence against them was circumstantial in many cases, but they were investigated as individuals, tried as individuals, and released when charges were not substantiated. In October 1942 Attorney General Biddle announced that all restrictions against Italians had been lifted, and by December 1942 Germans, too, were allowed to move freely.[51]

While the non-Japanese public applauded the evacuation orders, military and federal civilian agencies furtively whispered fears that mass relocation would be an exorbitant proposition both financially and diplomatically. If nothing else, mass detention would require the government to build reservations of some sort at the end points of this forced migration. The War Department initially instituted a program of voluntary migration to minimize the need for a reprise of the previous century's removal policy. The plan allowed Japanese participants to live as free people if they moved outside Military Area One of the Western Defense Command (Washington, Oregon, California, and parts of Arizona). Although this sounded simple enough, the path to freedom was wrought with unanticipated obstacles. No more than 8,000 of the almost 120,000 Japanese residents on the West Coast had the means to instantly pack up and leave, and many of those who could were barred from settling in the interior states. Arizona, Nevada, and Wyoming refused to admit people "too dangerous for California." Utah residents warned they were "considering their own means" of keeping the Japanese out if the state government failed to honor their demand that "if [the California Nikkei] are thrust on us we want them in concentration camps." Even the Ogden chapter of the Japanese American Citizens' League opposed admitting "troublemaking Californians" who might reflect badly on established Utah Japanese. Colorado and Utah bent to public pressure by closing their borders after absorbing four thousand voluntary migrants.[52]

The War Department, recognizing the failure of voluntary migration, terminated the program in March 1942 and turned the "Japanese question" over to the Interior Department. Suddenly, in addition to running the Office of Indian Affairs, the Interior Department controlled the War Relocation Authority (WRA), an agency charged with removing and detaining an estimated 120,000 western Japanese under civilian (rather than military) auspices. The Interior Department appointed Dillon Myer of the Department of Agriculture's Soil Conservation Service to replace Milton Eisenhower after his short stint as the inaugural director. Myer's supervision of the WRA was not only his first foray into managing communities, it was also his first encounter with people of Japanese heritage. The Interior Department, which oversaw the WRA, appointed Indian Commissioner John Collier as an adjunct advisor to Myer's agency and transferred a number of Indian Bureau anthropologists, sociologists, and social workers to develop a humane, yet efficient plan for the Japanese.

The collaboration generated more contempt than cooperation between the two men, because Myer saw the WRA "reservations" as structures to contain and Americanize an enemy race, while Collier sought to build havens from discrimination that would allow Japanese American culture, political organizations, and even small industries to flourish. Collier, like many fellow New Dealers, was a proponent of ethnic democracy who believed reservations could serve as arenas for vulnerable minorities to consolidate power, promote their political interests, and preserve their cultural distinctiveness within a multiethnic American polity. Myer's conception of the reservation was more traditional: to him, they were structures to protect the public from suspect races, incarcerate the hostiles, and turn the vast population of cooperative detainees into "real Americans" through rigorous education and training. All the while, FBI director J. Edgar Hoover and Attorney General Francis Biddle had misgivings about incarcerating an apparently loyal ethnic group as a form of preventative justice. The attorney general's obvious foot-dragging throughout the questionably constitutional process generated so much ire that the term "Biddling along" became California's new term for "foolish procrastination."[53]

The uncertainties of whether and how to execute the mass relocation program did nothing to slow the exiling of Japanese from the Western Defense Command. Almost overnight, workers from the Wartime Civil Control Authority plastered San Francisco's Nihonmachi with orders for all persons of Japanese descent—whether alien or citizen—to prepare to leave their homes and businesses, taking only what they could carry to wherever the government put them. Most people saw little room for choice in the matter and resolved to comply with the order. Still others saw cooperation as a way to prove their loyalty to the United States; as unjust as the order was, evacuation required as great a sacrifice as any other home front activity. In every case, the evacuation was deeply painful because it clearly confirmed that their neighbors viewed them as dangerous outcasts.

Fred Korematsu, a San Leandro shipyard worker, resisted the evacuation orders by posing as a Mexican laborer and denying his Japanese ancestry. Korematsu was not an especially political person, but he was angered at having been rejected from the army, thrown out of the Boilermaker's Union, fired from his job, and barred from his home state for being Japanese. His evasive measures were not confrontational but simply a strategy to allow him to work in a defense job and quietly move inland with his Italian American girlfriend. Neither the FBI nor the San Francisco district court saw it that way, so Korematsu was convicted and placed on a suspended sentence and five-year probation. He was released to an army transport unit, which took him to the WRA facility where he would spend the duration of his "probation."[54]

Mitsuye Endo, by contrast, followed the evacuation orders to the letter when she lost her civil service job, even though she thought them unjust. Neither the FBI nor military intelligence discovered a shred of evidence indicating that anyone in the Endo family was disloyal to the United States, and they made note of her brother's admirable military service prior to 1941. Yet when the ACLU demanded a writ of habeas corpus on Endo's behalf, the U.S. District Court ruled she was "not entitled" to this fundamental protection. The court argued that Endo had to employ first the WRA's "remedies" for addressing such complaints. It became clear that the government had drawn lines between the free citizenry, who continued to enjoy civil liberties and constitutional protections, and the wards of the WRA, with their truncated rights and freedoms. Although most were American citizens and the rest hardworking, law-abiding resident aliens (whose ineligibility for citizenship had been reaffirmed by the Supreme Court in 1921), the government had the apparatus in place to cast them as outsiders as soon as the dust settled on Pearl Harbor.[55]

By the time the evacuation began, there was little hope of stemming the tide. Even the reluctant Attorney General Biddle admitted there was little to be done. The Tolan Commission, a congressional committee charged with overseeing national defense migration, held investigations and hearings on the implications and implementation of Executive Order 9066. The commission concluded that the plan was a sound component of the wider wartime mobilization and was justified by the still unsubstantiated charge that Japanese American saboteurs participated in the attack on Pearl Harbor. Earl Warren, testifying as California's attorney general, urged immediate removal because "our day of reckoning is coming soon" and his state's survival depended on meeting an "invisible deadline."[56] The Wartime Civil Control Authority's "historic migration" proceeded so swiftly that Nihonmachi was a ghost town by mid-April. Junk dealers did a swift business hocking internees' abandoned belongings to newly arrived southerners recruited to work in defense plants. Even the San Francisco Park Bureau worked to eradicate the last traces of the Japanese by transforming the Japanese Tea Garden in Golden Gate Park into a generic oriental-motif garden, whose employees traded kimonos for khaki pants.[57]

The Japanese "migrants" boarded buses at gunpoint after undergoing registration and a humiliating search for contraband at the civilian control station. The Wartime Civil Control Authority assigned each family a number that it used to label internees' bodies as well as their baggage. The number tags, which hung from coat buttons, replaced names with government serial numbers, making America's Japanese citizens no different from prisoners or even government property marked at supply centers. With numbering came a novel class of citizenship: Japanese Americans became "non-alien Japanese." The term was absurd but its meaning profound: the government had successfully recast law-abiding Americans as internal enemies. They were so successful, in fact, that evacuees' own sense of their innocence was shaken. Ben Takeshita recalled, "[W]e had a strong feeling of shame. We felt we were going to be taken away as if we did something wrong." It was on this treacherous terrain that, in the words of one Japanese American historian, "thousands of Japanese-Americans would . . . begin other journeys in search for their place in America."[58]

The initial stop for the migrants was quite near. They spent the first several months living in animal stalls hastily made into barracks at the Tanforan racetrack until the long-term relocation camps were finished in the interior. Angelenos eventually destined for Topaz were housed at the Santa Anita fairgrounds. Although these internees remained in California, the distance across the barbed-wire fence from their home state was a world away. Residents could see life continue as normal without them, but they could not leave the grounds. While the assembly centers had established visiting hours, moreover, the crowds and bureaucracy made meaningful conversation all but impossible.[59]

The War Relocation Authority snapped the internees' remaining ties to their lives in California in September 1942 when it moved all the Tanforan internees and a portion of the Japanese Angelenos detained at the Santa Anita fairgrounds to Topaz. The flimsily built barracks city was far from luxurious, despite the claims to the contrary. Government planners allowed WRA centers only the "minimum essentials of living," which were limited to shelter; medical, dining, and sanitary facilities; administration buildings; WRA staff housing; post offices; storehouses; refrigeration equipment; and military police stations. If the residents wanted buildings for schools, churches, recreation centers, and "other community planning adjuncts," they would have to build them themselves. Army contractors broke ground for the bare-bones small town in July 1942, and six months later its crew of 800 laborers completed several rows of barracks at an initial cost to the government of $3,929.00.[60]

Topaz stood on federal land, part of which was confiscated from Sherman Tolbert, whom the government compensated with a cash payment and contracts to provide meat for the camp. Tolbert accepted the contract but resented what he saw as special treatment for "Japs" when "real citizens" endured rationing.[61] Lifelong locals like Tolbert benefited from the influx of government jobs, consumers, and cheap labor Topaz delivered, yet they also deeply resented the federal government for putting a reservation full of "undesirables" in their backyards. One resident stated frankly, "[W]e hated [the internees]. They were the enemy and they had to be behind barbed wire." Like Hall Kelley and the "Rogue River Citizen," who denounced the federal government for putting the well-being of enemy Indians ahead of that of citizen settlers, Tolbert and his neighbors perceived the WRA camps as a sign that the government was more concerned for the "enemy race" than for "true Americans" like themselves. In both cases, citizens in the West pressured officials in Washington to demonstrate that the reservations and the relocation centers served the interests of national security and did not extend "undeserved" rights of citizenship to those who were not squarely and unquestionably "American." For disgruntled citizens, the operation of the communities was less a measure of the government's capacity to protect national security and civil liberties and more a test of whether their government was as loyal to them as they were to it.

Rough Radicals in Middle-Class Portland

As the War Department moved soldiers to the battlefront and the War Relocation Authority sent the Japanese to the camps, American industry prepared for the race to build the ships, airplanes, and munitions necessary to win the war. The task was sudden and Herculean: years of isolationist policies and miniscule military budgets had left U.S. forces without tens of millions of tons in needed war matériel. Defense plants sprung up across the West, sparking a "second gold rush" that drew carloads of migrant workers along a second Oregon Trail to industrialize a region that Americans had come to farm and mine a century before. Continuing its long history of managing western lands and resources to further economic and national security interests, the federal government undertook in 1942 a haphazard demographic management plan to put the right number of Americans in the right places and ensure maximum productivity without compromising security.[62]

In the midst of mobilization, a young woman from Portland named Fred penned a letter to her friend Faith lamenting the changes befalling their city. Faith, a Japanese American, was detained in an assembly center while awaiting Topaz's completion. To prepare her for a changed postwar and postinternment world, Fred warned, "Portland itself has always been a quiet, sleepy, well-behaved town but it has changed over the past winter. The population is almost half-again what it was last summer—influx of Okies and Texans, for the most part, unfortunately, to work in the shipyards sprinkled along the water front. It is a twenty-four hour town now . . . it is very strange, swarms of roughly-dressed, roughly-acting people, all over the streets, and the streets darkened. I don't enjoy [Portland] so much anymore."[63] Fred, as a Portlander, shared San Franciscans' sense that an invasion was under way, but it was not the Japanese she feared—it was "rougher," working-class Americans from the South.

Portland was spared the physical devastation of the naval base at Pearl Harbor, yet in Fred's eyes the Japanese strike on the United States destroyed the things she held dearest about her town. White Portlanders like Fred understood the military necessity of developing war industries and recruiting the thousands of workers needed to run the factories, yet they steadfastly refused to allow the fearsome newcomers into their community. Although defense workers were mostly white, race proved an equally pervasive preoccupation among government officials and the public. If Indians' and Japanese Americans' isolation and homogeneity seemed to threaten disloyalty to the United States, Americans from diverse racial and political backgrounds concentrating in one place raised similar fears of antigovernment constituencies forming in America's defense industries.

Fred's letter could have been written by nearly any Portlander at almost any point in the city's history. Oregonians, and Portlanders in particular, had a customary wariness about large communities of newcomers, starting with the waves of European immigrants who came to work at the turn of the century. Prior to Pearl Harbor, there had been a great deal of anxiety about the number of labor activists among the Scandinavians, Finns, and Russians, whom established Portlanders pegged as "hostile enemies" in spite of their tireless work for the Allied war effort. The federal government was similarly anxious, and it heightened residents' fears by concentrating its investigative efforts on a growing number of European radicals in Portland. A 1930 Congressional report found that 60 percent of the mail sent from resident aliens in Portland was posted by people deemed "properly deportable," marking the quiet little city as a hub of subversive activity. The FBI and the Portland Police Bureau's Red Squad responded with continuous arrests and deportation proceedings over the next fifteen years, solidifying Portlanders' notion that outsiders posed great dangers to their community and their nation.[64]

Federal law enforcement activity in Portland shifted emphasis from red hunting to home-front security in 1942, when Portland joined the string of Pacific Coast cities slated for high-volume war industries. President Roosevelt's call for twenty-four million tons of military hardware in 1942 spurred the Maritime Commission to hire the Kaiser Shipbuilding Company to build and operate two new shipyards in the Portland area and to expand the capacity of their existing yard. Construction proceeded apace, but military recruiters and government removal of "potential disloyals" from war production centers were draining Portland's industrial labor pool. Because the city fell within the Western Defense Command, the Wartime Civil Control Commission was charged with moving 1,725 Japanese residents to WRA assembly centers. Mayor Earl Riley built on the removal trend by laying the groundwork for banishing Portland's Roma community. Citing their "unruliness" and "foreign influence" as security risks, he outlawed fortune-telling in 1942 and made arrangements to bus them to Texas in 1945. Federal and local law enforcement agencies continued to deport "undesirable aliens and (or) accused Communists," eliminating some labor radicals and, in the process, a number of Portland's seasoned industrial workforce.[65]

The tide turned rapidly when the War Manpower Commission (WMC) declared the Portland area a "zone of immediate need" of workers from other regions. The WMC granted Henry Kaiser's company special permission to recruit ten thousand workers to the Portland yards, with no regard to whether their race, nationality, or economic circumstances differed from those of the "average" Portlander. Full-page advertisements in newspapers across the country promised high wages, housing, and a train ticket to Portland for new employees. The first trainload of federally recruited Kaiser workers pulled into Portland's Union Station in October 1942, only one month after Fred wrote her letter to Faith. The trains unleashed a massive migratory wave that would add 160,000 newcomers to Portland's prewar population of 406,000 in four years. The drive for wartime workers left little time for extensive background checks into new recruits' political affiliations, deferring the question of labor radicalism for a less hectic period.[66]

The sheer numbers caused great alarm throughout the city. In particular,

Portlanders fixated on the newcomers' demographic composition — or rather, their *perceived* demographic composition. By September 1943 Kaiser and the WMC had recruited 7,760 northeasterners, 3,901 midwesterners, and 4,289 southerners to the area, and in spite of the fact that less than 37 percent came from the South, Portlanders scornfully referred to the entire cohort as "Okies" (as Fred did to Faith).[67] For Portlanders, the name was not just a term for the Oklahoma Dust Bowl migrant: a 1938 study of state policies toward migrant workers noted the city's singular practice of "render[ing] assistance and passing them on" out of the belief that poor southerners were looking to get something for nothing from Oregonians, who had been spared the worst ravages of the Great Depression.[68]

While an influx of "Okies" was worrisome enough for many people, the number of African American workers among the migrants was downright alarming — despite the fact that fewer than 1 percent of arrivals before March 1943 were black. Living in a city whose black community never numbered more than 2,500, African American workers were especially conspicuous to established white Portlanders. The migration would boost Portland's African American population to 11,000, a monumental demographic shift both statistically and in Portlanders' imaginations. The city's perception of itself as a quiet, orderly, middle-class family town crumbled after the arrival of thousands of single workers with Southern accents, work-worn clothing, and dark faces. These were the people Portlanders had imagined when they read of urban blight in the East and rural "backwardness" in the South.[69]

The federal government was similarly wary of Portland's new migrants. Congress's Tolan Commission monitored the progress of defense migration and any resulting community problems. The president's Committee for Congested Production Areas paid special attention to any hint of a correlation between the racial composition of newcomer populations and changing rates of homelessness, use of public services, aggregate education levels, and incidence of sexually transmitted disease. The FBI's "Racial Conditions Unit" (RACON) kept an eye on minority activists and groups considered likely to instigate race riots or engage in subversive activity for the Axis powers or the Soviets. The persistent stereotype of

African Americans as gullible, savage naifs subject to both the "evolutionary" influences of good whites and "corrupting" influences of bad ones shaped their profile as a potential danger. FBI memos alerted agents that some black workers would be drawn to German and Japanese propaganda assailing wartime rhetoric of "American democracy" with the hypocrisies of Jim Crow. They also warned that African Americans with more steadfast national loyalty were no less dangerous because they could still be beguiled by Communist agents promising political efficacy, economic power, and racial equality in their revolutionary state. What they failed to notice, however, was that the American Communist Party adopted a "Victory First!" agenda that placed black civil rights struggles on the back burner, which in turn caused rifts between black members and the party and among black organizations. (The Communists also endorsed the relocation of Japanese Americans, including their own members.) Fearing the deadly race riots that erupted in other defense centers (most notably in Detroit), RACON sent agents to Portland to report on black workers' activities and recruit informants from the burgeoning community.[70]

The Kaiser shipyard was plagued by social conflicts that had nothing to do with Axis or Communist activity. They stemmed instead from a 1941 agreement between the Kaiser shipyards and the Boilermakers' Union that gave the union sole jurisdiction over the workforce. As African Americans reported to work for Kaiser in greater numbers, the union established a black auxiliary called A-32, with an unelected, white union member as its head. The relationship between A-32 leadership and the black rank and file was similar to the one between Klamath superintendents and their Native American charges: A-32 had no grievance committee and could decide on a whim which workers received promotions and upgrades.

Many A-32 members felt duped by federal labor recruiters' promises of full union benefits, assurances that helped convince them to come to Oregon. Just as the Indian Bureau broke the Klamath treaties at will, the WMC produced a slate of broken promises, and A-32 members had about as much recourse to the law as the tribes. A-32 workers had the freedom to leave, however, and did so in great numbers. The Boilermakers tried to stem the loss of African American labor with promises of special training and promotions, but they switched course when an influx of white migrants in the late summer and early autumn made black workers expendable. A-32 jobs were downgraded to make higher-paying positions available to white newcomers, in spite of the fact that Executive Order 8802 prohibited discriminatory treatment of workers in war plants with federal contracts. Threats of strikes and riots pressed the union to stop the downgrades, but no amount of unrest could persuade the Boilermakers to include their African American coworkers as full members. One hundred black Boilermakers were fired on the spot in November 1942 for refusing to join the Jim Crow union. Mass firings continued through the next year, peaking in July with the dismissal of two hundred black workers from two Kaiser yards.[71]

Julius Rodriquez, a fired protestor, formed the Shipyard Negro Organization for Victory (SNOV) with the aim of desegregating the Boilermaker's Union and pressuring the Fair Employment Practices Committee (FEPC) to hold hearings on A-32 in Portland. On paper, the organization scored two victories. The FEPC not only held hearings in Portland, it ordered Kaiser and the union to comply with the antidiscrimination provisions of Executive Order 8802. Rather than eliminating A-32, however, Kaiser and the Boilermakers challenged the commission's legal authority to enforce such a decision on the grounds that racial discord in the yards was an internal matter that was not subject to federal regulation. To keep the peace, Kaiser made an empty promise to build quality housing for black workers. In the end, the promised housing never materialized, and RACON placed Rodriquez under surveillance as a "dangerous disloyal" with presumed ties to the Communist Party.[72]

Although Henry Kaiser skirted his promises to SNOV, he was forced to team with the Federal Public Housing Authority (FPHA) in early 1942 when an acute housing shortage threatened to drive off new recruits of all races. Hundreds of new workers camped in shacks throughout the city, which Portlanders decried as an aesthetic outrage. Kaiser recruits expressed their own discontent by quitting their jobs at such a high rate that one yard anticipated a 100 percent turnover every six months.[73] Plans for a dormitory in Albina, Portland's most integrated neighborhood, were met with outrage. Residents complained that it was they who had been betrayed by officials promising to end migration (echoing the ire of the "Rogue River Citizen"). As successive waves of black workers answered the WMC's call, white Albina residents demanded constant police protection from the "undesirables" and threatened to sue the government if ground was broken for the dormitory. In the midst of the protests, Oregon senator Charles McNary wired a message from Washington stating that the Federal Public Housing Authority had suddenly scrapped the project. Not even the threat of an Axis victory could move white Portlanders to renegotiate their racial lines.[74]

The dual threat of the war and Portland's racial and housing crises forged a natural alliance between the U.S. Maritime Commission, the FPHA, and the Kaiser Shipbuilding Company to build public housing for all Kaiser shipyard workers. Government-owned dormitories and apartment complexes were fast becoming a standard feature in American cities, but Portland's need was so acute, the demands on workers so great, and segregation so pronounced that Kaiser took the war housing concept a step further by planning an entire city to house and maintain its work force.[75]

Although this "worker's reservation" would differ markedly from the WRA camps, bureaucrats shared Myer and Collier's bitter disagreements about the ultimate purpose of a government-run community. Most officials saw no merit in social engineering goals beyond sheltering workers near the shipyards, keeping them at a comfortable distance from Portland, and keeping an eye out for "hostiles" who might slow production or engage in sabotage. Philip Klutznick, director of the Federal Public Housing Authority, shared fellow New Dealer John Collier's conception of controlled communities as structures for rehabilitation and empowerment. Faced with housing as many as 850,000 defense workers in projects across the nation, Klutznick rejected the model of "providing 'filing cabinets' into which [residents] could fit." He noted that rural Americans faced enormous adjustments to urban life, and that new arrivals to public housing projects would need to learn how to use gas ovens and flush toilets before they could begin to take their place among hardened city dwellers. Public housing could bring backcountry

America into the mainstream and, if undertaken properly, make marginal Americans full participants in political and economic life.[76]

At Vanport, as in other federal communities, the government pursued the incompatible goals of protecting the welfare of citizens it needed to move while curtailing activities that could make them a threat to national security. The town would heighten productivity and strengthen government influence by providing residents with housing, services, and jobs, making them political and economic dependents in the process. As at Klamath and Topaz, Vanporters' isolation and dependency allowed government officials to intrude on their political and economic activity by using resources as leverage, and by monitoring and shaping their behavior through institutions like schools and community policing. The resulting stigmatization and loss of economic and political power raised formidable barriers as war workers sought their place in postwar America: the experience prevented even many working-class white Americans from enjoying the benefits of full citizenship.

In addition to New Deal Progressivism, pioneering ventures in public housing owed much to the model of the company town. The isolated, single-enterprise community ran on paternalism instead of democratic or free-market principles. In towns built to house workers for private industries, employer paternalism would initially center on procuring the housing, services, and goods necessary to keep workers satisfied with their circumstances and free to work longer, more productive hours. Having devised systems that provided labor efficiency and relative comfort to workers, private industries held out their towns as models for the city of the future, where disorder and urban decay would be eradicated from the American scene.[77]

Over time, however, employers generally used the goods, services, and jobs they provided to intrude upon workers' private lives, lest their home and leisure activities compromise productivity in any way. Workers' subsequent loss of political and economic autonomy made them increasingly dependent on the company, which could decide whether it wanted to still employ and house them. For this reason, workers experienced extreme hardship when companies moved their operations and dissolved the towns. If Kaiser had been the owner and administrator of the new town, workers' experiences there would have been relatively unremarkable. Because the federal government was the paternal figure, however, it had the position of curtailing the freedoms of loyal citizens it was bound to protect. Although Kaiser's involvement made it seem like the government's power was not absolute, federal agencies and their local contractors were as engaged with the problem of national security and civil rights for Portland's war workers as they were with Indians and Japanese Americans. Although their reasons for living in a federal community differed markedly from those of the West's "hostile" minorities, war workers shared many of their experiences of marginalization, repression, displacement, and disillusionment with the federal government.[78]

The new city, named "Vanport" because it was equidistant from Portland and Vancouver, Washington, sat upon 650 acres of undesirable land on the Columbia River flood plain formerly known as "Drainage District One." An "impervious earth fill dike" was in place to protect the "miracle city" from floodwaters.[79] The prefab city shared a common purpose with Topaz and the Klamath Reservation: it would segregate and facilitate surveillance of minority populations of potential "hostiles" and "disloyals." But the FPHA's mission for Vanport was more complicated than the one the Interior Department had for its Indian reservations and internment camps. First, Vanport residents would not be moved forcibly to the town as a homogeneous ethnic group. The worker-residents would be multiethnic and largely white. The only selection criteria for Vanport residency were employment at the Kaiser shipyards and a willingness to live in public housing. Second, the development of Vanport was also seen as a pragmatic housing measure that doubled as an attractive employee benefit. Displeased workers could always leave, which could be as harmful to production as an act of sabotage. Third, Vanport had to project itself as a multiracial workers' utopia, where the toleration of difference and harmonious living as American citizens and proud industrial workers formed the reigning spirit, and where SNOV activists were unfortunate aberrations. The FPHA and Kaiser, in the rush to assemble a workforce, did not try to reconcile Vanport's competing agendas but took all of them on silently, putting their numerous social engineering policies on a collision course well before the project housed a single tenant.

Portland officials applauded the plan for a separate workers' city. Yet like Delta County residents near Topaz, they objected to the government confiscating local land to accommodate an undesirable group of people. The Federal Public Housing Authority leased the land from the county and established a local housing authority to "manage, operate, maintain and administer" the project. Mayor Riley selected the members of the Housing Authority of Portland's (HAP) board of commissioners from the leading local banking and real estate companies, adding one member of the American Federation of Labor. The commissioners set policy for all Portland-area projects (subject to the approval of the Federal Public Housing Authority) and supervised a project manager who, like Indian agents and War Relocation Authority officials, acted as an on-site headman, advocate, and disciplinarian. In sum, the Federal Public Housing Authority would be in charge of finances and major policy decisions, while HAP handled routine matters of maintenance, community programs, rent collection, evictions, and public relations. Difficulties awaited HAP from the moment of its inception because it was created to appease competing interest groups with different aspirations for Vanport. For Kaiser and the War Department, Vanport was first and foremost a tool for rapid shipbuilding. For Portlanders, it was a structure to isolate and contain the "undesirables." For residents, however, the federal enclave would be their home and community for the duration of the war, if not longer.[80]

Eternal Foreigners in the Manhattan Project

The stories of the Klamath Reservation, Topaz, and Vanport demonstrate a distinct pattern in the process of casting an identifiable "Other" as an internal enemy. In each case, race, class, newcomer status, political histories, and sheer numbers have made the inhabitants of these places conspicuous and therefore convenient objects of wartime anxieties about race, territorial vulnerability, and rapid social change. America's nuclear reservations also contained loyal citizens and law-abiding aliens deemed "potentially dangerous," but they were invisible to the American public. Instead, the scientists at Los Alamos raised anxieties in military circles about critical national security issues, including the trustworthiness of émigrés, leftists, and American Jews.

The tangled relationship between big government and big science, one of dire interdependency and deep distrust, has its roots in the very origins of the Manhattan Project. For most Americans, the Pearl Harbor bombing brought the first terrifying visions of invasion, but one Hungarian physicist at Columbia University had been afraid for some time. In 1939 Leo Szilard grew concerned that German scientists' recent discoveries in nuclear fission might allow the Nazis to build a bomb with a force so great that even New York City could be reduced to a hundred-foot hole. Szilard, already inclined toward jitteriness, was obsessed by the possibility that America could be destroyed and grew determined to advance his work with colleagues Eugene Wigner and Enrico Fermi toward harnessing the power of atomic energy for America's national defense. Apparently the only sure way to win against Hitler and his weapon of mass destruction was to beat him to the punch by building an American superweapon. Conversations among mid-level scientists did nothing to forge the necessary coordination between the government, the military, the American scientific community, and the growing number of foreign scientists like Szilard who had fled Hitler's Europe to live among the world's foremost defenders of freedom. As insiders to Germany's research institutes, Szilard and his fellow refugees knew very well how real the threat could be and were willing to sacrifice recognition, income, and even academic freedom in the interest of security. The scientific community implemented a self-censorship agreement in 1939, withholding findings that would have surely advanced their careers but potentially aided the Nazis in the race for the bomb.[81]

Although the scientific community then, as ever, wanted as little to do with government bureaucracy as possible, Szilard persuaded his mentor, Albert Einstein, to send a letter to the president alerting him that the nation's security rested upon government funding of an atomic project. The "Einstein Letter" did the trick. America's great genius warned, in measured prose, that the Germans had both the theoretical knowledge

Oliver Applegate with members of the Klamath tribal
police, Jeff Riddle (Modoc), author of *The Indian History of
the Modoc War* (1914), and Chaplain C. C. Hulet. Courtesy
of the Klamath County Museum.

Group photo foregrounding the orderly classroom and disciplined students at the Klamath Agency School. Courtesy of the Klamath County Museum.

Klamath residents, in a familiar lineup for government
services, attend a drawing for allotments run by agency
officials in 1908. Courtesy of the Klamath County Museum.

This panoramic view of Topaz was shot by government photographers in 1943, shortly after the camp was fully populated. Photograph by Francis Stewart. Courtesy of the Bancroft Library, University of California, Berkeley.

This WRA photograph of the Topaz Community Council
drafting a charter emphasizes expanded political
opportunities for one woman elected to serve without
noting the restrictions under which all council members
operated. Photograph by Francis Stewart. Courtesy of the
Bancroft Library, University of California, Berkeley.

This Vanport street scene bears a similar uniformity to
Topaz, but the built environment was far more pleasant.
Oregon Journal photograph courtesy of the Oregon
Historical Society, #c006 208.

A busy day at the Vanport ration counter, where a poster reminds residents to "Smile—Your [sic] in a Free Country." *Oregon Journal* photograph courtesy of the Oregon Historical Society, #CN006 178.

Aerial view of Los Alamos, 1946. Courtesy of the Los Alamos Historical Museum Photo Archives.

Two women stroll near the high security passage between the Tech Area and the main road. Courtesy of the Los Alamos Historical Museum Photo Archives.

and the uranium necessary to develop a bomb capable of destroying a port and surrounding territory. Einstein noted that such a bomb may be too heavy to transport or may lie beyond the realm of the possible, but he warned Roosevelt that the implications of recent German activity—including Germany's moratorium on the sale of uranium from Czechoslovakia while the son of the undersecretary of state pursued uranium research (pioneered in the United States) at the Kaiser Wilhelm Institute—should be "understood."[82]

Roosevelt convened the Uranium Advisory Committee to study the matter and activated the National Defense Research Committee to begin procurement and research efforts. Despite the urgency of the bomb project, the government was no better prepared to build an atomic bomb than it had been to build ships in 1941. The army stepped up the process by creating the Manhattan Engineer District (MED) in late 1942 with Pentagon-builder General Leslie R. Groves as the head. A multi-facility web of information, the MED was vulnerable to interception and eavesdropping in its fragmentary state. Simple consultations became military operations: scientists were spirited from one laboratory to another, and wire and mail communication had to be secured. The errors, awkwardness, and delays in these exchanges slowed the race for the bomb, placing the Allied cause in imminent peril.[83]

The MED untangled the web by concentrating much of the research and production efforts into three high-security, twenty-four-hour centers, where scientists and technicians could work undisturbed and the army could seal the project from leaks and infiltration. The government built a uranium enrichment complex at Oak Ridge, Tennessee, on 59,000 acres west of Knoxville. It housed 13,000 workers when it opened in 1942, later growing to 45,000 at the height of the project. A second facility at Hanford, Washington, necessitated construction of the city of Richland to support the 17,000 workers who would process plutonium as quickly and safely as possible. The laboratory complex at Los Alamos, New Mexico, was the most highly secured of the outposts. Locals knew about Oak Ridge and Hanford but not Los Alamos. Scientists would disappear into the desert for the duration of the war, breaking all contact with the outside world. Clearly, strict secrecy would be the key to preventing infiltrators from stealing information, kidnapping scientists, or discovering the project's purpose. But as with other federal communities, the agency also feared disloyalty among the top scientists, whose foreign origins or left-leaning politics raised concerns that American national security could be in the hands of Nazi or Soviet agents—or both. The number of alien nationals (roughly one-third of the top-tier scientists) and citizen radicals among the great lights of American science provoked fears that many Los Alamosans would be inclined to leak military secrets, could be hard to outwit, and would surely fight restrictions of their civil liberties.[84]

The MED, like the Indian Bureau, the War Relocation Authority, and the Federal Public Housing Authority, believed that an enclosed community with a self-contained political and economic system would provide the best means of keeping scientific workers productive and well secured without sundering the integrity of America's democratic principles. Although Los Alamos shared Klamath, Topaz, and Vanport's model of isolation and federal paternalism, there were some notable differences. The MED used elements of the reservation system and the company town model to enhance security and productivity, but it also relied heavily on structures from military installations to keep residents in order.

Although the government accorded its scientists far greater respect than Indians, internees, and shipyard workers, Los Alamosans also lived under the tightest controls and the strictest secrecy, leaving them unaware of some of the most egregious encroachments on their fundamental freedoms. Los Alamosans would have protested the extensive in-home surveillance had they known that their every word and action was being recorded. Scientists questioning health and safety standards in the laboratory were ignored while the level of radiation in their coworkers' bodies reached dangerous levels. The combination of secrecy and dependency made Los Alamos a disorienting place, and the degree of dependency the community engendered in the affluent, independently minded academics made it impossible for them to integrate their town into the rest of New Mexico at the end of the war. Although Los Alamosans' wartime experiences were markedly different from those of Topazians and Vanporters, they sustained similar economic, political, and social losses at the end of the war as a result of cooperating with government directives in the fight for global democracy.

Foreign scientists tolerated the conceptual inconsistency between America's war aims and their restricted freedoms as an acceptable alternative to what would have befallen them in Europe. Italian physicist Emilio Segrè was living in California in the months when Germans and Italians were under the same restrictions as the Japanese. This placed Segrè in "the ridiculous situation" of being privy to information too sensitive for Congress and high-level military officials to know but "too dangerous" to be allowed to take a walk after sundown or go to an evening movie.[85]

Enrico Fermi was enormously patient with the travel restrictions that made his frequent trips between MED sites so miserable. He became enraged, however, when mail arrived opened and censored. Fermi demanded that the Wartime Civil Control Authority explain to him the legal basis for invading his privacy. Civil Control denied Fermi's allegation, then admitted it (blaming a low-level employee), and dropped the issue on Columbus Day 1942, when Attorney General Francis Biddle lifted Italians' enemy status as part of the festivities. Fermi regained his right to move freely and correspond privately. But he remained a suspected fascist agent, despite pioneering the American atomic research project, which if successful would have blown European fascism off the map.[86]

As an East European with ties to Germany and a well-known irreverence for military discipline, Szilard appeared so dangerous to Groves that he advised Attorney General Biddle to intern Szilard as an enemy alien for the duration of the war. General Henry Stimson, commanding officer for the Western Defense Command, refused to sign Groves's order, as did Biddle, who noted Szilard was already subject to the same restrictions as Japanese, German, and Italian nationals. Szilard, however, ignored curfews, travel restrictions, and orders to account for his activities, giving Groves an excuse to place him under surveillance by army intelligence (or G-2.) The investigator's report revealed that Szilard, who was Jewish, usually ate in delis, walked when he could not get a taxi, was shaved by a barber, had mostly Jewish friends, and was absentminded to the point of frequently forgetting which way he intended to walk down the street. This, in addition to a War Department memo advising the

Manhattan Engineer District against placing Szilard and Fermi on the project together, led Groves to bar Szilard from Los Alamos. The memo warned that Fermi was "undoubtedly a Fascist" and that Szilard, while promoting the Manhattan Project, had "remarked on many occasions that he thinks the Germans will win the war." That Szilard had the expertise to accelerate the research effort mattered less than the MED's need to identify an internal enemy and exert control over him—or, barring his existence, create such an enemy.[87]

The MED was equally afraid of American-born scientists with histories of activism in progressive causes. The number of scientists involved in civil libertarian organizations, labor politics, and antifascist movements compelled the FBI to place nuclear laboratories under surveillance in the 1930s. The FBI zeroed in on Berkeley as the logical location for Soviet agents to infiltrate the American scientific community, and their suspicions were confirmed in the person of Giovanni Rossi Lomanitz. A graduate student in the University of California's Radiation Laboratory (Rad Lab), Lomanitz helped the Communist Party organize the newly arrived black workers at the local Kaiser shipyard. RACON agents reported that Lomanitz, on hearing of the Manhattan Project, had asked Party leader Steve Nelson for a permanent position as a shipyard organizer to avoid being sent away.[88]

Lieutenant Colonel Boris T. Pash, chief of counterintelligence for the Western Defense Command, launched his own investigation into Soviet espionage in the laboratory in the spring of 1943. He concluded that there was a cell within the laboratory organized by Dr. J. Robert Oppenheimer. The accomplished and popular professor had been under surveillance since at least 1941 for his personal involvement with avowed Communist Party members, who affectionately called him "the Big Shot" and "Oppie."[89]

Oppenheimer, though not one to march in the streets, supported the Spanish Loyalists in the 1930s and gave increasing aid to antifascist causes in response to the persecution of German Jews. He donated a large share of his family inheritance to the University of California to help graduate students finish their degrees during the Depression and cofounded a union for Berkeley professors, teaching assistants, and schoolteachers.

He became fervently anti-Soviet when he learned of Stalin's purges, stepping back from political and social movements altogether. This change did not persuade the FBI to erase Oppenheimer from the list of people subject to "custodial detention pending investigation" (on which local Japanese community leaders also appeared) in the event of a national emergency.[90]

The one thing that overshadowed Oppenheimer's "redness" was his genius as a theoretical physicist and as a manager of academic scientists and graduate assistants. For this reason, the federal government hired, rather than arrested, him — though not without controversy. Groves needed a scientific director for the main laboratory, and Oppenheimer had a record of success with similar projects. The director's ability to finish the bomb on time was critical to Groves's reputation: if Germany developed a bomb first, Groves feared he would spend the rest of his career answering to congressional committees. The FBI noted the political activities of Oppenheimer's ex-girlfriends, his wife's former husband, and his students, including Lomanitz, but Groves believed it was worth the political risk to appoint Oppenheimer as director. Invoking his powers to determine who was loyal and who was not (as he had with Szilard), Groves concluded that Oppenheimer, in spite of his questionable associations, was "absolutely essential to the project" and was appointed director on this basis.[91]

Oppenheimer's first task was to entice the nation's scientific talent to Los Alamos without telling them anything about their destination. Oppenheimer began his recruitment campaign at UC Berkeley's Rad Lab, knowing that scientists with whom he had a relationship would be most likely to devote their blind loyalty to the project. Intelligence agents watched every one of Oppenheimer's recruits. While they had no problem with Luis Alvarez and Edwin MacMillan, who were on record as "apolitical," they placed Philip Morrison, David Hawkins, and Robert Serber under constant surveillance for their varying degrees of involvement with activist causes. The only recruiting decision G-2 sought to influence was the one regarding Oppenheimer's brother Frank, who had been deeply involved with Communist organizations in the Bay Area. Interestingly, Oppenheimer was pressured to bring his brother to

Los Alamos, not keep him out. Army security for the Western Defense Command believed it was far safer to place Frank Oppenheimer under his brother's watch, in a confined, controlled setting. This way, the man with both a family connection to the project and the scientific know-how to understand and convey information about his brother's activities was in a place where he could put his knowledge to good use and remain unable to share it with others.[92]

Unlike the Office of Indian Affairs, the War Relocation Authority, and the Federal Public Housing Authority, the MED could not afford to make simplistic distinctions between dangerous and potentially dangerous government wards, so it used strategies like the one applied to Frank Oppenheimer for its scientists. Only the graduate students were numerous enough to selectively pre-segregate. "High-risk" students were drafted into the army by order of the Western Defense Command and sent to desolate posts, usually in Alaska or New Caledonia. In these remote locales, disloyal graduate students could not spread state secrets to Communists very easily and were not likely to be captured and interrogated by the Axis powers. Those deemed safe were asked to leave home, shut their mouths, and spend the duration of the war working on the project of a lifetime.[93]

By August 1943 Groves had a pool of international scientific genius, which he could only hope did not contain a giant Communist cell. As architects of the community in which these scientists, engineers, laborers, and security guards would work, Groves and Oppenheimer had a mission that was twofold: to ensure productivity at an unprecedented pace and to provide leak-proof security. In the minds of the federal bureaucrats and army officers in charge of the project, absolute loyalty to the United States was critical to the success of the project. The work environment and the townsite therefore had to nurture existing loyalty, cultivate it where it flagged, and root out disloyalty wherever it was detected. This unarticulated policy was so central to the workings of Los Alamos that it was in operation well before ground was broken for the secret city.

The site for the laboratory was selected from a number of "unpopulated" western lands. Los Alamos was the most remote area, set atop a high mesa, which was ideal for security. The landscape was magnificently beautiful and situated near the delightful town of Santa Fe, which was good for morale. Better still, there were very few educated English-speaking Americans in the area, making it preferable to Oak City, Utah, where a large Mormon community would have to be evicted. The Los Alamos site also included buildings from the Los Alamos Ranch School, a Progressive-era outdoor academy that turned sickly boys into great leaders, including one of Groves's lieutenants and Oppenheimer himself. The army sent the headmaster a letter informing him that the school was being condemned for military purposes and that they had two months to clear off the mesa. The government paid half its value and accused the headmaster of disloyalty when he attempted to negotiate a better deal. The old settler population of whites disappeared after a hasty February graduation ceremony, and Bences Gonzales, a cafeteria cook with extended family in nearby Espanola, was the only old-timer hired at Los Alamos.[94]

The MED told English-speaking locals that essential military work was underway on "the Hill" that was not to be discussed. This hardly put a lid on rumors, which ranged from speculation that the army was producing poison gas, jet propulsion rockets, or atomic bombs, to tales that the mesa was a haven for nudists, pregnant members of the Women's Army Corps (WACS), or the offspring of pregnant WACS. One child told his parents he was sure President Roosevelt had built "a Republican internment camp." Oppenheimer launched a disinformation campaign to make the public believe Los Alamosans were building a super-rocket. In any case, outsiders were never allowed close enough to Los Alamos to confirm their suspicions. Military police would patrol the area at all times with orders to go to any length to prevent intruders from seeing the town.[95]

Los Alamosans were also restricted from unnecessary interaction with curious locals and prohibited from revealing their identity or reason for being in New Mexico. Some banking services were filtered through a secret federal account, but all residents were instructed to maintain their hometown bank accounts. Drivers were issued bizarre licenses stating that their name was "Special List B" and that their residence was Box 1663, with a signature line stamped "not required." They could not appear on any public record, so no divorces, wills, adoptions, or marriages could be granted, certified, or enforced. Births were registered to families at Box 1663, and school-age children were registered by first name only so that batches of transcripts and other records would not reveal the population of the project. The more prominent scientists and their families could not use real names: the MED made the Fermis "the Farmers" and Niels Bohr "Nicholas Baker."[96]

Travel into Santa Fe was allowed but was closely monitored. The military policemen issued passes to each resident over the age of six, which allowed them to travel within a radius that had Albuquerque as its outer limit. For many, the area inside the fence was as large as their wartime world would be. Although Los Alamos's purpose was akin to Vanport's, security made the site so similar to Topaz that one MP destined for the mesa had been certain he was being briefed for duty at a WRA camp. Like Topaz, Los Alamos had to be equipped to meet residents' every need because they would have no means of accessing services outside the project.[97]

Meanwhile, the Manhattan Engineer District began construction at a pace as impressive as Vanport's but without the fanfare and public admiration. Once the site was secured, buildings were constructed without the benefit of a site plan. Groves ordered buildings from an army menu of flimsy, mass-produced, temporary structures. The laboratory buildings were of the "modified mobilization" style, and their generic blueprints lacked facilities for radioactive dustproofing, specialized ventilation, or air conditioning. There were, however, guardhouses, high razor-wire fences, and sophisticated listening posts everywhere. The differences between the commanding officer and the project director came to the surface during construction. Groves wanted a fortress, while Oppenheimer envisioned a research utopia where the finest minds lived and worked together in an attractive environment with few distractions.[98]

Groves and Oppenheimer got along reasonably well, but sharing power over a tightly controlled community and a high-stakes military mission made leadership a trying business for Groves. One of the earliest clashes came when Oppenheimer protested Groves's plan to have every scientist inducted into the army. Oppenheimer expressed doubt that many of the most-needed scientists would be willing to join the military. Thinking this was an issue of prestige, Groves arranged that they all be admitted as commissioned officers. Oppenheimer presented this proposal to prospective Los Alamosans Isador Rabi and Robert Bacher, who were unwilling to work within a military chain of command. They, like Szilard, refused to compromise the free inquiry and scholarly autonomy that formed the basis of good scientific work.[99]

Groves compromised, allowing scientists to remain civilians until the bomb was tested. Once the bomb existed, every scientist would be inducted immediately into the army as an officer and would then have to work in uniform, under military orders. Bacher signed on reluctantly, stating his intention to leave at the point of militarization, but Rabi remained a consultant, never joining the Manhattan Project.[100]

The softened security took its toll on Groves, with so many "enemy aliens" and "subversives" under his watch. In order to retain key scientists while maintaining a semblance of security protocols, Groves made each scientist vouch for a colleague with whom he had worked before. Somebody proposed an oath on the Bible, but Groves objected because "most of [the scientists] are unbelievers." An intelligence officer then proposed an oath on personal honor, but Groves insisted that the "longhairs" had none. They could, he decided, swear on their scientific reputation because "it seems to me it is the only thing they care for." Groves saw himself in charge of a community of less-civilized, potentially dangerous people, but unlike other project directors, he could make no claims to inherent racial or intellectual superiority. Having lost his mandate to make Los Alamosans into "good soldiers," his leadership hinged on making continuous shows of force in order to contain, if not reform, his wards.[101]

As scientists began to settle at Los Alamos, Groves's "longhairs" joined the West Coast Japanese, Vanporters, and reservation Indians in the cluster of people subject to federal demographic management (or, in Roosevelt's terms, "putting the right people in the right places").[102] The federal government had deliberately moved Indians, West Coast Japanese, industrial workers (black, white, radical, and otherwise), and the best of the nation's scientific talent pool to the places where, theoretically, they would do the least harm and the most good. As they began their lives in their isolated "little Americas," it became clear that they were, indeed, part of a real democratic experiment within the greater American one.

CHAPTER TWO

THE GREAT CITIZENSHIP PANTOMIME

Politics and Power in a Barbed-Wire Democracy

In 1946 War Relocation Authority (WRA) officials took stock of their relocation program. The "cultural structure of realistic democracy" spawned a system of homegrown, self-contained political organs that functioned separately from the American body politic, in which fully enfranchised citizens enjoyed real political efficacy. Historian Sandra Taylor, noting the differences between participating in a political exercise and exercising political power, quite aptly called Topaz "a barbed-wire democracy." In a barbed-wire democracy, Japanese detainees were expected to conduct public affairs as if they were living in any American small town, albeit one with a conspicuous, impermeable border. As Reveil Netz notes in *Barbed Wire: An Ecology of Modernity*, barbed wire is not the strongest physical barrier to movement, but it carries a threat of violence in its ability to wound. Tracing the invention of the barbed-wire settlement back to the Boer War and its widespread use to World War I, Netz asserts that such communities were powerful instruments of confining the enemy: containing people in small spaces by surrounding them with instruments of pain placed them under "relentless control." The politics of this sort of containment is part and parcel of the history of twentieth-century warfare—not of democracy, inclusion, or protection of the vulnerable bodies within.[1]

Ideally, the WRA's detainees would accept the government's fiction of "protective custody" and view their new communities as the western version of the New England towns of the eighteenth century, on which the nation's political culture of local control and full participation were built. They would elect their own leaders, hold town meetings, and engage in democratic processes to devise solutions to problems, but they would not regain their prewar political rights until the government determined it was safe (to the non-Japanese public) to restore them. To hasten the transformation, the WRA would establish "a pattern for government and the improvisation of community institutions within defined concepts of state and federal jurisdiction" that would afford Topazians as much democracy as "circumstances would permit."[2]

The most notable difference between small-town America and the barbed-wire democracies was that the federal government's power to act as *parens patriae* ("father of the state") granted the WRA "an authority to enforce discipline within a state administrative agency" such as a school, hospital, or prison, where citizens are incapable of acting in their own interest (as determined by the state).[3] Despite the authoritarian cast of this political arrangement, the WRA truly believed that, if all worked well, the contradictions between the democratic ideal of the small town and the totalizing effects of the prison would mold Japanese outsiders into capable American citizens. One WRA staff member mused optimistically in 1942 that "[t]here is an opportunity to share in the accomplishment of a modern miracle . . . the eventual return of every member of the relocated group to their normal place as members of the American Community not only as loyal citizens or resident aliens, but as *better* citizens, more realistically democratic in principle, in thought, and in effect: tempered . . . to carry forward the living principles of democracy which all of us, in our fashion, are fighting for now."[4] By this logic, the years spent in desolate camps offered just the extended civics lesson that a population so foreign would need to become fit for American citizenship.[5]

The WRA took credit for inventing these limited democracies, but there was nothing new about them; the Indian Bureau had been trying for decades to develop civic structures that were more pedagogical than politically efficacious in order to shape "savage" Indians into capable citizens and "competent" individuals. This fantastical reformist impulse had already been enacted at the Klamath Reservation well before Congress formally ratified the Treaty of 1864. Unbeknownst to the Indian signatories of the treaty, their reservation was being designed as a staging area from which Agent Lindsay Applegate, with the aid of his son Oliver, could judge each tribal member's loyalty to the United States. At the Indian Bureau, "loyalty" meant compliance with government directives, not devotion to American principles of freedom, equality, and democracy per se. Applegate absorbed the bureau's definition in his policies. For instance, he considered any Indian "not living in the place or places designated for them by treaty stipulation" a "hostile Indian" subject to military justice. Soldiers at Fort Klamath had standing orders to arrest all Indians outside the reservation boundary. Cooperative detainees were to be returned to the reservation for intensive Americanization. Indians who resisted arrest, however, were to be held as prisoners of war at Fort Klamath.[6]

Early on, government officials saw the reservation boundary as far more than a tool for separating Indians and whites. Agents watched how individuals situated themselves in relationship to the border to determine which Indians could be assimilated and which ones were eternally hostile and immutably foreign—and thus unfit to take part in the reservation's Americanization process. The stakes were tremendously high for Native peoples: those who complied with government directives held hope in the promise of greater self-determination, while those who fought for their freedom could count on remaining wards or prisoners of the U.S. government, unless they were hanged for their crimes.

The Klamaths' first great test came shortly after signing the treaty. Applegate called an assembly of cooperative around a fence post and announced that the reservation was to be democratized that day. No longer would kinship or heredity determine who had power; instead, a "president" and a panel of judges on a tribal court would lead the reservation government. The unusual feature of this "democracy" was that Applegate would supervise the new government, select a pool of appropriate candidates for election, and "correct" any errors in governance. Although these democratic structures emulated the functions of the executive and judicial branches in the American system, they were hardly designed to serve the will of the Klamaths, Modocs, and Yahooskins. At the Klamath Reservation, "government" was an exercise in procedure, rather than a mechanism for wielding power. Applegate, as the "teacher," held the real governmental powers, including that of the veto and judicial review. This living civics lesson was a mixed blessing for the Klamath Tribes. On the one hand, it gave active tribal members experience with the American political process and provided a platform to present issues to the agency. On the other, its abolition of traditional government structures made Indian political life subordinate to the absolute authority of the U.S. government.

To clear the way for a new political order, Oliver Applegate usurped power from the Klamath leader La-Lakes by declaring him incompetent. This assessment was based on La-Lakes's resistance to the agency's sweeping authority and his inability to control other "hostile" Klamaths (as well as his own Modoc opponents) under his rule. Applegate put forth an acceptable slate of candidates and endorsed a man named Allen David, whom the New York Times later described as "coming nearer than any other [on the reservation] to realizing the romantic ideal of the noble red man." The journalist was especially impressed with the strikingly "cavalier" way in which David wore his clean shirt, polished boots, sombrero, and scarf.[7]

David won the election that followed, but the final tally did not express the will of the people who protested the destruction of traditional governance. An Applegate relative wrote later that, "however bitterly the feeling of defeat may have rankled in the breasts of these lately savage citizens, the next scene in the drama shows that they had learned that fundamental principle of democratic government—majority rule." Applegate reinforced his civics lesson by instructing Indians to support their new "chief" and work toward the common good. Over time, this imperative proved more easily said than done for Yahooskins and Modocs who had to live beneath two tiers of foreign government as "citizens" of an ersatz American democracy headed by a Klamath leader.[8]

To deal with tribal members who did not work for the common good, Applegate established the first tribal court, whose handpicked judges were given instruction in American conceptions of crime and punishment. The judges' decisions were supposed to follow the basic principles of American jurisprudence. Because the tribal court was not connected to the American court system, its decisions were binding to the extent Applegate agreed to approve and enforce them. The judges heard cases and rendered opinions based on a set list of actionable offenses, which were divided into three categories. The first class of crimes encompassed acts committed against individuals, including murder, adultery, theft, witchcraft, and assault. The second included property crimes like arson, and the third set criminalized Indian customs including traditional marriages, cremation of the dead, shamanism, and dancing. The agency accorded Indian judges special status and personal favors for abandoning tribal traditions and for condemning everything from Native dress to Native philosophies of justice. The judges were left to deal with the social consequences when Applegate's agents arrested traditional doctors and broke up families united by traditional marriages instead of Christian ones.[9]

The first case before the tribal court was a divorce suit brought by a woman named "Little Sallie" who complained "in plain Boston" (meaning English) that her husband had purchased a second wife over her objections. The second case was that of a man who stole the daughter of a subchief. The court sentenced him to wear six feet of log chain on his leg for nine months, cut his hair, and chop wood for tribal leaders, who would board and clothe him in the meantime. Such sentences made the territorial superintendent complain that Indian jurists were treating the justice system as a game by hearing silly complaints and meting out absurd punishments. He also blasted the court for its ineffectiveness at subduing a group of Modocs who continually disobeyed the agents. The tribal judges had much to gain by meeting the agents' demands, but whether the Indian Bureau realized it or not, relocation did not ease the long-standing rivalry between Klamaths and Modocs. In fact, tensions only grew worse during their shared confinement. Klamath leaders knew heavy-handed punishments would spark something more akin to a revolution than a citizenship lesson.[10] Despite the limitations of the reservation's new legal system to deliver justice and keep public order, the court undermined traditional systems of justice and immersed the Klamath Tribes in the language, if not the practices, of American jurisprudence.[11]

There was no democracy lesson in the world that could divert attention from the fact that the Indian Bureau did not fulfill its treaty obligations. Provisions were often short, leaving people hungry and fearful of what their dependency on the U.S. government could bring. Worse, the government neglected its promise to provide the security necessary to protect the Klamaths and Modocs from one another. The Modocs claimed that they were not given the protection from the Klamaths they were promised as a condition of moving from their *own* homeland to the Klamath's much-reduced one, which the latter grudgingly shared. Skirmishes between the tribes began to escalate, but as the territorial superintendent noted of the court, tribal institutions were unable to devise meaningful solutions to the problems that plagued the rival tribes.

Reservation politics quickly shifted from the government's great democratic pantomime to prosecuting the Modoc War (1872–73), which was a real political contest involving the exercise of genuine political power. When the Klamath Agency failed to respond to Modoc leaders' reports of harassment by Klamaths, a band of approximately sixty members of the tribe led by Keintpoos (or "Captain Jack" to non-Indians) abandoned their treaty obligations as well. Modocs had been forcibly removed from their homeland in the Lava Beds of Northern California in 1869 and had been restrained from demonstrating resentment in the intervening three years. Pushed to the limit by humiliations and economic deprivation, the dissident Modocs made their first show of resistance by crossing the reservation boundary and returning to the Lava Beds, which were off-limits according to the Treaty of 1864.[12]

The Oregon superintendent's office was quick to grasp the broad political implications of the dissidents' actions. Officials sent an urgent memo warning the officers at Fort Klamath (whom Modocs referred to as "The Colonizers") that the Modocs were so enraged that Keintpoos and his men would lay their lives on the line if they thought they could take out several U.S. soldiers in the process. The memo also emphasized, however, that the U.S. government could not afford to exterminate a tribe it had just made a treaty with, no matter how hostile. After all, the legitimacy of the entire Indian program rested on the government's claim to be the guardian-protector of the indigenous Americans-to-be.[13] The Indian Bureau opted to negotiate a peace settlement with the Modocs to save face, but it was humiliated when an antisettlement faction of the Modocs (who had broken from Keintpoos) ambushed the federal agents in the peace delegation. A letter from Colonel Alfred B. Meacham reprinted in the New York Times—under the headline "SAVAGES. Letter of Mr. Meacham Detailing the Brutal Treachery of Modoc Jack—Latest from the Front"—reported that the Indian commissioners and soldiers had "gained several points over the Indians looking to a peaceful solution." It also stated they had "thwarted all [the Modocs'] schemes of treachery" with the aid of their Modoc interpreter Toby Riddle (whose birth name was Winema). The delegation was caught off guard when the Modocs arrived at the appointed meeting place with "eight armed instead of six unarmed Indians" and the firm demand that the United States withdraw its soldiers from the area. The delegates refused, insisting the Modocs settle for their offer of "amnesty, a suitable and satisfactory home, and ample provision for their welfare in the future." General Edward B. Canby tried to persuade the Modocs that such an arrangement would provide security for Indians and non-Indians alike, but before he could finish two more armed Modocs rode into the meeting. Canby demanded an explanation from Keintpoos. Keintpoos raised a pistol to Canby's face and shouted an order, "in Indian," to attack. Canby was killed and Meacham nearly scalped.[14]

The New York Times criticized the agents for failing to see that Keintpoos was "an intense liar and a great politician" who was plotting a treacherous act, implying the Modoc leader was simply hostile by nature (although he was not part of the guilty faction) and beyond the reach of reason or civilized politics (even though he had been willing to negotiate at several points).[15] To compensate for the error, the army chased down the Modocs, trapped Kientpoos and his men, and returned them to Fort Klamath in chains, where Kientpoos and six of his men were tried and executed for the ambush. The Indian Bureau insisted that everyone suspected of supporting Keintpoos's cause view the execution so that they understood the consequences of resistance and dissent. The army then separated the loyal Modocs from the irredeemably disloyal and removed the latter to the Quapaw Agency in Oklahoma for life. (The government barred the descendants of the Oklahoma Modocs from returning to the Klamath Reservation until 1909.) Increasingly, federal agencies made identification and segregation of hostile or disloyal subjects a central purpose for building new isolated enclaves. One agent and an array of scaled-down democratic institutions might be able to assimilate outsiders or instill democracy where it might not otherwise exist, but they did not have the power to quell dissent and disorder that could turn the community against the federal government. Dissenters who refused to recognize the absolute authority of the United States government went from being citizens in the making to exiled (or executed) prisoners of war.[16]

It is worth noting the cost of the Modoc resistance movement for both sides. Press reports and oral traditions relay indiscriminate slaughter, as in the case of the elderly Indian man who was bludgeoned to death and burned as he tried to show American soldiers he was unarmed. Reporters found his charred bones as well as corpses of Modocs and U.S. soldiers littering the Klamath Basin. Twenty years later, historian Hubert Howe Bancroft referred to the Modoc War as being "in some respects the most remarkable that ever occurred in the history of aboriginal extermination." The loss of life disheartened the Modocs tremendously and threatened to undermine the Indian Bureau's stated aim behind the reservation system. The Modoc War demonstrated that reservation life could just as easily raise anti-American sentiment as any desire to Americanize.[17]

Once the army eliminated the hostile elements of the tribal population from the Klamath Reservation, the Applegates shed their role as Indian fighters to resume their position as Indian agents. Their work was simplified by the Indians' loss of recognition as sovereign peoples in the post-treaty period. Once Indians were subdued and made into wards of the government, agents could disregard treaty provisions if they impeded plans to reform the reservation. Their task was to restructure reservation institutions in order to nurture residents' nascent loyalties to the United States and speed the process of Americanization. Having just ended a war, the reservation agency was also responsible for maintaining strict security to assure nearby citizens their right to live free of fear of Indians. Repressive management strategies were not used exclusively at the Klamath Reservation, however. They were borne of and bolstered by federal initiatives to put a final end to Indian uprisings across the reservation system. As a result, according to one scholar, reservations became more like prisoner-of-war camps. While Indians were encouraged to proceed with their everyday lives, soldiers from Fort Klamath kept the peace through regular patrols of the area, keeping the reservation under armed guard. The fort was equipped to jail, try, punish, and even execute Indians who interfered with their white neighbors or made similar "treaty violations." The presence of the military garrison at Fort Klamath came to mean very different things to Americans and Indians in the area. For whites, it was a reassuring symbol that their government was protecting them. To the Indians, however, it was the place where the U.S. Army executed dissidents who attempted to hold the government accountable for its failures. It was the place where people were punished for engaging in meaningful politics.[18]

To reduce both the tensions and the security costs resulting from the Modoc War, the Klamath Agency allowed procurement officers at Fort Klamath to purchase meat and produce from the developing reservation agricultural training program and to employ suitable tribal members as casual laborers. The Applegates promoted the fort to the tribes as an example of market-driven mutuality, and they lauded the enhanced quality of life such trade relationships would bring. The Indians were not convinced. When Fort Klamath extended its goodwill mission so far as to recruit young Native men as cavalry scouts, most refused out of suspicion that this sudden desire for "inclusiveness" was a government ploy to send young "hostiles" away to die.[19]

The Indian Bureau interpreted Klamaths' resistance to military service as evidence that discipline was lacking. The experimental remedy was to make the Klamath Reservation among the first to have an agency-supervised tribal police force. The idea of Indians policing Indians gained currency in the late 1870s, when the Indian Bureau asked reservation agents to establish permanent, official forces who would be paid a small salary, issued uniforms, and given badges. In addition, Indian police acted as the reservation vice squad, apprehending bootleggers, illegal grazers, poachers, adulterers, and fighters. Perhaps the most symbolically significant function of the tribal police was to maintain the integrity of the reservation boundary that had so recently been breached. The Indian Bureau authorized tribal police officers to arrest Indians leaving the reservations and non-Indian trespassers alike. In addition to being enforcers, however, Native policemen were expected to serve as translators and cultural mediators between the agency and less Americanized Indians.[20] Policing, unlike some of the early fencepost-era institutions, afforded selected Indians an opportunity to wield real power, albeit over errant Indians, and not over agency or Indian Bureau decisions. Native officers would enforce rules set forth by U.S. officials, thus making them allies in the project of Americanizing the community and, on the flip side, effective agents of de-Indianization.

Agency staff selected officers from the growing biracial population and gave these new employees conspicuous markers of their special status. This is not to say Indians were vested with full police powers. They worked under the supervision of the chief clerk, who was a career bureaucrat and not a law enforcement expert. While tribal police handled everyday crimes and infractions of the law, the Indian Bureau had special officers to deal with large-scale federal crimes, including shows of resistance to government authority.[21]

The agency also established a special Klamath Court of Indian Offenses to adjudicate cases involving Indians' refusal to abandon traditional practices. Oliver Applegate boasted years later that he selected the justices of the reservation court from the "most capable and progressive Indians" to create a class of "resolute men" who were ready to support the government authorities even if it meant suppressing tribal leaders. For the government, having Indians police Indians allowed officials to claim that the reservation's disciplinary spaces were Native creations and that heavy-handed Americanization programs were tribal initiatives. To the outside world, tribal policing awarded greater legitimacy to federal law and policy on the Klamath Reservation for making them seem approved by Indians themselves.[22]

As with all federal programs, however, the Klamath tribal justice system was subject to budget cuts with each new session of Congress. When budget cuts reduced tribal policemen's salaries to less than five dollars per month, the agency proposed a reorganization of tribal law enforcement so that lower-paid deputies could be added to expand the force. The agency bestowed these honorable commissions upon two "loyal, intelligent and progressive Christian men" as well as a promising student at the agency school named Jesse Kirk. As an intelligent, disciplined son of an Indian minister, Kirk embodied the promise the Applegates held out for their work. Such accomplished youngsters seemed to prove the Indian Bureau's theory that the educational and disciplinary structures of reservation programming could make capable, cooperative citizens of the Indians in as little as one generation.[23]

Despite the Indian Bureau's many layers of social engineering, democratic experimentation, military intervention, and the emergence of men like Allen David and Jesse Kirk, the reservation system became an embarrassment to the federal government by the mid-1880s. Reports of corruption, violence, aimlessness, and deplorable living conditions seeped into the public dialogue through reservation grapevines and government reports. By 1890, following the official closing of the frontier and the cessation of large-scale Indian conflicts, the War Department wanted out of reservation security and frontier operations generally. Progressives of all stripes railed against different elements of the reservation system: some complained that Indians were too poor, others that they received too much from the government; some that Indians were destined to die out, others that they must be saved; some that they were future Americans, others that they were subhuman species unfit for citizenship. Helen Hunt Jackson roundly condemned the government's conduct of Indian affairs on the Pacific slope in the opening sections of A Century of Dishonor:

> There is not among these three hundred bands of Indians one which has not suffered cruelly at the hands either of the Government or of white settlers. The poorer, the more insignificant, the more helpless the band, the more certain the cruelty and outrage to which they have been subjected. This is especially true of the bands on the Pacific

slope. These Indians found themselves of a sudden surrounded by and caught up in the great influx of gold-seeking settlers, as helpless creatures on a shore are caught up in a tidal wave. There was not time for the Government to make treaties; not even time for communities to make laws. The tale of the wrongs, the oppressions, the murders of the Pacific-slope Indians in the last thirty years would be a volume by itself, and is too monstrous to be believed.[24]

All sides agreed, however, that Washington had to adopt a new approach to "the Indian question." The federal government could no longer squander public resources or the nation's credibility as a defender of freedom on a system that made people impoverished, dependent, "backward," and, from some points of view, perpetual prisoners.

Indian reservations were not the only places where government institutions proved inadequate to the task of democratization. Land scarcity and wild boom-and-bust cycles increased the ranks of the discontented working class, for whom the revolutionary promise of ownership and independence was still an expectation. A renewed vision of freedom, independence, and social equality was articulated in the Homestead Act of 1862. The act opened public land to settlement by any citizen (or alien intending to become a citizen who had not borne arms against the United States) who could afford the eighteen-dollar filing fee and had the wherewithal to develop, make productive, and live upon their 160-acre plot for five years. The land would belong to the homesteader, who could legally transfer it to his (or her) heirs. With this promise of upward, intergenerational mobility, homesteaders who existed on the margins of respectable life in the East could attain full equality in the West. As one boosterish publication put it, "There is no landlord, no rent to pay, nor are any church rates exacted. He himself is lord of the manor, and peer of his fellow-citizens of all classes."[25]

Although historians generally agree that the Homestead Act ultimately made land available to speculators and monopolists, its rhetoric reestablished the Jeffersonian yeoman farmer as the embodiment of American freedom. Through ownership, hard work, and a venturesome spirit, anyone — regardless of background — could achieve independence, prosperity, self-determination, status as a first-class citizen, and true efficacy in American political life. In its own hands-off way, the federal government put forth a utopian vision in which land and labor together would transform wage slaves and aliens into free and full citizens. American utopias had no fences, masters, or limits on what an independent, self-determining individual could do with his talents and resources.[26]

The General Allotment Act of 1887 (or the "Dawes Act") also sought to reinforce the ideals and habits of American citizenship by placing Indians on individually owned 160-acre plots. The theory was that owning a little property would make Indians desire more, which would provide the incentive to live like white homesteaders. Indians would naturally be motivated to adopt habits of thrift, hard work, and an appreciation of American technology, family structure, education, and systems of law that protected property rights. In addition to providing a conduit to rapid assimilation, the Allotment Act was also intended to make Indians self-supporting, saving the U.S. Treasury millions of dollars per year.[27]

The Allotment Act required the Indian Bureau to parcel out 160 acres for each tribal member, allowing each allottee to pick his own plot. Beyond acreage, the similarities between the Homestead Act and the Allotment Act were few. The Allotment Act placed all land titles in trust to the Indian Bureau for twenty-five years to prevent premature dissipation of allotments, which were highly coveted by settlers and speculators alike. The Indian Bureau was authorized to sell unallotted parcels "for the Indians' benefit," thus granting non-Indians access to land that fell inside the original reservation boundaries. In addition to their allotments, each tribal member received a semiannual payment of their per capita share of tribal income through the sale of timber and other community resources. Per capita payments were to be disbursed at the discretion of Congress, the Indian Bureau, and the agency superintendent, and they could be withheld at the discretion of these government agents. Allottees whose use of resources demonstrated they had fully embraced the "habits of civilized life" would be deemed "competent" to assume the duties of full citizenship. This tentative return to Justice Taney's theory that Indians could be naturalized like immigrants turned on an agent's ability to determine who among thousands of allottees merited naturalization.

Making such determinations required government intrusion into Indians' economic affairs to a degree that would have been decried as tyranny if imposed on white Americans.[28]

The Allotment Act, with its mixed land use policy and vague social programming, sent a garbled message to the Klamath Tribes. While Indians were supposed to consider themselves independent property owners, it was hard to forget that government officials made their most important decisions for them. The Allotment Act would make citizens of the Klamath Tribes, but they would be second-class citizens whose status would always depend on judgments made by officials from the Indian Bureau. At the moment when the Homestead Act was realizing its utopian ideals of an independent citizenry, it was becoming apparent that allottees might never regain their lost powers of self-determination. The Allotment Act was the inverse of the Homestead Act, and the stark differences between the reservation and the prosperous towns surrounding it reflected this ever more clearly over time.

The first problem with the Allotment Act was its presumption that all reservations had vast tracts of arable land. The Klamath Reservation held rich forest, grazing, and mineral lands but did not have enough acreage to provide farmland to everyone. Agency officials asked Washington to help develop stock raising operations that would make the Klamath Reservation economically self-sufficient, but it was nearly impossible to sway policymakers in the East from their vision of Native yeoman farmers taming the uncultivated west. Preexisting agricultural policies were already failing miserably, so the land squeeze only raised the ire of Klamath farmers long frustrated with the agency and the Indian Bureau.[29]

It is hard to discern the degree to which tribal members approved of the Allotment Act, but numerous accounts indicate that officials gave them the hard sell. Agent Applegate's overblown promises of economic gain allowed him to report to Washington in 1888 that he finally got eight hundred reservation residents to sign up for allotments once the advantages of doing so were "pointed out to them." By 1890 each adult tribal member held a 160-acre plot of land, which they could farm, use to raise livestock, or rent for grazing or other uses.[30]

While surveyors remapped the reservation, the Klamath Agency re-created its political, educational, and social institutions to resemble more closely those of a real American small town. The Indian Bureau directed reservation agents to reform defunct tribal governing bodies for a closer resemblance to America's governing institutions. Superintendent H. G. Wilson, in a manner reminiscent of Applegate's fencepost meeting, announced in August 1908 that all adult males on the reservation (approximately 267) were to gather the general council to vote on membership of the tribal council, which would serve as its executive committee. Superintendent Wilson chaired the initial meeting and opened the proceedings by explaining how the U.S. House of Representatives operated and what American citizens expected of their representatives. He closed the meeting with a directive from Washington ordering the tribal council to conduct itself according to the model of the House.[31]

The leadership of the new tribal council took its duties seriously, but in doing so they could not help but notice some striking differences between the way it functioned and what they understood about the House of Representatives. Superintendent Wilson, though nominally a "non-governing member" of the council, oversaw all proceedings, determined meeting agendas, acted as a "guide" to correct procedural errors, and signed off on all the minutes to indicate his approval.[32]

The paternalist structures of the reformed reservation democracy were obvious to everyone, yet the new tribal leadership sought to make the most of the opportunities the governmental reforms appeared to offer. Many among the Klamath Tribes came to believe that in order to regain their independence, they had to develop proficiency in American political procedures and take a greater part in managing the reservation's resources, because that was where the real power was. The tribal council conveyed this outlook in its crafting of initiatives that created a tribal business committee within the general council. Instead of denouncing the Indian Bureau for assuming dictatorial power over tribal economic affairs, the drafters emphasized how placing competent Klamaths on the business committee would accelerate progress toward the assimilationist goals of the Allotment Act:

We the undersigned treaty Indians of the Klamath Indian Reservation Oregon most respectfully petition to your honor to grant us the privilege to appoint the Councilmen 23 men by the majority votes of the male adult Indians over 18 years of age, to transact the tribal business affairs of this reservation with you, said councilmen shall be appointed annually subject to approval of the commissioner of Indian Affairs Washington D.C. before it [goes into] effect. . . . We believe that will incourage [sic] us into citizen-ship which is near at hand. It's time for us to learn how to execute as such privilages [sic] which will be vital important [sic] to us in the near future.[33]

The tribal business council was formed as part decision-making body, part advisory body, and occasional rubber stamp for the Indian Bureau's more controversial land use policies. Most importantly, however, it presented clear evidence that the Klamath Tribes were absorbing their lessons in American politics—possibly too well for the liking of some white observers.

A Klamath tribal member named Robert Wilson (no relation to the superintendent) served as the first elected chair of the reformed tribal council, and he was instrumental in furthering Native participation in reservation affairs. He led a campaign in 1909 to establish a fund that would send tribal delegates to Washington to advocate for the Klamath Tribes on pending legislation. After the funds were in place, Jesse Kirk capitalized on the momentum of these political victories to successfully lobby the Indian commissioner for an additional appropriation to fund a new public park. Kirk stated his case boldly and brilliantly. Americans-in-the-making, he argued, must have a suitable place to play baseball and properly celebrate the Fourth of July. The Klamath Tribes had gradually accepted that pushing the federal government to honor the Treaty of 1864 would only bring crippling restrictions of resources and freedoms. Adopting American political ideals yielded great results, and Klamath leaders became increasingly adept at using democratic rhetoric to assert their own political agendas.[34]

This was not the sort of political participation that officials at the Klamath Agency had envisioned when they called Klamath leaders to the fencepost convention. After forty years of political education, Klamath leaders had changed remarkably. For some white observers, the transformation was as unsettling as negotiations during the treaty period. A journalist attending Fourth of July festivities in 1903 witnessed an "admixture of savagery and civilization" that caused "one's harmony of thought [to be] constantly disturbed." While she was impressed with founding father Oliver Applegate's presentation of the Declaration of Independence and the evident athletic training of the young Native "inmates" (who did not stoop like the "old squaws"), her encounter with a "son of the forest" named Dennis O'Toole raised anxieties that savagery and civilization were housed within a single person. For this correspondent, Independence Day 1903 did not help her see members of the Klamath Tribes as fellow citizens but as a dangerous race on the way to extinction. She concluded that in 1903 "only a few [Klamath] like 'Long Jim' and 'Dikkos,' whose personal recollections antedate the times of peace, have power to stir our imagination or chill our blood with their war whoops. Soon these will pass, and the race will cease to be."[35] Yet in 1909 this "vanishing race" was standing on the Capitol steps and writing confounding political treatises. Without question, the spirit of democracy, independence, and self-determination had taken hold on the Klamath Reservation and continued to blossom into the mid-twentieth century.

Despite all the flaws in the reservation system, the federal government returned to the model of the rehabilitative, isolated community during the New Deal to solve problems related to demographic distribution, suspected subversion, or socioeconomic vulnerability within a population. The New Deal brought a wave of similar communities that aided and reformed farmers, homesteaders, migrant workers, and participants in the Civilian Conservation Corps by providing prefab housing developments, structured work routines, and social programming to help down-and-out citizens get back on their feet and into the mainstream. But when federal officials looked for a model in Boulder City, Nevada, which had been built to house the labor force for the Hoover Dam project, they found "no parallel to wartime relocation centers" because such communities offered no "comprehensive legal or political statements of policy to provide guidance to the WRA."[36]

Politics, Power, and Pioneering at Topaz

One hundred years after a settlers' petition called on the government to contain the "Indian problem," westerners called on Washington for protection from a local Japanese population that might, they feared, house an enemy within. The Roosevelt administration, also fearful of internal sabotage, turned to its time-honored systems for managing suspect populations. Experts from the Office of Indian Affairs, led by John Collier, were mobilized to adapt the reservation model into what officials would hold up to the public—without so much as a hint of irony—as a model for "ideal cities."[37] All the while, seasoned experts in Indian affairs questioned the efficacy of the proposed relocation centers. E. R. Fryer had been temporarily transferred from his post as general superintendent of the Navajo Reservation to serve as regional director of the WRA. In a report to Solon Kimball, who was himself "on loan" from the Indian Bureau to the Community Analysis section of the Colorado River Relocation Center, Fryer noted "the difficulty of creating a normal community when many external aspects resemble a concentration camp." He concluded that the "presence of troops, guard towers, restrictions on free movement and the imposition of rules and regulations without consultation are all evidence of the fact that evacuees are not free persons." Indian Bureau personnel would never claim they could make ideal cities out of concentration camps, but their long experience in managing the internal contradictions of inverse utopias brought numerous wartime transfers to every level of WRA administration.[38]

When the West Coast Japanese were moved from their homes to internment facilities in 1942, the Indian Bureau was called in to replicate the "model democracies" they had developed at reservations like Klamath. It seemed, at first, like a simple prospect. Landholding would not be an issue—the "evacuation" was intended to be temporary, and westerners complained that the "Japs" owned too much land already. All that the community councils and citizen judiciary boards would have to do was give the camps a semblance of democracy and provide a vehicle for citizenship education to root out the presumed Japanese racial predisposition to fascism and anti-Americanism. The WRA downplayed the fact that the camps were disciplinary spaces designed to wash out disloyal tendencies. A government film introduced the public to the new "pioneer communities" in which their Japanese neighbors would live as Americans and "reclaim the desert." The rhetoric sounded like that surrounding the Homestead Act, but in reality it was much closer to that of the Allotment Act—absent the figure of the independent ethnic landholder.[39]

It was clear within moments of arriving at the assembly centers that the Japanese were far from the promised land. The first stop for the future Topazians was the Tanforan or Santa Anita assembly centers—both popular racetracks only weeks before. The army converted horse stalls into housing with a bit of flooring and a hasty paint job. Newcomers were fed starchy meals before moving into unventilated barracks that smelled of horse manure. They were surprised to discover that the lavatories were merely open toilets with no privacy. Meal times were no better. Residents stood in endless lines only to guzzle their unappetizing chow. The hardest part was being placed under constant surveillance; Caucasian camp police constantly patrolled the barracks. The worst moment for many came after the flurry of move-in activity had subsided, when sadness, loneliness, and uncertainty set in. When Grace Oshita, her mother, and her grandmother opened their wire cots in their new "home," the three burst into tears, Grace thinking, "This is it."[40]

According to government officials, one of the benefits of the internment was that these suspect individuals could prove their loyalty and fitness for citizenship by contributing their labor (and all their unstructured time) to America's war effort, particularly in the production of camouflage nets. Articles 31 and 32 of the 1929 Geneva Convention explicitly forbade using incarcerated foreign nationals (in this case, the first-generation Issei) for the production of war matériel of any kind, but there was no language governing the use of incarcerated "non-aliens" as a ready labor force. At Santa Anita, the army classified Nisei net makers as "volunteer workers" and put them on a forty-four-hour schedule. Over 1,200 of these "volunteers" earned forty cents an hour in a badly ventilated workshop where burlap dust entered their lungs. When they organized a strike to demand better pay, shorter hours, and safer conditions, camp officials closed the schools, making scab laborers of students and teachers.

Workers who refused to sign statements declaring they were volunteers were threatened with placement on a blacklist. Although the strikers won a shorter workday, a slight wage increase, and eventually an end to the net-making project, Santa Anita residents saw how fully their civil liberties were subordinated to shifting federal agendas. The incident also raised doubts about the larger promises of the work program.[41]

Political activity was risky because federal agents closely monitored residents' past and current associations. The House Committee on Un-American Activities had been monitoring suspected front organizations like the Japanese American Committee for Democracy (JACD) and the Young Democrats, a socialist organization whose call to dismantle systems of racial inequality appealed to Nisei radicals. Even decades-old associations imperiled some residents. Yamato Ichihashi, who had been a professor of history at Stanford University prior to becoming a resident of Santa Anita, was one of many internees arrested from an assembly center without warning or explanation. When Ichihashi learned he was being held in suspicion for having served as a translator at a 1922 disarmament conference, he wrote in his diary that "the present set up of the community is illogical and impossible; this is made more so by the attitude and handling of affairs by the management—autocracy enforced by a veritable Gestapo."[42]

WRA officials did not look to Hitler's Germany for a model community but to their Interior Department colleagues in Indian Affairs. Anthropologists and sociologists from the bureau developed training materials for WRA project directors, who would fill the same role as agency superintendents on reservations. In many instances, general information about negotiating cultural differences was useful, but in others, it was clear that agents' approaches to forming Native communities in the nineteenth century might not make sense for communities of Japanese American urbanites in the twentieth. One WRA manual instructed project directors to introduce themselves to the elder residents as the "village headman" with duties similar to community leaders in rural Japan. Although this worked reasonably well when Applegate established a new political order at the reservation fence post, very few San Francisco Japanese had even visited rural Japan, so most had no idea what WRA officials were talking about. When the WRA drew up plans for the relocation centers, there was no mention of Japanese village life.[43]

The WRA did assemble a staff of seasoned Indian Bureau employees and sent an untested group of conscientious objectors to the camps for wartime service. Myer's office selected the former director of a Boston settlement house, Charles Ernst, to be project director for Topaz, which indicates a commitment on the part of the WRA to rehabilitating a troubled (and troubling) urban population. Ernst was most interested in working to ensure the welfare of Topazians, which included making sure that every loyal resident was on the path to "first-class citizenship." If the residents became disorderly, however, Ernst's responsibilities would change from taking care of Topazians to suppressing the unrest, through force if necessary. Ernst, for his part, seems to have seen himself as a benevolent reformer and did not consider that, as the embodiment of *parens patriae*, he appeared to many Topazians as the man who took away their freedoms.

The relationship between Ernst and his charges was somewhat like the one between the Applegates and Indians on the Klamath Reservation: it was largely friendly, but there was a greater degree of distrust among the residents than Ernst seemed to realize. Although there were no property transactions or per capita distributions at Topaz, project directors were considered heads of families. They arranged for student transfers, hospital care, disposition of the remains of the deceased, and had to approve any request to move to another project or visit a family member on an emergency basis. The San Francisco office of the WRA was also the custodian of living persons and was responsible for having evacuees committed to psychiatric institutions, placing children in foster care outside the camps, decisions concerning orphans, and other matters of family law. One young nurse's aide found that the San Francisco bureau often made cruel decisions, particularly in sending away sick or disabled internees to area state hospitals without provision for families to visit or participate in their care. Project directors were responsible for the usual governmental procedures surrounding deaths in a project, including arranging an inquest where no physician was in attendance, filing death certificates, and notifying the census bureau. In addition, project directors decided how to dispose of the remains unless the family wished to make other arrangements. In his capacity as the head of the family, an individual project director issued specific instructions for getting bids on funeral services. Families had to pay for funeral services and interment if they wanted burial outside the center cemetery. As the architect of the work program, however, the project director could take the WRA's suggestion and make the construction of a crematorium an evacuee work project.[44]

While Ernst thought he was building cooperative relationships with Topazians seeking self-improvement, residents involved themselves in these projects to prevent the imposition of repressive measures, not to partake in his reformist agenda. This confusion and distrust lay beneath the surface for most of the camp's history but in times of stress threatened to spark clashes between the people and their governing authorities in Topaz's barbed-wire democracy.

Topaz opened officially to the evacuees, administrators, guards, and social scientists on September 11, 1942. After four months of struggling to make a life at Santa Anita and Tanforan assembly centers, internees had to start again in a strange place that seemed to defy description. One WRA pamphlet called it a "pioneer community, with basic housing and protective services provided by the Federal Government," while others referred to it as a "city," "municipality," "camp," and "metropolis" (noting that Topaz was Utah's fifth-largest city). To Tom Kawaguchi, Topaz stood not on a promising frontier but "at the end of the world." Kawaguchi's first glimpse of the "pioneer community" overwhelmed him with a "complete sense of loss."[45]

Topaz was not one of the camps located on confiscated portions of Indian reservations (as the Arizona camps were), but it had a very similar landscape: rugged, empty, and treeless, with fine alkaline soil and nothing to stop the desert sun from beating down in the summer and bitter winds biting in winter. Its dusty, square-mile area included residential, administrative, and service buildings. These were connected by streets assigned names drawn from the natural world that the older generation of Japanese could not possibly pronounce, such as "Tamarisk," "Malachite," and "Cinnabar." The separation between Caucasian and Japanese areas made an immediate impression on new arrivals like Michi Kobi, who "felt the hard impact of apartheid" when she saw the sturdy white administration offices and WRA housing clustered near the exit road, set apart from the hundreds of identical, flimsy black barracks.[46]

New arrivals found conditions at Topaz cruel and disorienting. Many were greeted with blinding, choking dust storms, which remained a constant hardship of camp life. They were herded through the WRA bureaucracy once again, each person having to register with project administrators, undergo an examination for communicable diseases, and receive assignment to a barrack. One Topazian remembered reading, "You are now in Topaz, Utah. Here we say Dining Hall and not Mess Hall; Safety Council, not Internal Police; Residents, not Evacuees; and last but not least, Mental Climate, not Morale." Camp publications encouraged readers to buy war bonds on one page, while warning them to stay away from the fence to avoid being shot on another. Security regulations were inconsistent and confusing: sometimes WRA staff would take evacuees on hikes beyond the fence, even as the guards arrested little old ladies for crossing the camp boundary.[47]

Structures of surveillance and control were as visible at Topaz as they had been in the early days of the Klamath Reservation. Instead of a full garrison like Fort Klamath, Topaz was ringed with guard towers manned by inexperienced armed guards who resented being left behind while their comrades fought "real Japs" in the Pacific theater. The guards' collective boredom, lack of experience, and zeal to discipline their "prisoners" fueled nine incidents of guards shooting at residents, one a child collecting scrap lumber to make furnishings for his mother's barrack. The WRA said little about these incidents, continually referring to the military police as the Topazians' protectors, ignoring the fact that the guns were pointed toward the residents, not the imaginary gangs of invading vigilantes.[48]

Inside the barbed wire, WRA workers in every department compiled as much data as they could find on the internees for purposes of planning and surveillance. Topaz teachers, with the aid of teachers from the Navajo schools, kept meticulous student files that revealed as much about the adult family members as the students themselves. Students were polled on such questions as "Personal Adjustments Found Most Difficult" and "Parent's Use of English," which reflected the family's degree of compliance with the evacuation and degree of assimilation—the standards by which the WRA measured "loyalty" and "progress."[49] Outside the schools, teams of anthropologists and sociologists from the Interior Department compiled data and observations of community life in regular community analysis reports sent to Washington, where Myer's office sought to gauge the outcomes of the government's great experiment.

By the end of 1943, Ernst and every other project director had full community analysis files with detailed information on each resident's education, employment history, relatives in Japan, knowledge of the Japanese language, financial assets in Japan, organizational affiliations, religious preferences, and special aptitudes and hobbies the government found noteworthy. Some files included reference letters attesting to residents' socioeconomic status and personal history, and others held intelligence reports on prewar associations or activities deemed "inimical to the interest of the United States." Ernst's office had the added burden of gathering information for the government about Fred Korematsu and Mitsuye Endo, who awaited the Supreme Court decisions at Topaz. The stakes were high for the WRA in both cases; if the Court ruled that the forced removal of the Japanese was unconstitutional, the agency would have to close the camps and somehow resettle the tens of thousands of displaced people in its charge. The more immediate concern for Ernst, however, was investigating Korematsu's behavior, which was a salient issue in his arrest and subsequent legal challenge. He would have to determine once and for all whether Korematsu was a patriot, a saboteur, or a devoted boyfriend. Such inquiries required a fair amount of government intrusion into the life of the individual.[50]

Once the "barbed-wire" elements of the community were firmly in place, the WRA established policy to develop the "democracies." The WRA decided each camp would have a governing body of residents selected by popular vote, whose powers would be accorded "as is consistent with sound administration" of the camp. John Collier, whose recent experience reforming tribal governments under the Indian Reorganization Act gave him a wealth of knowledge about community planning, worked with like-minded colleagues like Native American scholar D'Arcy McNickle to develop democratic procedures and protocols for the internee community government. Collier proposed that camp community councils (much like the Klamath Tribal Council) be empowered to pass laws governing community affairs, and that they serve as advisors to project directors on matters of camp policy (a recent innovation in reservation government). To ensure proper civics training, community councils had to adhere to a set of by-laws and consistent procedures (such as Robert's Rules of Order) and were required to hold regular meetings under the supervision of the project director. If democratic processes brought political change for Americans outside the barbed wire, at Topaz, they only yielded "advisories" that WRA officials could adopt, ignore, or nullify at will.[51]

While Collier's model looked restrictive to the WRA's incoming citizens, to Myer it was all too permissive. Myer saw no reason to give the Japanese *any* say in camp management, and he objected strenuously to Collier's plan. He insisted that, as a government agency, the WRA had an overriding responsibility to "maintain ultimate control over the management of the relocation center." An administrative policy statement on community government in the relocation centers made Myer's point very clearly:

> Community self-government among the evacuees is not being instituted as an end in itself, even though it is rich in intrinsic values, but is rather a means to the larger end of effective administration of the whole program of the War Relocation Authority. The best way to achieve discipline and order in relocation centers . . . is what is being sought, and the program offered by Administrative Instruction No. 34 constitutes no Utopian's dream of an ideal government, but rather a practical administrator's attempt to preserve order in a somewhat special type of community.[52]

While the WRA remained true to its aim of instilling a democratic ethos in the camps, community self-government would never become an instrument of community self-determination.

Ultimately, WRA policy reflected a compromise: project directors were required to hold free elections for community councils, but they could also appoint "evacuee representatives" on an informal basis if the director believed the non-elected person's participation in government was important for some reason. In addition, project directors could nullify community council resolutions at will, without an appeal process or an explanation. This scheme bore clear resemblances to reservation governments, but instead of adopting the newer "House of Representatives" model, the WRA reached back to the era when agency superintendents determined what political outcomes would be, like Applegate did with the Allen David election. The limitations on the powers and functions of these bodies dashed any pretense of the council functioning as an organ of the popular will.[53]

Knowing that visible democratic institutions would be critical to getting internees to buy into the culture of realistic democracy, the WRA divided Topaz into blocks of barracks that functioned as small political units. Each block contained 250 to 300 housing units and shared laundry and toilet facilities, with a mess hall and recreation center nearby. The residents of each block elected managers (often called "blockheads") to represent them at the camp-wide community council and serve as liaisons between the residents and administration. Their duties were similar to those of both the Klamath Tribal Council and the tribal police: representing not only the people but also Ernst and the government, block managers had to conduct head counts two times per day and supervise the evacuee nurses, clerical workers, and janitors who served the block. Placed in the odd role of concierge, congressman, and WRA subagent, one "blockhead" found himself "the butt of many jokes and hostilities" because of his conflicting responsibilities to both the WRA and his neighbors. The elected leadership at Topaz had little power to do anything except take the heat for whatever went wrong in the camp. As one resident remarked cynically, "when the administrators screw up they can say, 'well, the citizen's committee said it,'" thus making the Japanese responsible for their own victimization.[54]

The WRA required that project managers appoint an internal security force consisting of the "best men" in the community. Topazians responded to this measure in much the same way Klamaths did: they saw it as a sign of the government investing power in the people but also as a mechanism for stirring up internal conflict by promoting a sort of competitive assimilation. Caucasian police trained the evacuee force in project security and specialized points of police work such as interrogation, evidence handling, and classifying fingerprints in preparation for detaining and prosecuting their fellow Topazians. Successful trainees were issued metal badges and whistles to heighten the officers' profile and boost their morale. The WRA system of dressing selected wards in the trappings of officialdom may have raised some Japanese officers' morale, but it brought trouble to the community as a whole. Ernst received complaints from residents about one evacuee guard, a "fresh young punk" who used his position to "kick his elders around." The young officer's behavior was so outrageous that a rumor circulated throughout the camp that a group of older men had raided the mess halls for meat cleavers to put the guard in his place. The plot was stopped, the story goes, by other Topazians who suggested they wait until Topaz had closed and then surreptitiously throw the guards out of the transport trains.[55]

In spite of the strict limitations on its governing authority and the way that power often worked *against* the community, the leaders at Topaz took their offices very seriously. George Shimamoto openly opposed the internment, but he believed that by creating a spirited community life, Topaz would "show [that the] Japanese [have] a big heart" and that Topazians could be model small-town Americans as well as anyone else. Council members took immediate advantage of the wealth of political and organizational experience they brought with them to Topaz to win improvements in the quality of food, health care, working conditions, and camp safety standards. In less than a year, the council had established a scholarship fund, a tofu factory, fire prevention week, regular war bond drives, and a working relationship with the Spanish consul responsible for monitoring the condition of Japanese nationals on behalf of the Japanese government. That the community council's political vision and initiative vastly exceeded what the WRA had imagined for Topaz suggests that the Japanese had a greater appreciation for the workings of a small-town democracy than their village headmen from Washington DC.[56]

Segregation, Surveillance, and
Citizenship in the Miracle City

Any Topazian who spent a day at Vanport would instantly notice that life there was remarkably freer but not appreciably more democratic. New arrivals did not have numbered tags or armed guards like the Japanese; Vanporters flocked freely to the project when it opened in the spring of 1943. For many, the modern conveniences and the relative permanence of their tenancy gave them comfort and stability that had been unimaginable during the Depression. Each unit had a living area connected to a dining room, kitchen, and bathroom, with one to three bedrooms depending on the number of family members. The floors were covered with varnished fir, and the walls with fireproof Sheetrock and papered knotty pine, with screened louvres for cross ventilation. Each bedroom had a closet, a dresser, and beds equipped with mattresses and blankets, so no one at Vanport had to take time to build scrapboard furniture and stuff straw ticks. Hotplates — used surreptitiously at Topaz — were standard-issue equipment in Vanport kitchens. Vanporters less enthralled with their government-issue appliances shared Topazians' dismay at the architectural and environmental monotony of their towns and the dreariness of government installations, where "everything was the same and everything was grey." Many Vanporters responded to the dullness of their government-issue town as their Nikkei counterparts did, hanging curtains and planting flowers to individualize and brighten their exteriors and fashion lives for themselves that met the elusive "American standard."[57]

Vanporters took advantage of all the available conveniences to mitigate the discomforts of dislocation and project life. They flocked to the twenty-four-hour movie theaters, played team sports, and attended weekend dances and shows by Portland entertainers. The cafeterias made table space and sodas (never beer) available to inspire wholesome interactions among Vanport neighbors. Lacking the usual working-class gathering places — churches, bars, and the sidewalks of the old neighborhood — the laundry became the center of continuous social activity. Vanporters from every shift would wait to use the machines not only to do the wash but also to gather in the one place that, for many, felt free of the omnipresent gaze of Housing Authority officials.[58]

Although Vanport was never encircled with barbed wire, residents' opportunities for political participation were clearly limited. Vanporters retained their freedom to move in and outside of the project, but they still experienced some of the isolation of their contemporaries in closed communities like the Klamath Reservation and Topaz. Multnomah County officials attempted to relegate the first wave of war migrants to second-class citizenship by refusing to appropriate $1,500 to set up voter registration centers for fifty thousand newcomers. Without ready access to a polling place, Kaiser workers simply could not find the time to cast ballots in Portland. When asked about the hardship this posed to war workers who wanted to vote, the Multnomah County clerk retorted, "They're just Okies. They're not fit to vote. Why bother about them?" As temporary wartime laborers and non-homeowners, Vanporters did not pay local taxes, which legitimated their continued alienation from the political process. The federal government made payments in lieu of taxes to Multnomah County at a rate of 8.5 percent of the total annual dwelling rentals, but this only reinforced Portlanders' view of Vanporters as government wards, not first-class citizens. This was only one of many ways in which Vanporters were caught in a web of half-developed rules and regulations that compromised their rights as citizens, made them vulnerable to injustices, and afforded them few legal or political remedies.[59]

Despite their tax-exempt status, Vanporters could vote in national elections if they could find a polling place. But their short residency and inability to purchase real estate barred them from voting in local elections. Vanporters could lay no claim to being "taxpaying Oregonians" in making appeals for better service or treatment. Their position was similar to that of the Klamaths vis-à-vis their white neighbors in Klamath Falls. While they were integral to the labor pool and consumer market, Vanporters were easily shunted to the political margins as "non-taxpaying federal dependents."[60]

Vanporters' inability to acquire property also limited their political power within the project itself. Residents lived by the law of the lease, which was a very flimsy code. Instead of standard leases, tenants were issued "revocable use permits," allowing the Housing Authority to evict without cause with as little as seventy-two hours' notice. The landlord was both lawmaker and enforcer at Vanport, with eviction serving as the ultimate punishment for wrongdoing and random fines redressing the balance for "lesser crimes." The Housing Authority of Portland (HAP) authorized project officials to enter apartments without warrants, cause, or advance notice, though they were supposed to limit entrances to emergencies or "reasonable hours." Late rent-payers came home to padlocked doors, their apartment and contents inaccessible until they paid all back rent and fees. Having just recently escaped the ravages of the Depression, Vanporters generally had very little, making the confiscation of the contents of their apartments a total loss. There were no standards to govern when eviction was permissible, and there was no recourse if a resident wanted to protest an eviction; HAP would gladly hear a complaint but was unlikely to make a ruling against its own agents and policies.[61]

As with subjects on the Klamath Reservation and at Topaz, Vanporters faced an array of restrictions that would be unthinkable in nongovernment towns. While Vanporters were freer than Topazians to come and go, HAP was more likely than the WRA to use Vanporters' housing as leverage to force compliance with social controls and standards of labor discipline and to impose racial segregation. When local newspapers reported rampant absenteeism among Kaiser employees who had been brought at government expense and provided good wages, housing, and support services, HAP called for a joint investigation of Kaiser's attendance records. After determining which residents "make [absenteeism] a habit," HAP moved to dislodge them to open a spot in their unit for "the more conscientious type of war worker."[62]

Bound by its selection criteria to admit any Kaiser worker, HAP could not recruit "good citizens," so it attempted to use project life to mold its industrial workforce into the model of a dutiful citizenry. The community council was the cornerstone of the "instructional communities" built by the Office of Indian Affairs and the War Relocation Authority for their residents, but Vanporters could be neither coerced nor enticed into forming a government. This was not for lack of pressure from federal authorities. John Jessup, commissioner of the Federal Public Housing Authority (FPHA), insisted that war housing projects form tenant governments to preserve "our heritage of democratic action, symbolized by the New England Town Meeting [because] if we ever lose sight of that symbol, democracy will be in danger." Community government, to Jessup and the FPHA, was "[t]he school in which true democratic action is learned" through cooperative problem solving by elected boards of tenant representatives.[63]

HAP, in turn, pressured Vanport project director James Franzen to organize an election in Vanport for a five-member "advisory council." Like the Klamath Tribal Council and the Topaz Community Council, the Vanport Advisory Council would relay tenant concerns to HAP, oversee special committees and run project-wide elections, and promote volunteer beautification and neighborhood improvement programs. HAP believed that meeting with the advisory council occasionally would reduce staffing needs. In such a scheme, there would be fewer individual complaints, and residents would be in charge of administrative and maintenance functions that would otherwise have been carried out by lower-level HAP personnel.[64]

HAP also believed an advisory council would compensate residents for the political privileges they lost at Vanport, and it anticipated that residents would eagerly stand for election. Surprisingly, the call for elections drew a lackluster response compared to that at Klamath or Topaz; Vanporters were so thoroughly engaged with shipbuilding (many worked between forty-eight and sixty hours per week) that community activities seemed impractical. Neither the Housing Authority of Portland nor the Federal Public Housing Authority could press the issue too hard, given the repetitiveness of their "ships first!" refrain in Vanport's orientation literature.[65]

In contrast to the Klamath Tribes and the Japanese internees at Topaz, whose home communities were relocated en masse to federal reservations, Vanporters migrated as individuals. Residents were complete strangers to one another, and they did not see themselves as a coherent political unit or even as a cluster of Vanport constituencies. Other federal projects relied on newspapers like the *Topaz Times* to guide residents as they imagined their communities, and Kaiser used the shipyard publication the *Bo's'n's Whistle* to promote loyalty and unity in the shipyard. Oddly, however, the FPHA refused to subsidize a newspaper for Vanport, citing prohibitions against federal agencies involving themselves with the free press, though such provisions had not restrained the government in the past. HAP recognized the benefits of a project newspaper but could not figure out how to finance such a venture, since it was not fiscally prudent for a private publisher to start a paper in a temporary town. HAP continued to worry that the absence of a community bulletin of any sort would compromise morale and slow any attempt to promote community spirit among Vanporters.[66]

Vanporters did, on occasion, form organizations to confront community issues, but the groups fell apart within months because of a lack of direction or purpose. Earnest citizens who wanted to engage with the government met constant frustration. On the one hand, they thought they were fulfilling the Housing Authority's wish for citizen participation in project development. Yet on the other, HAP was never bound to *follow* the will of the people, only to witness its expression. With ships to build and families to raise, Vanporters had no use for unproductive dialogue or government propaganda about local self-government. Instead, they left Franzen's office to make all the decisions — including those that HAP and the FPHA would prefer to attribute to residents.

Vanporters' withdrawal from so-called "community governance" was, in fact, a meaningful act of retaliation against HAP officials who were willing to listen but refused to act. The absence of resident response to the question of whether Vanporters had to register their firearms put HAP in a difficult situation. On the one hand, the government feared firearms restrictions would encourage the use of concealed weapons, leaving law-abiding gun owners at a disadvantage. Multnomah County sheriff Martin Pratt, alarmed at the thought of forty thousand armed Vanporters in his jurisdiction, requested blanket permission to enter apartments to confiscate whatever firearms he could find. When HAP's chief commissioner reminded the sheriff that he would need a warrant, other commissioners suggested a renewed effort to form a community council so the residents could develop solutions and, as Kenji Fuji noted about the Topaz Community Council, be held responsible for undermining their own civil liberties.[67]

Anecdotes from the annals of law enforcement illustrate the thorny problems of maintaining order and protecting civil liberties at communities like Vanport. HAP's odd position as residents' liaison to Washington and referee for complaints against the Federal Public Housing Authority, conflict among residents, and grievances against HAP itself made the wheels of justice turn poorly. Even simple cases threw the agency into a confused, defensive posture. William Potter made a claim against HAP following a break-in due to "negligence on the part of an employee of the Authority" who entered Potter's apartment without permission. Potter lost $116 in cash, a Shriner's ring, and a box of 38-caliber shells. While HAP never doubted the negligence of the employee or the value of the lost articles, it denied Potter's claim on the basis that other tenants would make similar appeals, which would raise the cost of burglary insurance for Vanport. HAP advised Potter to sue for recourse, knowing he had neither the time nor money to do so. The decision preserved the FPHA's bottom line, but as with the administration by the Office of Indian Affairs and the War Relocation Authority, principles of democracy and justice became flexible once government interests were at stake.[68]

Law enforcement was an equally thorny problem. Policing for Vanport was pieced together using HAP's disciplinary powers and a contract with Multnomah County for sheriff's deputies to patrol the project. In contrast to OIA and WRA programs, HAP did not generally encourage Vanporters to serve on the internal police force. The one exception came in mid-1944, when HAP recommended "several colored men" be hired onto the sheriff's staff to monitor activities among black Vanporters. Although HAP commissioners made no mention of programs for "minorities policing minorities" run by the Bureau of Indian Affairs and the War Relocation Authority, their reasons for raising a small black police force were similar to those motivating officials to create the Klamath Tribal Police and the evacuee police unit at Topaz. All three programs called for model community members to keep their dissident members in line. Community policing also provided good public relations material for the

Interior Department and the Housing Authority, who held up their ethnic officers as "proof" that barbed-wire democracies went beyond teaching civics to fostering radical social equality. Federal agencies were sometimes beguiled by the spin they put on race in their respective communities. HAP all but ignored Commissioner Klutznick's directive to hire not just a handful but "several intelligent colored people, who understand the negro problem," for positions on Franzen's staff. It was quick to note that the agency employed four African Americans—including two new deputies—but slow to acknowledge the difference between hiring a black policymaker and hiring black men to enforce white bureaucrats' directives.[69]

In truth, political matters had far less urgency at Vanport than at Klamath or Topaz because it was easy enough to replace a single agitator with an apolitical worker who wanted Vanport's many benefits. Vanport shared Klamath's and Topaz's segregatory function, but Vanporters, as individuals, were not considered "dangerous" in the same way that Klamath Basin Indians and the West Coast Japanese had been. The boundaries were perfectly permeable, the labor pool was vast, and it was easy enough to detain a Vanporter suspected of the sort of treachery the government feared from Indians, Japanese, and increasingly Communists. All the government needed from the FPHA's "new citizens" was steady work at the shipyard, an attitude of cooperation and patriotism, and adherence to the terms of the lease. There was no place at Vanport for engaging substantive questions of race, government powers, or civil liberties. After all, it was the Shipyard Negro Organization for Victory that made Vanport a government necessity. And if Julius Rodriquez would have settled in Vanport, it is unlikely that he would have found organizing block parties or serving as a token black police officer satisfying exercises in American democracy.

American Life in the City of Secrets

Officials of the Manhattan Engineer District (MED), like those at the Indian Bureau, the War Relocation Authority, and the Federal Public Housing Authority, believed that an enclosed community with a self-contained political and economic system would provide the best means of keeping scientific workers under surveillance and control without sundering the integrity of America's democratic principles. Although Los Alamos followed the Klamath, Topaz, and Vanport model of isolation and federal paternalism, there were some notable differences. The MED used elements of the reservation system and the company town model to enhance security and productivity, but it also relied heavily on structures from military communities to keep residents in order. This was due in part to the very clear security concerns that accompanied the creation of an atomic bomb, and in part to the fact that if Julius Rodriquez had been a nuclear physicist, the MED would have had no choice but to bring him to Los Alamos. Such was the case with many of the project's leading lights. The MED excluded Leo Szilard, but it could not afford to keep Enrico Fermi, Emilio Segrè, and the Oppenheimer brothers off the project.

If anyone was surprised that Los Alamos was organized as a barbed-wire democracy, it was at the "democracy" part as much as the barbed wire. Officials did not hide the fact that Los Alamos would be a fortress. They also did not commit resources to institutions like community councils, educational programs, or community cooperatives. Residents came with very strong ideas about how community institutions should be run, and the military had its own nonnegotiable limits on how much power residents could wield over community affairs. The tensions between the rhetoric of American freedom and the reality of life at Los Alamos were matters of overt discussion and constant negotiation. Armed with extensive education and political experience, Los Alamosans skillfully parlayed their affluence, racial privileges, and their desperately needed scientific expertise into political power, opening limited channels of free speech, creating an infrastructure the army thought frivolous, and holding the government to providing a decent standard of living.

While Los Alamos was distinctive for the extremity of its security policies, it also differed from Klamath, Topaz, and Vanport in the residents' power to challenge government policies. Scientists, like shipbuilders, were necessary to the war effort, but individual shipyard workers could be fired and more easily replaced if they protested workplace or townsite policies. Few of the Los Alamos scientists were dispensable, and leaders like Oppenheimer and Fermi were irreplaceable. Los Alamosans used their expertise and the project's secrecy to negotiate for more democratic practices without provoking stricter government controls. With Oppenheimer at the lead, the scientists engaged in an ongoing process of building freedom and democracy, which had been left out of the army's social blueprint for Los Alamos, into community life.

Oppenheimer pursued democratic reforms in the laboratory, where his power was more evenly matched with that of Groves. He began by appointing a governing board and a coordinating council, where division leaders (between eight and ten) and group leaders (approximately fifty) developed policy. Initially, the governing board worked on problems of housing, laboratory construction, personnel matters, and security, but its focus narrowed over time to bomb building. The coordinating council directed the flow of information laterally between work groups and vertically to Oppenheimer and Groves. The environment was far more open than Groves ever intended, but the "need to know" rule remained in effect, creating an awkward work culture in which scientists could talk freely to a point but usually had to stop before fully explaining themselves. When the FBI interrogated Robert Marshak in 1950 about a box of Christmas candy he had sent to convicted spy Klaus Fuchs, Marshak said he could not know what information Fuchs had because scientists "formed the habit of not questioning each other relative to their activities, because it puts the other person in an embarrassing position."[70]

Oppenheimer's first free speech campaign began at a meeting of the governing board in May 1943, when physicist Hans Bethe suggested a colloquium to improve efficiency and morale. Groves understood the value of the leading researchers seeing the entire project, but he would not allow implementation of the "antithesis of compartmentalization." Oppenheimer defended the colloquium by agreeing to limit its size, requiring participants to vouch for one another's loyalty, and strictly limiting discussions to scientific matters. The scientists hailed the colloquium as a victory for science and democracy. The obstreperous Richard Feynman, who put aside his doctoral thesis to fight the Nazis with his professors, described Los Alamos as "very democratic" because scientific meetings were open. He marveled that "everybody was allowed to say anything to anybody, so it wasn't the kind of hierarchy where you had to know your place." British scientist James Tuck shared Feynman's view, expressing delight that, "I, an almost unknown scientist, came here and found that I was expected to exchange ideas with men whom I had regarded as names in textbooks. . . . Here at Los Alamos I found a spirit of Athens, of Plato, of an ideal Republic."[71]

Even the most exuberant young scientists were quick to note that the ideal republic extended no further than the Tech Area. Los Alamosans were faced with the challenge of creating an all-American town in un-American circumstances. Citizens' freedom of movement, speech, and association as well as their right to due process were sharply curtailed. There was no free enterprise, no home ownership, no free press, and no forum for decision making and conflict resolution. Dissent was neither tolerated nor practical, given Los Alamosans' invisibility and disloca-tion from the American body politic. Space, like time, was segmented between the Tech Area and the townsite to keep everything extraneous to the construction of bombs away from the laboratory. Each day was segmented by sirens that told residents when to wake up, go to work, and return home. Los Alamos, like Vanport, was a labor-efficiency sys-tem that, like all inverse utopias, subordinated individual freedom to the fufillment federal policy aims.[72]

During the first days of settlement, Oppenheimer encouraged resi-dents to develop institutions for community government, public services, and conflict resolution. As at Topaz, accommodationists and agitators alike jumped at the chance to improve community life and stave off the dispiriting effects of conditions at Los Alamos. The town council, which was organized by Oppenheimer as soon as the first families moved in, was the liveliest public body on "the Hill." Although Oppenheimer never intended to serve on the council himself, he knew that residents would have to have some means, no matter how small or artificial, of exer-cising a degree of control over their hermetically sealed environment. Just as heavy work on the bomb commenced, Oppenheimer held an ad-hoc meeting at his house, instructing the first residents to schedule an election, write by-laws, and identify issues of concern that the council might address.[73]

Residents, quick to note that as nontaxpayers, nonresidents, and, on paper, nonexistent persons, they had entered a "political no-man's land" where there was scant hope of securing voting rights, even as an absentee. Security restrictions prevented most Los Alamosans from voting in the 1944 presidential elections. The MED divided voters into three categories: those whose identity might give away the secret, those who came from states with absentee ballots, and those who met state residency requirements in New Mexico. Group one could not vote. Group two applied for absentee ballots. Group three attempted to register in Sandoval County, but if the vote were contested, ensuing publicity could blow the secrecy. Members of this group also could not use the abbreviated federal ballot because the procedure required legislative action, and the session was over.[74]

The council, despite its limited powers, provided the only arena of political participation for Los Alamosans. Setting criteria for council membership generated one of the body's first contentious debates. The first election notice stated that, "[s]ince it is difficult for officers or enlisted personnel to act in an advisory capacity on the council, and to maintain their status as a part of the military administrative organization of the Post, only civilians will be eligible for election." Most civilians agreed with the underlying premise, which was that the military had powers and duties that posed conflicts of interest with council membership.[75]

Still, many were uncomfortable with the fact that the growing number of enlisted men drafted from classrooms to assist in the laboratory would be left with no means of political participation. To democratize the process, Los Alamosans reserved one-third of the council seats for military personnel and another third for Tech Area employees, with the remaining third open to any candidate. The measure passed easily, but it was not enacted until the MED approved the change some months later, reminding Los Alamosans of the limits of their political efficacy.[76]

The town council also assumed limited judicial functions, the most important being the traffic court because, according to Alice Kimball Smith, "[t]he Army was well equipped to deal with spies and saboteurs but had apparently neglected that most common of modern malefactions, the improper operation and disposal of a motor vehicle." The members developed procedures for hearing cases and levied fines, which it donated to the Red Cross. Interestingly, Los Alamosans engaged in heated political activity concerning issues of animal control. The first animal-related council meeting centered on a "mad" Airedale who had bitten a child. The MED summarily banned pets from Los Alamos, but the town council insisted that, as a community issue, the animal problem required public discussion and a vote on the ban. The MED retained the right of approval of all council decisions and allowed the meeting to go forward.[77]

The dog belonged to Bob and Schatzie Davis, and it had not been rabid after all. Ultimately, it was not the public health problem but the political one that drew Los Alamosans to the Airedale issue, and the meeting attracted one of the largest crowds ever. Attendees saw in the meeting a rare opportunity to challenge the MED's absolute authority and arbitrary decisions. One pet supporter made a pre-meeting speech cautioning the MED to "[t]ake our freedom, censor our letters, work us day and night if you will, but do not interfere with our immediate families or our pets!" Ninety percent of the town fervently agreed and arrived at the meeting ready for a fight. Instead, an army spokesman announced the ban had been called off, and "peace again reigned."[78]

The town council continued to challenge unfair military policy and was particularly vigilant in watching prices at the post exchange and the commissary, which were the only two places they could shop. When prices spiked up, the council demanded that the MED post recent financial statements for the project stores. The MED initially refused, stating that commissary prices reflected the additional cost of the special arrangements necessary for getting supplies to a high-security facility. Finding the explanation unsatisfactory, the council pushed harder by accusing the army in writing that it exploited the absence of market competition and gouged Los Alamos consumers. Sensing the issue was becoming both persistent and heated, the MED agreed to give the council notice of impending price changes and have a federal inspector audit post operations, but it never fulfilled the council's request for audit reports.[79]

Housing became an increasingly difficult issue as the need for more minds and hands in the laboratory expanded the population more quickly than the MED could build homes. As more scientists, research assistants, and lab techs came to "the Hill," the MED called in scores of Women's Army Corps members and security agents, for whom it could only supply the crudest dwellings. To minimize the need for outside government contractors, the MED planned to move the local labor pool out of the pueblos and villages and into Los Alamos, so they could work on round-the-clock construction projects. Of course, there was not enough housing prepared for them, but the MED planned to crowd groups of workers and their families into the tiny hutments originally designed for single enlisted men in the Special Engineer Detachment. Town council members, though harboring similar prejudices, would not tolerate such inhumane conditions in their community, but they did not know how to win a political battle without votes or funds. Bences Gonzales threatened to organize a letter-writing campaign to Congress and thereby spark investigations that would expose Los Alamos to public scrutiny.[80]

Gonzales's strategy was on target. Hispanos complained to New Mexico senator Dennis Chavez of racial discrimination on a federal project, which was both illegal and an embarrassment to the government. Chavez alerted the War Department, which demanded an explanation from the MED. The army denied any racial basis for the move, stating that the more commodious Sundt housing was reserved for scientists and skilled personnel of "higher-salaried brackets." They avoided further questioning by fusing huts together to make family-sized dwellings.[81]

White Los Alamosans adopted Gonzales's strategy in July 1944 when, due to a clerical error, fourteen families were accidentally placed in Sundt apartments instead of the smaller Morganvilles. When ordered to move, the "Fourteen Furious Fighting Families" drafted a statement to the town council, the housing office, and the army alleging that the MED's shabby treatment of personnel slowed progress on the bomb by undermining morale. The aggrieved Sundt-dwellers threatened to leave in a raging huff, while their supporters waved the Bill of Rights. The Fourteen were victorious that evening, when the army admitted to an "unfortunate misunderstanding" and allowed residents to keep their spacious apartments.[82]

This tactic worked again when the MPs started conducting searches of dormitory units after laboratory equipment had gone missing. Residents had cooperated with the more frequent car searches and closer gate scrutiny because, though annoying, they were implemented universally. The council denounced dormitory searches for targeting working-class Los Alamosans and denying their Fourth Amendment protections against unreasonable search and seizure. Army representatives put the matter "under study" without issuing a further response.[83]

While the town council unified Los Alamosans, it could not achieve a balance of power with the MED. Like the Topaz Community Council, the town council would survive only as long as the military could tolerate and profit from its presence, so all council rulings were subject to army veto. The council provided a controlled forum for Los Alamosans to sound off and a way to work on the issues the MED considered trifling distractions. One council member felt she had rejoined the student council, where members might resolve to "abolish examinations, permit smoking in chapel, or move the college to New Haven, but political imagination was inhibited by the matter-of-fact attitude of faculty and administration." Another resident wondered if the council's purpose was to "make us feel better about not being allowed to vote because of security. Here we could make our voices heard in our small community even though they must be stilled in local or presidential elections."[84]

Town council members worked within the constraints to foster a "spirit of cooperation" and found ways to meet the needs of a community that the MED had no interest in. They established a radio station, a public library, a swimming pool, playgrounds, and a car-sharing program. They sought to improve the magazine selection at the PX, where residents hoped to replace an overstock of comic books and outdated journals with newsmagazines and the *New Yorker*. The council issued a formal request that desserts and breakfast fruit be served in separate dishes in the mess hall, making it a more attractive place to eat. It did not enjoy the same success bringing pinball machines and jukeboxes to the mesa. The army took the request under advisement indefinitely, though they did not ban jukeboxes outright, as the housing authority would at Vanport. The MED did not worry about dance music promoting promiscuity or race rioting in white, middle-class Los Alamos, but it frowned on requests to commit resources to activities outside of the scientific mission.[85]

Residents often acted independently of the town council when military policy put their families' well-being at stake. Mici Teller organized women to sit under the tree that shaded her son's play area to prevent the MED from removing it, realizing that power politics at Los Alamos involved making such a nuisance of oneself that it was cheaper and easier for the army to relent.[86] In one of the most heated demonstrations, angry housewives slapped handfuls of poor quality hamburger from the commissary on an officer's desk, shouting "dog meat!" It may have been unbecoming to throw meat at an army officer, but Los Alamos housewives knew from experience that if they brought a fresh-meat measure before the town council, they would probably end up vegetarians for the duration. The council may have had the MED's official recognition, but it did not have the power to make changes that the army did not approve of or care about. Los Alamos housewives were among the first to learn that real power came from unladylike rebellion instead of orderly participation in the established "democratic" process.

The barbed-wire democracies in all four communities offered residents some influence in local policy decisions, but these highly mediated models of representative government afforded their citizenry no meaningful political power. The reigning doctrine of *parens patriae* made political efficacy a matter not of natural law but of authoritarian rule that was inimical to America's mission as defender of freedom. This parental model, often compared to the governing structures in prisons, hospitals, and schools, took away the power of the individual that made popular sovereignty and individual initiative possible. Instead, in order to exercise real power, residents had to escape and resist as the Modocs did, tolerate futility like Topazians, opt out of the system as Vanporters did, or resort to throwing infantile tantrums like some of the most effective Los Alamos politicians.

Despite its many efforts, the government's self-contained communities were not "little Americas" but inverse utopias in which an idealized American small town functioned in complete opposition to the rest of the nation. Politics was not the only arena that operated in the inverse; the gap between the government's wards and the "real" Americans outside widened in economic life, education, and every aspect of daily life. This divide only became larger over the course of the war, eventually destroying visionary officials' fantasies of rehabilitative, disciplinary spaces as the key to achieving a secure, inclusive American society.

CHAPTER THREE

CULTIVATING DEPENDENCY

Economics and Education in America's Inverse Utopias

"American freedom" rests on two pillars: citizen participation in the democratic process and economic independence, which includes equality of opportunity and upward mobility. This vision has been revered and re-embodied across time, from Thomas Jefferson's image of the yeoman farmer to Frederick Jackson Turner's intrepid frontiersman, and from the GI Bill's suburbanite veterans to President George W. Bush's triumphant claim to laying the groundwork for unprecedented minority homeownership.[1] The true fulfillment of the American promise, however, is the ability to transcend one's economic and social class and move as far as one could along a theoretically even playing field. John Studebaker, writing in his capacity as commissioner of education under President Franklin D. Roosevelt, asserted that full civic participation was critical to achieving "the freedom we want, which is security and opportunity—the abundant life . . ."[2]

When the economic shocks of the Industrial Revolution caused hardworking, loyal Americans to lose their footing on the path to abundance, Congress passed the Homestead Act of 1862 and expanded public education to free working families from the bonds of wage slavery and urban poverty. When the homesteaders' grandchildren lost their homes, farms, savings, and jobs in the Great Depression, the Roosevelt administration provided subsistence homesteads (among an array of planned communities) to replace the stable foundation lost to economic forces beyond their control. Subsistence homesteaders received low-cost land to cultivate, a small house, schools, agricultural processing facilities, and community centers. Although the homesteads were equipped to allow a jobless family to live at subsistence level, most were located near cities so subsistence homesteaders could take every opportunity to work their way back to abundance.[3]

The government's communities for suspect populations were quite different. By isolating "potential hostiles" from the body politic, they pulled them off the path to prosperity. Klamaths, Topazians, Vanporters, and Los Alamosans were also hard-working, self-sufficient people who sought to improve the lives of themselves and their children. They cherished their independence, and by the time FDR was inaugurated in 1932, they had a long record of loyal service to the nation. Although the government agencies in charge of their communities spoke often of helping the residents achieve full independence, many sustained debilitating losses. The contrast between the government's utopias and its reservations for potential hostiles showed itself most clearly in the way it led each population toward the abundant life. Where the government's homesteading utopias promoted financial stability, gainful labor, ownership, and education for economic success and political efficacy, its inverse utopias separated people from markets, meaningful work, and the self-sufficiency that comes with ownership and entrepreneurship. The loss of self-sufficiency was especially devastating to the vast majority of the government's subjects who had previously sustained themselves through indigenous economic systems, solid employment histories, or family-owned businesses.

Having less and less to pass on to their children, parents relied on the government to fulfill its commitment to public education. Since the common school movement, public schools have been the instrument for erasing social inequalities through common learning. The lone teacher in the frontier schoolhouse, through standardized lessons from readers like McGuffey's, could offer the same education as a teacher in an urban schoolroom. Public education could even America's playing field, making differences of class, region, and national origin irrelevant to a hard-working youngster's quest for the abundant life. The ascendancy of progressive education at the turn of the century placed appreciation of one's individual strengths, critical thinking, and community engagement at the center of an education for citizenship. These reigning philosophies of common instruction for individual efficacy shaped public school pedagogy across America, but especially in government-run communities.[4]

In the inverse utopias, however, government teachers were primarily concerned with students' presumed deficiencies rather than their individual talents. Believing their parents' suspect racial or political "tendencies" had some inherited component, educators prepared students for citizenship by pressing them to conform to prescribed modes of thought and behavior (Los Alamos schools being the notable exception). The emphasis on their difference led many students to believe they could never be "first-class" Americans, resigning some to second-class citizenship and sparking resistance and a general resentment toward the government in others.

The federal government's utopias were not perfect; they, too, often did not yield the results planners in Washington sought. Rarely, however, did the government's allocation or management of homesteads and homesteading communities set people back, preclude their economic independence, or stigmatize them as "second-class citizens." For all the government's rhetoric about Americanization in the inverse utopias, its programs for independence ultimately fostered the very dependence and stagnation inimical to being a "true American." In much the same way barbed-wire democracies demanded citizens engage in politics without exercising power, economic activity in the inverse utopias took adults and children farther afield of the abundant life.

The federal government's utopian vision was clearly laid out in the homestead acts of the nineteenth century, during the very same moment that experts in other corners of Washington were hatching plans for the reservation system. Like much of the federal government's Indian policy, the Homestead Act of 1862 was written with multiple goals and interests in mind. Stephen C. Foster, a Jacksonian-Democrat-turned-

Republican congressman from Maine, cast homesteading as a critical component of America's unique conception of freedom and to its eventual realization:

> The history of the world has been a history of injustice and oppression of the poor. The rulers of the world have ruled for their own advantage, and the rights and interests of the people have been sacrificed without scruple on the altar of individual ambition, or to promote the welfare of a favored few. But a better day is dawning. The era of kings and oppressors is passing away, and the era of the people is approaching. Governments are now instituted professedly for the benefit of the governed, and there is reason to hope that the day is not distant with the universal diffusion of knowledge and the freedom of the press and of speech will reduce theoretical justice to practice.[5]

The homesteader, therefore, was not just a down-on-his-luck American seeking a government handout and a shot at the Main Chance; he was the bearer of the American promise and the agent of America's historic destiny. When they piled into their wagons, they went to America's frontier, not its margins.

The Homestead Act was also the product of national security concerns. It was designed to populate newly acquired territories that, despite all legal language, remained contested by the British, Russian, Mexican, and Native nations. Conceptions of American freedom and American security meshed fairly well; homesteaders staked their claims and proceeded to work on them as they saw fit. Like the immigrants to Oregon during the joint occupation with British monarchists, men armed with plows—as well as rifles—solidified the American presence on western lands.[6] Meanwhile, the Indian Bureau parceled out reservations in Indian treaties. On the surface, treaties embodied similar goals as the Homestead Act, with the exception of immediate economic independence. The government's mandate to maintain rigorous social controls on reservations required federal agents to manage economic affairs on both the individual and tribal levels.

In his speech before Congress on the merits of the Homestead Act, Foster considered the possibilities inherent in parceling unwanted land to the Indians. Underscoring the threat hostile Natives posed to home-steaders and settlers already on the frontier, Foster argued,

> These Indian savages are few in numbers, but their trade is in war, and their means of subsistence altogether precarious. They are not engaged in cultivating the earth, nor even in pastoral pursuits. Their habits are those of mere savages, and their pursuits, hunting, fishing and war. When the first two fail them, they resort to the third. They rob caravans, they murder and despoil emigrants, and they attack settlements.

Also noting America's commitment to redemption and reform, Foster added shortly after,

> But what is to become of the Indians? I would not ignore their rights . . . But I do deny the right of a handful of savages to monopolize a continent, when millions of men, more intelligent and better every way, need homes. I would pay the Indians liberally for their lands, and secure to them and their posterity perpetual homesteads, and I would extend to them every facility for learning the arts of civilized life . . . They should be assigned a permanent home, and confined to it. They can never become civilized until they become fixed to the soil, and learn to live by its cultivation.[7]

These interventions, originally designed with national security and social control in mind, ultimately fostered dependency, even when fed-eral agents sought to "civilize" Indians by assimilating them into the wider free-market economy. In the case of the Klamath Reservation, it was the tribal economic resources, consumer base, and labor pools that were integrated into the wider economy. The Klamath Tribes found that access to capital, quality education, and true independence was long in coming. The treaty kept the Klamath people alive, but it did not level the playing field as it did for the homesteaders, and it closed off the option of returning to the pre-treaty economic practices.

Indian treaties were not, as Native signatories might have believed, contracts to ensure an equal exchange of money and goods for land. The Treaty of 1864 set forth a schedule of substantial payments to compensate

Klamaths, Modocs, and Yahooskins for seized lands, but these payments would not go to the tribes. Instead, the funds would be "applied to the use and benefit of Indians by the superintendent or agent having charge of the tribes." This language put the tribes and its members in an impossible bind: the government demanded that Native peoples "earn" their autonomy by demonstrating their capacity to be economically independent while its agents held all the money and made all the decisions concerning the use of tribal members' assets. The government's inclusion of a separate clause in which the Indians "acknowledge their dependence on the government of the United States" seems a bit like overkill: every request to the agency made it more than obvious that adult tribal members were no more self-sufficient than many white children.[8]

The Office of Indian Affairs expected its "children" to grow up, and officials envisioned hard work as the route to cultural and political maturity. The Treaty of 1864 provisions included $35,000 in goods and infrastructure that, at face value, seemed part of a long-range economic self-sufficiency plan. Mills, shops for a blacksmith, carpenter, wagon maker, and plough maker, and a hospital would be provided and operated by the Indian Bureau for twenty years. A farming superintendent, a blacksmith, a carpenter, some sawyers and plough-makers, and a doctor would be employed to build the infrastructure, teach the Klamaths how to use it, supervise operations, and either leave or be paid by the tribes (not the Indian Bureau). Most importantly, the Klamath Agency would establish a manual labor school to train young Klamaths to continue work on these tribal ventures.

Among the earliest features on the reservation's built landscape was the sawmill that would employ Klamath men and supply the Klamath Agency, Fort Klamath, and the local timber market with cut-rate lumber. The mill, in addition to introducing Indians to new technologies, would familiarize them with American work routines. The agency extended tribal members' "educational opportunities" to stock raising, rail splitting, and construction on government projects. White families also "did their part" by employing Klamath youths as domestic servants and casual laborers through an agency-run placement program in conjunction with the manual labor school. This meant that the treaty payments prepared

Native youths to be a source of inexpensive products and services for non-Indians and did not necessarily promote economic development on the reservation. Native employees received only a fraction of the going wage for their work, but they participated in this labor system because it was the easiest way to get a coveted pass that allowed the bearer to venture outside the reservation. Working off the reservation may not have brought prosperity, but it did add a precious bit of freedom and an occasional tinge of adventure to their lives.[9]

The tenets of the General Allotment Act of 1887 required Indians to do more than wage labor to become self-determining citizens. Tribal members had to develop their 160-acre allotments as homesteaders would, making the land productive as proof that they could function independently in American economic life as determined by a government competency board (or, in other words, that they had reached "economic adulthood"). Jefferson's revolutionary ideal of the independent farmer clearly influenced the Indian Bureau's vision, but it did not square with the environmental realities in the Klamath Basin. Klamath peoples had both cultural and environmental reasons for not farming. The arid climate yielded some good grazing areas, and Klamaths and Modocs in particular were able stockmen. No less determined to make farmers of the "Bloody Point savages," Indian Affairs pushed them into agricultural work, going so far as to use the tribal police to enforce compliance.

The agency boasted nonetheless that it had converted 90 percent of all able-bodied Klamaths to farming within a year of implementing the agricultural program.[10] However, a subsequent report submitted to Congress by the secretary of the interior in 1874 noted that 500 Klamaths, 475 Modocs, and a number of Yahooskin Snake Paiutes had worked hard at cultivating their 1,056,000 acres, but that harsh weather conditions had made farming operations "a failure." Native workers, well aware that southern Oregon was not especially suited to agriculture, went about restructuring the economy around the sawmill (filling a contract for 210,000 feet for Fort Klamath) and ventured into raising stock, owning three hundred head of cattle. Although the observer credited Klamaths for being "unusually free of vices," the report did not acknowledge their superior wisdom concerning the productive use of land and labor.[11]

Markets for reservation goods and services were as poorly planned and stringently controlled as the Indian labor system, leaving tribal members few opportunities to develop the sort of independent ventures that formed the foundation of early American capitalism. Instead of allowing a free market, the agency gave selected vendors exclusive contracts to sell goods to or on the reservation. Privileged merchants enjoyed monopoly status and captive markets with guaranteed money on hand, whether at the agency level from timber sales or individually when tribal members received per capita payments. (As "interested parties," the merchants were privy to the disbursement schedules.) Klamaths were all but locked out of their own markets, closing off the time-honored tradition of gaining independence through individual enterprise, if that was what one chose to do.[12]

Even if the government had surrendered Native market controls to the invisible hand of capitalism in the post-treaty period, its social controls were far-reaching enough to curtail meaningful economic freedom at the Klamath Reservation. In the 1870s the U.S. government supplanted nation-to-nation relationships with more overtly paternalistic approaches; increasingly, officials and observers referred to Indians as "wards," implying that the government was the parent or guardian of an immature person. The conception of reservations as bridges between removal and assimilation eventually gave way to the sentiment that reservations must serve as permanent homelands. One of the most striking expressions of this change was in the degree to which reservation agents tightened controls on commodities and subsistence payments rather than encouraging Native economic self-determination. This shift reflected the knowledge of both the government and their Indian wards that Native communities had sustained so much damage from warfare, removal, and reservation life that they were dependent on the government for their survival.

Once the reservation system was well established and the treaty period had ended, Washington had fewer concerns about the consequences of breaking Indian treaties. By the mid-1870s federal reservation policy and local administrative practices were based increasingly on expediency and less on treaty language. Indians became wards of the state, and reservation agents were no longer so much government emissaries as parental figures. Reservation agencies were no longer responsible for delivering commodities in payment for Indian lands but for coercing Indians into full compliance with reservation policy. Both Congress and the Indian Bureau expected agents to maintain order and progress by any means necessary, which could include withholding commodities and other forms of compensation for lost tribal lands as punishments for failing to comply with agency rules. Such retaliatory acts constituted clear treaty violations, but the formal replacement of government-to-government relations with the doctrine of *parens patriae* made legal breaches into mere disciplinary interventions.

Lindsay Applegate had stopped considering the treaty only a year after drafting it, making a regular practice of using commodities as disciplinary tools. He discovered the political power of food when tribal leaders, whose subjects were no longer allowed to hunt for, gather, or prepare native foods, demonstrated enough disaffection with the superintendent that he pressed for sufficient supplies on hand to quell any political ferment. Subsequent officials presented annuities not as a debt owed the Indian but as a favor or gesture of care bestowed generously by the U.S. government on its hapless and helpless wards.[13]

In fact, treaties fell out of public discourse in Indian affairs. Instead of viewing transfers of goods as a contractual obligation, an increasing number of Americans saw them as a harmful form of charity. The disbursement of commodities became controversial not out of concern for the questionable quality and value of the goods, but because the public, fearing it would extinguish incentives to work, perceived it as dangerous. Addressing public criticism instead of the real problem, Washington issued directives that commodities should not be issued to Indians who did not work. Annuities became something like contemporary emergency welfare grants, paid only to those the superintendent judged physically unable to work, and to areas of the reservation where crops failed. By the end of the nineteenth century, government annuities made up less than 20 percent of the Klamath Reservation economy, meaning that the tribes were providing for their own subsistence, yet there was no corresponding reversion of land or extension of freedom on the part of the United

States. The Klamath peoples could be prosperous but not independent, making progress toward "maturity" almost impossible to discern.[14]

The problems of the nineteenth century persisted into the twentieth. The reformist vision that guided the Allotment Act failed to account for the numerous factors that led Indians toward poverty and away from the independence required for citizenship. Though exasperated, the federal government remained concerned about Indians' well-being, and it continued aggressive land management, forestry, and extension projects to improve infrastructure and productivity on tribal lands. It also allowed allottees to sell or lease their allotments to raise capital for other investments such as housing or farm equipment. Often, however, the money went to food and clothing or to pay old debts at a nearby general store. The reservation's expanding economic relationship with area whites had a paradoxical effect on Klamath families. While the tribal entity gained wealth from transactions with whites, individuals grew poorer from land losses. Landless tribal members became dependent on per capita payments as their primary income. Unable to work the land according to the guidelines in the Allotment Act, only a handful of the reservation's residents secured citizenship and voting rights. The Allotment Act was supposed to have granted greater powers of individual self-determination, but the Native community faced being overrun by whites on the reservation. For the majority of tribal members, freedom and independence remained elusive as ever.[15]

The American promise guarantees prosperity to no one, but it does hold that if one works hard and educates their children, future generations will attain the status, prosperity, respectability, and the full privileges of American citizenship that they did not enjoy. The nation's faith in the transformative power of public education to develop one's god-given abilities melded with assimilation policies to form the highly specialized Indian school system. Indian schools, like the common schools, were unified around a central educational outcome. Where the common school sought to make every child fully part of America, Indian education was initially designed to make children "less Indian." Colonel Henry C. Pratt, founder of the Carlisle Indian School, summarized this principle as "kill the Indian, save the man." De-Indianization was a bit different from Americanization; it tried to pull Native students away from their elders and traditions and bring them into the laboring class. This way, they could engage in "realistic" economic pursuits, which would lead to economic independence. Citizenship education was only a distant second goal.[16]

The agency built the first Klamath schoolhouse in 1874. Like schools on nearly every other reservation, it had one teacher, very few students, and no resident Christian minister to oversee it. Educational resources remained modest in 1875, and the student body consisted of children of tribal members employed by the agency as well as a small number sent by order of the superintendent. The curriculum centered only on basic literacy and skills in manual and domestic labor, both of which prepared young Indians for their role as allottees. In addition, students received rigorous lessons in proper comportment and Christian morality once Methodist missionaries were assigned to the reservation.[17]

To ensure that all Klamath residents enjoyed the full benefits of Indian education, the agency established two boarding schools by 1883, and it enforced compulsory attendance laws in order to guarantee every Native child was rescued from parents' and grandparents' traditionalist influences. Parents who failed to comply had their children taken forcibly on orders of the agency.[18] Like the reservation itself, the agency schools were designed to instill lessons in good citizenship, preferences for American culture, and disciplined work habits. Students were roused early from the dormitories, dressed in uniforms, and sent to chapel before their breakfast. The school day began with a few hours of academic lessons before the more rigorous vocational training began. These "lessons" were conducted in the kitchen, laundry room, garden, and school facilities needing maintenance. The teachers who presided over vocational classes demanded perfection. One student recalled with horror the day her sewing teacher hit another student for making crooked stitches. The force of the blow knocked the girl to the floor, giving her a nosebleed. She retaliated by lunging at the teacher and seizing her by the hair while she kicked and bit her. When the teacher called for help, the other students refused to respond. The student warned the teacher never to hit another girl and never returned to class.[19]

Students, skeptical of the educational value of the "vocational educa-tion programs," viewed their mandatory attendance at the agency school as a form of punishment for being Indians. They were not alone in this critique: in the South, black parents insisted on academic training for their children over the prescribed "manual schools" because freedom included the right to choose one's occupation from the same array of options available to every other citizen. Some northern educational leaders agreed that freedom was rooted in choice and the possibility of upward mobility, which was denied children from communities that were arbi-trarily relegated to a perpetual working or servant class.[20] Speaking Indian languages brought cruel and unusual punishments, such as making the offender walk around a tree stump for an hour while carrying a fence rail on his or her back. Disobedient students' "wildness" was managed with brutal whippings, locking them in their dormitories every night, or placing them in "solitary confinement" for extended periods. On good days, school was onerous hard work, and on bad days it was onerous hard work coupled with physical and psychological abuse.[21]

The deplorable conditions in the schools added to the misery of families separated by the agency's compulsory education rules. Students survived on a steady diet of biscuits (with syrup for a special treat) and vegetables from the garden. Hungry students often fled the school grounds long enough to catch and cook a fish to keep them going. Inadequate health services left sick and injured students without adequate treatment. The emphasis on work discipline made school officials read requests for visits to the doctor as a ploy to avoid work. When one student informed her matron that she had a fever, the matron refused to dismiss her from class, stating, "You Indians [are] always complaining about something." Days later, she was covered with spots from scarlet fever. The student was admitted to the agency hospital for two months, but only after the disease had permanently damaged her kidneys.[22]

The educational outcomes for the Indian schools were as negligible as those of the Allotment Act generally. Even students sent to the more prestigious Chemawa Indian School near Salem came away with little to help them achieve independent living. One forlorn student wrote of his upcoming graduation, "I don't think that am able for graduate so I have to do it just as he say. Although my time up for going home, and I cannot say nothing to him or any body. The reason is that I am not smart enough for business then I can't help it. The teacher gave me subject for my oration and I wrote some of them but not correct though I have tried thrice and I have not get it yet." This student was fortunate in one respect. Parents across the Klamath Reservation mourned the loss of children who died in Indian schools with little explanation of what happened. This poorly prepared student accomplished something in having survived his ordeal.[23]

Opportunity for educated Klamaths was almost nonexistent, even for those who managed to make great academic achievements. Claudia Lorenz grew up near the reservation, and she recalled most high school and college graduates taking jobs in logging and farming. A few women trained to be teachers, but the public schools rarely hired Indians. Two young women artists whose work was well regarded by gallery owners could not get teaching jobs or funding to continue their work. Some graduates looked for work in Los Angeles, Oakland, or Portland, but found that what little vocational training they had was inadequate, and they languished in Indian ghettos until they returned home in a worse frame of mind than when they left. Hundreds of young Klamaths were disillusioned after following the Indian Bureau's program for assimilation and independence only to find themselves adult wards of the government. Like their ancestors who were subject to the Treaty of 1864, a new generation of Klamath Reservation Indians acknowledged their own dependence on the federal government as they entered adult life in the twentieth century.[24]

There were also students who would not accept the status quo and who pushed their government "parent" to practice what it preached. This new generation surprised Oliver Applegate, who followed in his father's footsteps to become superintendent in 1898. On the surface, little had changed. Indians gained various degrees of "civilization," but poverty, dependency, and despair remained persistent problems. The one thing that had changed was the sophistication with which tribal leaders articulated political issues and employed expanded modes of political expression. As the Americanization program pushed the Klamath Tribes toward poverty and dispossession, residents performed everyday acts of resistance on an increasingly regular basis. Parents kept children home from school with false reports of illness. Biracial families sent their children to non-Indian boarding schools to demonstrate that the superintendent did not, in fact, have absolute power over every tribal member's affairs.[25]

The most stunning act of resistance came when the agency selected Clayton Kirk to attend the Carlisle Indian School in Pennsylvania. Instead of playing the exemplary Klamath, he embarrassed the agency by running away. Kirk, the son of the minister and tribal leader Jesse Kirk, had been chosen by his peers to be the runner because of his status as the agency's most promising student from an "advanced" family. His defiance made a very bold statement about the realities behind the rhetoric of "progress" on the reservation. When the Indian Bureau demanded an explanation of the incident, the Klamath Agency reminded Washington that Kirk's grandfather had been a "resolute old war chief" and that his rebelliousness may be truly immutable. No one framed Kirk's protest within the American tradition of dissent against tyranny, yet Indian education appeared to be making Thomas Paines out of Captain Jacks.[26]

Meanwhile, on the reservation, Jesse Kirk started an independent activist organization in 1890, when the federal government failed to correct mistakes in drawing the reservation boundary lines, leaving the Klamath Tribes with less land than the area designated in the Treaty of 1864. Instead of pretending the agency would respond to the tribal council, the group gathered funds to send Kirk, Henry Jackson, and wealthy cattleman William Crawford to Washington to settle the matter directly. Congress listened to the first delegation's boundary disputes and misconduct charges against the Applegates with polite tolerance. The secretary of the interior, however, condemned the "reprehensible custom" of addressing Congress directly and ordered that all governmental issues be settled through the agency, unless the Interior Department granted Klamaths special permission to go to Washington. In other words, Klamath political leaders were not to speak until spoken to.[27]

The Indian commissioner's backlash did nothing to deter Kirk and his followers from assembling delegations to draw attention to everything from land policies, the state of Indian education, and tribal members' misgivings about the character, motives, and competence of Superintendent Oliver Applegate. Applegate, stunned by the betrayal of his "friends," was particularly disappointed that the young man selected for a special police commission in the 1870s used his leadership skills to organize against the Applegates. Pulling no punches, Applegate attempted to ensnare Kirk in indebtedness by extending bank loans to him without his permission.[28]

But Kirk, whose faction grew steadily to include Carlisle graduate Charles S. Hood, questioned Applegate's decision to change the tribal police and judges from elected offices to agency appointments. Hood went further, demanding to know why a stockman with a family to support was serving an extended jail term without a scheduled trial. Applegate, apparently shocked at being asked by one of his charges "by what process or authority" he held an Indian in jail, said simply the suspect was a flight risk. He then deflected criticism by casting the most accomplished Klamath Reservation citizens as displaying "civilized" behavior as a cover to develop savage acts of treachery against the agency. Fearing widespread disorder on the reservation, Applegate alerted Washington that Kirk's hostility was "now boldly asserted, though for a long time treacherously veiled," and predicted it would become necessary to "restrain him in some way or remove him from the reservation."[29]

Kirk and his faction were never removed, nor were they deterred from writing President Theodore Roosevelt about Applegate's mismanagement at the agency. Tribal leaders, educated in civics, handy with a pen, and well versed in the language of democracy, independence, and assimilation, sought political powers instead of empty titles. Their campaign captured Klamaths' political imagination, and in 1904 they staged their most effective demonstration against agency rule over tribal resources. When the Indian Bureau ordered Applegate to sell 87,000 acres of reservation timberland to a large lumber company, he complied without question. A group of Indians, many employed by the agency, erected a shantytown (called "Slabtown") around the agency complex to protest their imminent dispossession. The demonstrators were ordered not to "loiter about" the agency buildings and were forcibly removed. While the "rebels" crafted a petition condemning Applegate's actions, a "loyalist" faction publicly condemned the demonstrators. Applegate transferred to another agency in exasperation.[30]

Tribal factionalism intensified during his absence, deepening rifts within the Indian population along personal, familial, and cultural lines. Some flatly opposed the presence of the federal government in any capacity, while others believed the Indian Bureau had simply imposed unfit leaders on them. Some activists wanted to fight for government accountability for treaty violations, and others thought additional government protections were in order. Some Klamaths were individualists, while others thought and acted tribally. Some wanted to preserve the reservation, and others came to believe that assimilation was the only way to security and prosperity. The variations in individuals' political outlook were numerous, but everyone agreed the Klamath peoples must have greater control over economic resources and their private lives.[31] Increasingly, as reservation programming for economic independence and universal education raised barriers to economic self-sufficiency, Native leaders focused their efforts on gaining control of tribal resources and demonstrating the conflict between rhetoric and reality in their inverse utopia.

New Deal Homesteads and Wartime Reservations

When government planning experts gathered to create Topaz, Vanport, and Los Alamos, they had an array of models from which to draw, including the Homestead Act, the reservation system, and the newly constructed subsistence homesteads and similar New Deal communities. Like the homesteads and reservations of the nineteenth century, FDR's utopian vision was a response to a "national security threat" — in this case, the one the global depression posed to the nation and its independent citizens. He vowed to defend the American people by ensuring "security of livelihood through the better use of national resources of the land in which we live, the security against the major hazards and vicissitudes of life [and] the security of decent homes." The president then created and deployed the Division of Subsistence

Homesteads to develop and manage ninety-nine new homesteading communities across the United States.[32]

The homesteading program of the 1930s embodied the same ideals as the homestead acts of the 1860s. In both programs, the federal government made land available to use and easy to acquire so that Americans most vulnerable to economic slumps would have the opportunity to secure their economic independence and build a foundation for their children's success. Subsistence homesteading differed markedly, however, in the degree to which government agencies participated in shaping family and community life in the homestead areas. Where nineteenth-century homesteaders would tame the land as individuals, subsistence homesteaders would do it as tightly knit, highly structured communities of select individuals and families. Under no circumstances, though, would homesteaders engage in collective farming or any other anticapitalist pursuits. The purpose of the program was to develop the qualities that would transform unemployed urbanites into independent landholders able to supplement wages with subsistence produce and, in a good year, make a little extra selling their surplus. In both cases, government did its duty by creating opportunity, as opposed to giving out charity or annuities on demand.[33]

The target population included underemployed city people and struggling rural families who made too much money to qualify for existing forms of relief but did not have the resources to acquire homes and farms. Residents were free to come and go, especially if they were moving to pursue job opportunities. They were free citizens, after all; the fact that they were hit hard by the Depression did not indicate that they had wavered from the bedrock American principles of hard work, independence, and modest spending habits. There was no reason to put constraints on their path to prosperity and self-fulfillment.[34] The New Dealers' greatest hope, however, was that the subsistence homesteaders would purchase their parcels and secure themselves against economic hardship by combining wage labor, small-scale agriculture, and modern home economics. The government provided a thirty-year purchase period on the $3,000 parcels, which allowed the hard-pressed homesteader to progress toward home ownership at the rate of $12.65 per month.[35] Roosevelt, like Congressman

Foster in 1860, envisioned homesteaders as the heroes of American freedom whose hard work, venturesome character, and optimism would preserve the American way of life through good times and bad.

Each homestead was part of a cluster ranging in number from twenty-five to three hundred. Homesteaders could begin cultivation immediately because their acreage came with a "modern but inexpensive house and outbuildings." Although the houses were small, government designers had been instructed to "provide for privacy, comfort, convenience, and attractiveness insofar as cost permits" and to be attentive to "local and regional needs and traditions" in customs and architecture.[36] Planners also put great care into the surrounding landscape so that the built and cultivated elements of the homestead enhanced the homesteader's productivity and prosperity. One government pamphlet explained, "Economy of effort is important. The use of land should be planned so that the work can be done with the least possible effort. This means that the vegetables and berries that need the most attention should be closest to the house. . . . Trees require the least care and . . . should be located farthest from the house."[37]

Among the architects of this grand plan was Elwood Mead, head of the Bureau of Reclamation from 1924–36. In his early career as chair of the California Commission on Colonization and Rural Credits, Mead founded two multifamily farming colonies in 1918 and 1920. While governments experimented with such settlements across the industrialized world, Mead's innovation was the inclusion of community centers, recreational facilities, and cooperatives for seed, machinery, stock breeding, and distribution of the communities' products. Mead's planned-community concept gained its greatest support from Washington at the end of World War I. Fearing that landless veterans would become revolutionaries instead of farmers, the Department of Labor and the Interior Department actively promoted state-sponsored settlements. On realizing that American doughboys were fairly short on revolutionary potential, the forces of antiradicalism cast government settlements as "paternalistic" and—worse—"socialistic." By 1923 even Mead's original California farming colonies fell apart. Mead's conceptualization of the rehabilitative planned community remained a fascination among

Washington progressives, and it was readily adopted by the Roosevelt administration as a component of New Deal programming.[38]

Eleanor Roosevelt was also instrumental in the planning and design of the subsistence homesteads, being most directly involved with the development of homesteads for displaced coal miners in Arthurdale, West Virginia. As soon as resident selection began, the first lady received suggestions from several women about what the homesteads ought to include to help inhabitants "at last become self-supporting citizens."[39] In a jointly authored letter to Mrs. Roosevelt, the future female homesteaders of Arthurdale asked for multiple bedrooms large enough for every family member to have his or her own bed as well as a living room and a large kitchen with bins for apples and potatoes. They requested closets and cupboards in most of the rooms, storage space for preserves, and a basement shower and toilet instead of the standard tub, though some women wanted upstairs bathrooms. (The walls of all bathrooms were supposed to be painted, not wallpapered.)[40]

Homestead women's concerns extended beyond the home. The women asked for a nearby schoolhouse, as all the children would be required to attend classes. In the tradition of the common school movement, every child would be prepared to meet the demands of taking over the homestead and becoming effective citizens. Being a Progressive project, however, the new schools would also emphasize the student-centered techniques of John Dewey, who promoted community schools in which learning happened outside the classroom as well as within. Progressive teachers would help students appreciate their own individuality and push them to their full potential, in keeping with the mission of "provid[ing] outlets for creative energy." Dewey rejected the rote learning and uniformity of the "conventional type of education which trains children to docility and obedience," a model "suited to an autocratic society." Students would not learn passively but think independently and tie class lessons to the realities of their community life. Progressive education contained the same promises of a level playing field and the possibilities for economic mobility, which made it greatly appealing to parents.[41] The Arthurdale women wanted a community center to be used for kindergarten in the morning, recreation in the evenings, and church services on Sundays.

They closed by saying, "These are the most important things needed by the average family among us. We thank you sincerely for all that you are doing for us, and we hope that we shall be able to help you build a happy and hard-working community."[42]

Eleanor Roosevelt took all such requests seriously, locking horns on several occasions with Secretary of the Interior Harold Ickes over whether to install refrigerators and indoor plumbing or to keep costs at their $2,000-per-unit limit. When homesteaders in other communities asked for assistance in establishing community governments, community newspapers, cooperative stores, processing centers, and other institutions that residents believed would help them gain self-sufficiency, Roosevelt and Ickes saw that they got it. If residents were to regain their lost powers of self-determination and rediscover their faith in government, it was incumbent upon leading officials to be responsive to what they were saying.

President Roosevelt emphasized this point in his "Four Freedoms" speech to Congress in January 1941. Aware that the United States was on a near-inevitable course to war, the president reminded the isolationist nation of the bases for their freedoms, their promise to extend these freedoms to the world, and the reasons for defending the American way of life from political foes—just as the New Deal was fighting off the ravages of the global economic depression. Referring to both struggles, Roosevelt asserted that

> there is nothing mysterious about the foundations of a healthy and strong democracy. . . . They are: equality of opportunity for youth and for others; jobs for those who can work. . . . The ending of special privilege for the few; the preservation of civil liberties for all [and] the enjoyment of the fruits of scientific progress in a wider and constantly rising standard of living. . . . The inner and abiding strength of our economic and political systems is dependent upon the degree to which they fulfill these expectations.[43]

Like Foster's intrepid pioneers of the nineteenth century, Roosevelt's subsistence homesteaders were the common men and women who formed the backbone of democracy and embodied the promise of American egalitarianism. These were the people the government sought to protect from invasion, subversion, and sabotage.

The subsistence homesteads were New Deal utopias, and the wartime communities bore some resemblances to these earlier settlements. Daniel Rodgers describes how the New Dealers saw planned communities as "not merely emergency shelters against the decade's storms" because, "[t]o their architects, they were templates of a better social order than price and property alone could devise."[44] The director of information for the Division of Subsistence Homesteads was Milton Eisenhower, who served very briefly as the WRA's first director before Dillon Myer assumed leadership. Eisenhower received instruction to restore the social order after Pearl Harbor, but the plan for these citizens did not call for "modern decent housing; land for subsistence gardens to supplement cash income; and a community social-environment to restore and expand morale, confidence and self-reliance which were considered to be the imperative ingredients of a full and free life."[45]

John Collier, Dillon Myer, and their colleagues at the Interior Department spent comparatively less time considering how to raise the morale of their Japanese residents and notably more energy addressing how goods should be supplied and how people in the WRA camps might best be employed. The WRA did not share the Indian Bureau's goal of making Native yeoman farmers, and it had no interest in seeing the Japanese own any more land than they did in California (which was very little, given the Alien Land Laws). But it did hope to teach the Japanese a thing or two about American enterprise and the American work ethic. No one ever asked the Japanese women what they would need to run a productive household or to educate their children properly. The built environment was uniform, prefabricated, government-issue construction that had, as art historian Lucy Lippard says of bounded communities, "the architectural homogeneity of company towns, where ethnic tastes and decoration are suppressed." The uniformity carried over to Vanport and Los Alamos; one is hard-pressed to distinguish between the three clusters of government-issue structures in photographs.[46]

Only weeks after branding the California Japanese a danger to public safety, Utah governor Herbert Maw came to see them as a cheap labor force. When Topaz opened, Maw proposed that all able-bodied internees be conscripted into the army as a farm labor corps. The WRA rejected Maw's plan, but it did permit local sugar beet growers to recruit 250 field hands, which opened the door for apple, carrot, and potato farmers to recruit from Topaz as well. Tomoye Takahashi joined Mexican and Indian field laborers outside the barbed wire in the Food for Victory program. When she introduced herself to two Indian girls, she was stunned by their response: "We heard about you. You have to live in reservations now just like we did." Although field work allowed internees to cross the barbed wire and make contact with Utahns, most Topazians had been merchants and professionals and had no hope of any long-term benefit from agricultural work.[47]

Nevertheless, Topazians worked so energetically and efficiently that they garnered great appreciation for saving the sugar beet harvests of 1942 and 1943. The WRA touted their achievement as proof that the camps were producing good citizens. Eager to build on this success, Ernst encouraged Topazians to raise crops and livestock in the camp to supplement the mess hall rations. Such a program was logical for most camps, as 45 percent of the West Coast Japanese had been farmers before the war. Most Topazians, by contrast, had been urban dwellers and had about as much farming experience as the Klamath Tribes had when the Indian Bureau implemented the Allotment Act in 1888. Despite this lack of experience, Topazians raised $100,000 in agricultural goods, remarkably reducing the cost of their own detention.[48]

The WRA's need for in-camp labor was as great as its desire for good public relations. Topazians were hired for jobs ranging from maintenance to medicine at artificially low salary rates. The rates were set at twelve dollars per month for apprentices, sixteen per month for semi-skilled jobs, and nineteen per month for professional services. There was no structure for advancement or provision for maintaining a presence in one's professional community (though they were required to renew their licenses with the state of California, where they were barred from private practice). In addition to providing income, a way to show loyalty, and a hedge against boredom, the evacuee employment program also reinforced the racial order. Caucasians held supervisory positions even if a Japanese employee had more experience. In some cases, a racial hierarchy was built into the system through seemingly innocent policies, though it was clear that this government initiative did not serve to even the playing field between Japanese and Caucasians. Postal workers, for example, were stationed at several small pick-up stations, but there was only one at which an internee could buy money orders, register mail, or buy stamps and war bonds. Caucasian postal workers, employed by the post office, worked the main station where financial, administrative, and personnel matters were handled. The branch workers were unbonded Topazians.[49]

Although the WRA presented Topaz as an arena for self-improvement, camp employment programs served government interests. One publication described camp work programs as merely a way to "use the combined effort of all persons on the payroll toward the general operation of the center," noting that questions about the experience, training, and job satisfaction were of little importance. Putting residents to work would yield more political benefits than economic ones. Leaving internees idle for an indefinite period would surely breed disorder and rebellion, which federal officials could ill afford. Residents were hurriedly assigned jobs and had to spend several hours in service to the community. The lack of coherent policy bred a system of arbitrary rules, abuses of authority, and weeks-late paychecks resulting in "unhappy situations" like work stoppages and violence.[50]

The WRA earnestly hoped that all political tensions would center on the agendas raised by the community councils and block managers, but because most evacuees' concerns were related to the "essential services" the WRA provided to sustain them, quality of life was always a political flashpoint. Topaz, like all the WRA camps, was well below "the American standard" in the world outside the wire. (The only places of comparison were the Indian reservations on which two WRA camps were located—Gila River and Poston.) Every Topazian agreed that housing units were unreasonably small, and the tar-papered two-by-fours did not protect residents from the desert dust or the blowing snow. While each barrack was equipped with cots and some bedding, Topazians had to build their other furniture from an inadequate supply of scrap lumber at one end of the camp. The potbelly stoves that heated each barrack were old "black beauties" that lived up to their name by belching soot into the room, and they often did not keep a flame long enough to bother with lighting it at all.[51]

The mess hall held significance for Topazians that went far beyond being a feed station or even the principal communal space for the block. The evacuee chef and mess hall workers had little experience feeding 250–300 people at a time, and their mistakes produced laughs at the dinner table, as when kids held contests to see who could bounce a spoon the highest from the too-hard Jell-O. The steady ration of beans disagreed with many diners, and outbreaks of food poisoning led older diners to suspect the WRA was trying to starve them. Food became a center of political activity at Topaz, much as it did at the other WRA relocation centers, Indian reservations, and federal nuclear reservations. When a disgruntled art teacher was elected to the community council, he initiated a campaign to inundate Myer's office with telegrams complaining about the endless streams of heart and tripe cooked in ketchup or soy sauce. The stakes could be as small as getting specific dishes or as critical as convincing the WRA to provide living conditions that approximated the "American standard."[52]

Community analysts warned Washington that poor quality food and dining facilities would be a continuing source of unrest and disorder. A 1943 memo asserted, "Unless the chief steward has the confidence of his cooks, who in turn have the respect of the blocks, food riots or strikes are going to occur sooner or later in the project." The WRA capitulated by commandeering 40 percent of the nation's rice crop and issuing civilian rations of fish, meat, and vegetables for the mess halls to prepare as they chose. Still mindful of public scrutiny, the WRA kept tight controls on ration points and food stocks, revising menus to keep costs down. In spite of the WRA's efforts, Topazians continued to suspect they were shunted the worst-grade government food, and Utahns continued to believe Topazians were being wined and dined at public expense.[53]

As an extension of its Americanization program, the WRA allowed evacuees to operate supervised consumer cooperatives in order to make goods available to Topazians that fell outside the WRA's "basic needs" category. Like the community council, the co-op was supervised by a WRA agent who had an educational mission in mind. The co-op supervisor's loftiest goal was to introduce "foreigners" to the principles of American business (including the Hadley Company accounting model used at army post exchanges). There were, of course, a few oddities to this conception. A WRA poll revealed that 93.7 percent of co-op participants had been independent businessmen before the internment, so the co-op held little educational value. Even if Topazians needed instruction in mainstream economic practices, American business does not operate on a cooperative basis—only Indian reservations held communal capital.[54]

It is unclear how the WRA reconciled itself to promoting an essentially anticapitalist economic model in its barbed-wire democracy. The official explanation was that private enterprise could not exist on federal property, particularly in communities where economic inequality would create social tensions. The unofficial explanation was that the WRA had a talent pool of internees whose business skills offered a cost-effective alternative to hiring more Caucasian professionals to supply the camp.[55] In any case, the co-op filled a demand for a wider variety of consumer goods. Miné Okubo wrote humorously of the ill-fitting pea coats and other government-issue garments that kept Topazians warm in winter but feeling silly all the while. The ladies' sections of the *Topaz Times* and the literary magazine *Trek* suggested how to alter the garments for flair and a better fit, but the solution of choice was to order from catalogs. While it was nice to have new clothes, there was a sort of uniformity that continued to unsettle people like Harry Kitano, who recalled, "It is frightening to think that the big excitement in one's life would be the Sears Roebuck catalog. That was fantasy land. You looked at it and you thought, 'gee, I wish I could have all these things.'" He heard later that Sears saved the best stock for regular customers and made the unsold items available to customers in the WRA camps, which created uniformity of dress all over again. Okubo took note of this, writing, "Everyone was dressed alike, because of the catalog orders and the GI clothes."[56]

The members of the co-op saw the program for what it was, but they used the otherwise unfulfilling jobs as a way to improve Topazians' quality of life and transform prisoners into active community members.

Co-op leaders were as eager as the WRA for Topazians to make a good impression on the outside world, and residents were truly happy to regain some range of consumer choice. Dissatisfied with their passive role as WRA poster boys, managers cultivated business relationships with department stores, made an effort to have friendly interactions with Utahns generally, and brought items to lift residents' spirits. Knitting supplies, special magazines, and hobby items went a long way toward making their confinement bearable, yet these products would never be on the government's list of essentials.[57]

The cooperatives took on important internal political dimensions as well. The WRA incorporated egalitarianism in its mission through its mandate to elect a board of directors, but it maintained full control over the money and power. The co-op board was responsible for collecting membership fees and running the business in the black. It was also a lender, auditor, supervisor, and employer of hires chosen by the board. The board determined which Topazians would be full, voting co-op members as well as the more controversial matters of policy and procedures. The exercise, then, was fundamentally political, and the reward for doing well was a more comfortable life in camp and "proof" that the Japanese could "learn" how to function in American economic life. Interestingly, like Indian tribes with resources to invest, Japanese internees put a great percentage of their income into war bonds, both as a postwar investment and to demonstrate their loyalty by being a high-spending group. This fact was acknowledged in government reports, but it was never considered in the development of camp programming.[58]

Topazians would face tremendous hardships after the war that had nothing to do with their absorption of the WRA's "lessons" in economic independence. Over the course of the internment, the WRA lost track of thousands of dollars worth of evacuees' personal property that the government had agreed to store safely for the duration of the war. Making matters worse, the California State War Board contacted the WRA in early 1943 to inform them that the state would requisition all property that could aid war production, particularly vehicles and expensive farm machinery. The state would send purchase offers to the owners, who would have ten days to respond or lose their right to compensation. The board reported in December 1943 that "only" thirty-eight such requisitions had been made, but this constituted a significant loss of assets for these families. There were also numerous cases of "friends" and neighbors offering to hold property for internees only to appropriate or sell it for their own benefit.[59] If the internment was really intended as a living civics lesson, one must wonder how this wholesale seizure of private property by government agencies and fellow citizens fit into the WRA's picture of American life.[60]

In addition to providing "adult education" in politics and business, the WRA had to provide schools for a population of children whose degree of assimilation was unknown to government officials. The Interior Department transferred educational specialists from the Navajo Reservation to the WRA to implement classroom techniques from the Navajo Agency schools, which integrated academics with "a planned community life." In this model, teachers "instill the social competencies thought to be necessary for living in contemporary society." The veterans of the Navajo schools saw Japanese pupils in the same light as Indian students, as "racially disadvantaged" and politically suspect. Instead of approaching students in terms of their gifts, as one would see them in a public school or a school on a New Deal resettlement project, reservation schools took the student body's "deficiencies" as their pedagogical point of departure. Using reservation students to understand Topaz students ignored not only critically important cultural and historical differences but also the fact that Japanese children had much stronger academic backgrounds and were assimilated into the American educational mainstream.[61]

On paper, the Indian Bureau and WRA shared Topaz parents' desire to maintain students' academic progress and help students cope with the stresses of the internment. With the tenets of progressive education at its core, the curriculum prepared high school students to meet state and college entrance requirements and included the option of a half-time vocational education and apprenticeship program. The school year would run eleven months, leaving parents free to work, maintaining students' social supports, and offering regular guidance counseling. In addition to extending the instructional time for students who had been "miseducated" in Nihonmachi, students would receive special instruction in keeping "emotional control" while being chronically sleep-deprived in their cold and noisy barracks. Such lessons were vital to living at Topaz, but they would not prepare them for lives as citizens in a normal American town.[62]

The curriculum in Topaz schools, like adult programming, was intended to Americanize the California Nikkei. But no amount of patriotic pedagogy could distract the students' attention from the obvious contradictions between camp life and any conception of American democracy. In spite of the fact that over eight hundred Topazians held college degrees, Caucasians were brought in as head teachers; Japanese teachers served as teachers' assistants even when they possessed better credentials. Each day, Topaz students received lectures on equality and racial diversity from teachers who were clearly placed in a rigid racial hierarchy.[63]

Students not only witnessed the hypocrisies of the internment, they lived by its confused dictates. They were escorted to the fields during spring and summer sessions for a "garden project," only to find that their "botany lesson" involved hard agricultural labor, angering students who saw themselves as "suckers" for trusting their teachers. When Myer made his first visit to Topaz, grade-school students asked why there were guard towers at the edge of the playgrounds. Myer said they were built to protect them and their families, but nine-year-old Lee Suyemoto was skeptical. Suyemoto saw everything at Topaz as a punishment for being Japanese, from the armed guards to the racist slur of a Caucasian teacher in class. Rather than accept his teacher's behavior, Suyemoto led the entire elementary school in a walk out. The teacher was replaced after two days of discussion by the principal and faculty, but many students remained distrustful of the school and its officials.[64]

Student activism was all the more pronounced at Topaz High School, where some students found more opportunity to participate in "Caucasian" activities like student council and cheerleading, while others chafed at the limits on free expression. When Minoru Kiyota suggested the United States might be considered an "aggressor nation," the enraged teacher demanded to know if the seventeen-year-old was a fascist. Kiyota followed his "no" with a question about how the internment fit into the American democratic tradition. The war of words escalated until

Kiyota walked out. He returned to school a few days later to complete his graduation requirements and his application to attend college in the East, leaving with the impression that he and his teacher had made amends. Kiyota was scheduled for an interview with the Student Relocation Council to discuss his placement options. He was surprised to find an FBI agent, not a student relocation official, on the other side of the desk. The agent, after pounding his fist on the table and shouting "you dirty Jap!" denied Kiyota educational leave because he spoke Japanese and studied *kendo* as a child, making him "a perfect candidate for sabotage." Kiyota was later cleared to attend college, but he never stopped pondering the crude lessons in democracy, both formal and informal, he learned at Topaz High.[65]

Graduating seniors used commencement speeches to challenge WRA rhetoric on race and democracy. Rather than waxing sentimental about her school days, valedictorian Rhoda Nishimura encouraged classmates to overcome an "evacuation mind" so absorbed with anger, fear, sloth, and alienation that young Topazians risked falling into unending apathy. Succeeding classes compared their experiences to those of African Americans, Native Americans, and German Americans during World War I. Instead of railing against the United States government, speakers underscored their faith in America's tradition of correcting mistakes. Not recognizing that it was the WRA, not the students and teachers, who promoted the negative outlook, Topaz director Charles Ernst accompanied transcripts of the speeches to Washington with a note reading, "The kids sound as tho they had been studying psychology. It doesn't sound particularly healthy to me. I think it is about time to play down the minority group psychology." No curriculum reform could persuade Topaz's students that they were first-class citizens. While they remained patriotic, many young Topazians modified their daily pledge of allegiance with "liberty and justice for all, except us!"[66] They realized, even if the WRA did not, that while the president built communities for "real Americans" to prosper, Japanese Americans were placed in communities where they were losing wealth, falling behind in educational achievement, and unwittingly becoming entrenched in systems of government dependency for the first time in their history.[67]

Vanport resembled the subsistence homesteads more closely than any of the other three communities because its residents most closely matched the profile of the hard-working Americans they sought to help. The vast majority of Vanporters were rescued from the ravages of the Great Depression by both their jobs at the Kaiser Shipyards and the War Manpower Commission's offer to transport them to Oregon. Vanport housing was far better than anything many families had been able to provide for themselves. While the circumstances of Klamaths and Topazians declined, newcomers to Vanport enjoyed great economic improvements.

Unlike Klamaths and Topazians, Vanporters had well-paying work. (This was slightly less true for African Americans, who found the Fair Employment Practices Committee to be generally ineffective enforcing the antidiscrimination laws in the unions and the yards.) Once their wages started to roll in, there was little for Vanporters to do but put their money away and save it for when their "real lives" began after the war—by sending it to where they came from, traveling to Portland to deposit it in the bank, or by stashing it in coffee cans in their apartments because there was no bank at Vanport (and many distrusted banks after the run in 1929).

Banks were not the only businesses in short supply at Vanport. In sharp contrast to the internee-run Topaz cooperative, Vanporters were prohibited from engaging in on-site commercial activities, particularly in the apartments. Outside solicitors were forbidden from trading in Vanport unless they had made formal arrangements to do so with the Housing Authority of Portland (HAP). HAP established contracts with merchants who had preexisting business licenses to operate in the project shopping centers, an arrangement reminiscent of the permit system for outsiders conducting commercial activity at the Klamath Reservation. This prerequisite barred newcomers from operating small businesses, which made sense for the shipyard workers, but it prevented trailing spouses or older children from improving their lots through free enterprise.[68]

Approved merchants paid rent to HAP on a sliding fee scale based on their monthly net profits, and HAP reviewed the books and reports on day-to-day operations. Peddlers were licensed by the same criteria and barred from trading on the project if their products were available from existing merchants. HAP met some consumer demand on its own by operating cafeterias and concession stands, and it controlled supply, distribution, product inspection, and general economic oversight. By eliminating market fluctuations and consumer choice within Vanport's boundaries, HAP retained full control of the project. Established merchants enjoyed captive markets, and while Vanporters' economic agency was better than before, it was still narrower than that of their neighbors in Portland. Although their shipyard jobs most certainly improved their economic circumstances, this prosperity rested on the government's wartime demand, the unusually high demand for labor, and the availability of affordable housing with exceptional support services at Vanport.[69] These working families were more prosperous, but they were not fully self-sufficient and had difficulty achieving full economic independence. As communities of future owners instead of temporary workers, subsistence homesteaders had abundant infrastructure and incentives to be independent participants in the economy as soon as the opportunity arose.

Social control was not the sole impetus for all this economic management. Public relations played a large part as well. A small-scale crisis erupted when the maintenance supervisor broke HAP's confidentiality rule prohibiting workers from speaking publicly about Vanport's inner workings. He made boastful statements about the amounts of government money spent on Vanport, admitting that HAP employed 834 people, mostly as maids and laborers. Subsequent stories of Vanporters living like kings grew more numerous and colorful, leading HAP to fear that continued publicity "gave an incorrect psychological picture in reflecting the humoring of tenants and accentuating the amount of money spent on the project." HAP put its employees on notice that all statements to the press must be cleared by its offices, submitted exclusively to a "Mrs. Hedges." Portlanders were infuriated, believing, as Sherman Tolbert did about his Topaz neighbors, that the government was taking better care of the nation's "undesirables" than it was its better citizens.[70]

The supervisor failed to note, however, that the maids were not personal housekeepers to the tenants; they simply maintained the public spaces (so Vanport would not be the eyesore Portlanders feared) and prepared

new units for fresh arrivals. Nevertheless, the perception that Vanporters lived high on the hog threatened to reignite the old animosities that
had forced the project outside the city. Maintaining the peace required
clear demonstrations of government thrift, but putting on this show
also made life at Vanport unnecessarily constraining economically, and
it ultimately fostered closer economic ties between the workers and the
government that housed them.

New Frontiers for Children and Housewives

Vanport adults, for all their perceived problems, were clearly
able get along in the labor market. Children became the government's
greater concern, having only known the do-nothing days of the Depression and the upheaval of migration to the shipyards. Worse, they lived in
a community that in no way resembled the quiet suburbs to which they
were supposed to aspire. Education and child development were critical
to developing the next generation of decent, hard-working, and self-
sufficient citizens at Vanport. Left to their parents, they might perceive
government handouts as an expected source of income, unemployment
as nothing unusual, and migration from one workplace to another as a
normal way to support a family.

Political and economic life at Vanport was relatively unstructured
because the adult population found more meaningful engagement and
investment in their work at the shipyards. The children, however, spent
all their time in the community. So while tenant government, community
policing, work programs, and structured recreational activities were
central to operations at the Klamath Reservation and Topaz, children's
programs were the focus of community activities at Vanport. For the
FPHA, childcare was critical to the war effort, both to free mothers' labor
for the shipyard and to inculcate habits of good citizenship in America's
postwar generation. Ideally, FPHA-sponsored day care emphasized "fair
play, the rights of others, tolerance of others, [and] the give and take
which are the keystone of democratic living." Taking its parental role
seriously, Vanport's child services programs were among the first in the
United States to provide individualized services to children with special

needs while integrating children from all walks of life into its child-sized, multiethnic, all-American village. Attendance was not mandatory, project director James Franzen asserted, but "as a citizen of Vanport you will place the welfare of your child first and cooperate fully in this respect."[71]

As with Vanport itself, the child service centers put national security objectives ahead of progressive social policy. Although the press cast Kaiser and the FPHA as the heroes of such innovative family-centered institutions, Portland teachers and social workers had to "push—push anybody doing anything [about childcare] to get women to work and also to give the proper care at the same time." The decisive blow came in June 1943, when the Women's Advisory Committee denounced Kaiser for failing to provide the day-care services recruiters promised, even after having solicited funds from the U.S. Maritime Commission. At the same time, young families found that the childcare problem was as serious as the housing problem had been prior to the construction of Vanport City. Only when pollsters discerned a connection between women's high rates of absenteeism and the shortage of quality childcare did Kaiser order facilities built at Vanport.[72]

The planning and design of the child service centers took place just where they had for both Vanport and the subsistence homesteads—in the meeting rooms of visionary architects and social engineering experts. The six centers were laid out hexagonally, with classrooms along the exterior. The inner space was divided into "paddocks," or confined playground spaces where children played freely and could be easily supervised by childcare workers. Each day, tiny Vanporters followed a regimented schedule in the confines of a specially designed building complete with child-sized sinks, toilets, and closets, so children could take care of dressing and hygiene independently. In tightly organized fashion, the children had health inspections, indoor play, an educational story, outdoor play, naps, and a spoonful of cod liver oil. Each activity had a particular developmental benefit; outdoor play emphasized sharing to prevent "spoiling" children, while naptime was intended to instill "good habits of sleeping and dressing" in addition to providing a short rest.[73]

While professionals hailed the arrival of modern childcare technologies, some mothers were reluctant to leave their children at first. Some

African American mothers never imagined that state-of-the-art centers were truly available to their families, while others feared overt racism would damage their children more than government educational programs could help them. Parents of all races found tuition to be expensive if they had several children, or they shuddered at scattered references to Vanport's "Sovietized nurseries." Government educational specialists' mass childcare system was not based on Soviet practices but on those of the Indian Bureau and the WRA. Vanport children, like children from the Klamath Tribes and Japanese American community, were placed in a structured setting designed to instill American middle-class values under the supervision of government agents who would make them into better citizens than they believed the parents could.[74]

The aim of the daily routine was not merely keeping children safe, supervised, and focused on their lessons, but to reverse the damages of "poor parenting," which included everything from actual abuse and neglect to having lived through difficult circumstances (such as the Depression) or being raised according to ethnic or regional customs. The center's program director used the case of six-year-old Gary to demonstrate the wonders of their services to readers of *Architectural Forum.* The boy's family arrived at Vanport exhausted and disoriented after their long drive from North Dakota. Gary's father brought him to the center while he arranged for housing and a work assignment. Not only was Gary tired, dirty, and hungry, he and his siblings had no mother. The head nurse took the children from the father for the day, which ended with a family reunion between a well-employed father and children who were rested, bathed, fed, and had new female figures in their lives. The Vanport Child Service Center did not just watch Gary; it transformed his life — and that was only day one.[75]

The child service centers' long arms reached across the divide between what, in normal circumstances, would be considered "public" and "private." In some ways, this was necessary and welcome. Childcare workers mended children's clothes, prepared hot meals for take-out, and made a team of counselors available to help with parenting problems that arose in Vanport's odd environment. One of the cornerstones of children's programming at Vanport was its extensive nutrition program, designed to ensure children were well nourished and to teach them to aspire to a better standard of living than most of their parents provided. Teacher training emphasized the "highly organized and structuralized program with nothing left to chance" because "food influences behavior." Teachers saw working-class living habits as "detrimental" to Vanport children and sought to eradicate them, just as Klamath Agency teachers turned students from traditional lifeways and Topaz teachers chided parents to "say it in English." With Vanport students, food was a marker of relative "backwardness" and was the subject of much ethnographic observation. The official Vanport school publication reported that most children's lunch boxes contained "an array of bread, sweet rolls, cookies, cream decorated pies and pop" because, according to the children, "Daddy gets the fruit in his lunch box" or "Mother and daddy eat the meat; they work." After several meals at the child service center, however, children reportedly exclaimed, "Golly, I never knew this stuff could taste so good! I don't like it at home."[76]

Food became Vanport's currency of care and the standard by which parents were judged. Inevitably, the school had more and better offerings than working parents. Children were instructed to bring the benefits of middle-class life home by telling their parents to buy vegetables and cut out sweets. Similarly influenced by government education programs, some Klamath kids scorned wocus and Topaz students turned up their noses at miso. In all three cases, there was little parents could say about the state's subversion of parental authority because the distance from family and community networks made them dependent on government childcare.[77]

While HAP portrayed the child service centers as places where small children's problems were solved instantly and expertly, the schools that were built for their older brothers and sisters were conceived as places where tougher, more deeply engrained social problems would be rooted out. Officials referred to the Vanport Public Schools as "living centers" that would give students whose families had "abandoned them for the shipyards" a place to anchor their lives. School would become Vanport children's wartime community, encouraging good health and citizenship and curbing unruly behavior: "For adults, the community would be chiefly a place to eat and sleep. . . . But their youngsters would be living in this community. Their life must center somewhere — either around gangs of their own making or in the school." While Vanport schools shared the reformist elements of those at Klamath and Topaz, their goal was not to civilize or Americanize the children. Rather, it was to bring working-class children to the "American standard" of social conduct lest juvenile delinquency make them into "dangerous outsiders."[78]

Days in Vanport schools were as regimented as those at the shipyard and the nursery. Play times and lessons in the three R's were punctuated by the arrival of the snack cart and its attendant lessons in hand washing and good nutrition. Older children received instruction in cooking, grocery shopping, and childcare, since these tasks had fallen to them in the home, in those places where there was a gap between the family's ability to manage household affairs and Vanport's actual ability to deliver "complete and constant services" to workers. Commissioners extended the policing program to include a "boy's patrol" in which boys reported vandalism and other small crimes committed by Vanport's youth, a strategy akin to the "minorities policing minorities" systems in place at Klamath, Topaz, and the Vanport deputy station.[79]

Classes were deliberately integrated, and children were encouraged to learn about one another's backgrounds (which accounts for children remembering Vanport as integrated and harmonious, and adults recalling it as segregated and tense). Field trips to ship launchings, local farms, and Portland cultural institutions were an integral part of the curriculum, as were art and music classes. Community service and awareness of current issues helped train the students to become good citizens of Vanport and the United States.[80]

Children with special needs received generous personal attention. Part and parcel of the individualized care and instruction devoted to each child was the "diagnosis" of academic deficiencies or problems of adjustment. Frequent absences, behavioral problems, or simply having a family structure that differed from the two-parent norm was reason for a visiting teacher to make an unannounced call at the family home. Visiting teachers conducted home inspections and interviews with each family member, which were recorded for submission to the students' files. Teachers openly stated that part of their mission was to keep tabs on parents who seemed likely to cause problems for the Vanport community, just as they did for the children who disrupted the harmony of their miniature Vanport, or the "living center" community.[81]

While programs of racial integration and special education put the Vanport schools at the forefront of progressive pedagogy, too often cultural differences became the basis for a diagnosis of "mental retardation." The link between racism and misdiagnosis appears clearly in the case of Bobby, whose miraculously reversed "retardation" was closely related to his ethnic identity. The Vanport schools glowingly reported the case of "an Indian boy" who had appeared "very nervous and seemingly mentally retarded. He had been placed in the fifth grade because of his age [sixteen]. . . . The teacher reported back that Bobby would scarcely answer a question, and then in so low a voice that the answer could not be understood. . . . His lunches came from home and each day . . . the boy would wander off and eat in solitude. A test showed he had not been endowed with much mental ability." When remedial reading and math teachers intervened, Bobby made "amazing progress," which culminated in his "fervent hope" that his family would not return to their Montana reservation.[82]

The physical condition of the Vanport schools could not have been more different from those at Topaz. Vanport's teachers, buildings, curriculum, and special programs were designed to enhance each child's physical, psychological, emotional, and intellectual growth, in addition to preparing every one of them for the responsibilities of good citizenship. Students in both school systems were taught that America was a multiethnic democracy where equal treatment was a fundamental national value, but once they left the classroom, they entered communities whose policies and structures segregated citizens by race, according to the design of the federal government. Their teachers told them to respect their parents while showing them that the government was the better "parent." Despite their interest in each child's individual gifts, Vanport educators expended the most effort on only one—their capacity to serve as "civilizing agents" of the adults in the project.

Of all the inverse utopias, Los Alamos was the most concerned with security and productivity and the least geared toward "rehabilitation" or "reform." General Leslie R. Groves wished dearly that he could turn the "longhairs" into disciplined, God-fearing, all-American boys, but even he gave only the slightest consideration to reform or rehabilitation in the course of planning and managing Los Alamos.[83]

This difference is due in great part to the fact that Los Alamosans enjoyed the greatest economic stability of any population in government communities. Scientists with academic positions continued to draw salaries through an arrangement with the University of California, and the vast majority had homes, assets, and other resources awaiting them at the war's end. Even those who took pay cuts did so for the great reward of working with the world's greatest scientists on the most important project of their time. This, for an academic, was what "doing better" was truly about. The government considered most Los Alamosans politically suspect but by no means part of a larger economic and social problem. So community features, including the closed market and the peculiar labor system, were designed to promote efficiency and secrecy, not to build nest eggs, develop job skills, or impart the American work ethic.

Long accustomed to exercising consumer choice, many new arrivals had trouble adjusting to the lack of goods, services, and amenities. They also noticed immediately that their power to "vote with their dollars" withered away when they entered the gates. Los Alamos's economy was the most highly managed, self-contained system of all the federally run communities. The army post exchanges provided a limited stream of supplies selected by procurement officers on the basis of availability, not demand. The scientists and their families understood this to be a function of project secrecy and security, and some even appreciated the simplicity of the system. Alice Kimball Smith noted quickly that her new life was far less complicated than that of her "urban sisters" because, "[if] there was no chicken at the store, you ate something else because there was no other store to check. If you ran out of gas, you walked to work. . . . If you had no cigarettes, you rolled your own."[84] The MED's lack of transparency about the operation of the commissary made issues of supply and demand increasingly political.

Los Alamosans were highly attuned to shifts in the quality, supply, price, and availability of consumer goods, ever suspicious that the federal government might be gouging or withholding various items as a form of social control. The town council continually monitored prices, in what became a sort of a citizens' watch against government abuses of power in an arena where protest was relatively safe. Groves and J. Robert Oppenheimer could tolerate the occasional consumer complaint. They could not, however, allow any conditions that might shift focus from the bomb. Both leaders harbored grave concerns about two populations that could, if not constrained within some form of community discipline, create dangerous upheaval on the project: the locals and the scientists' wives. They both made sure that the scientists' wives and local pueblo dwellers whose social and economic networks had been disrupted had jobs on the project. This was due in part to the enormity of the project and the need for all available hands, which were few in the secret city. Yet more often than not, Oppenheimer and Groves expressed concern that idle women and curious locals might be tempted to undermine the project or worse, talk about it. Giving everyone positions as hard-working stakeholders in the Los Alamos project (whatever they believed it to be) made it easier to capitalize on all available labor and served the security interests of the MED, if not the real economic interests of the women, Indians, and Hispanos themselves. The women were already under surveillance, as were the Indians to some degree, and neither the Indians nor the Hispanos spoke English well enough to pick up or convey sensitive scientific data.[85]

Before the Manhattan Engineer District broke ground on the mesa, federal agents encountered Indians and Hispanos who were hostile to American encroachments on their land. Bences Gonzales was one of hundreds of local Indian and Hispano villagers recruited to work as wage laborers on "the Mesa" but the only one recruited from the old Los Alamos Ranch School. The army employed people from the villages and pueblos to provide inexpensive manpower to the project and with the pretext of assimilating native New Mexicans into the mainstream economy. The MED had no interest in Indian affairs aside from making sure pueblo dwellers were cooperative neighbors. The initial encounters between the MED and the local residents were not promising. The Gomez family, who were bean farmers, returned from the market one day to find MPs blocking them from their land. Pete Gomez, like Topaz neighbor Sherman Tolbert, was shocked that the U.S. government expected him to surrender his land and his independence for the benefit of a government project no one could even explain to him. Tolbert was at least given a month's notice and the option of refusing his contract to supply meat to Topaz.

The Gomez family was informed of their fate, which affected the entire village, for which beans were the main cash crop. At the same time, young men from the villages were drafted into the armed forces while able-bodied, draft-age Euro-Americans streamed into the area. The loss of manpower further destabilized family economies, while the loss of young villagers fueled racial resentments. The MED, having little interest in the crises in the pueblos, required the new corps of maids, furnace stokers, and maintenance workers be fingerprinted and vouched for by someone the army trusted. Groves was confident they were safe because even if their loyalty was not heartfelt, the language barrier created an effective wall of secrecy.[86]

Indians and Hispanos occupied the bottom rung of the civilian labor hierarchy. The MED bused them in each day to perform maintenance and domestic services for a small wage. Some pueblo dwellers believed "that place in the mountain is a blessing" for its promise of jobs, education, and new inroads to industry and technology that BIA policies could never provide. Farm equipment, furniture, and cars became available for the first time in many of their lives but at tremendous personal and social cost. The shift from agriculture to wage labor changed gender dynamics dramatically because there were far more domestic service positions open for women than manual labor jobs for men. Phyllis Fisher recalled a conversation with Appolonia, a San Ildefonso woman assigned to provide housekeeping and childcare services, in which she asked what her husband did. Appolonia answered, "[B]y custom, men do the hunting." Unsatisfied, Fisher pressed her a bit, until Appolonia added,

"[O]h, sometimes I gave him money. He go to the store. He buy food. It's all right" — though clearly it was not.[87]

Cleto Tafoya, the governor of Santa Clara Pueblo, took a construction job at Los Alamos in 1943 and was hired permanently as a cafeteria server along with his three daughters.[88] The MED never consulted him on matters of shared concern because the MED had no intention of negotiating with Native communities. The pueblos' many wartime contributions went unacknowledged, with officials in Washington scolding them for their dependence on "government generosity" and their "refusal" to work anywhere other than Los Alamos. The sacrifices of the San Ildefonso and Santa Clara people were enormous: the short-term economic gains could never compensate for the profound disruption of the traditional web of social and economic relationships that had sustained the pueblos for generations.[89]

The scientists' "republic of Los Alamos" had strict geographic boundaries that extended no further than the outer edge of the laboratory. Being walled off from the laboratory bore heavily on the scientists' wives, who gave up their careers, social ties, and civil liberties to mark time while their husbands immersed themselves in a career-making opportunity. The women's grudging acceptance of the MED was mutual; the MED only accepted women and children as a recruitment measure. The MED, drawing on stereotypes, imagined a group of intelligent women corralled in a sterile enclave being quarrelsome and gossipy, carelessly leaking secrets during bouts of hysteria.[90] Oppenheimer and Groves both saw potentially disastrous problems if the "woman question" were not adequately addressed. The two differed remarkably, however, in their approaches to the problem. Groves never wanted to house them in the first place and hoped they might just stay home, while Oppenheimer committed himself to integrating them into the project. Oppenheimer, worried that the intensity of their husbands' work schedules and the security restrictions would unleash an epidemic of depression and disruptive behavior, consulted a psychiatrist who recommended that the women be put to work to give them a stake in Los Alamos and to "keep them out of trouble."[91]

Oppenheimer made women's first public responsibility the organization of a school system, knowing the MED refused to bear the expense and security risk of hiring teachers from the outside. Most women on "the Hill" had college degrees or professional experience in the arts and sciences. The scientists also agreed to give guest lectures. Despite makeshift conditions, pupils at Los Alamos received a good education, particularly compared to students in other inverse utopias. Teachers led field trips into the woods, along the mesa, and into Indian communities, resulting in an incredibly rich, community-based education completely free of the government's intrusive, reform-oriented "citizenship" lessons that drove the curricula at Klamath, Topaz, and Vanport.[92] The MED said little about the schooling of Los Alamos youngsters and was not terribly concerned about the teacher shortage that inhibited quality instruction in several subjects. As long as the women who taught were busy, happy, and not gossiping, the Los Alamos educational system fulfilled its main purpose.[93]

Some women appreciated the opportunity to channel their energies and abilities into the school. Others did not and resisted pressure from the MED to become educators. Bernice Brode did not mind working but resented being told she had to be a schoolteacher. After all, in America people chose their occupations, and Brode had serious objections to teaching school. Her refusal to join the school was misunderstood as shirking, so she quickly took a job in the Tech Area, where there was increasing demand for research assistants. Although they were often blamed for miscalculations, the Tech Area's female labor force excelled at their work and made enormous contributions to the work of the lab. Most of these jobs involved adding strings of numbers and similarly dull tasks. Some women made tremendous professional strides, like Elfriede Segrè, who compiled a widely used isotope chart, and librarian Charlotte Serber, who prepared and stored manuscripts of laboratory findings for postwar publication. This was a very fortunate circumstance: unlike most other American occupations, these jobs had nothing to do with economic gain or self-improvement but with staving off boredom, depression, and foolish behavior.[94]

The jobs of most women, like the chemist's wife who was "shang-haied" into driving the mail to Santa Fe twice a day with armed guards and a locked briefcase handcuffed to her wrist, were less gratifying. There is no indication that the mail carrier ever grew to like her job, nor did it give her the fringe benefit of more time with her husband, which was a precious perk to Los Alamos women. Bernice Brode enjoyed the challenge of her new work but lamented that she was "not essential." Although the history books would acknowledge the value of women's contributions to Los Alamos's success, Brode's statement reflects the truth of the matter at the time. Hiring wives served similar functions as hiring local Indians: it ensured their cooperation, reduced their idle time, and deepened the MED's presence in the private lives of people whose malice or ignorance could harm the bomb project.[95]

Eleanor Jette shocked recruiters by refusing to work outside her home so she could stay with her six-year-old. The MED branded her unpatriotic, but she stuck to her guns because there was not sufficient community infrastructure for working women with small children. Although maid service and year-round school were provided, both were unreliable. If the maid missed the bus, she could not get clearance to enter the compound, and when the school called its impromptu one-week vacations, mothers had to choose between going to work and supervising their children. Many worked to stave off depression and anomie but were dismayed at the anxieties that working life created.[96] Despite some vocal objections to the Los Alamos labor system, it brought as many as 75 percent of Los Alamos women into the work force at the height of the research and development phase of the project.[97]

Groves' and Oppenheimer's recruitment strategies gave Los Alamos a special corps of manageable defense workers. Scientists had contracts with the University of California and settled problems through their administrative channels. Most other personnel were military or married to scientists, and the Indian labor force was subject to economic and bureaucratic controls from the MED and the Office of Indian Affairs. By August 1944 enlisted men constituted almost one-third of the scientific staff, and ninety highly educated Women's Army Corps members joined Los Alamos wives in covering administrative and clerical duties.

The official military history of the army's involvement with Los Alamos notes that by not hiring regular workers, Los Alamos avoided the labor unrest that plagued towns with booming defense industries.[98]

While economic participation, productive labor, and education had been arrayed so carefully in the Homestead Act and the subsistence homestead programs, they were used as social controls in the inverse utopias. Economic activity was without gain, particularly for Topazians who lost the fruits of a life's labor while working for nineteen dollars a day at a WRA job during their internment. Some Vanport and Los Alamos parents held out hope that their children would have better opportunities in their own working lives as a result of their first-class education. Yet other Vanport parents saw their children fall behind like their counterparts at Topaz and Klamath, where students were being educated for life as second-class citizens.

The cumulative effect of the barbed-wire democracies, government-run capitalist systems, unprofitable economies, and confused public school systems was a life fraught with daily ironies. Demonstrating loyalty through cooperation undermined residents' independence, and in most cases it forged temporary and sometimes long-term ties of dependency with the government. Living day-to-day meant negotiating strange contradictions that ultimately made American life more foreign, not more familiar. Upon leaving the inverse utopias, residents faced the ultimate irony: the gap between themselves and Americans in the mainstream had only widened as a result of the government's project to unify America's insiders and outsiders.

The contrasts between the government's subsistence homesteaders and its "potentially dangerous wards" were subtle but significant. Homesteaders, from the outset, had a sense of ownership over their communities. The experience of "building a happy and hard-working community" alongside the first lady and the secretary of the interior was qualitatively different from being rounded up and placed inside a government-controlled community for one's own good and the security of the nation. Subsistence homesteaders asked for many of the same features that the government installed at Klamath, Topaz, Vanport, and

Los Alamos. They wanted community councils, cooperative stores, and educational programs, and for good reason: they had a great deal of control over both how the programs were run and their participation in them. The fact that such structures were imposed on inverse utopias and remained impervious to citizen input made the homesteaders' communities worlds different than the government's settlements for the presumably "hostile" and "uncivilized."[99]

CHAPTER FOUR

TRAGIC IRONIES

Everyday Life in an Inverse Utopia

During the 1913 commemoration of the Modoc War, Oliver Cromwell Applegate, speaking as former superintendent of the Klamath Reservation, lauded the unusually bright "race of fighters" who, after having "finally succumbed to the control of our race" became one of the wealthiest, most "advanced" tribal groups in the reservation system. Nevertheless, the agency could not yet certify their competence for citizenship because "'fire water' has become with them, as it had before with any other tribes, the greatest menace to their progress." This mixed image of the vanquished savage perpetually treading the line between fulfilling white America's hopes and dashing them utterly legitimated the government's continued segregation of the tribes while holding them to their obligations as citizens in the making.[1] The impossible task of Americanization within a system built for the enforcement of racial isolation and perpetual "Otherness" brought ironies, absurdities, frustration, heartbreak, and the occasional pang of antigovernment feeling as residents struggled to live as exemplary Americans.

Nowhere was this clearer than on the battlefields of World Wars I and II. The onset of global conflicts — at least in theory — presented America's outsiders the rare opportunity to transcend their Otherness by joining the nation as brothers in arms. The government mobilized Indians for the war effort in the belief that military and home-front service was the path to rapid assimilation. As never before, military service became paired with citizenship, making World War I seem like the opportunity for non-whites to demonstrate their loyalty and, through what Lucy Salyer terms "blood sacrifice," earn full political and social equality with whites (for those who made it home from the battlefield). Native people everywhere hoped their patriotism would push the government to honor its treaties, but many at the Klamath Reservation were highly suspicious of the deal being offered. Community elders never pressured young men to join the army because they openly suspected that recruitment was another scheme to remove young men from their communities and have them killed. Still, the government's promise to reward Indian recruits' loyalty made service in the Great War an attractive prospect to Indians nationwide. Young Native Americans believed military and defense jobs offered them a rare chance at relief from chronic poverty and isolation. The most optimistic among them hoped that Indian soldiers and war workers would improve the political and social status of all Indian peoples by showing the American public they could be loyal and dutiful citizens.[2]

Indian commissioner Cato Sells, who doggedly promoted Native enlistment, was praised for instituting wartime programs that served both Indians and non-Indians. His massive reservation agricultural program put tribal members to work growing crops for military and home-front supplies, answering the eternal criticism that "lazy Indians" had squandered reservation land. Nationally, Native Americans produced $7.9 million in agricultural products, led in the production of processed moss for surgical dressings, and boasted some of the highest participation rates in blood drives. Schoolchildren at Klamath conserved vital timber supplies by helping with planting, pest control, and pledging not to mutilate or destroy any trees. Their mothers and grandmothers helped by manning the lookout towers in the place of firefighters gone to war. The Klamath Tribes answered Commissioner Sells's call to purchase liberty bonds to demonstrate they had both the patriotism and "habits of thrift" essential to good citizenship. One Klamath woman, known as "Princess Ah-tra-ah-saun," joined her Cherokee husband Chief White

Elk on tours to sell liberty bonds that yielded $1.8 million per week and brought favorable attention to America's most "exotic" patriots.[3]

Indian doughboys were similarly revered for their exemplary service and the mysterious "warrior spirit" they brought to the front lines. The general public welcomed them home with fanfare infused with fascination and awe. Their home reservations welcomed them a second time, often with traditional ceremonies for returning warriors. But when the parades and ceremonies died down, many veterans were confronted with the fact that neither the conditions on their reservations nor their status as citizens had changed. Congress rewarded returning servicemen with the Indian Citizenship Act in 1924, which granted citizenship to all veterans and competent allottees. The act did not, however, remove impediments to Oregon Indians exercising their voting rights. Eligible Indian voters had to negotiate a confusing bureaucratic process with the Naturalization Service to get on the rolls. Once they did, they encountered a new set of state voting laws in 1925, subjecting Indian voters to literacy tests with no standards for their content or administration. In much the same way that Jim Crow laws prevented African Americans from exercising their newly acquired citizenship rights after Reconstruction, the 1925 statute rolled back voting rights to prewar status for poorly educated Indians.[4]

Indians' postwar economic fortunes were no better than their political ones. Federal bureaucrats stayed firmly in control of tribal assets, and allotments remained in government trust until agents judged allottees competent to manage their own affairs. The pliable term *competency* stretched far enough to encompass hazy notions like "mental fitness," "adequate financial means," and "Americanism." Demoralized veterans from the reservation expressed their dismay in government questionnaires intended only to record the nature and duration of Native veterans' service. After filling in all the identifying information, one Modoc respondent from the Klamath Reservation attached a statement expressing resentment at being used and studied but never receiving the opportunities promised him: "I know a lot more then [sic] the paper can hold—but I'm keeping it to my self. Seeing it will benefit me in no way what so ever

[sic] if I told it all. it [sic] will only enrichen some body—who may want the data to make a book."[5]

Veterans like this man were angered that their military service had not provided more opportunity. The camaraderie veterans shared with whites in the army did not extend to the Klamath Basin home front. Skills gained in military training and defense jobs did not translate to peacetime opportunities. Wartime images of assimilated Indians gave way to the old images of backwardness that justified every formulation of federal Indian policy. The same Oregon newspapers that lauded Klamath soldiers in the 1910s reported in the 1920s that the Klamath Reservation was rife with axe murders, beatings, alcohol, poverty, interracial conflict, and family breakdown. The dual image of the Klamath Tribes as well assimilated and collectively rich on the one hand, and as dependent, dangerous, and eternally uncivilized on the other, perpetuated Indian officials' practice of issuing contradictory policies that always worked to Indians' disadvantage.[6]

The entire reservation system came under scrutiny in 1928, when Interior Secretary Hubert Work engaged the Brookings Institution to conduct a nationwide survey of conditions on reservations across the United States. Their final product, the Meriam Report, found that federal management strategies created deplorable living conditions in nearly every reservation community. The majority of reservations were just plain impoverished, but the Klamath, along with other prosperous reservations, contained the deepest paradoxes of reservation engineering. The oddities of living in a "democracy" with an authoritarian power base, a controlled economy that made the tribe rich and individuals poor, and an education system that taught children to emulate their white neighbors who shunned them, made full citizenship all but impossible. The investigative team of Native and non-Native experts recommended a profound restructuring of the reservation community in which a government-regulated incorporation scheme would replace the collection of landholders playing at democracy. Klamath tribal members, as stockholders in the reservation, would share tribal assets and participate in economic planning in a manner that more closely approximated the workings of American democracy and corporate capitalism.[7]

The prospect of Indian management of natural resources piqued the interest of enterprising tribal leaders like Wade Crawford. Crawford lived just outside the Klamath Reservation, made money in livestock (as had his father), and lived completely in the mainstream, except when acting as self-appointed spokesman for the tribes. Crawford helped the tribal business council devise a plan to organize the reservation as a corporation with a board of directors elected by, and accountable to, its fellow shareholders. The Klamath Agency would remain in place only as a hired consultant whose decision-making power would diminish as the tribal leadership gained experience managing their resources independently.

These plans became the basis for the Klamath Incorporation Bill (S. 4165), sponsored by Oregon senator Charles McNary and endorsed by Indian commissioner John Collier. Collier, a New Deal liberal, was a proponent of ethnic democracy, a philosophy unlike that of his predecessors. Where "democracy" had been conceptually married to "assimilation" in the past, Collier envisioned a multicultural citizenry in which all ethnic groups could organize their families and communities as they chose and each community had equal standing in the American polity. Collier thought reservation Indians were especially well suited to leading Americans toward a cooperative commonwealth because they had been experimenting with cooperative, democratic community systems for decades. To most Indian commissioners, reservations were supposed to absorb white influences. Collier believed that the rest of America would find examples of true democracy in well-planned Native communities like that on the Klamath Reservation.[8]

The bill passed with the addition of a three-person board of supervisors drawn from government service to act as advisors and to protect tribes from bad decisions—keeping federal paternalism in place for the time being.[9] Yet incorporation made the Klamath unique among reservations. Most tribes were adopting the provisions within the Indian Reorganization Act (IRA), which, as part of the Indian New Deal, required tribes to reorganize their governments under constitutions they wrote, unless they voted to reject the act altogether. Collier intended the act to stop Indian land losses and give tribal leaders some say in how their reservations would be run. Critics pointed out that the tribal governments would remain subject to Indian Bureau controls, making them too autocratic, and that their communal holdings would keep them in a Communist system.[10]

Although the Klamath Reservation rejected the Indian Reorganization Act in favor of incorporation, the tribes were profoundly affected by Collier's system-wide policies. Collier hired nearly 2,000 Indians to the 5,000-person Indian Bureau in an attempt to expand opportunities for educated Indians to bring their expertise to problems affecting reservation life. In 1933 Collier put the Klamath Reservation to a test by recommending Wade Crawford for a presidential appointment as superintendent of Klamath Agency. Roosevelt took Collier's suggestion and made history: Crawford became the Klamath Reservation's first Native superintendent, and the only Indian assigned to his home reservation.[11] The Klamath Reservation was to have its first governor, and, Collier believed, its first experience of political self-determination.

The announcement of Crawford's appointment, however, was met with at least as many groans as cheers. Part Klamath, part Modoc, part Caucasian, and well-known in Washington for his opposition to non-Indian encroachment on the reservation and his complete distrust of the Indian Bureau, Crawford had long been the object of controversy, both on and off the reservation. An older woman complained to Collier that Crawford had her son beaten and arrested at a general council meeting for taking the opposing position on pending congressional legislation. Most recently, the tribal council had recalled Crawford from Washington for presenting himself as a council representative and misrepresenting its position on the disposition of forest and grazing lands. Collier still set great hopes in Crawford, advising the new superintendent that if he could maintain diplomacy among tribal factions, his administration would be "a historical success."[12]

Collier focused his concerns on social and community issues, while Crawford remained concerned with economic ones. Crawford applauded Collier's statement that "one is entitled to get from his property not only material benefit but experience and self-confidence, and life; and they are not even getting that—they are not getting life." Crawford was keenly interested in the question of "material benefit," while Collier emphasized "experience and self-confidence." This persistent difference in outlook caused the two men to clash almost immediately. Crawford, for his part, could not have taken on his economic agenda at a more challenging moment. The Great Depression brought timber cutting to a near standstill, which required both the tribal business council and Indian Affairs to make difficult decisions about forest management. In addition, the federal budget crunch reduced law enforcement staff to one constable and one tribal policeman. Klamath County refused to lend any aid apart from suggesting that the army resume its old law-and-order function on the reservation.[13]

Tribal leadership fractured even further when a corruption scandal involving three members of the tribal business committee erupted in 1934. The committee members accepted $1,600 from lumber companies to lobby allottees and the general council to give them highly profitable timber cutting contracts. Collier removed the three councilmen for their ethical violations, but Crawford demanded additional legal action. The tribal court appears not to have pursued the matter, perhaps because there were no federal or tribal statutes prohibiting tribal officers from acting as paid lobbyists. Crawford blamed Collier for the court's inaction, which evolved into renewed charges that he deliberately failed to protect the Klamath people and that he was the most paternalistic commissioner ever.[14]

Crawford's distrust and disdain for the people he led extended from public to private matters. He granted privacy to state-sanctioned unions, but he was so openly intolerant of custom marriages that he was rumored to have monitored domestic conduct by peeking in the windows of residents' homes. He then complained bitterly to Collier that the courts declined to prosecute a couple married by Klamath custom, putting the commissioner in the odd position of defending traditional lifeways to an indigenous leader. When Collier suggested putting more reservation citizens on the tribal police force, Crawford refused, claiming corrupt tribal council members would use their influence to bribe or blackmail Indian officers. To Collier's dismay, Crawford embodied the worst of the Indian Bureau's influences, and he diminished the chances of the

Klamath Tribes gaining control of their reservation by casting them in the worst possible light. Collier sent him a series of letters offering advice, which Crawford perceived as Collier's attempt to interfere with his rightful authority.[15]

Collier's refusal to discipline Crawford led to the passage of two anti-Collier resolutions by the tribal council. The first called for his ouster for having ignored numerous complaints and petitions presented to him. The second denounced Collier's support of Crawford's order that parents receive merchandise orders instead of cash for their minor children's per capita share of tribal assets. The council argued that the new policy laid unnecessary hardship on struggling families and would invite abuses. While recognizing that Crawford implemented the policy to prevent parents from squandering their children's resources, critics charged that a responsible leader would look for ways to make families economically self-sufficient, rather than punishing destitute parents. Crawford, impervious to criticism, strengthened his authority on the reservation and made continual pleas to Washington that it also take a firm hand in reservation discipline.[16]

Angry Klamaths went over Collier's head by petitioning President Roosevelt and the congressional committees on Indian affairs to force Collier to fire Crawford. Residents charged Crawford with illegally conducting timber sales, refusing to comply with the general council's harvesting guidelines, suppressing reports documenting his own wrongdoing, and using tribal resources for threats and bribes. The petition complained that Crawford's "dictatorial policy" made it "impossible for many Indians to survive." The general council then made a formal call for Collier's ouster in May 1934 when their petition received no response. The council condemned Collier for ignoring the will of the majority, alleged that Crawford confiscated income from tribal members when he did not approve of how they spent their money, and complained that he attended general council meetings with a loaded gun.[17]

Collier's hopes for a self-governing reservation were dashed when he admitted to the Interior Department that Crawford was unable to manage administrative and personnel issues on the reservation. The turnover rate at Klamath Agency reached 200 percent, with most terminations based on Crawford's suspicions that employees were affiliated with the Communist or Nazi parties. When Crawford was finally dismissed from his post in 1937, he demanded a hearing to have his name cleared. When his request was denied, Crawford accused Collier of trumping up charges against him because he refused to join the Communist Party. Crawford closed with, "The Klamath Reservation will never become a part of Soviet Russia or its principles. . . . I have found out that your mind works on the same twisted principles as does your legs, when you are sitting." Secretary of the Interior Harold Ickes relayed a final reprimand and barred Crawford from consideration for a future post. He was granted a hearing before the Senate Indian Affairs Committee, which was dominated by testimony about timber contracts and lost profits, with some discussion of Crawford's personnel policies, Collier's "Communist agenda," and his alleged retaliation against Crawford for allowing the Klamath Reservation to reject the Indian Reorganization Act.[18]

Although there is little question that his agenda was consciously self-serving, Superintendent Crawford was also very much a product of Indian Bureau political education and influences. He fully absorbed the white supremacist teachings of reservation life and reaped the rewards of being highly assimilated. Crawford saw how other superintendents played to the wishes of powerful outside interests and used those interests to exert control over Indian people and resources. And in a political tradition dating back to Oliver Applegate's near-appointment of Allen David as the reservation's "president," Superintendent Crawford ignored, interfered with, or took control of the tribal government when its democratic processes proved a nuisance. The intrepid politician suffered a defeat, but he was no less deterred from pursuing greater political ambitions. Ever confident of his skills as a politician, Crawford made a bid for the House of Representatives in 1938 but was handily defeated in the Klamath County Democratic primary. Crawford was without a place in institutional politics, so he followed his failed election bid with a career as an independent activist on the reservation.[19]

The Indian Bureau replaced Crawford with a white bureaucrat and never assigned another member of the Klamath Tribes to the superintendency. Crawford gave the Indian Bureau a glimpse of its progress toward the "Americanization" of Indians, which showed that superficial markers of assimilation could be deceiving. Unfortunately, it did not spur Congress or the Office of Indian Affairs to study the inner workings of the community before making similarly dramatic policy changes for the Klamath Reservation.[20]

For all the effort to bring American ideals of independence and democracy to the Klamath Reservation, six decades of experimentation in artificial institution building and unfocused assimilation programs sent the residents hopelessly confused and contradictory messages about how to regain their powers of self-determination. Klamaths lost land to whites who made them outsiders in their own homeland. Military recruiters saw them as fully competent citizens in wartime; then civilian bureaucrats deemed them incompetent in peacetime. They understood the capitalist system from their exposure to the timber and livestock industries, yet individuals lived from one per capita payment to another, which was an insufficient household income. Their tribal funds purchased better health care than other reservations, but Klamath Indians still died much younger than their white neighbors. While the Klamath Tribes may have had an impressive tribal government, its resolutions could be ignored by the superintendent or vetoed by federal officials who knew little about Klamath people or tribal affairs. Conditions of life did not meet the standard set in the Treaty of 1864 or in the U.S. Constitution.

As the reservation began its recovery from the upheavals of the Crawford administration, the Pearl Harbor bombing opened new questions about Klamaths' role as American citizens and the place of the reservation within the nation at war. Answering the call for unity, Klamath draftees willingly went to the battlefront while workers took jobs in defense industries. Tribal members who remained on the reservation became civil defense workers, making themselves and their resources available in the war for global freedom and democracy. They had been full legal citizens for twenty years and now became full participants in the American war effort, which meant that questions about Indians' place in America as self-determining individuals and communities demanded a postwar resolution.

Collier saw in the war emergency the same opportunities for Indians that he saw for Japanese Americans. Reservations and internment camps could serve as enclaves for building solid ethnic communities whose contributions to the war effort would place them within an emerging ethnic democracy. The inclusive democratic spirit surrounding the war mobilization expanded opportunities for Indians to join the military and the industrial labor force, creating new paths into mainstream economic and political life. Indians, as a racial group that Americans and federal agents found nonthreatening, were not to be confined but sent into the mainstream in large numbers.

Collier instructed superintendents to bring reservations in line with other American small towns by mobilizing people and resources for war. Superintendent Bert Courtright, one of the most avid promoters of Klamath assimilation, appointed six Klamaths to be civil defense coordinators and to implement home-front education and information programs. Klamath residents would also receive training films on how to identify aircraft, read maps, disarm incendiary bombs, and provide first aid for poison gas casualties. Separate corps of Indians served as reservation air-raid wardens, while others conducted blackout drills and watched for the Japanese incendiary bombs that occasionally drifted onto the Pacific Coast. The reservation had its own "Rosie the Riveters" in the teams of women who manned observation towers on the lookout for forest fires. The reservation itself showed an increased military presence, as the air corps installed observer systems and aircraft warning devices at strategic points on Klamath land.[21]

The Klamath Tribes wholeheartedly supported Courtright's efforts to place Klamath people, land, and resources in the service of the war effort, but their wariness of his absolute authority did not disappear. While the Klamath Agency welcomed the county draft board onto the reservation to induct young tribal members, Courtright worked to secure draft deferments for agency staff. The federal government alleviated the deficit of on-reservation Indian labor by enlisting conscientious objectors to help with administration, fire suppression, agriculture, and other maintenance and development projects. The Klamath General Council approved a government request to locate a conscientious objectors' camp on the reservation but noted with irony that their own young people were being drawn off those lands to foreign battlefields and equally foreign defense plants.[22]

As the reservation reorganized itself for war, security and surveillance became increasingly important agency functions. The FBI was not nearly as concerned about fifth column activities among Native Americans as it was among Japanese Americans, African Americans, European immigrants, and citizens with Communist allegiances. Nevertheless, the FBI augmented security and surveillance structures from the reservation's earliest days. Washington alerted Oregon superintendents that their reservations were "embraced in one of the 'States of Hazard'" and must be monitored for "overt acts of aggression or subversive hostile acts."[23]

The Indian Bureau's Special Agent John Arkell, in addition to his peacetime cases of drug trafficking and organized crime, was in charge of rounding up Indian draft resisters and turning them over to the Klamath County sheriff. Both Courtright and Arkell tended to see AWOLS as "primitives" and "shirkers," instead of dissenters or even disloyals. A Klamath AWOL named Joe evaded Arkell for several weeks until the young man (whom Arkell and the sheriff referred to as "our little friend") was arrested and incarcerated off the reservation. Four months later, the young man escaped from Camp White and led the Oregon State Police on another extended search. Throughout the ordeal, no one considered that Joe might have refused military service for political reasons; his flightiness was seen as a racial characteristic that was especially pronounced among indigenous southern Oregonians.[24]

The government viewed the tribal police as key to curbing draft dodging and disorderly behavior that detracted from the war effort. The Office of Indian Affairs encouraged reservation agents everywhere to give tribal police officers special commissions, which brought no extra compensation but would be an honor bestowed by the agent and the tribes. The "special officers" would assist with the usual duties, such as suppressing liquor traffic, and with wartime ones, like apprehending draft dodgers and subversives. In addition, the OIA requested Courtright forward commissions for six deputy special officers and appoint a non-Indian chief of police to aid in wartime security. Among the leading candidates was a former Klamath Falls police officer returning from service as a guard at the War Relocation Authority (WRA) internment camp at Tule Lake. The U.S. attorney urged Superintendent Courtright to send tribal police officers to a weeklong FBI training program to prepare them for the demands of wartime policing—special searches and seizures, civil defense, the mechanics of arrest, and handling bombs, explosives, and firearms. The memo also noted the peacetime applications of these skills in a community where law enforcement personnel were always stretched thin.[25]

Wartime measures went beyond aiding the Allies' cause abroad to accelerating the government's assimilation campaign on the reservation. Congress outlawed traditional "custom marriages" in 1943, and the agency set a deadline of June 13, 1945, for couples to "separate or be dealt with according to the law." Traditionalists on the reservation confronted cacophonous messages of appreciation for their part in the war effort and disdain for their "backwardness." Assimilationist tribal members supported the government's position, and tribal officers were placed in charge of policing their traditionalist compatriots.[26]

While Courtright kept tabs on the wartime activities of Indians on the reservation, county and federal agencies tracked the activity of tribal members living outside the reservation. This new partnership between the superintendency and the county extended the reach of government control when Indians left the reservation, as in the case of two Klamath County Indian girls who were frequently absent from school. Courtright engaged Klamath County law enforcement and social service workers to monitor the girls' school attendance, attire, hygiene, and to determine whether their mother, who was Caucasian, maintained a "good home." Courtright decided he would reduce the family's per capita payment by one dollar for each day the children were absent from school, disciplining the family with a tactic from the Applegate era.[27]

Courtright also followed Collier's example of promoting America's "warrior exotics" as fully loyal citizens, and he began by registering young Klamath men for the draft. It is hard to know what young Klamath men thought when the county draft board arrived on the reservation. Their anger at Germany's racist policies and Japan's direct attack on the United States motivated dozens of men from the Klamath Reservation to enlist, and the government's promises of new opportunities for dedicated soldiers were undoubtedly enticing to those just entering adulthood. To the slightly older recruits, however, these were the same promises that their fathers heard during World War I before receiving paltry economic supports, the ineffective Indian Citizenship Act, and a greater sense of isolation and exploitation by the federal government. Still, those who served did so in defense of freedom, with the hope of perhaps enhancing their status as patriotic American citizens.[28]

Courtright did his share to promote the Klamath as America's most advanced reservation. When asked whether Klamath boys would be interested in attending training for civil defense and war industries at Chemawa, Courtright replied that Klamath was an unusually wealthy reservation community that, while committed to national defense, was composed of the "advanced type" of Indian who already had university training. Although Courtright's description of the Klamath population was greatly exaggerated, some tribal leaders shared his belief that good public relations would pave the route to full citizenship. A member of the tribal business council went so far as to tell a reporter that the Klamath Tribes were more independent and advanced than most others and that their per capita wealth of ten thousand dollars made the reservation "the richest community in the world."[29]

In reality, most members of the Klamath Tribes still had no meaningful access to the privileges of American society and almost nothing to call their own, aside from the right to live on the reservation on considerably less than ten thousand dollars. No matter how much money accrued to the reservation, Klamath residents would have a long way to go before Americans recognized them as full citizens. Although it seemed like presenting Klamaths as competent citizens would change Anglos' attitudes toward their Indian neighbors, Anglos proved just as inclined to reject them for being rich and competent as for being poor and shiftless.

Part of the problem was that the government and the American public had so many conflicting ideas about Native Americans that every attempt to present them in the context of wartime ethnic and industrial democracy "read" in a garbled, confusing way. When Kaiser's Swan Island yard prepared to launch a destroyer named *Modoc Point*, planners asked Courtright to arrange for some "Klamath Indian women" (not Modocs, if they were aware of the difference) who were "of suitable type and qualifications" to attend the christening in Portland. Courtright eagerly forwarded the names of five candidates, some of whom were "college women" and others "of good standing, appearance and ability" at the ready to sing and serve as flower girls.[30]

Kaiser held the "Indian launching" on the same day the company's Oregon Shipyard held the "Negro launching" of the *Tuskegee Victory*, which was attended by Father Thomas Tobin, several Tuskegee graduates, and legions of black shipyard workers (many of whom were undoubtedly Van-porters). The day was set aside to "celebrate the cooperation of all races and creeds" in building the arsenal of democracy. The press was taken with the "comely Modoc maiden" dressed in the fashion of the day as well as Modoc basketball star Clyde James, who gave the keynote speech. This launch was as much a celebration of minority groups' (perceived) decision to place national unity ahead of their own civil rights struggles for the duration of the war as it was a recognition of their contributions to their American democracy.[31]

Courtright continued to ride the wave of interest in Indian patriots by drumming up national press for major reservation events. He presented the Klamath Tribes as being the richest and among the most patriotic Indians in the United States, which made them a curiosity. He sent press releases to all the newsreels inviting journalists to cover the dedication ceremony for the reservation's new airfield and the christening of the reservation's new airplane, the *Klamoya*. The agency press release proudly noted that Klamath tribal leadership built the first Indian airport, which could only have been achieved by America's "richest Indians." He also pointed out that the Indians were not just wealthy but were esteemed patriots who purchased over one million dollars in war bonds and were honored by having three bombers and a government steamship named after the reservation tribes. The agency planned a program to appeal to white audiences by presenting Klamath residents as both traditional reservation Indians and contemporary American citizens. Placed among the military machines and signs of conspicuous wealth would be Klamath cowboys, soldiers, and Indians in teepees (instead of the *wikiups* their ancestors actually built.) The agency's display of stereotyping and conspicuous consumption showed the American mainstream that the Klamath Reservation made significant contributions to the most important facets of American life. It also began to raise questions about whether such accomplished people should be allowed to live so comfortably on what observers misperceived to be "government expense."[32]

The American public got a second look at the Klamath people when the Jacques Tourneur western *Canyon Passage* was filmed in southern Oregon. Oregonians were thrilled by press photos of Hollywood stars learning archery from war-painted Klamath extras and took pride in their enchanting landscape and charming Indians. The Native actors' charm was forgotten by the time Governor Earl Snell went to Hollywood to formally invite the studio to hold the premiere in Oregon. Portland put out the red carpet for stars Ray Milland, Yvonne De Carlo, and Hoagy Carmichael for a gala that promised to "capture the spirit of pioneer Oregon" and, true to history, relegated Indians to the background.[33] *Canyon Passage*, like the Kaiser launchings and the airport dedication, served to build and satisfy whites' nostalgia for the Old West, when pioneers pulled together like World War II Americans to advance the march of "civilization."

Behind the images of Klamaths' successes, however, were hundreds of people living the same reservation realities that had existed before the war. A young Klamath extra in *Canyon Passage* participated because he sought a professional acting career. When Courtright asked Yakima actor Nipo Strongheart if he might assist the young actor in some way, Strongheart advised that only independently wealthy Indians could make a living in Hollywood. Once there, the young man could join the vast pool of on-call Native extras. Strongheart also advised against acting lessons, because regardless of how much training an Indian actor had, his "native appearance" was all that would interest a casting director. Exploitation of Native workers was hardly exclusive to Hollywood. Indians were pushed and pulled to and from centers of opportunity at Chiloquin, Klamath Falls, Vanport, and Washington DC.[34]

The pushes and pulls intensified during demobilization as the Indian Bureau rushed to determine which Indians had most fully assimilated into wartime society. Klamaths made a good showing on the battlefield and the home front, with 121 of 167 Klamath GIs remaining on active duty in 1946, and two Klamath women returning from the WACS and WAVES. The future looked bright for veterans returning to the reservation, with forty-eight Klamath residents landing jobs off the reservation and sixteen applying for Indian Service jobs at home. Prospects dimmed a bit as approximately half of those who worked for off-reservation employers returned to Klamath. As wartime unity waned, tribal members had trouble staying in the mainstream, leaving the government uncertain about how to position Indians in postwar society.[35]

One of the biggest problems for Native veterans was the federal government's confusion about whether the Veterans Administration or the Interior Department should provide transitional services for them. The VA was provisionally assigned to aid Indian veterans, which it did by ordering superintendents to establish veterans' centers on the reservations. Even with the reservation centers, only two Klamath veterans were able to draw benefits from the GI Bill. One received the education benefit, the other a home loan. Edison Chiloquin, descendant of the great Klamath chief whose mark appears on the Treaty of 1864, returned from the war without resources to reestablish his life. He suffered terribly from alcoholism, and for many years the honorably discharged veteran was walking aimlessly around the reservation in shabby clothes and glasses with one lens missing. Another Klamath soldier reunited with his family at Vanport. The young man was well liked among Vanporters and spoke often of attending college, but like many Indian veterans, he suffered from feelings of aimlessness and alienation while attempting to reenter civilian life. Before he could get his bearings, he died suddenly. The word around Vanport was that he died of alcohol poisoning at an especially wild party in the complex. It is hard to know what might have become of this Klamath veteran had he lived to old age. Although the war opened new vistas for young Indians from Vanport to Hollywood and beyond, they were still not much closer to being "first-class citizens" than their elders after World War I.[36]

Service, Sacrifice, and Segregation

The Japanese Americans at Topaz also built an all-American community only to find that their continual shows of loyalty meant little in the government's determination of when and how they would regain their lost liberties. Topazians of all ages defied the hostile landscape, cruel living conditions, and confused community ideals to nurture bonds of community. They founded Topaz chapters of the Red Cross, Boy Scouts, and Girl Scouts. Spectators from every barrack turned out to watch intramural sports like A-League baseball, with teams drawn from the motor pool, hospital, wrecking crew, and community welfare office. Mess hall employees competed in "best meal" contests, which did more than the WRA could to improve the quality of meals. Topazians maintained a library; organized dances; held holiday celebrations for Christian, Buddhist, and secular occasions; planted gardens; and built an ice rink. Resident music and theatrical groups traveled to nearby towns to entertain Utahns as part of an exchange program. Everyone collected tissue paper for the women who made artificial flowers to have on hand for funerals and participated heartily in war bond drives. While their years in camp were the among the worst of their lives, one Topazian looked fondly on "the creativity of people who made beauty out of nothing, the nobility of people who made a life and a community in the middle of a desert behind barbed wire."[37]

Topaz gained recognition as one of the WRA's model relocation centers, but the federal government was finding that even the best camps caused more problems than they solved. Some critics attacked their "luxuriousness," others their shameful injustice, but everyone agreed that internment became a greater political liability the longer it continued. Not only was the program expensive to run, the FBI concluded that the Japanese American community had no part in the Pearl Harbor bombing, meaning the WRA was managing a nonexistent risk. The House Committee on Un-American Activities was particularly alarmed that the WRA and the Japanese American Citizens League (JACL) allowed judo and goh tournaments and "un-American" cultural performances of Japanese music and theater. Representative Karl Mundt, who sat on both the House Committee on Un-American Activities and the Indian Affairs Committee, denounced the use of taxpayer money for another system of ethnic reservations in the West. The committee's line of questioning intimated that anti-internment civil rights activists like Carey McWilliams might capitalize on the disorder in the camps to build Communist cells in the Western interior (despite the fact that McWilliams was not, in fact, a Communist).[38]

In spite of the Interior Department's experiences with the reservation system, agents grew dismayed that the WRA relocation centers failed to evolve into "socially sound or healthy communities." Instead, they saw an alarming trend among internees to demand greater amounts of government assistance on the grounds that its decision to cut them off from economic and political life obligated the government to take care of them. The Interior Department warned that Japanese Americans, who almost never engaged the welfare system or social services before the war, could go the way of the Crow and Blackfoot Indians, who had strong individual initiative until the reservation system instilled a "typical wards-of-the-government outlook on life." One Topazian made the same analogy, noting that "eventually you just follow orders, even the dumb orders [and] you just shrug your shoulders and say, 'Well, okay, that's the way it is going to be.' There was no way to plan for today or for the future." Another resident lost his sense of purpose in life while at Topaz because "[y]ou had four walls around you. You could do only so much work and come home. Then they would have dances and that sort of thing, but your heart really wasn't in it. You knew it was just a facade, the whole thing." WRA officials worried that the internees' low morale and collective discontent might breed the very disloyalty the camps were supposed to extinguish.[39]

Just as the camps were fully populated, WRA director Dillon Myer announced a shift in the internment policy: "safe" Japanese would no longer be detained but dispersed to eastern cities where they could study and contribute to the war effort. The promise of rapid assimilation through government-sponsored resettlement might have appealed more to Topazians had the WRA not also guaranteed the same result from evacuation.[40] The promise immediately proved hollow when mayors of eastern cities, faced with having their first substantial Japanese populations, echoed Utah officials' objections to welcoming Japanese deemed "too dangerous for California." The difference, this time, was that the Socialist Party, the NAACP, the JACL, and now the federal government worked to stem the resurgence of the anti-Japanese stereotypes that seized the public imagination after Pearl Harbor.[41]

Even if resettlement worked as Myer had envisioned, the fact remained that most Nisei were full participants in the American mainstream before the evacuation. Although they relished the freedom to find good jobs, rejoin the American citizenry, and contribute to the war effort, they were disheartened at the restrictions against returning home to California. The decision to keep Area One of the Western Defense Command closed had less to do with the federal government's earlier concerns about security than its fear that vigilantism, race rioting, and political problems would follow if it "failed" white Californians. To prevent similar problems from developing in the East, Myer recast the internees as loyal citizens and those who impeded resettlement as disloyal bigots. In an early plug for the resettlement program, Myer asked a radio audience to avoid dealing with Japanese reintegration "as Hitler would handle it under his Nazi regime, or as Tojo would deal with it in Japan. Let's do it in the American way." By this, Myer perhaps meant "the peacetime way," because by 1942, racial discrimination had become very much a part of "the American way."[42]

Believing only the Nisei could be "sold" to Californians as suitable relocatees, Myer ordered WRA Community Analysts to gather data proving their high degree of assimilation. This study used many of the same markers of Nisei assimilation that social scientists at the Office of Indian Affairs used to determine a reservation's success: the Nisei greeted people with a handshake instead of a bow; they wore blue jeans; and they enjoyed basketball, hot dogs, and swing dancing. Although they were familiar with Japanese customs, the Nisei practiced them awkwardly and spoke Japanese very rarely. The WRA and the Office of War Information used this information to promote Nisei relocatees as supremely loyal, highly productive, and infinitely sacrificing American citizens.[43]

While the WRA depicted the Nisei in a positive light, it was never fully convinced that they were (or had become) a uniformly loyal group. Federal agents were especially concerned about the Kibei, American citizens educated in Japan who allegedly instigated the most frequent and serious disturbances in the camps. The question became more pressing in February 1943, when Roosevelt announced the formation of the 442nd Regimental Combat Team, a segregated all-Nisei combat unit. Like Indians in World War I—and indeed, like their own fathers before them—young Japanese men were called to make a blood sacrifice to become true Americans whose loyalty would never be questioned or tested again in a relocation center. The president seemed to have forgotten the unfulfilled promises of World War I when he roundly declared that "Americanism is not, and never was, a matter of race or ancestry," but younger Topazians questioned why they were being segregated like African American soldiers. Older Topazians shared Klamath Reservation parents' fear that their sons' new "equal opportunity" was being among the first soldiers on the front lines. Rumors flew through the barracks that the Nisei unit would be sent on suicide bombing raids over Tokyo or simply loaded on a ship that the navy would sink in the Atlantic.[44]

The impetus for the War Department to reclassify the Nisei (all of whom were 4-C, or "enemy aliens") came from Elmer Davis of the Office of War Information, who was concerned about Japanese propagandists' frequent mention of the relocation centers in broadcasts to Asia and Latin America. Davis advised that a firm endorsement of Nisei loyalty from the president would be the most effective countermove against Japan's indictment of the U.S. government's white supremacist policy. While the president proclaimed the loyalty of the Nisei and welcomed them into the armed services, government officials held fast to stereotypes of the Japanese as inscrutable, treacherous, and bloodthirsty. As a security measure, the War Department developed what it thought was a simple, straightforward questionnaire that would survey each internee's loyalty and establish their fitness for resettlement and military service. Among the several questions about their degree of assimilation were numbers twenty-seven, which asked if young men would be willing to defend the United States under any and all circumstances; and twenty-eight, which asked respondents to foreswear all allegiances to Japan.[45]

Question twenty-seven was a loaded one for Nisei and Kibei men who would be called to serve in the armed forces. While most young Topazians had hoped to join the military in December 1941, their experiences in camp made some feel it was unreasonable to be asked to serve in combat while their families were being held behind barbed wire. Many of their parents encouraged their sons to answer yes, and to claim their place as full citizens. They did so, however, while swallowing their rage at the government for taking their children, after having taken everything else.[46]

Older Topazians were especially distressed by question twenty-eight, which was sprung like a trap for the noncitizen Issei. Immigration law prohibited Japanese nationals from naturalization, so asking them to sever their ties to Japan was asking them to make themselves stateless. Nonetheless, federal officials interpreted a "no" response to question twenty-eight as a declaration of disloyalty, which made them subject to segregation at the high-security internment camp at Tule Lake, near Klamath Falls. There, "dangerous hostiles" from the ten WRA camps would await repatriation to Japan, much as the dissident Modocs were expatriated to the Quapaw Reservation after their defeat in the Modoc War.[47]

Morgan Yamanaka initially understood the question to be, "Do you want to go out [of Topaz] or don't you?" Even in this simple form, the question was alarming and difficult to answer. While the Yamanakas wanted to leave Topaz, they "didn't know a damn thing outside of San Francisco." As he thought about it, Yamanaka saw the questions as being less about making suitable resettlement plans and more about race and citizenship, which made him all the more resentful of the process. Karl Akiya never imagined he could pass the loyalty test because he spent part of his childhood in Japan and most of his adulthood in the Young Democrats. A leader of the Americanization program, Akiya formally renounced his Japanese citizenship and adopted a strong pro-American ideology to persuade the WRA that it was safe to allow Americanization teachers to deliver information in Japanese. Military intelligence called on Akiya, who it saw as a reformed radical, as an informant during the registration process. Akiya refused to identify Topaz's "disloyals" and asked to be inducted into the 442nd instead, but he was rejected as a riot risk, which marked him for enhanced surveillance at Topaz as well.[48]

Registration provoked similar dilemmas in every Topazian who received a questionnaire. Topazians fought among themselves, with family members, and with their own conscience as they pondered the questions, causing tremendous personal pain, familial strife, and heightened animosity toward the WRA.[49] Violence broke out at some WRA centers, and wars of words at others. Topaz was noted for its calmness during registration, but Topazians far from passively accepted the government's insult. Topazians renounced their American citizenship at ten times the number the Department of Justice anticipated. Government agents were horrified that their simple bureaucratic procedure set off political firestorms in the camps — some blazing, others smoldering. Charles Ernst, in his alarm, assumed his authoritarian role, announcing that noncooperative Topazians would lose all their civil liberties and be treated as subversives according to the provisions of the Espionage Act.[50]

Topazians responded to their dire situation by holding mass meetings to discuss the meaning of compliance as well as its potential consequences. One ad-hoc activist group, the Committee of Nine, drafted a resolution to Secretary of War Henry L. Stimson. The document made the patriotic assertion that, "[w]e, the citizens of the United States of America, residents of the Central Utah Relocation Project, Topaz, Utah, in order to perform our duties as loyal citizens of the United States and in order to uphold the principles of democracy as established in the Constitution of the United States" recognized no legal or moral basis for government to suspend the rights of any citizen on the basis of race. The resolution concluded with an impassioned call for restoration of the Topazians' freedom of movement (even to California) and for the president to reclassify the Issei as "friendly aliens." A small opposition group challenged the Nine with the simple statement, "[W]e shall register, we are loyal, we shall fight for the United States." Ernst responded with a vague assurance that the WRA would proceed with registration, resettlement, and segregation "in a spirit of fairness and justice."[51]

Topazians lost faith in the WRA's assurances on April 11, 1943, when a military policeman killed sixty-three-year-old James Wakasa while he was taking a stroll near the fence. The sentry testified before the WRA and the War Department's joint board of inquiry that he had ordered Wakasa to halt three times but Wakasa would not obey. The board of inquiry, composed of WRA and War Department officials, ruled the MP followed procedure, but the Millard County coroner's report showed Wakasa was shot in the front and fell backwards, indicating that he had been facing the guard tower, not running from it.[52]

Wakasa's death heightened Topazians' awareness of being isolated, unarmed, and under the guard of lawless soldiers who could make egregious human rights violations with impunity. When residents' hostilities became apparent, the army issued a two-day general alert, during which time MPs patrolled the camp armed with tear gas and submachine guns. The army's repressive gesture was met with Topazians carrying pipes, farming implements, and anything else that might serve as a defensive weapon. Once again, the OWI had to minimize the propagandistic mileage Japan could get from a racially charged incident in a WRA center. The War Department was equally alarmed, fearing that Wakasa's violent death might be used as justification for harming Americans in Japanese internment and POW camps.[53]

Ernst quietly informed a select group of community councilmen of the shooting and pled for their assistance in identifying the body, breaking the news to the community, and making funeral arrangements. The council cooperated with the hope of gaining greater access to tightly held information and having a role in the investigation. The councilmen appointed an all-Issei Committee of Ten to lead an investigation, which included sending two Japanese physicians to examine the body, putting residents' questions to the head of army security, and requesting the Spanish consul to lend aid on behalf of the Japanese government for its slain citizen.[54]

Tensions rose at Topaz as Wakasa's funeral drew near. The editors of the *Topaz Times* protested a WRA news release reporting that Wakasa was shot while crawling through the fence, after failing to heed four warnings from two sentries in two different towers. Residents staged work stoppages and were unmoved by Ernst's announcement that strikers would be docked pay for each day they refused to work. The most worrisome event, however, occurred when the Spanish consul and the Red Cross delivered humanitarian aid packages from the Japanese Empire to Japanese nationals in WRA camps. One Nisei with few cultural ties to Japan recalls being very moved when her parents received a block of Japanese *miso* with a message that even as Japan struggled to feed its own people, it would never forget the unfortunates in the relocation centers and would make sure they were not neglected.[55] The WRA had to be extremely thoughtful about how they treated the residents from then on. If the Japanese government were to position itself as the provider in U.S. government camps, both the security and Americanization missions would surely be doomed.

The community council and residents of Wakasa's block battled WRA restrictions against holding Wakasa's funeral at the place where he died, which was part of Japanese tradition as well as politically resonant. To reduce the riot risk, Ernst approved the location and gave workers and students time off to attend. The three-hour, resident-organized ceremony was a triumph for Topazians as well as an opportunity to reflect on their general condition. Confrontations between residents and the WRA were frequent and pointed in the weeks following the funeral, as Topazians saw nothing to lose in cornering WRA officials on the legality of the evacuation, civil rights of evacuees, and, to quote one WRA report, "other over-all unanswerable topics." As angry as Topazians were, however, confrontations rarely approached violence. Instead of starting the race riots the government desperately feared, Topazians' protests were well within the venerated American democratic tradition of resisting tyranny through reason.[56]

Topazians' smoldering anger motivated the WRA and the FBI to heighten surveillance and place controls on political activity. The community council resisted Ernst's measures to curb its political efficacy when the WRA announced plans to send Topazians to Tule Lake as scab laborers during the Nikkei potato growers' strike in 1944. Most Topazians were unwilling to go, and council member George Ochikubo stated his own objections during a closed-door council meeting. Shortly after the meeting, Ochikubo was detained by the FBI for having made the subversive statement, "let the potatoes rot in the field for all of me!"[57]

The FBI's charge alarmed the council because no Caucasians were present when the "rotten potato" statement was allegedly made. The council meeting minutes said nothing of rotting potatoes, so the FBI built its case by attacking Ochikubo's credibility by branding him a crusader who "becomes wrought up to a high nervousness over disturbing affairs in the center." Fearing he might put the community council in danger, Ochikubo resigned his seat. All remaining members sent a letter to the FBI asserting the charges against Ochikubo were clearly false and resigned their council seats to protest the FBI's implication that one of them must be the "informer." Ernst hurriedly called a special election to reconstitute the council before John Provinse, chief of Washington's Community Management Division, arrived to conduct a question-and-answer session with residents about resettlement and the removal of military police from Topaz. Topazians unanimously reelected all the former councilmen, including Ochikubo and four members who refused to stand for reelection. The election did not bring an end to the conflict, but it readied Topaz for its meeting with Provinse.[58]

He opened the meeting by asking Topazians to approve the withdrawal of the military police. Instead of the simple "yes" they expected, Ernst and Provinse were barraged with questions about their reasons for seeking approval on such an uncontroversial point, especially when the WRA ignored residents' opinions on most other matters. When Ernst refocused the discussion on the MPs, Chairman Masanori Iriki asked him how he planned to control violent incidents without MPs. When Ernst answered dismissively, "the same as if we were outside," the chairman shot back, "Suppose some people happened to be killed. What would happen?" Ernst, having apparently forgotten James Wakasa, upbraided Iriki for imagining that such a thing could happen at Topaz. Topazians' strong political showing led to enhanced surveillance and expanded dossiers, starting with Iriki's, which was updated to note he "worked closely" with Councilman Ochikubo using "the dictator method."[59]

Topaz's outspoken leaders and impassioned activists had much more in common with the Kirk faction, the stumptown campers, and Indian school rebels from the Klamath Reservation than with any dictator or subversive. They respected the community council and the democratic process and engaged with both as the federal government intended. But when issues of civil and human rights were concerned, activists stepped off the set, went off script, and used what few powers they had to force the government's hand. In both communities, wielding power required great care and precision: Klamaths and Topazians could intimidate government agents by assuming the posture of "hostiles," but if they took the protest too far, or used it on the wrong issue, they faced a crackdown on freedoms and access to resources. Once Topazians figured out that the WRA's power was negotiable within bounds, they became effective politicians. They enjoyed greater success than the Klamath Tribes because Topazians had previous experience in the political mainstream and did not have community property and assets to be used as leverage against them.

The first in a series of major confrontations between Topazians and the WRA came in September 1944, when a general strike threatened to stall the relocation program. The trouble began with disgruntled auto mechanics. Shouting the slogan "self help is forced labor," they argued that if the WRA forced them to live at Topaz, it should provide the labor to run the camp itself. Their discontent became a full-blown labor dispute when an MP was mistakenly stationed at the truck gate shortly after the WRA promised to cease inspection of incoming freight for contraband liquor.

Angry workers protested the perceived betrayal and the WRA's discriminatory prohibition policy, which did not extend to the WRA's Caucasian staff. The Caucasian supervisor, unimpressed, ordered them to "get to work or get off the lot." The mechanics chose the latter option, agreeing to return to work when the supervisor was fired and made to issue a written apology to the workers. Community analysts in Washington sent advisories stating that the entire community would be insulted when workers were mistreated in a labor dispute, and Topazians had proved them right. Within hours of the mechanics' walkout, three hundred Japanese maintenance men, carpenters, plumbers, and transport crew struck in sympathy, which shut down camp operations, including the transfer of "disloyals" to the high-security segregation center at Tule Lake.[60]

Ernst called in the labor committee to aid negotiations and immediately replaced the guard, but the mechanics remained angered by the supervisor's refusal to apologize. Interestingly, Topazians overwhelmingly withdrew their support for the workers after Ernst straightened out the problem with the guard, because the legal committee of the community council found that most of the supervisor's objectionable actions did not violate any laws. Without community support, the workers returned to work peacefully, in part because the garage supervisor had been drafted into the military (though he returned to the Topaz garage after several weeks, having been rejected from the army for unrelated reasons.)[61] Oppositional politics became part of the permanent landscape at Topaz, not because Japanese Americans gravitated toward confrontation with government authorities but because the real power was far more effective and expressive than the constraining system of WRA councils. Realizing that acting the political parts according to the script did nothing to make them "fully American" in the government's eyes, most Topazians became cynical about the system. Some played along while others did not, but nearly everyone came to have less faith in the government they had trusted prior to the war and would fear by its end.

Negotiating the Color Line That Never Was

If Vanporters' citizenship status was never in question, the placement of the color line always was, generating disharmony among a population of "Americans all" ostensibly united in patriotic labor. The fluctuations of a racial boundary that, given the antidiscrimination requirements in Executive Order 8802, supposedly did not even exist, produced an ever-present dissonance for Vanporters of all ages. Schoolchildren experienced racial equality at school, only to be released to segregated sections in the project. In spite of the Federal Public Housing Authority's (FPHA) antisegregation policy—which was designed to prevent strikes and deflect Axis propagandists who reveled in reports of American racism—the Housing Authority of Portland (HAP) was extremely conscious of where in the project black and white families were placed. As late as July 1944, HAP pored over maps indicating where black and white families lived before deciding where to house incoming families, and project manager James Franzen was required to report the number of vacancies in "units which were held for colored people." Vanport would never be a multiethnic utopia: it was a desegregated city by law that was segregated through policy and custom, making it possible to transcend its origins as a way of segregating the "undesirables" from Portland.[62]

Vanporters' shorthand for the area between Cottonwood and Broadacre streets was "the black section of town." Although most of the housing units in the "black section" were similar to those throughout the project, they were located an inconvenient distance from essential project services. The *Observer*, Portland's leading African American newspaper, noted Vanport's "black section" was a mile from the post office, making it impossible to send and receive mail regularly. The article further speculated that the reason the streets were unlit was that HAP was testing the army's theory that "Negroes had excellent eyesight in the dark." Rather than working to better integrate Vanport, HAP stated that because federal policy did not allow discrimination or segregation in war housing, the segregation African Americans were experiencing did not exist.[63]

Behind closed doors, HAP commissioners devised the intricate segregatory schemes that were unquestionably real. The HAP board responded to "frequent requests" from residents for jukeboxes by banning them in common areas and private apartments alike. A perceived correlation between jukeboxes and gambling was cited as the reason, but the minutes of the HAP Board of Commissioners also note that "the negro is very fond of music," which made "installation . . . unanimously considered undesirable." The commissioners and Franzen's office were alarmed at the recreation staff's plans for "mixed dances." Franzen, when called to account for allowing such a "dangerous event," explained that "the colored people in the project" effectively duped his staff by including the dance in the "entertainments" accompanying a weeklong war bond drive. HAP employees were shocked to find black and white Vanporters buying war bonds and dancing "promiscuously" but were powerless to stop a widely advertised war bond drive, which would have made for horrible public relations. Sheriff Pratt ordered a ban on mixed dances and implementation of a curfew for teens to keep white girls away from black men, should another interracial social event occur again.[64]

In the wake of the dance, HAP called for a policy in September 1943 that would bar integrated dances without violating Executive Order 8802. This was important not only to maintain the integrity of the order and the project but also to avoid further charges of discrimination, since a black minister had just sent a letter of protest to the office of Commissioner Philip Klutznick of the FPHA complaining of discrimination and segregation in Vanport. The solution was to order all Vanport staff to cease support of integrated dances and to set aside Recreation Building Number Five for events initiated and attended by black tenants. Sheriff Pratt would also begin attending staff meetings at Franzen's office to keep policing a central component of managing the "Negro problem" at Vanport.[65]

Segregation was readily apparent in these resolutions, yet HAP insisted that black residents deliberately created enclaves for themselves where they could be more comfortable. This ruse broke down in 1943, when Franzen, Sheriff Pratt, and the director of community programs approached the commissioners with the "problem" of disturbances at Vanport stemming from residents' disapproval of a black man living with his white wife and her sister in the project. Eviction appears to have been the first and only solution discussed. It was considered feasible because the man was no longer employed in the shipyard, though it is likely that the sisters were Kaiser employees.[66]

Given white Vanporters' attitudes about race relations, one could hardly blame black Vanporters for seeking distance from the white majority. In a 1944 survey of complaints about the project, respondents listed "Negroes and whites in the same neighborhood" ahead of "fear of fire," and "Negroes and whites in the same school" ahead of "lack of telephones." In that same year, 30 percent of Vanport arrests were of black residents, even though the project census showed that only 12 percent of the project's entire population was African American. Residents responded with alarm to rumors of "Negro crime waves" but paid little attention to a white maintenance worker who assaulted a black woman during a service call to her apartment. The woman ran to the administration building for help but received no meaningful assistance. A citizens group complained to the sheriff, who referred the matter to the HAP Maintenance Department. Not surprisingly, the maintenance department chose not to bring suit against itself on behalf of its African American tenant.[67]

The FPHA and the War Manpower Commission always worried about race riots, but federal agencies also feared the consequences of harmonious encounters between African Americans and Communist Party members at Vanport. Although surveillance of black Vanporters was covert, all black war workers knew they were suspect. So too were white Vanporters who crossed the color line. The *Observer* reported in August 1944 that a black Vanport deputy arrested white Vanporter Sam Markson during a visit to the home of a black friend. The deputy confronted Markson as he walked to the house, demanding he identify himself and explain what he was doing in the "colored section." FBI agents and sheriff's deputies questioned Markson about his political beliefs and his reason for being in the "Negro section." The sheriff explained to Markson's angry friends that they merely worried that "fraternization between the races could provoke white southerners to violence."[68]

Black Vanporters were understandably fed up with HAP assurances that they were being treated as full first-class citizens while experiencing such blatant discrimination. Residents confronted HAP with questions about substandard facilities in Broadacres-Cottonwood, white-on-black crime, abuses by HAP officials, and the string of suspicious arrests (particularly those made by black deputies). A group of residents formed the Vanport Interracial Council to discuss issues of concern to all Vanporters. Although these tactics illuminated problems of social inequality at Vanport, they did not alter the status quo. They did, however, interrupt the stream of double-talk to which black shipyard workers had been subjected since the day the Kaiser labor recruiter came to their town. So while the federal government retained its absolute authority, Vanport activists shined a light on its agencies' antidemocratic actions, making HAP's egalitarian rhetoric increasingly transparent.[69]

Vanport's racial dynamics grew more complex with the announcement of a joint agreement between the WRA and the FPHA to resettle Japanese American internees from the ten relocation centers in vacant war housing units in their hometowns. Portland's prominent civil libertarians, ashamed of their silence during the evacuation, jumped at the chance to help the WRA "undo" the internment by finding transitional housing, jobs, and social services for their returning Japanese neighbors. Portland's general public, however, was no more prepared to integrate its Japanese old-timers than it had been to accept its African American newcomers. The Oregon Property Owners Protective League angrily demanded WRA director Dillon Myer's resignation, and both Mayor Riley and Sheriff Pratt gave a cold welcome to the relocatees, claiming they had been released from "protective custody" too soon to guarantee their safety. Vanport again became the arena for an experimental ethnic democracy, the aim of which was to fulfill the federal government's war aims while managing local government's concerns about race and disloyalty.[70]

Vanport was well equipped to serve the government's needs in this delicate relocation scheme. Federal desegregation policies ensured that the dispossessed would be offered leases and that the project had the amenities to support them. At the same time, existing systems of segregation, surveillance, and the insulation from hostile whites quelled racial anxieties. In less than a year, over 300 of the 1,500 relocatees in the Portland area lived in federal housing, the majority at Vanport. The Citizen's Committee, with the help of the HAP Board of Commissioners, simplified the task by passing a resolution allowing immediate, unrestricted rental of available Vanport units to relocating internees regardless of whether or not they worked in war plants.[71]

Japanese Vanporters — unlike their African American counterparts — were all but invisible community members. The Portland newspapers printed occasional stories about Vanport families' Nisei heroes in the 442nd Regimental Combat Team, but otherwise the former internees were moved in quietly. Japanese teachers, who were among the first to relocate to Vanport, had to pass as "Chinese" for their safety. The superintendent of the Vanport Schools, seemingly unaware of the extent of anti-Japanese feeling at Vanport, assured Japanese parents that their children would find "friendly, democratic treatment" at school. Teachers redoubled their efforts to form an inclusive children's community where good citizenship was a core value, though often in strange ways. They posted copies of Roosevelt's speech in which he declared that "Americanism is not, and never was, a matter of race or ances-try" — perhaps without realizing the president delivered it at the request of the Office of War Information and the War Relocation Authority to encourage Nisei internees to register for the draft.[72]

Project manager James Franzen resigned his position in the midst of Vanport's transitional phase and its attendant problems of community governance, social service provision, and racial discord. He explained in his September 9, 1944, resignation letter that his position as an on-site project manager was no longer needed because the Vanport community was now "fully developed." Instead, the board of commissioners would govern the community directly, making Vanport the only federal townsite with such volatile racial conditions and neither a community government nor a project manager available to resolve conflicts on a twenty-four-hour basis.[73] Unable to make its rhetoric match racial realities, government officials left Vanporters to their own devices to sort out the problems created by their own poorly conceived policies.

Los Alamos: Heroes of Democracy in an Atomic Cage

The Manhattan Engineer District may not have had the evident racial tensions of the Klamath Reservation, Topaz, or Vanport, but power struggles were being waged in every corner of the community. Los Alamosans' freedom of movement, speech, and association as well as their right to due process were sharply curtailed among a popula-tion that cherished academic freedom. There was no free enterprise, no home ownership, no free press, and no forum for decision making and conflict resolution. Time was organized and marked by siren wails to keep everyone on task. Space was similarly segmented between the Tech Area and the townsite to keep everything extraneous to bomb building away from the laboratory.

Los Alamos received its first settlers on April 15, 1943. New arrivals found a large laboratory enclosed in barbed wire, with a sort of plywood village of apartment buildings clustered haphazardly. Different contrac-tors built apartments in increasingly speedy phases, the quality of the units declining with each successive wave. The spacious log cabin–style cottages from the Ranch School—dubbed "Bathtub Row" because they had baths instead of drizzly showers—were reserved for the project VIPs. Most of the senior scientists and their families lived in Sundt apartments, which were compact and thin-walled, with the same sooty "black beauty" stoves Topazians struggled with. Newer units, known as "McKees" and "Morganvilles" (a play on "Hooverville"), housed junior scientists and engineers and were more like Topaz barracks in their small size and crowded quarters. Young bachelor scientists lived in dormitories, and on-site laborers and other nonscientists lived in hutments (Quonset huts made of plywood and corrugated metal) that were sixteen square feet.[74]

The army-issue furnishings, all marked "USED" for "United States Engineer District," provided something far from the homey atmosphere Kaiser and the FPHA created for Vanporters. Los Alamosans, like Topazians, began their new lives battling dust and mud to make their dwellings habitable. One new resident found a soot-dusted set of rooms with army cots and Sheetrock dining room furniture that had to serve until her own arrived. She spent the next day laying linoleum and scrubbing down the walls with the only cleaning equipment available at the PX—a nailbrush.[75]

Self-service laundry stations and a network of icehouses dotted the housing clusters. On the laboratory side of town sat the Los Alamos hospital, at the ready to deliver babies and attempt to treat radiation sickness. A fire station, motor pool, and rows of barracks and military mess halls completed the setting in which bomb building and community life would take place. The entire area was encircled with barbed wire, twice around the Tech Area, with guards watching the perimeter and guard posts at the one entrance and exit from the site.

As they arrived, Los Alamosans reacted to their new surroundings in a variety of ways, depending on their prior wartime experiences and the amount of information they had about Los Alamos's purpose. Many were pleased by the magnificent landscape, open spaces for children to play, and the fact that colleagues and families would continue to be together. Some liked the array of services and conveniences the MED provided, while others remarked on the simplicity of life in such a small, closed-in space.[76]

The majority of newcomers, however, were thoroughly dismayed at the living conditions. The non–Bathtub Row houses were given the generic term "the crackerboxes," which reminded some residents of the worst aspects of urban life. Bernice Brode wrote to a friend in Berkeley that "we resemble an Eastside slum area, washing hanging out over balconies, bedding put out to air, children and dogs making a racket in the cleared off area between 3 of the 4 family apartments. Women call to them from the windows but in Harvard accents, or cultured foreign accents!" Jane Wilson remarked that her new home had a nice enough interior and a gorgeous mountain view, but her neighborhood consisted of "rickety houses" that reminded her of tenements in "a metropolitan slum area."[77]

There was no welcome wagon at Los Alamos. Instead, MPs greeted new arrivals by confiscating their cameras and firearms and fingerprinting, photographing, and recording the body scars of each family member. Residents read the newcomer's handbook on arrival to learn about their relationship with the MED. The cover was blotched with red-ink "restricted" stamps, and the text barked "YOU WILL" directives and enumerated a long list of project "don'ts." Most regulations were designed to protect the project's secrecy, which made sense to most residents, but they questioned the degree to which security regulated private life. Los Alamosans had to change the way they interacted with the outside world—or else "G2 will get you." All personal communications to and from project residents would be censored, and mail with return addresses reading anything other than "PO Box 1663, Santa Fe" would not be sent. Under no circumstances could a Los Alamosan post mail from boxes outside the project. Residents were issued cards informing their families that their mail was censored, with no further comment or detail. Letters could only be written in English, French, German, Italian, and Spanish, with no X's or scribbles that could be taken as encryption.[78]

The army monitored private conversations with as much diligence, if less success, than the mail. Groves pounced on Elfriede Segrè, Enrico Fermi, and other Italian physicists for "speaking 'Hungarian' in public."

Telephone calls were subject to preemptive censorship. If an outside caller asked a resident where they went for a picnic, the censor would cut the connection to prevent an indiscreet answer and remind the resident of the censor's presence. Although the censor allowed reconnection of the lines, this was usually not successful, making meaningful communication with people Los Alamosans left behind all but impossible.[79]

The most controversial issue between Oppenheimer and Groves concerned the compartmentalization of information. Compartmentalization was designed to thwart "hostiles" by providing only the information any scientist, engineer, or machinist needed to do the task at hand, and nothing more. Information flowed through a direct chain of authority so that subordinates only spoke to superiors about problems and findings. Mid-level supervisors sent information up the chain to Oppenheimer, who assembled all the pieces and relayed the big picture to Groves. Even blueprints had to be separated and pieces distributed to different contractors or research divisions to prevent spies from seeing the layout of the laboratory. In the rare cases where lateral exchanges of information among the divisions were absolutely necessary, scientists could petition the military for permission to speak to their colleagues. This rule proved absurd in the case of one physicist who headed two departments and theoretically required the army's permission to talk to himself.[80]

Scientists had a hard enough time bearing surveillance, restrictions, and censorship, but compartmentalization was, to them, the army's assault on the world of ideas. They could not conceivably operate without knowing the desired theoretical outcome. It was even worse to guess the unknown consequences of innocently speaking the wrong words to the wrong person. The foreign scientists found this especially troubling. While they saw the need for background checks, isolation, and tight security, the scientists resented being suspected even as they contributed to the war effort.[81]

Innocent reports of everyday life were suddenly fraught with sensitive military secrets. Los Alamosans could not discuss the size of the project, its physical characteristics, the number of people working on it, or the extent of security measures. They could not mention their neighbors, the work they did, what their housing was like, or "any material which may be in use at the Project." This obviously referred to uranium and plutonium, but to a nonscientist of the pre-atomic age, "any material" could refer to any and all tangible things. Sending photos to relatives was impossible; scientists could use cameras to photograph their families, but they were prohibited from capturing anything else. The cramped conditions made it difficult to keep every building or piece of machinery out of the shot. It also took a great deal of mental dexterity to sustain a line of conversation without accidentally shedding light on the shadows of secrecy over Los Alamos.[82]

The army helped assure secrecy by placing counterintelligence agents, posing as bodyguards, on every Rad Lab transplant and foreign scientist. The scientists were told the bodyguards were assigned to protect them from the very real threat of kidnapping. Their main purpose, however, was to report the scientist's every move to army officials. The army took pains to find compatible bodyguards with enough scientific training to elicit both professional and personal conversation, which would curb any inclination in the scientists to discuss their work with colleagues, friends, wives, strangers, or spies. The bodyguards also became confidants, traveling companions, and, in the case of Fermi's bodyguard, interpreters of the scientist's shaky spoken English. In Los Alamos's world of secrets, bodyguards became the closest friends of many scientists, who mostly had no idea they were intelligence agents.[83]

Historian Martin Sherwin points out that security systems are both the implementation and expression of larger policy objectives. The Manhattan Engineer District's system at Los Alamos quickly shifted its mission from keeping atomic secrets to controlling the activities of the scientists and their families.[84] Counterintelligence agents regularly searched residents' apartments to determine who fell out of compliance with security regulations, and occasionally they dropped in on residents to ask what they heard of their neighbors through their thin walls.[85] Counterintelligence agents watched mid-ranking Los Alamosans on the mesa and in Santa Fe, where they posed as hotel clerks, bell captains, tourists, electricians, painters, contractors, and gamblers, packing cameras and hidden recording equipment. Security did not always have such a friendly face. Los Alamosans remember the Oppenheimers as the town glamour couple with the nicest house on Bathtub Row, but one man from the pueblo felt sorry for them because "there were two military policemen with dogs that walked around his house all night, twenty-four hours. And when they went shopping in Santa Fe, Mrs. Oppenheimer would have one MP in front of her and another behind with submachine guns. And everybody would wonder if they were prisoners or something." Groves expressed his intense anti-Communist feeling in security policy that put agents on the lookout for misbehaving "longhairs" instead of Nazi spies.[86]

In short order, Los Alamosans like Jane Wilson found that "it isn't a pleasant or easy thing to surrender one's rights as an American citizen." European émigrés like Laura Fermi also had a hard time because "living inside a fenced area reminded [Europeans] of concentration camps." Mici Teller not only felt she was in a concentration camp but was anguished by the security protocols preventing her from finding out about her family in Hungary, who might have been confined in the Nazi extermination camps. Claudio Segrè, whose Italian relatives were known to be in Hitler's camps, sensed his father's anger at the "restrictions of garrison-style living" because he came to the United States to enjoy freedom of association, movement, and expression, only to find himself under heavy-handed authority. After a few months' confinement, citizen and alien Los Alamosans shared Phyllis Fisher's suspicion that "we were the prisoners, the dangerous ones [and] 'they' were the safe ones, outside."[87]

One of the treasured beliefs among Los Alamosans was that the mesa was immune to the problems associated with the urban poor, such as crime, family violence, and juvenile delinquency. In an enclave of early- to mid-career academics and military officers, Los Alamosans enjoyed a pleasant homogeneity with "no invalids, no in-laws, no unemployed, no idle rich and no poor."[88] Parents let their children run around unsupervised, and no one locked their door. The MED never considered raising a citizen police force, perhaps because there was no distinct minority community and military discipline ensured civil order. Protecting citizens from harm was never a thought.

The military police were shocked when the parent of a three-year-old girl reported that a man tried to lure her into a shack. This was followed by some incidents of women's underwear being slashed on clotheslines. The head investigator, having almost no experience dealing with sex crimes, attributed them to a lack of recreational variety and free time allowed at other installations and a shortage of chaplains and other support resources. He concluded that the isolation, stress, and close quarters combined to bring out psychotic tendencies that went undetected in screenings.[89]

The search continued secretly until the perpetrator was caught and sent to a psychiatric hospital, with no trial or public notice of the crime. The army promoted law and order and mental hygiene, but without the benefit of shared state jurisdiction, state and local social service systems were not available to the project. Anything other than housing, medical care, procurement, and some recreation went beyond what the army had planned for its installations. One resident remarked of law enforcement that, "had anyone felt impelled to beat his wife or steal a neighbor's spoons there was not much the Army could do but deposit the culprit on a pink promontory or tufa outside the gate, to be picked up, perhaps, by a New Mexico officer of the law out hunting cattle rustlers." The MPs' pattern of removing offenders and restoring silence might have thwarted spies, but it did nothing to prevent crime or aid Los Alamosans in distress.[90]

Laboratory safety raised other strong points of contention. The MED gave the impression all along that the medical staff was prepared to treat radiation exposure, but in truth neither the health hazards unit nor the general practitioner had any protocols in place for uranium accidents. The closest thing Los Alamos had to a radiation hazards laboratory was the corner of the hospital where animals that had been irradiated by accident were observed until they died. By 1944 the ill effects of radiation exposure were showing themselves, but compartmentalization limited the flow of information between the laboratory and the hospital about what ailed sick Los Alamosans, which made treatment nearly impossible.[91]

Glenn Seaborg was one of the first scientists to raise concerns about the MED's failure to plan for the safe management of enormous quantities of plutonium. Noting that the MED planned security and labor efficiency to the last detail, he asserted the same care should be given to protecting everyone handling dangerous materials. Seaborg's warnings came too late to protect the enlisted men who already had been exposed to dangerous levels of contamination. Machinists collected plutonium particles that dusted the cracks between floor tiles, hardened on beakers, or floated in waste liquids (both laboratory materials and urine, when Tech workers ingested large amounts.) They had twice-daily nose swabs, but no one knew how to interpret the plutonium count. Still, the work never slowed and conditions never improved as scientists continued to use the primitive open hoods and respirators.[92]

All the scientists were aware of the risks of plutonium exposure, "but there was a war going on," and their fear that the Germans might have a bomb at the ready made their own safety seem trivial. Top-level scientists also had the benefit of information about uranium, its properties, and how to reduce exposure risks. One of the ways the MED reduced the risk to the irreplaceable "idea men" in the Tech Area was to make the easily replaceable enlisted men handle radioactive material on a day-to-day basis.[93]

Compartmentalization kept lower-level scientists and technicians dangerously in the dark. Security protocol prohibited disclosure of the name and nature of any substance workers handled. Bill Gibson was told he would work with a "new man-made element." He assumed he would suffer radiation sickness if he ingested large quantities, but he placed great faith in the ability of MED physicians and safety officers to keep him out of harm's way. The first eight grams of plutonium that Gibson worked with hit the floor. He and his coworkers spent frantic hours recovering every bit of the precious element, worrying all the while that every minute searching was a minute away from completing the project and ending the war.[94]

Gibson's health was the least of his concerns until 1945, when a piece of contaminated glass lodged in his thumb and the medical staff discovered that his plutonium levels were dangerously high. They immediately excised his wound, but Gibson's urine assays showed a rapid increase in plutonium levels between 1944 and 1945. Gibson and three other overexposed workers were dismissed from the laboratory but became permanent government test subjects, as they were rare specimens of irradiated humans. Time passed, workers' exposures increased, and Groves's promise to oversee construction of a medical research facility never materialized.[95]

Despite the residents' many hardships while confined at Los Alamos, they, like other residents of inverse utopias, composed a vibrant community, which helped residents feel their lives had become somewhat normal. While the bomb's mysteries unraveled in the Tech Area, families grew bigger, and larger groups of children gathered to play cowboys and Indians and GI Joe versus the fascists (not knowing who the "fascists" were).[96] Between two and five students graduated from Los Alamos High School each year, while their mothers taught, worked, kept house, gave tea parties, and formed social, recreational, charitable, and religious organizations.

Town characters made everyday life colorful, like Arno Roensch of the Army's Special Engineer Detachment, who led the project's most popular swing band, and Otto Frisch, who gave regular piano recitals over the weak little Los Alamos radio station. Genia Peierls was a self-proclaimed broadcast service who made daily rounds from house to house gathering and disseminating information and gossip. She was also a very clever shopper and made delicious dinners from whatever rations were available. Richard Feynman perfected his techniques for frustrating the MPs, and as his coup de grâce he draped lingerie in his dorm room to avoid being assigned a roommate. In addition, he and his friends had the regular pleasure of watching the MPs search for nonexistent women. Los Alamos was an odd little town, but residents had come to see it as their own.[97]

Even Los Alamosans who did not know that the first atomic bomb had been successfully detonated in the Trinity Test of July 1945 — the vast majority — felt they belonged to a special community with a special purpose. Over the next few years they, along with Topazians, Vanporters, and eventually the Klamath Tribes, would experience the loss of their special communities. Although these enclaves were home to no one, they were the only places the residents had. The final irony was that displacement from these inverse utopias became as great a hardship as being uprooted from their home communities. They had spent the war as outsiders, and their "Americas" had been so vastly different from that of their mainstream compatriots that these places were, ironically, quite foreign. Entering the mainstream of postwar American life would entail far more than merely crossing the perimeters of the Klamath Reservation, Topaz, Vanport City, or Los Alamos.

Billboards celebrated the Klamath people's many
contributions to the war effort—from forest
products to war bond sales. Courtesy of the
Klamath County Museum.

The Klamath Honor Roll projected patriotism and the
strong identity of the reservation community. Courtesy of
the Klamath County Museum.

WRA photographers framed this scene of boys playing
with a football in the desolate Topaz camp as typical of
a sunny day anywhere in America. Photograph by Tom
Parker. Courtesy of the Bancroft Library, University of
California, Berkeley.

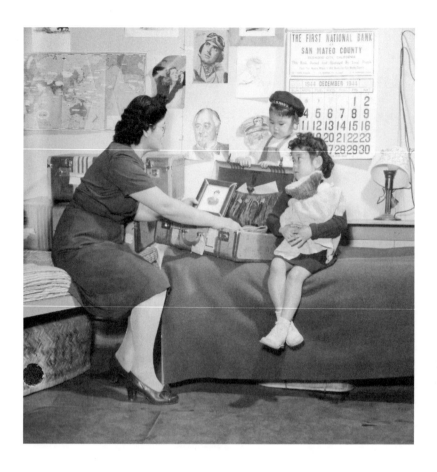

The WRA commissioned a series of photographs that
highlighted Japanese Americans' family values and
patriotic service to promote its resettlement program to
the wider public. The government's caption to this photo
of the Arimoto family reads (in part), "Daddy will be
glad to know we're going home. So said Mrs. Marianne
Arimoto to [daughter Deanne, four, and son Dennis,
twenty-one months] as she packed a photograph of Pvt.
Edgar Arimoto, army volunteer in France." Photograph
by Charles E. Mace. Courtesy of the Bancroft Library,
University of California, Berkeley.

Flood waters submerged Vanport completely, pulling
housing units off their foundation, killing fifteen people,
and leaving homeless survivors with the barest of
personal belongings. Courtesy of the Oregon Historical
Society, #CN006 189.

African American Vanporters gathered in front of a
Portland vfw post. Most were forced to settle within the
existing black community, which was confined to North
Portland. *Oregon Journal* photograph. Courtesy of the
Oregon Historical Society, cn#006 200.

Flood victims—black and white—called on government officials to investigate the Vanport flood, hold responsible agencies accountable, and provide a decent standard of living for homeless Vanporters. Courtesy of the Oregon Historical Society, CN#006 198.

Interior of a Los Alamos efficiency apartment, ca. 1946.
The apartments were sparse but spacious and airy
compared to the barracks in the relocation centers.
Courtesy of the Los Alamos Historical Museum
Photo Archives.

Maj. Gen. Leslie R. Groves presents J. Robert
Oppenheimer with the Army-Navy "E" Award for
Excellence in War Production, October 16, 1945.
Oppenheimer accepted the award on behalf of the civilian
personnel on the Manhattan Project for their "determined,
persevering, unbeatable American spirit." Courtesy of
the Los Alamos Historical Museum Photo Archives.

New Mexico governor Thomas J. Mabry (second from
right) and a delegation from the Hill putting Los Alamos
County on the map (literally), ca. 1950. Courtesy Palace of
the Governors Photo Archives (NMHM/DCA) #053108.

CHAPTER FIVE

FROM BARBED WIRE TO BOOTSTRAPS

Freedom and Community in Cold War America

In April 1944 *Fortune* magazine warned readers that "the 'protective custody' [of the Japanese] of 1942 and 1943 cannot end otherwise than in a kind of Indian reservation, to plague the conscience of Americans for many years to come."[1] The War Relocation Authority (WRA) had the same concerns; throughout the political tumult of the segregation crisis, the Wakasa incident, and the general strike, Topaz's resettlement program continued apace. It took no time at all for WRA officials to change their policy from containment of the Japanese masses to dispersal of individuals and small nuclear families to live as self-sufficient Americans.

As dramatically as the hot war turned cold in 1945, the government's view of its "ideal cities" shifted from social engineering marvel to political and economic scourge. The depopulation current grew stronger as discussions about Indian reservations turned from lamentations over poor conditions to fear that the United States was operating Communist enclaves within its own borders. Vanport and Los Alamos raised no fewer concerns; in the postwar era, no one wanted a potential "welfare colony" full of people one tended to associate with prewar Communism. By 1953 liquidation fever had spread to the House and Senate Committees on Indian Affairs, spurring legislation to terminate treaty relationships and "emancipate" Native people by dissolving their reservations. Cold War freedom was centered squarely in individualism; government sponsored collectivism of any kind was, in this new political environment, read as a rejection of Americanism—and of America itself.

Yet it was hard for government agencies to get past the fact that these populations had been isolated for what they once saw as very good reasons. Ostensibly, the nation's security and the project of making good citizens relied on these out-of-the-way, government-run colonies. Unwilling to fully abandon their functions as overseers and caretakers, the agents in charge of America's inverse utopias refashioned their paternalist relationships with their wards as they ventured out to the mainstream. They took clear, deliberate measures to extend their ties into the world outside the perimeter, but when it came to determining when and how to cut those ties, tensions between the agencies, the residents, and the American public became immediately evident. Leaving Topaz, Vanport, Los Alamos, and Klamath was far more complicated than simply packing up and moving on; it demanded extensive negotiations about how long federal paternalism would govern one's life.

The question first arose at Topaz in 1943, when the WRA granted leaves to college students for whom the Japanese American National Student Relocation Council had arranged transfers to eastern schools. For these Nisei, the prospect of living outside the barbed wire was a glorious one, but college life would not bring complete freedom. Topazians at eastern universities would be free to study what they wanted, but decisions to move, transfer, drop out, or visit their parents at Topaz required the WRA's approval, which it was unlikely to grant.[2]

Although the Student Relocation Council steered Nisei students toward supportive campus organizations and local congregations, it could not shield them from the myriad forms of prejudice that made their education "a tangle of opportunity and oppression." Yoshiko Uchida felt guilty about leaving her parents and her second-grade classroom behind when she left Topaz to resume her education at Smith College. Uchida found tentative acceptance, but she arrived in the wake of another Topazian whose enrollment was met with calls for her immediate expulsion as a Japanese. More tolerant colleges allowed Topaz students to be full participants in campus life once they rejected their Japanese heritage. Mary Iijima received the ultimate "compliment" that she was "just like an American" with mixed feelings of flattery, relief, and shame. In spite of the difficulties, students had the best chance at fully recovering from the internment. As youngsters, the Nisei took fewer financial losses in the evacuation process, while resettlement channeled them toward good jobs, increased their social and cultural capital, and integrated them into civil-libertarian networks.[3]

WRA director Myer, hoping to build on the success of the student relocation program, expanded the pool of prospective relocatees to include "safe" agricultural and industrial workers. Defense industries and growers outside the Western Defense Command lined up to recruit workers to relocate for employment in their factories and fields. The WRA established group leaves to make much-needed hands available to local growers at harvest time. The Nisei population continued to dwindle as young professionals sought positions in the firms of their East Coast colleagues. The shrinking numbers who remained started to stand out. Some stayed behind to care for older family members, while others, like Mitsuye Endo, had to remain an internee until the U.S. Supreme Court made its ruling on her case. Her relocation clearance arrived months ahead of the justices' decision.[4]

Miné Okubo, for her part, saw no reason to rush from Topaz. Until *Fortune* magazine offered her a job as an illustrator, she had nothing better to do in the East and had no chance of returning to California. Moreover, she had three meals a day and a group of close friends at Topaz. As much as Topazians suffered during the internment, Topaz was the only community they had, and few were willing to leave what they had built to start anew in unknown, hostile terrain where they had nothing of their own.[5]

Okubo realized well before leaving Topaz that being outside the barbed wire would not free her from the WRA bureaucracy. Before receiving their resettlement assistance grants, relocatees had to sign pledges to travel only to the destinations designated by the WRA. Each relocatee had to sign a loyalty oath; citizens swore to defend the United States however called upon, while aliens promised to cooperate with the American war effort and abide by the laws of the United States. After that, candidates for resettlement watched nine training films with titles like *This is America* and attended lectures on topics such as "How to Behave in the Outside World." As the day of their departure approached, resettlers were assigned a "relocation worker," which, to many, sounded like a euphemism for "parole officer." Once cleared to depart, each Topazian received a train ticket and twenty-five dollars (plus three dollars a day for meals while traveling), four typewritten postcards to inform the WRA of the their whereabouts, and orders to read one final informational pamphlet.[6] The purpose of these preparations was not to orient "foreigners" to life in America. They were, after all, either citizens or longtime residents. Instead, the sessions were designed to establish government paternalism in their lives outside of Topaz: they would make relocatees believe that they could not independently navigate their lives as free people, and that they needed a federal agent to help them find their way as they tread the path to assimilation.

Similar ties of paternalism bound members of the 442nd to the bureaucrats "at home." The fresh young recruits were the first and largest group to leave Topaz, but they remained vital community members. News of the bravery, patriotism, and extraordinary capabilities of the 442nd brought honor to the Nisei, the WRA, and the Roosevelt administration. Even some Utahns who resented Topaz's presence saw the 442nd as the pride of America and proof that a few "Japs" were really loyal to the United States. Sherman Tolbert, still bitter that the WRA "coddled" the internees, spoke fondly of his Nisei farmhands who he believed had been drafted as cannon fodder without hope of returning alive. The army stepped up the pace of Nisei recruitment, which in turn raised the number of stars on the Topaz service flag from 400 to a crowded 1,250 between March and July 1944. Memorial services and posthumous medal ceremonies became a regular part of life at Topaz; no one failed to note the mantle of grief that had fallen suddenly on the camp.[7]

The WRA and the army identified each soldier by the camp he came from, just as the Office of Indian Affairs identified Indian soldiers by tribe or reservation, bringing pride to Topazians and good public relations for the project administration. The soldiers, for different reasons, came to see Topaz as "home."[8] Several maintained a newsy correspondence with project director Charles Ernst, who remained a paternal figure in absentia by writing letters of encouragement and offering fatherly advice. Occasionally a Topaz soldier's "letter home" expressed deep disillusionment about his military service in light of the experiences of evacuation, registration, and being "given" his citizenship by exercising his "right to serve."

Many Topaz GIs were embittered by placement in a segregated unit in which opportunity outside the infantry was extremely rare, even for those with specialized education or skills. One soldier wrote Ernst: "we think the idea of drafting niseis under the illusion that they are on equal terms with whites *just stinks*. I never fully realized how little democracy meant until I got into the Army. When they ask me what I'm fightin' for and against whom, i tell them that my first enemy is right here in the US — the American Legion, the short-sighted American public, etc. The Germans are only secondary."[9]

A second letter reported very little battle fatigue among the Topaz boys, but it reveals war-weariness in the Nisei soldier's fight for social equality:

What am I fighting for? For the chance of returning to California? I may never reach there! Regardless of uniform I'm called a Jap. Yep, let's face it! Wot am I fightin for? [sic] I'll tell you! I'm fighting so that my parents can live here — I'm fighting so my kid brothers and sister can get an education here! . . . Sure, I'll be called a Jap, but what of it? We'll be called that for generations to come. But that's a small detail. My parents were given a home and a living far superior to Japan. They (US) gave me an education and chance to prove I got what it takes. That's what I'm fighting for! To reclaim myself! I don't' blame this country, I never will. The evacuation was a *military* necessity, not because the caucasians hated us — get that out of your heads. Disregard the petty discriminations . . . fight for the opportunities that are plentiful. But don't expect them to come to you! What do you want, service with a smile? I sound nuts and illogical yet that's how I feel. If they don't understand it's too late, you're indirected.[10]

While Ernst may have corresponded with Topaz GIs to fulfill his role as "village headman" or Americanization coach, for Topazians he was the one federal agent with whom they had a personal relationship. In railing against the military, Topazians could air complaints freely to a federal official without immediate repercussions. The substance of their complaints, however, also applied to the injustices they experienced at Topaz. The letters thus served a dual purpose: to rant about the military through civilian channels and to confront Ernst indirectly by dressing their grievances about the internment in descriptions of the army's discriminatory practices.

Topazians on the home front did everything they could to ease the soldiers' dual burdens of being internees and infantryman. Everyone worked to make the camp a homey place for their GIs on leave, but the WRA's rush to empty the camps led to the implementation of a forty-cent per day visiting charge to deter residents from returning to Topaz. Complaints from insulted parents of servicemen changed nothing, which demonstrated to Topazians once again that expediency in meeting government objectives was always more important than the well-being of Topazians—even those in uniform. The longer their relationship with the WRA wore on, the less Japanese Americans could believe in the promises of freedom, democracy, and equality their president said they were fighting for.[11]

Despite the frontline rhetoric of camp as a "home place," Topazians were quite willing to resettle. They had the second highest response rate to the resettlement program because an unusually large percentage could pursue their lives and livelihoods in eastern industries and universities. Most Topazians who stayed behind were older, struggled with English, knew only California, and relied on Japanese community networks to get along. Federal paternalism would not be enough to shield them from their economic, political, and social vulnerabilities on the outside. Their property in California disappeared because of trusted caretakers who sold their real estate; careless storage practices in WRA warehouses; or the California State War Board's brief campaign to requisition evacuee property, such as farm machinery, to aid war production. Even the highest paid Topazians earned too little to keep up payments on insurance policies, mortgages, and taxes, resulting in the loss of holdings they might otherwise have retained. The WRA calculated individual property losses to range from a few hundred to many thousands of dollars, but it did not consider ways to assist internees in their economic recovery, pushing them out of the camps to sink or swim.[12]

Agents used a third of the column space in the *Topaz Times* for "relocation education," offering constant reports on successful relocatees, accompanied by a few accounts of racial violence with admonitions to relocate more quickly as a show of force against racial intolerance. The paper also presented disincentives from wanting to return to California such as headlines reading, "New Slum Area: SF Nihonmachi." The article used race-baiting tactics to discourage Topazians from returning home, describing their former neighborhood as "a menace to the city's health and welfare" where the African American residents would harass and perhaps even harm them if they tried to return to San Francisco.[13]

Ernst's office countered the bad news from California with spirited information sessions, pep talks, and in-depth interviews to determine the earliest possible release date for each resident. Those unmoved by resettlement propaganda were compelled to leave by the rapid disappearance of project services, such as recreational facilities, schools, and mess halls. A faction called the "Stand Pats" resisted rapid resettlement, arguing that the federal government owed them more than a placement and a train ticket for withholding their rights and disrupting their lives for so long. The WRA, incensed at their refusal to cooperate with such an urgent measure, denounced anti-resettlement activists for their "shortsighted resistance to freedom."[14]

Topazians who accepted the WRA's offer of assisted freedom were carefully scattered eastward by resettlement officers to avoid creating new Nihonmachi, with Chicago, New York, Ogden, and Salt Lake City the most common destinations. Disorientation, economic hardship, and racial prejudice posed formidable obstacles to new arrivals, whose WRA resettlement grants ran out on arrival. Jobs in defense industries for unskilled relocatees were much harder to get than WRA agents had indicated.

Chicago offered mixed blessings to its new Japanese residents. The city had never had a substantial Japanese population and hence no history of anti-Japanese sentiment. Additionally, racial tensions between white and black Chicago ran very high, had been long in the making, and lay at the center of the city's social landscape. New Topazians faced the challenge of fitting into the preexisting racial order. While they were clearly not regarded as "white," they were not considered "black," either. Japanese Americans still found housing relatively easily, though it was housing in neighborhoods where black and white enclaves abutted, and Caucasians wanted another racial group to hold the color line. Topazians were able to find jobs, but they generally worked "black" jobs in domestic service and as unskilled factory labor, which opened when African Americans migrated to new defense plants and were drafted into the armed services. The workplace became the locus of discrimination, as white employers found comfort in having nonwhite workers in "nonwhite" jobs and continued the pattern of asserting their dominance over an equally vulnerable racial group.[15]

Young Topazians found greater acceptance in Chicago, particularly newlywed couples who, to Caucasians, showed promise in their quest to attain middle-class respectability. WRA relocation workers steered new arrivals to churches and civic groups that agreed to help the WRA both support the Nikkei in their transition and watch to make sure they did not revert to "clannishness," which the WRA believed had caused the internment. Relocatees enjoyed friendly relationships with Caucasians, frequently attending mixed social gatherings. Nevertheless, WRA agents and resettlement workers monitored their social interactions and provided correction whenever they fell into being too "Japanesy." Japanese American Chicagoans lived in a world of resettlement workers rather than friends.

The older Issei bachelors, who settled in the Newberry Park area, fell through the cracks completely. Their one-room apartments resembled their Topaz barracks: they were dark, poorly ventilated, badly maintained, and barren except for a bed, table and chair, dresser and a small cook stove. Most worked in restaurants or hotels, or received public assistance, and spent their spare time gambling and drinking. Their poor showing was an embarrassment to the WRA; resettlement workers continued to monitor workers' progress while turning a blind eye to the elderly bachelors, who became the silent shame of the resettlement program. While some of these older internees might have demanded better treatment in the camps, in Chicago they had no one they could easily complain to and, they believed, no one who cared. One seventy-six-year-old man told a journalist for the *Pacific Citizen*, "we bachelors are failures, and we know it . . . [y]et we do not have the courage to commit suicide. For us, life has no significance or positive meaning. We are only waiting now to die."[16]

Topazians who stayed in the West did not fare much better because the internment had perpetuated the long history of anti-Japanese prejudice and extended it to new populations of westerners. Still grieving their losses at Bataan, the Navajo Tribal Council recoiled at the possibility of "California Japs" settling in their area. When the Interior Department presented plans to transfer Nisei teachers to the beleaguered Navajo schools, the tribal council formally barred hiring Japanese teachers because "the idea of placing aliens over our people in our schools simply is slighting our people." White westerners continued to use their Japanese neighbors as a cheap, dispensable labor force while segregating them from the community. When the WRA abandoned its segregatory function, employers and real estate agents used selective hiring and redlining to keep resettlers "in their place." While Topazians might have guessed that white Utahns would be somewhat hostile, many were unable to find the adequate housing and jobs they were promised by resettlement agents.[17]

Ernst may not have been aware of the extent of Topazians' difficulties when he sent a survey to all resettlers asking about their progress and prospects for their post-camp lives. One Topazian residing in nearby Delta ignored the printed questions and vented his frustration at being "dumped" in a strange place with no hope of finding adequate housing or a good job. The writer did not just criticize the resettlement program; he placed its failings in the context of the internment when stating, "The whole setup, right from the time of evacuation has been done in an Undemocratic and Hitleristic way. Why don't the WRA come right out and admit their mistakes, instead of alibiing and trying to cover all the mistakes with a lot of hot air and MALARKEY!" Another disheartened relocatee wrote, "It is too late to suggest or criticize after being placed in camp life and have to start out in life again. I really feel sorry for myself, but particularly for my children." Ernst might have empathized with the plight of his former charges, but WRA agents did not. John Embree, chief Washington analyst at the WRA, was bemused at the failings of America's "adolescent race" and noted in his early report on resettlement that "life on the outside was more difficult than they expected." He subtitled the section, "The Great White Father."[18]

Neither prejudice nor compassion for the Nikkei could slow resettlement at the end of 1944, when the Supreme Court handed down its decisions in the *Korematsu* and *Endo* cases. The Court held Fred Korematsu criminally liable in failing to report to the assembly center because military judgments may override other constitutional considerations in a national emergency. *Ex parte Endo*, however, found the federal government had no basis for incarcerating loyal citizens and called for readmitting all loyal Nisei to the Pacific states.[19]

The *Endo* decision pleased Topazians, but it also posed wrenching dilemmas. Larger families had children in the East and lacked the means to reunite in one region. The WRA, shifting its role from jailer to social worker, did what it could to help families solve their relocation problems, but the difficulties were legion. In November 1943 a WRA welfare worker accompanied a woman resident and her two sons to San Leandro to visit their dying father. Shortly after they arrived at the hospital, a deputy sheriff—having received a tip from the hotel owner that Japanese people would be there—threatened to arrest the WRA worker, the doctor, and several hospital staff. The WRA found another hotel for the family, but the sons were so rattled they retreated immediately to Topaz. An Oakland policeman later warned against bringing Topazians to the area again.[20]

California was no less hostile two years later. In 1945 elected officials denounced the return of their Japanese constituents, with one representative warning that those aiding the returnees were "advocating bloodshed" because "the only good Jap is a dead Jap, and that is just what is going to happen to every one of them."[21]

The prewar Nihonmachi was gone, with businesses boarded up for years and Japanese homes occupied by African American defense workers who were barred from white neighborhoods (just as black Vanporters were barred from most of Portland). During the migration, the Tolan Commission believed most workers would return to their home states after the war. This was not the case for the many black workers who found better jobs, less discrimination, and few incentives to return to the Jim Crow South. In addition, black workers made less money than whites and often did not have means to return to the South. Released internees who were unable to find space in Nihonmachi were slated for transitional housing in federal defense housing projects, like Hunters Point in the Bay Area, just as Oregon's resettlers were housed at Vanport. Ironically, the federal government had built the projects to house black workers unable to move into Nihonmachi or other better-integrated areas. This unforeseen level of contact between African and Japanese Americans raised anxious questions about how this new racial dynamic might play out in the immediate postwar period.

Alarmists cried that race war was imminent, but a survey in the *Crisis* revealed Bay Area blacks were "surprised . . . at the idea that they are supposed to be resentful about the return of the Japanese." In fact, the majority of San Francisco's African Americans had great affinity for those suffering under what they called "Jap Crow." Arthur Caylor's prediction that African Americans and Japanese Americans would form alliances based on an understanding that "there is less difference between brown and black than black and white" had come to pass. What Caylor did not acknowledge, however, was that their mission was not to undermine the American way but to defend its bedrock principles from government race-baiting and discriminatory policy making.[22]

In spite of the difficulties, San Francisco County regained 62 percent of its Nikkei population; San Mateo County, 54 percent; and Alameda County, 52 percent. The WRA reported that returnees owned either businesses or homes, were only eligible for public assistance in their county of origin, feared moving to a strange place, or had helpful Caucasian friends. Yet Topazians without such strong pulls also returned to stand against racist Californians who tried to drive them out and the federal officials who denied them their constitutional rights and protections, including the freedom to live in their communities.[23]

On October 31, 1945, the last of the nearly ten thousand Topazians left the camp forever, free to resettle where and how they chose. As the WRA wrapped up its administrative loose ends, Myer cautioned against managing people this way again except during natural catastrophes, when there was no time to prepare anything else. Myer's view stemmed from the widening realization that the federal government's attempt at blending national security objectives with social reform was nearly as disastrous for the West's Japanese population as it had been for Native Americans. The process of rounding up America's most feared racial minorities restored the public's confidence in the government's ability to protect them in the wake of Pearl Harbor, but for the Nikkei, it raised the same questions about the meaning of American freedom and democracy that Indians had been pondering for nearly a century. It was abundantly clear in 1945 that residents of both Topaz and the Klamath Reservation lost their independence and self-determination to federal agencies that ruled by force and fostered economic dependency in people who had previously been able to sustain themselves.[24]

Community life in both federal enclaves was designed to inculcate a set of values, but the government sent contradictory messages to Klamaths and Topazians: they must aspire to full citizenship, but Indians and Asians were not fit for full citizenship; and while they must demonstrate their commitment to America' highest ideals, they could not expect social equality from the population at large. These contradictions undermined every attempt residents made to become fully participating community members. Federal agents insisted residents serve as governors, but they did not allow them to govern. They insisted that Klamaths and Topazians work but made it impossible for them to attain economic self-sufficiency. Youngsters were sent to school, where lectures on freedom took place within view of guard towers. While the vast majority of Klamaths and Topazians remained loyal throughout their ordeals, they had serious doubts about the government's ability to protect their civil liberties as well as it did other Americans'. Instead of learning unflinching obedience to the U.S. government, the Klamath

Tribes and Topazians alike developed an array of resistance strategies to federal authority, with the aim of protecting principles of freedom and equality when the government agents betrayed those values in the "little Americas" of their own making.

Life and Death in the City with Everything but a Future

The government's race-consciousness was so engrained in its community-building practices that federal agencies incorporated systems of segregation, surveillance, and reform into wartime communities with multiracial populations. As the case of Vanport demonstrates, the government employed structures for security, surveillance, and celebration of the American way in order to prevent interracial conflict from diverting the forty thousand shipyard workers in residence from the tasks of war production. Although industrial workers were not considered a class of "hostiles," the isolation, institutional life, and heavy-handed government controls reflected the same concerns about security and democracy that drove policymaking at Klamath and Topaz. The government did not use reservations and internment camps as formal blueprints, but their influence is clearly evident in Vanport's management policies and community institutions, even as the war emergency and the shipyard labor shortage came to an end.

Vanporters received the news of Hiroshima and Nagasaki bombings with mixed jubilation and shock. Everyone reveled in the overwhelming spirit of triumph—against all odds, Kaiser workers had built enough ships to aid the Allies to victory on both fronts. But the age of atomic bombs and iron curtains shifted defense priorities from shipbuilding in Oregon to plutonium processing at the MED facility at Hanford. Vanport housing units were repurposed for the burgeoning atomic city, while other federal projects and key wartime programs, like the Vanport Child Service Center, were slated for quick termination to cut costs and convince residents to leave.[25]

The Housing Authority of Portland (HAP) informed the shipyard workers, now Vanport's "old-timers," that even if the town remained, it would no longer be for them. HAP bombarded residents with reports of better opportunities elsewhere as enticements to leave, even as it quietly removed housing units from the site. This push saddened many Vanporters, who like Klamaths and Topazians had made these artificial communities their own and looked forward to starting their postwar lives on their own terms.[26]

Meanwhile, just as the Federal Public Housing Authority (FPHA) began considering what to do with "the city with everything but a future," Portland was overwhelmed by yet another housing crisis. Mirroring the 1942 in-migration, both 1945 and 1946 brought waves of veterans to Portland in search of the housing and educational benefits promised in the GI Bill. Portland was short on both. Portlanders rented out every last bit of space in their homes to newcomer veterans, while area colleges and universities processed unprecedented numbers of applications for admission with no plan for accommodating so many students. Once again, war housing expeditiously solved the problem. In December 1945 HAP redesignated a cluster of Vanport units as the "Veteran's Village." Villagers—who were mostly young white families—immediately distinguished themselves from the old-timer "transient element" by displaying all the trappings of permanent suburban homes. They painted and landscaped their units; put up small picket fences; and organized to demand improved community facilities, better schools, and a new recreation center from HAP.[27]

Fulfilling the government's promise of a college education for every veteran was more difficult because Portland's few institutions were over-enrolled with the first wave of returning soldiers. In a statement echoing those by early supporters of Vanport's construction, one official warned it would be a far worse error to deliver "too little too late" on the GI Bill than to overinvest in educational facilities. They quickly set to work, crunching numbers to make estimates, and after refurbishing old child-care facilities, they recruited seventy-five faculty members from area colleges and universities. Clocking in on time and on budget, Vanport College held its official opening on May 25, 1946. It was one of the few times when federal community planning placed human need ahead of budgets, politics, and public relations.[28]

Villagers' presence as Vanport's "model citizens" motivated tremendous policy change. In 1946 HAP reversed its position on community newspapers, making funds available to hire a retired editor from a Hawaiian naval base to supervise the *Voice of Vanport*. The mimeographed newsletter reported mostly on events at Vanport College, the comings and goings of recruiting sergeants, teen events, lighthearted gossip, new project regulations, and Vanport's projected longevity. Even if an editorial page and hard-hitting stories had been added, the paper would have never been an organ for discussion and dissent. HAP retained editorial control and remained concerned that community politics not evolve into rebellion or social disorder.[29]

As questions arose about whether and how Vanport facilities would be funded, residents assumed an increasingly active role in shaping decisions about the future of their community. Campus veterans founded a Vanport chapter of the American Veterans Committee in the fall of 1946 to solve community problems and pressure the government to honor its promises of affordable housing and full educational benefits in the GI Bill. When the Vanport schools refused to let the college use some of the Child Service Center buildings, two students ran for seats on the school board and changed the building use policies.[30]

In some areas, however, the federal government held tenaciously to its policymaking privileges. The FPHA was unmoved by villagers' protests against the prohibition of alcohol in the project. Villagers, arguing that responsible adults should not have to sneak a beer at the end of a school or work day, persuaded HAP to allow operation of a bar. The FPHA, however, would not budge. The issue deepened the rifts between the local and federal agencies and showed the villagers that as long as Vanport remained a federal project, the FPHA set the limits on residents' decision-making powers, war emergency or no. Residents were undeterred by HAP's shows of force. Neighborhood bulletins warned that HAP and the FPHA projected a three-year life span for the project, further cautioning that if the residents did not play a constructive role in community affairs, government agents would drive them from their homes. Vanporters became increasingly politicized as they made claims to ownership and rights in their government-issue town, and with twenty-four-hour work schedules a thing of the past, residents had more time and interest in political participation.[31]

The Vanport funding crisis inspired creative political activism. In perhaps the most astounding incident, the school principal, Laura Kellar, found a way to give herself voting rights without leaving Vanport. Kellar was determined to vote in a tax levy to keep the schools open when federal funds were cut for the 1946 school year, seeking a way around the property qualification. She noticed four tiny plots of nongovernment property in the project where Pacific Telephone and Telegraph equipment stood. Kellar purchased one share in PT&T, making her part owner of their property in Vanport, which made her eligible to vote. Other Vanporters followed Kellar's lead, and by 1948 the Vanport voter roll jumped from one to 149.[32]

The Vanport Tenants League—a tenant's advocacy group affiliated with the Communist Party—won meaningful change by directly challenging HAP's unlawful policies. The League staged large demonstrations when HAP prepared to raise rents in defiance of the Federal Public Housing Authority's "hardship clause," which required housing authorities to adjust rents for residents in cases of unemployment or other circumstances that threatened their tenancy. Initially, HAP denied any improprieties in its rent scheduling, but the Vanport Tenants League found that other Portland projects were being scheduled at adjusted rates. They contacted the Federal Public Housing Authority directly, found that HAP had no right to restrict hardship adjustments to veterans, and staged a demonstration to expose HAP's wrongdoing and demand redress. Their action was so effective that the Communist Party and the Vanport Tenants League organized residents in other HAP projects, creating a community of interest that extended beyond Vanport's city limits.[33]

Despite residents' concerted efforts to build a viable permanent community, Vanport's fate was determined in 1946 when the Federal Public Housing Authority replaced Commissioner Philip Klutznik with Dillon Myer, who needed a job after the last WRA relocation center was dismantled. Myer's success had little to do with the way he ran the internment camps; he was the toast of Washington because he quickly and efficiently resettled the entire population of West Coast Japanese. Myer had very little experience with human services, but his bureaucratic skills were much in demand, and over the next ten years he fulfilled the Eightieth

Congress's mandates to disentangle the federal government from federal communities by emptying FPHA projects and Indian reservations as head of the newly renamed Bureau of Indian Affairs from 1950 to 1953.[34]

Before Myer could apply his experiences at the War Relocation Authority to the public housing program, Vanport was washed off the map by floodwaters that burst a railroad fill used improperly as a dam. Several nearby communities were evacuated within a few days of the rise in water levels, but HAP chose not to evacuate Vanport, believing that people could be moved quickly enough if a true emergency arose. Residents received written notice that "[t]he dikes are safe. . . . You will be warned if necessary. You will have time to leave." The advisory proved disastrously wrong as residents were caught in a wall of water that smashed housing units to kindling in a matter of minutes. Bewildered Vanporters had no possessions and no place to go, save for higher ground in Portland.[35]

Making homes in old trailers, homeless Vanporters relived the miserable experience of their arrival in Portland, this time with neither a "miracle city" nor a well-paying job awaiting them. The federal government announced that it would make trailers available at low rents but only to private property owners and their renters. These rules were especially burdensome for black Vanporters, who rarely had the means to return to their state of origin ("Kaiser Specials" were one-way trains) or to dodge restrictive covenants. Most black Vanporters had to start life over in Albina, where they knew they were unwanted.[36]

A group of former tenants led by Vanport College students, labor activists, and members of the Progressive and Socialist parties formed the Vanport Citizens' Emergency Disaster Committee (VCEDC) to pressure the government for permanent housing and full compensation for flood losses. They petitioned Mayor Earl Riley for more comprehensive, "humane" flood relief, including implementation of emergency rent controls and the removal of several HAP officials deemed most negligent in the disaster. Riley eschewed all responsibility for the federal enclave aside from "a moral responsibility on the part of our citizenship to alleviate suffering."[37]

Riley's dismissal of the Vanporters did not make them go away. Three hundred Vanporters held a mass meeting to air complaints of rent gouging, racketeering, profiteering, and looting, which led chairman Spencer Gill to conclude that officials at all levels of government had "an immunity to the needs of human beings." VCEDC representative Victor Todd confronted the Portland City Council's dismissive attitude with a petition for improved living conditions, fair compensation for flood losses, and the "outright dismissal of the housing authority of Portland," while seventy-five picketers took to the sidewalk demanding a "Marshall Plan" for Vanport. Riley, incensed by the picketers' applause for Todd's presentation, abruptly ended the meeting. HAP announced later that "Todd is a communist" who was "playing his war record" to earn support for flood relief and, by extension, the Communist Party. HAP's quick resort to red-baiting reveals a clear change in the overall community ethos. HAP became the adversary, rather than the advocate, of dissenting Vanporters when residents were no longer willing to put government interests ahead of their own. Vanporters calling for redress and government accountability for poor management policies were no longer slapped with eviction notices but given the more damning and permanent label "un-American."[38]

The VCEDC pressed on all the way to the state capital, organizing a caravan of flood victims to travel to Salem to speak with Governor John Hall. An advance telegram, signed by three Veterans Villagers, requested that the governor call an emergency legislative session and stop throwing up the "red smokescreen" to avoid responsibility for the stricken Vanporters. Hall refused to meet with the VECDC on grounds that the federal government was responsible for the Vanporters, and that VECDC leaders were "allied with the Communist party or closely associated with it." The governor received more support than disapproval from Oregonians, who generally viewed the Vanporters as outsiders who expected handouts. Although these thousands of people were veterans or defense workers who had either fought or labored (or both) for the preservation of democracy, many found themselves impoverished and stigmatized for demanding emergency housing—an odd condemnation, given that Dillon Myer supported prefab communities to house victims of natural disasters in his speech condemning WRA-style projects for all other purposes.[39]

Vanporters spent the next four years seeking redress, but they received neither monetary compensation nor an apology from any government agency despite filing 712 suits for damages totaling $6.5 million under the 1946 Federal Tort Claims Act. The act, which waives sovereign immunity provisions, allowed individuals to sue the government in a narrow range of government-approved circumstances. Unfortunately, flood damage did not make the list. The ninety-man legal team representing the Vanporters in one of America's first class-action suits did not argue the government's liability for the flood. In a last-ditch legal strategy, Vanport lawyers argued before the federal district court in Portland in *Clark v. United States* that HAP made "negligent misrepresentations" in the May 30 memorandum assuring residents that the dikes were safe and instructing them to remain in the town. The court heard testimony for two months and deliberated another ten before ruling against Clark. The judge explained that HAP's actions were honest and competent, and that the federal government had no control over the course or intensity of the floodwaters. Nor did the government have any control over the condition of the railroad fill that HAP had misused as a dike. The fill belonged to the Spokane, Portland, and Seattle Railway, so the federal government was not at fault for the break. The SPS Railway did not operate Vanport, so it was not responsible for the welfare of the people, thus leaving no one legally responsible for residents' losses and displacement from their homes on the floodplain.[40]

The court faulted the Federal Public Housing Authority's paternalistic management practices, citing bulletins from Washington in which "the thesis seems to be that the people in housing projects are like children; they really do not know what they want or what to believe [and] the designated managers of the housing project should [therefore] accept the challenge and give them guidance and directions, all in accordance with the mandates from above, contained in the housing regulations." When the flood hit, the court argued, HAP presented itself as "omniscient and radiated an atmosphere of confidence which the situation did not justify," and it encouraged tenants to abrogate all responsibility for their personal well-being in a dangerous circumstance because "the kind, paternalistic government would take complete direction of its children and protect them." Vanporters followed HAP's instructions even when the bowl-shaped lay of the land and its proximity to two swollen rivers should have made the flood danger plainly obvious. Although the Federal Public Housing Authority and HAP were declared blameworthy, the seven hundred plaintiffs were awarded no damages or compensation of any kind.[41]

Klamath Indians and former Topazians were probably not surprised by the verdict, given that they, too, felt cast away by the federal government. Los Alamosans also experienced an abrupt turn in their relationship with the federal government, beginning the moment news of the Hiroshima and Nagasaki bombings reached the home front. The $56 million, 6,000-person town became suddenly visible to the world, and its anonymous inhabitants turned into national heroes overnight. The enlisted men held jubilant celebrations, while many scientists soberly contemplated their creation. A wave of Los Alamosans streamed off the Hill to resume their prewar positions or accept the offers that followed their newfound fame. Many younger scientists who had followed their mentors to the project took permanent Tech Area jobs as employees of the University of California, and hundreds of discharged research assistants were hired as civilian replacements. The laboratory adopted a forty-hour workweek for the first time, and a trickle of journalists, traveling salesmen, and mothers-in-law appeared on the mesa, making peacetime unsettling for those who had grown comfortable in their cocoon.

Power, Privilege, and the Politics of Enclosure

At Los Alamos, more than at Topaz or Vanport, officials had to grapple with how—and how soon—to cut the ties between the government and its wards. Secrecy remained desirable, but dependency was not. In spite of the town's shrinking population and increased visibility, life in Los Alamos remained insulated. Even President Harry S. Truman, whom General Groves had promised the first full tour of the Manhattan Project, was barred from entrance. The army flew Truman to Albuquerque, where he toured a military airfield before being flown to the plutonium processing plant at the Hanford Nuclear Reservation. There, a brigadier general of the Engineer Corps said sternly to the president that he and his companion Senator John H. Tolan, as the first outsiders allowed in a Manhattan Engineer District (MED) project, would ask no questions, and if they did, even the president would get no answers. Although Truman started the tour in New Mexico, he never saw Los Alamos and apparently never asked why.[42]

Restrictions loosened a bit for Los Alamosans, however. They were finally free to write "Los Alamos" on the datelines of their letters, if not the envelopes. Censors continued to read residents' mail, but they were less certain of what was okay to write. The Army Corps of Engineers issued a stern warning that "[l]oose talk and speculation, particularly by individuals now or formerly connected with the project, jeopardize the future of the nation and must be controlled" and that the government would use the provisions of the Espionage Act to punish anyone who said the wrong thing. Los Alamosans took their freedoms where they found them. They continued to avoid speaking foreign languages, submitting to frequent searches, and exercising caution in their social contacts.[43] Clearly, the MED had a challenge on its hands: it sought to organize the town around the very democratic-capitalist principles it had been designed to undermine.

The process was aided, however, by residents' decreasing tolerance for unreasonable security measures and far-reaching federal paternalism. The town council demanded that the MED no longer make residents present commissary ID cards for purposes other than purchasing food at the commissary, a request that gained widespread popular support. Originally, the cards were used to identify legitimate users of the commissary so that "outsiders" would not raid supplies. Over time, it became customary for officials to ask for cards to ride the bus, purchase "bottled goods," and vote in school board elections. They also asked that the army change the sign at the commissary from "[a]ll items purchased here must be consumed on the project. Violations may result in loss of Commissary privileges" to "all food purchased here must be consumed by residents of the project." The friendlier sign, they argued, would prevent MPs from seizing food from picnickers at nearby Bandelier National Monument.[44]

Although the commissary issues seem like minor complaints, in federal communities the smallest matters often had the greatest political significance. American citizens living outside the barbed wire did not have to identify themselves to officials to conduct normal activities such as making purchases and boarding public transport. In the free society Los Alamosans had just worked to save, market forces, not procurement officers, guided economic conditions. Other Americans could choose what to do with their purchases; Los Alamosans had as much choice as the federal government would give them. While Los Alamosans had anticipated a turn toward greater freedom and a normal American life following the war, the increased use of the commissary card seemed to indicate a return to wartime controls.

There were some great advantages to living in Los Alamos, however. Housing, though rental only, was priced on an affordable sliding scale, medical care remained free, and the government made payments to New Mexico in lieu of state taxes. At the time, though, it was hard for residents to discern whether the community infrastructure was intended as a perk, as compensation for having been uprooted, or as a form of social control that made dependent wards of atomic scientists. The question was thorny enough when the project was invisible and Los Alamosans and the MED were working it out for themselves. Now that Los Alamos was in the public eye, the government had to be mindful of the way it managed its atomic reservations as well as its atomic bombs.

The federal government wanted to be sure the public understood Los Alamos was not a haven for state-sanctioned Communism. The first War Department press release confirming the existence of Los Alamos emphasized its modern family housing, shopping facilities, schools, recreation programs, public library, and the town council. The memo concluded that "[t]he community may be isolated, but the personnel has not given up living as any American group would anywhere else in the nation." Even if there were some Los Alamosans who were not especially interested in living like all other Americans, they would have to adjust quickly because the MED was preparing to replace free health care with a fee-for-service system. The nursery school was swiftly eliminated, and the Tech Area mothers were sent home to raise their small children.[45]

Despite pending cutbacks in social services, progressive journalist Carey McWilliams was extremely impressed with the absence of want at Los Alamos, where there was no need for a welfare apparatus because only persons connected with the project or their dependents could live there. In addition to perpetual full employment, residents had affordable housing, healthcare, and excellent schools. McWilliams's glowing utopian view may have impressed a few socialists, but the newly formed Atomic Energy Commission (AEC) had no intention of perpetuating these "un-American" community features. The challenge, however, was to reduce residents' dependence on the federal government while maintaining sufficient controls on Los Alamos's potentially dangerous population.[46]

Uncertainties about the future of community life, paired with a burning desire to get out from under military control, fueled a swift exodus that shrunk Los Alamos's population from 8,200 to 6,524 in three months. J. Robert Oppenheimer was one of those who left, and Norris Bradbury was appointed his successor on his return to Berkeley. Bradbury slowed the exodus by announcing plans for the laboratory to spearhead development of the hydrogen bomb and research the effects of nuclear fallout, joining forces with General Groves to convert Los Alamos into a peacetime defense project. He called on the MED in 1945 to make improvements in housing, utilities, and community facilities—particularly "recreational facilities for single persons" to make Los Alamos attractive to America's top scientists. While this strategy worked for the first wave of recruitment in 1942, scientists—both current and prospective—were more interested in establishing academic freedom at Los Alamos than basketball courts.[47]

In Washington, legislators, army officers, and scientists argued over the soundness of placing Manhattan Project facilities under civilian control. Increasing support for the May-Johnson Bill, which kept atomic energy facilities under military control, politically galvanized Los Alamos scientists, who organized to defeat the bill and bring freedom of speech to the mesa. Enrico Fermi, Oppenheimer, and a few former Los Alamosans regarded the bill as reasonable, but many others considered militarization unacceptable in peacetime. An additional offensive provision assigned penalties for security violations, which could be as great as ten years in prison and a hundred-thousand-dollar fine.[48]

Meanwhile, a number of remaining veterans of the bomb project organized the Association of Los Alamos Scientists (ALAS) in response to the bombings of Hiroshima and Nagasaki. Their original mission was to use their information about atomic energy for the good of humanity. When it looked as though May-Johnson was destined to pass, ALAS launched a public education campaign on the uses and dangers of atomic energy. They made Congress their first students, issuing a formal statement denouncing military control of the atomic energy program as inefficient and dangerous. In addition, ALAS held regular public meetings in which scientists answered Santa Feans' questions about atomic weapons, potential radiation risks, Hiroshima and Nagasaki, and the perils of hoarding atomic secrets from other nations.[49]

Congress passed the Atomic Energy Act in 1946, which trumped May-Johnson by placing the atomic energy program under the control of the Atomic Energy Commission, a five-member civilian board. The commission would have the support of a military liaison and a general advisory committee, but President Truman's intention in signing it was to place civilian scientists and politicians in charge of America's nuclear arsenal. With the president as head overseer, the AEC would give scientists and technicians in its employ whatever they needed to fulfill their mission of designing, testing, and producing more weapons. Los Alamosans were also supposed to understand that part of serving the public trust meant acting as "a gigantic strong-box" for military secrets.[50]

Most ALAS members were heartened by Truman's appointment of Oppenheimer, Fermi, Isidor Rabi, and Glenn Seaborg—each of whom had been politically troublesome at some point during the Manhattan Project—to the AEC's General Advisory Committee. The committee's first task was to advise the AEC on how to balance academic freedom with security protocols.[51] Newspapers everywhere applauded the AEC for balancing the voices of government, science, industry, and the military. The exception was the *Baltimore News-Post*, which predicted a "bitter fight" over confirmation of "certain key members" for their "internationalist, pro-Soviet and leftist affiliations." The *Daily Worker* chimed in by accusing the AEC of nuclear imperialism in keeping the "American monopoly" of atomic energy.[52] With every new phase of Los Alamos's evolution, concerns about Communism complicated progress of the atomic energy program. This time, the anxieties did not just lie with the FBI and military intelligence but with the public as well.

Meanwhile, back at Los Alamos, residents and lame-duck MED officials faced the Eightieth Congress's "year of readjustment," which involved dissolving federal communities of all kinds. Dillon Myer had liquidated the WRA camps and cut back FPHA war housing. The AEC was in the unusual position of having to transform its flimsily built atomic cities into full-fledged small towns. The AEC charted an unusual route to normalcy. Rather than turning the town over to the state of New Mexico or the Los Alamos citizenry, it entered a contract with the Zia Company to perform all the MED's management functions.

Although Zia was created to serve Los Alamos, the MED had a long relationship with its parent company, McKee Company, which built the second phase of Los Alamos housing—the famed "McKeevilles." McKee's contract for new Zia housing construction grew to include maintenance, providing utilities, collecting rent, and supplying consumer goods in the new project stores. At the close of contract negotiations, Zia handled everything from bookkeeping and landscaping to hiring medical staff and providing traffic control, which reduced the number of companies doing business in an "open" Los Alamos to one. This way, the introduction of new residents, workers, and business interests would be gradual, making the transition to a postwar security system simpler and more orderly. As with Vanporters and the first wave of Los Alamosans, all nonscientific workers would be managed by a single authority, which kept wartime structures of surveillance and control in place.

Zia transformed Los Alamos from a military installation into a federal company town like Vanport. Both single-enterprise towns consisted of worker housing, management infrastructure, and a small-scale internal economy. Employer paternalism remained the ruling force in Vanport, but it was especially prominent at Los Alamos, where it drew greater criticism from outsiders. As Kaiser employees, Vanporters were more closely tied to the mainstream economy, but Los Alamosans appeared to be living in a completely separate world at the taxpayers' expense. Conservative detractors labeled Los Alamos a dangerous "socialist" experiment in which an autocratic government stifled the free market. In truth, Los Alamos was no more "socialist" than Vanport. Federal agencies, like managers of company towns, simply provided the means for workers to stay close to the workplace and achieve maximum productivity without presenting a hindrance or danger to the enterprise. Government autocracy was a turn not to the left but to the right, as the AEC and Zia adapted the Federal Public Housing Authority's relationship with Kaiser to get the most from their much-needed labor force.[53]

Los Alamosans were acutely aware of their unchanged living conditions, even as Zia made its first cosmetic changes to Los Alamos. Despite Groves's call for attractive family housing, the AEC turned to Hanford and the WRA for stopgap units, renewing the government-issue feel of the town. The Zia bureaucracy was often more muddled than the army's had been. One woman came home to find a Zia electrician installing an electric outlet in the mantle. She told the electrician she had not ordered an outlet there because it was an absurd place to have one. Zia replied that the man who designed the mantles had an electric clock on his, so every mantle had to have the same outlet. Because Zia had to maintain every home in identical condition, all the houses needed the outlets, whether the occupant (who was, after all, not the owner) approved or not. In attacking the absurdity of the policy, she unleashed her fury at Zia, the AEC, and the government's unreasonable control over ostensibly private space. Her complaints on these loftier matters were met with silence.[54]

Los Alamos's political development also embraced democratic principles, even if the town council was not always able to implement democratic policies. The staffing needs of the Zia Company were so great that Zia workers became an important segment of Los Alamos society. Los Alamos came to see itself politically and socially as a three-sector community in which the University of California scientists and AEC officials formed an upper-middle class and Zia employees composed Los Alamos's lower-middle and working classes. The three entities pulled together to bring about some remarkable changes in 1946 and 1947. Christian residents petitioned the army for a chapel, the central feature of every real American small town. The AEC would not approve construction of a new chapel while the laboratory was moving to the next mesa, but the army allowed Zia to move the chapel from a nearby army hospital to Los Alamos. The chapel stood as a symbol of Los Alamosans' unity, both in the struggle to have a chapel and as a home for all denominations. Even Jewish residents, who had been worshipping together informally, used space in the church to organize the Los Alamos chapters of B'nai B'rith and Hadassah. AEC funds, Zia facilities, and UC journalists made the Los Alamos Times the first local newspaper, and every imaginable civic, recreational, and social club suddenly had a Los Alamos branch, with members from all three segments of the community.[55]

Even the town council changed its structure, designating seats for University of California, AEC, and Zia employees. This decision did not come easily, however. When a UC employee declined his appointment as chairman of the town council's safety committee, he cited the addition of Zia seats as a reason. His letter stated that Zia workers were newcomers who had nothing in common with the "real" Los Alamos residents they were there to serve. Zia enfranchisement was a recipe for tyranny, he argued, because the company controlled all public services and outnumbered UC and AEC employees. The councilman was not alone in his disdain for Zia workers. The wife of one prominent scientist suggested that the way to improve "civic pride" in Los Alamos was to instruct the domestic help not to eat their lunch on private property (wherever that might be).[56]

Far more substantial political issues lay outside the fence. Los Alamosans still did not have legal standing in New Mexico, and they could not be tried in their community by a jury of their peers, make wills, get divorced, or arrange an adoption. They could, however, be taxed and tried for misdemeanors. The first sign that Los Alamos was in political peril came in the 1946 town council election, when twelve nonscientists who were allegedly backed by a member of the New Mexico state political machine submitted petitions for candidacy. The allegation was never proven, and perhaps it was a product of "old-timer" Los Alamosans' multiple political anxieties. They chafed against wartime political constrictions, and their discomfort was heightened by anxieties about how newcomers would change political life on the mesa and what would happen when Los Alamos reintegrated with the rest of America.[57]

Increasingly, Los Alamosans turned their attention from town council voting blocs to restoring the voting rights they lost during the 1944 presidential election. This became an even more pressing issue after the war, when Los Alamosans lost their leverage as keepers of wartime secrets. Disgruntled citizens could no longer threaten to tell the world they existed if the AEC stocked the commissary with bad meat or placed workers in substandard housing. The League of Women Voters spearheaded a study of local government and brainstormed ways for Los Alamosans to engage in state and county politics. The League worked tirelessly, trying everything from traditional voter registration to political theater when Los Alamosans responded with disinterest. At one point the League tried to shame Los Alamosans into action by raising picket signs that looked like little headstones with epitaphs reading, "This is the end of Murgatroyd Moocher who wasn't concerned about his town's future." Some of the League's tactics may have been silly, but their cause was serious. Los Alamos activists feared that years of learned helplessness and government dependency had allowed a dangerous, unbreakable apathy to take hold of the community.[58]

They could not have been heartened by early signs that the AEC had retained the MED's "school principal" authority in thwarting community objectives that interfered or compromised government objectives at Los Alamos. When Zia prepared to pave and put signs along Los Alamos's unnamed streets, the AEC asked residents to submit their nominations for street names. "Hiroshima," "Nagasaki," and "Slotin" (after the first scientist killed in a laboratory accident) were moderately popular choices, yet they never made the ballot. As at Topaz, where wilderness names reinforced the WRA's vision of a pioneer settlement (and reminded Japanese speakers that they needed practice with words like "Tamarisk" and "Cimarron"), the AEC only allowed street names that conveyed an unproblematic view of the Manhattan Project. In the end, the main arteries were named "Central Avenue," "Canyon Boulevard," and "Trinity Drive." Although the names of streets are largely symbolic and have little bearing on residents' quality of life, the AEC's ability to ignore residents' comments showed that the federal government would still give residents only as much choice as suited it.[59]

Los Alamosans' political problems were compounded by confusion on all sides over whether the federal government had sole jurisdiction over Los Alamos. Sandoval and Bernalillo counties took advantage of this ambiguity by summarily eliminating Precinct Seventeen (where Ranch School voters had been registered) and refusing to register more than a few Los Alamos voters. Like Utahns with Topazians and Portlanders with Vanporters, New Mexico's established population resisted the newcomers at Los Alamos. Their concerns were less rooted in racial fears than concrete demographic ones: Los Alamos was large enough to swing elections in Sandoval County. New Mexicans could not imagine that a bunch of California academics would have the same interests as Hispano or even Caucasian old-timers. The Zia workers were unionized New Mexicans who voted straight Democratic tickets, but the UC group was unpredictable. They tended toward conservative social policy but favored tax increases and large federal budgets for fairly obvious reasons. New Mexicans also anticipated that Los Alamosans, like Anglos everywhere, would not tolerate being subject to the political whims of the state's Hispanic majority and would therefore build an unbeatable ethnic voting bloc.[60]

Los Alamosans' intentions may have been unclear, but the 1946 town council election made it apparent that the Sandoval County political machine would not allow Los Alamos to wrest control from them. The League of Women Voters and a group of male supporters (mostly from the town council) organized a campaign to persuade the federal government to cede jurisdiction of Los Alamos to the state of New Mexico.[61] When the AEC failed to respond, the campaign returned its focus to the local level. Town councilman Henry Trujillo, who had extensive experience with New Mexico politics, brought a state supreme court justice to a December 1946 council meeting to discuss ways Los Alamosans could attain voting rights. Since canvassing boards had made rejecting Los Alamos registrations standard procedure, the judge suggested Los Alamosans move into the homes of sympathetic Santa Feans, or that the three thousand adult residents purchase a house off the mesa that they could claim as an address. The plans were abandoned when one audience member questioned whether mocking state law was a desirable political goal. Instead, he argued, the state and county governments should be compelled to make provisions for Los Alamosans to vote.[62]

As Los Alamosans gained a better understanding of the machinations of state politics and the fact that federal "normalization" would not restore their political power, they developed more effective strategies of political empowerment. A group of legislators presented a bill in 1948 making residents of federal reservations New Mexico citizens for the purposes of voting only. The town council used Los Alamos's air of mystery as a political tool by arranging special security clearance for legislators supporting the bill so the council could entertain them at Fuller Lodge. Los Alamosans had their first political success when the voting rights bill passed and Precinct Seventeen was reinstated. The first registration was held at Los Alamos with much anxious anticipation. Sandoval and Bernalillo county residents feared that the anticipated 4,500 "outsider" votes would overpower their electorate, who, with a 55 percent turnout, cast 2,700 ballots in the 1946 election. They need not have worried: political apathy continued to reign at Los Alamos, and less than 1,800 eligible voters made the effort to register.[63]

Los Alamosans' relative political disengagement and New Mexicans' relentless defense of their political dominance combined to make Los Alamosans' status as citizens perpetually unstable. When Los Alamosans went to the polls for the first time in June 1948, they helped elect the Democratic challenger to the machine-backed incumbent for the second district judgeship. When the incumbent saw he lost in Sandoval County, he petitioned the New Mexico State Supreme Court to have the votes declared illegal. The court found for the incumbent, arguing that Los Alamos, as a federal reservation, could not be considered part of New Mexico. Both the AEC and the Los Alamos town council demanded a resolution of the issue of federal jurisdiction with something firmer than haphazard special provisions.

Their voices were joined by the growing number of state legislators who, in looking to the future, saw their political fortunes tied to atomic energy development instead of the old political machine. The political winds shifted so dramatically that Sandoval County surrendered all claims to Los Alamos, allowing the mesa to be a separate county. That way, Los Alamosans could vote without interfering with the Sandoval County political machine. Los Alamos County was written onto the political and geographic map in June 1949, under a county classification created specifically for the federal city-county.[64]

Los Alamos's political muscle grew stronger in New Mexico not from the town's voters but through its politically advantageous situation. Its unending federal support freed the community to pursue issues beyond those of mere survival that plagued America's poorest counties. While the rest of New Mexico struggled to fund schools, Los Alamos had some of the best schools anywhere, with no expenditure of political energy on residents' part. Rather than accept political charity from their educated white neighbors, New Mexicans evened the score by reducing state educational funds to Los Alamos and implementing redistricting plans that put different parts of Los Alamos in congressional districts with pueblos that outnumbered them, thus splitting the mesa vote. Instead of strengthening ties with their neighbors, Los Alamosans attributed New Mexico's political behavior to envy of their resources and turned inward.[65]

While Los Alamosans worked to structure themselves politically, the AEC tried to develop appropriate economic structures for America's "not exactly socialist" town. The transfer of the project from the army to the AEC brought an end to the much-despised commissary and the PX, but instead of developing a free market, the AEC established a concessionaire system, with storefronts clustered in a "community center." Shoppers enjoyed the convenience of a bank, drugstore, newsstand, post office, movie theater, library, hospital, and grocery store in a single cluster of uniformly plain buildings. Further, the AEC's elimination of "unnecessary stores" would save "downtown Los Alamos" from "the clustered appearance usually noticed in a city of this size." Part mini-mall and part town plaza, the $4 million facility was promoted in the press as trendsetter for all American business, with the media overlooking the elements of government control.[66]

Initially Santa Fe businesses clamored for concessions. The highest bidders believed it would be worth the considerable price and the onerous

AEC regulations to have a captive market of well-paid consumers in Los Alamos. Much to their horror, Los Alamosans continued their wartime practice of catalog shopping supplemented by trips to Santa Fe, which had a better selection and where residents could escape the mesa for a bit and even have a drink. Business might have boomed had the AEC allowed alcohol sales in eateries and grocery stores, but permits were restricted to a few "responsible entertainment clubs." The AEC shared the Federal Public Housing Authority's belief that "the town could better carry out its [military] mission," which took precedence over fostering a favorable business climate.[67]

The AEC exercised its power to raise rents and terminate contracts at will, creating an "aura of fear" in the business community. These fears were compounded by the AEC's demand that Zia regulate prices so that they match those in Santa Fe, even though it cost more to rent space and transport goods to Los Alamos. The Los Alamos Merchants Association complained that the government-run "company town" had been designed to "pamper" young scientists, whose special privileges made them unreasonably demanding. Residents' constant complaints to the AEC's Community Management Branch resulted in over-supervision of concessionaires, leaving merchants feeling like "second-class citizens and a necessary evil." Frustrated with the lack of commercial or social progress, the Merchants' Association lashed out against the town as "a throwback to the socialistic communities [of] Robert Owen and Charles Fourier," where capitalism and democracy were doomed to fail for those outside the AEC's protected circle.[68]

Normalization would always be something of a misnomer as long as Los Alamosans remained engaged in highly secretive work. For decades to follow, they would remain subject to a strange brand of federal paternalism that put national security and scientific progress ahead of civil liberties and individual welfare. The iconic American neighborhood policeman was unknown at Los Alamos. The demand for a regular system of law enforcement was met with the appointment of a federal commission to hold court two and a half days a week. After some discussion of deputizing MPs as state police, the federal government authorized park rangers and forest service agents to assist the New Mexico State Police with law enforcement, reestablishing federal authority on the mesa.[69]

Los Alamos's new criminal justice system had its first major test in March 1947, when two Zia employees were brought to trial for the attempted rape of a seventeen-year-old girl. The girl broke away from the men and informed the military police, who held the men overnight before turning them over to the U.S. attorney. At a hearing before federal commissioner Albert Gonzales, they pled not guilty, and they were indicted and remanded for trial in federal court. Both defendants were found guilty of "rape and assault on a federal reservation," which carried a penalty of approximately half the maximum sentence issued defendants in non-federal communities. The judge was empowered, however, to adjust sentences according to the needs of the federal reservation in question, but Gonzales declined to do so in this case. Los Alamos's law enforcement mechanisms promoted policing as much as its economic system encouraged commerce. The AEC's conflicting aims of normalization and retaining authority made building a community where human rights superceded national security objectives an extremely slow-going process.[70]

Los Alamos's emergence from the shadows of wartime secrecy did not bring an end to experimentation, secrecy, and high security on the project. The heavy cloud of mystery and anxiety that engulfed the mesa during the Manhattan Project weighed on the community's collective psyche in the postwar years with the onset of the arms race and controversy over whether to develop a hydrogen bomb. Security and surveillance tightened as astonished Los Alamosans followed the espionage trials of British Mission member Klaus Fuchs and machinist David Greenglass, a member of the Army's Special Engineer Detachment and brother-in-law of Julius Rosenberg. It turned out that military intelligence had been so busy preventing Europeans from speaking "Hungarian" and surveilling the Oppenheimers' bedroom conversations that disgruntled underlings could pass secrets with little difficulty because they did not fit the profile of a Soviet spy. Fuchs and Greenglass were quiet, compliant, and not card-carrying members of the Party; they were spies who simply did not do anything to align themselves with the official profile for a "subversive."[71]

Oppenheimer, however, was brought before the AEC on charges of being a spy for the Soviets. In hundreds of pages of files replete with transcriptions from wiretaps on his phone, summaries of his travel, and renewed inquiries into his prewar associations, no conclusive proof emerged to indicate that Oppenheimer volunteered his services to the Soviets (though investigation of this question continues as the Venona intercepts and Soviet archives become available). Oppenheimer's resistance to hydrogen bomb research, his use of his scientific position to promote international control of atomic energy, and his history of leftist political associations became the basis for the AEC stripping him of his security clearance in 1954. Without access to top-secret information, Oppenheimer was effectively banned from all involvement in atomic research and policy until his untimely death in 1967.[72]

Los Alamos transformed itself from one inverse utopia to another: the first compromised individual freedom to protect the mesa's secrets from Hitler, and the second—while more open and more democratic—was so fully geared toward beating the Soviets in the arms race that individuals themselves became expendable. Fatal plutonium accidents took the lives of two young scientists within eighteen months of the war's end. After helplessly watching the two young men die slowly and painfully over the course of several days, the medical director of Los Alamos called for increased disclosure from the AEC on laboratory health hazards as a means of regaining the confidence of residents harmed by failed safety and security procedures. New aid stations popped up across the mesa, and doctors started a "milk route," collecting urine specimens from UC employees who forgot to give samples at the lab. Some scientists refused to submit to testing, charging that with little reliable information concerning the effects of radiation on humans, the urine assays were useless except as morale-boosters. Other scientists complied but kept the open secret that the AEC monitored radiation hazards so vigilantly only to prepare for the lawsuits it anticipated from people affected during and after the Manhattan Project.[73]

Los Alamos's new "American-style democracy" experienced its first great test when the AEC declared it an open city. Like Klamaths and Topazians, Los Alamosans were unprepared to return to the mainstream without a transition period. They feared being swallowed into the mass and losing what benefits they retained in their isolated enclave. In spite of the discontents of living in a closed city for so long, Los Alamosans feared opening "their" city. An alarmed letter writer to the *Los Alamos Times* asked, "Do we really desire an 'average' community? . . . must we accept and endure the unwholesome and sordid aspects of the average town? . . . The average city is not, in my opinion, particularly desirable. Remember, it also has slums, rows of unlovely tenant houses, unbeautified areas, untended parks, advertising sign boards, garbage dumps, political racketeering, nepotism, civil corruption, economic uncertainty!!"[74]

Beneath these rallying cries, Los Alamosans whispered fears that "their" mesa would be "infested and invaded by all the Spanish out of the bottom of the Hill" and sought a home rule amendment to avoid integration with New Mexico. They also resisted integrating a growing number of African American Zia employees. In 1950 (in a scene reminiscent of Portland in 1942) six barbers refused to give security inspector William G. Stone a haircut because he was black. The AEC, as a federal agency, had to enforce nondiscrimination policies and insisted the barbers serve Stone. The barbers not only refused; they walked off the job, which resulted in their eviction. (Only those working for Zia, the Lab, or the AEC qualified for housing or commercial space in Los Alamos.) The barbershop manager, in a frantic effort to save his concession, advertised for new barbers, but none of twenty-nine applicants would agree to serve black customers. As a compromise, the barber offered to cut Stone's hair in a separate location if Stone would agree to stay away from his shop. Stone refused, stating, "Either you believe in democracy or you don't." Unmoved, the result was that "everyone else in town either went shaggy or drove 34 miles to Santa Fe and the nearest pair of clippers." Instead of desegregating the barbershop, the AEC allowed the barbershop to close after making halfhearted efforts at enforcing nondiscrimination provisions for federal projects.[75]

Los Alamosans' conflicting sentiments about life in a "normal" community were met with an equally ambiguous statement from the Atomic

Energy Commission in 1952. The atomic cities were placed on the fast track to self-governance and private ownership — except for Los Alamos, where there was no separation between the laboratory and the townsite. The resulting blend of limited new freedoms and unchanging wartime restrictions preserved the distinctiveness of inverse utopias until the 1960s, when the residents gained meaningful political and economic control over Los Alamos. Until then, the open gates continued to lend an air of freedom to the town, but they did not produce the same sense of political efficacy enjoyed by residents at Oak Ridge and Hanford. Nor were Los Alamosans fully free of all the wartime security restrictions and social controls. Although Los Alamos had been integrated into the state's political geography, it remained, in the words of an AEC historian, "an American anomaly" that still bore the hallmarks of "an island of socialism in the midst of a free enterprise economy," one "bred in extraordinary scientific developments . . . isolated by security barriers, and protected by unprecedented national legislation."[76]

While Los Alamos's glacially paced "normalization" process quieted the AEC's anti-Communist critics on the outside, it did not bring democracy or civil rights protections to Los Alamosans. The federal government changed the character of its involvement with Los Alamos throughout the Cold War, but the fundamental characteristics of inverse utopias — isolation, dependency, and subordination of essential civil liberties to national security objectives — remained firmly in place.[77]

Throughout the processes of resettling Topazians, repopulating Vanport, and "normalizing" the atomic cities, Dillon Myer received accolades from every branch of government for the speed and economy with which he dismantled the War Relocation Authority. Other government agencies adopted Myer's strategies for dissolving communities under government auspices, making Topaz (and the other WRA relocation centers) a blueprint for the Klamath's termination, just as reservations like Klamath had been a model for creating Topaz. Though Myer was roundly criticized for his mistakes in running Topaz and the nine other camps, both the Federal Public Housing Authority and the Bureau of Indian Affairs (BIA) courted him as he worked to make his position at the WRA obsolete. Myer took the reins of both programs, working to dismantle public housing programs from 1946–47 and to terminate the Indian reservation system when he replaced John Collier as commissioner of the BIA in 1950. After years of wrangling with Collier about the nature and function of federal communities, Myer had the final say about what "ethnic democracy" would mean in the postwar world.

CHAPTER SIX

TERMINATION OF THE KLAMATH RESERVATION

From Inverse Utopia to Indian Dystopia

Americans everywhere celebrated the dawn of a new era of peace and prosperity in 1950. In contrast, many former Topazians, Vanporters, and Los Alamosans struggled to recover from a decade of displacement, stigmatization, and involuntary dependency on government agencies that left them abandoned and alienated. Washington's zeal for dissolving collectivist enclaves soon reached Indian Country as well. Ten years after Dillon Myer announced the closing of the WRA camps in 1943, the federal government formally adopted a policy of termination in 1953. The destructive policy called for the dissolution of tribal entities and national homelands and the integration of labor and resources into the free market. Proponents argued that termination would liberate Indians from the shackles of federal dependency just as global capitalism might one day liberate the millions in Europe and Asia enslaved by Communism. The termination of the Klamath Reservation left individuals to sink or swim in the turbulent American mainstream, and they would go forth without a tribal land base, tribal institutions, or tribal community and culture as a life preserver. Like the Issei bachelors before them who languished in Chicago, Klamaths were set adrift by the federal government.

Presented as a new progressive policy for Indians, termination was for most residents of Klamath the culmination of decades of failed policies and bungled social engineering experiments that brought Indians from the dispossession of the 1840s to a tragic new phase of dispossession in the 1950s. The process of termination responded to the same historical forces behind the founding of the reservation, only this time Indians were enmified as "collectivists," identified as useful to urban labor markets, dislocated in the name of demographic management, and "civilized" in a crash course on living as a mainstream wage laborer. Instead of isolating the tribes from the rest of America, termination made Klamaths invisible within it. Detribalization was more complex than the postwar changes in Topaz, Vanport, and even Los Alamos because of the longevity of the reservation system and the problem of Indians, and not just federal agencies, as landholders. Nevertheless, Klamath termination followed the larger patterns of inverse utopian history, as a full, detailed examination reveals.

Well before the end of the war, federal legislators and bureaucrats began to consider which tribes might be prepared to live independently of their reservations and their "paternalistic" treaty relationships with the federal government. Congress and the OIA—renamed the Bureau of Indian Affairs (BIA) in 1947—placed the Klamath Reservation near the top of the list because of its wealth, its forward-thinking incorporation plan, and even the fact that Wade Crawford had served as superintendent. Like the Japanese internees and the valiant men of the 442nd Regimental Combat Team, Klamaths had proven their loyalty though military service on the battlefield and the home front. Government officials and the general public saw Native participation in wartime as progress toward assimilation that had to be continued, not squandered on quasi-Communist reservations.

Historians may never reach a consensus about how Indians' participation in World War II altered—or failed to change—Native life, but most agree that it paved the way for the federal government to implement the relocation and termination policies in the 1950s. The government pursued both policies to sever the ties between Indians and their land, identity, and treaty rights. The War Relocation Authority had just dissolved its internment camps, and Vanport and Los Alamos were slated for disposal or normalization, so termination was part of a larger campaign to dissolve all special relationships between specific communities and the government. When Dillon Myer took John Collier's position as commissioner of the BIA in 1950, he implemented the relocation and dispersal plans that garnered him such praise in bureaucratic circles.

Attaching Indian reservations to the wave of federal community terminations might have seemed appropriate and opportune, particularly for reservations with a financial and statistical profile like that of the Klamath. Federal officials seemed not to recognize, however, that despite the similarities between the various federally managed communities, the government's unique treaty relationship made a quick and simple severance impossible. In using external markers of tribal wealth and highly mediated images of the Klamath Tribes, the BIA also ignored the complex difficulties of individual Indians struggling within the confines of the reservation system.

As early as 1944, the Interior Department reported that the Klamath Tribes assumed all costs for law enforcement and social services, paid a tuition fee from personal funds for children's education in public schools, and covered all health care except the salary of one field nurse. They were hardly wards of the government any longer, inasmuch as they were paying most of their own way, yet these statistics do not show the unusual government controls over the lives of the tribal members and their families. Agents had a hand in determining individuals' finances, employment, exercise of rights as citizens, and care of children as well as judging the validity and morality of sexual relationships. Financially, the tribes had attained independence on paper only. Socially, politically, economically, and culturally, many Klamath residents were unequipped for life as self-sufficient Americans; they would need education, training, technical assistance, economic supports, and a number of other transitional aids if they were to join the surrounding community.[1]

One of the factors that influenced government assessments of Klamaths' preparedness for independence (its overall influence is a matter of robust debate among historians) was the state of the regional timber market and the degree to which reservation timber would aid the industry as a whole. The postwar housing boom sent demand for lumber soaring, as the Northwest's ability to produce waned. President Harry S. Truman's 1945 Reorganization Act eliminated forest management programs at both the Interior Department and the BIA, leaving Indian timberlands more vulnerable to quick-profit schemes. The wartime emphasis on Klamaths as generous "timber barons" reinforced perceptions that their status as government wards was unwarranted. They appeared to be well assimilated and not in need of government assistance. The point of public welfare, after all, was to help disadvantaged Americans survive, not get rich. Only rarely did the laudatory literature on Klamaths explain that Indians received government supplies and services in exchange for land they ceded in the Treaty of 1864, not simply as "free money." By and large, the legal ramifications of treaties went unexplained even as the government met public scorn for meeting its fundamental treaty obligations.

When Collier resigned from Indian Affairs in 1945, his vision of an ethnic democracy gave way to mounting calls for Washington to extricate itself from "the Indian business." Western senators who disapproved of the socialist elements of communal property ownership and the paternalistic relationship between tribal members and the federal government cast the reservation system as something analogous to southern plantations and used this sketchy parallel as the basis for their "emancipation" campaign. The possibility of the government liquidating Indian assets and dissolving tribal entities had been part of the discourse on Indian policy for decades, argued in various permutations with varying degrees of intensity. Both the liquidation programs of the 1920s and the emancipation campaigns of the 1930s lobbied for the payment of all outstanding Indian claims against the government as a means for dissolving the treaty relationship. Congress's emancipation program had similar elements, but it was billed as Indian people's just reward for their loyal and faithful service in World War II. They had defended civilization, made the world safe against the forces of fascism, and taken a stand against racist systems of oppression. For this, they were to lose their treaty rights, their corporate land-ownership, and recognition of their tribal identity.

Washington's "emancipators" had help from a number of Klamath tribal members who mostly lived away from the reservation and had considerable financial resources and fruitful business relationships with non-Indians.[2] For all their independence, Klamath tribal assets remained under government control. Angered at the government's encroachment on both tribal assets and individual freedoms as off-reservation residents, this constituency sought to separate itself from government paternalism, even if it meant releasing reservation residents without government protections before they were fully self-sufficient.

Prominent among the off-reservation constituency was Wade Crawford, who continued to engage Congress with plans to reduce Washington's control over Klamath tribal business long after his controversial term as superintendent had ended. Having held numerous official positions on the reservation, he concluded that the only effective way to effect change was to go directly to Congress. He made so many appearances before Congress that they never questioned his claim to being spokesman for "the Klamath people." Crawford regained enough political clout to build momentum behind an emancipation bill, and Congress was glad to be able to claim that it severed treaty ties at the request of "the Klamath people." Increasingly, tribal politics became a matter of groups of "delegates" or "spokesmen" presenting themselves before congressional committees and bickering among themselves, some elected to appear for the Klamath citizenry, and others going independently to air their own grievances on behalf of "the tribes." The scene was confusing, but it was a convenient confusion that afforded congressmen sufficient "proof" that tribal members supported termination.[3]

Republicans on the Indian Affairs Subcommittee of the Senate Committee on Public Lands, in consultation with Wade and Ida Crawford, entered an "Emancipation Bill" (S. 1222) in 1947. "Emancipation" involved declaring tribal members competent to manage their affairs within in a mainstream-American context and dissolving the relationship established by the treaty. They stated that the purpose of the legislation was to turn the reservation over to the Indians and to end the most damaging federal policies, particularly those restricting Indians' sale and use of land.

The first hearings on the matter were held before the Senate on Public Lands, which heard testimony from Superintendent Bert Courtright, the Crawfords, and general council members Jesse Kirk and Boyd Jackson. To most outsiders, Utah senator Arthur Watkins's call for emancipation of Klamath aviators, movie actors, war veterans, and timber barons seemed unquestionably reasonable. The Crawfords bolstered Watkins' arguments by declaring emancipation to be the only way for Klamaths to take their place as full American citizens.[4] They railed against the BIA as strongly as Watkins praised Klamaths' achievements, focusing on the ways federal paternalism had cut them off from the political, economic, and social systems in which they were to exercise their freedoms.[5]

Watkins's straightforward arguments against federal paternalism were complicated by testimony from Oregon senator Guy Cordon. The committee expected to learn from the testimony that the residents of the Klamath Reservation were either entirely ready to manage their own affairs or that they were completely incapable of doing so. Instead, they heard individual Indians testify to their particular circumstances, exposing vast differences in each person's readiness for detribalization and opinion on the emancipation issue. One member described the Klamaths' preparation for independence in terms of being "able to do it, mentally" but not "prepared by experience." Another tribal member challenged the Klamaths' preparedness for political participation with the observation that in "the way of managing our business, we do have a certain amount to say; but after all, the Government really has the say-so as to whether we do what we would like to or not."[6]

Two older women, Mrs. Ike Mose and Mrs. Ellen Hecocta, talked about the irony of being a "rich Klamath Indian" with nothing to live on. Mrs. Hecocta testified that "[t]his day I have no way to live" even though she had her allotment and at least four hundred acres of inherited land. Mrs. Hecocta may have had valuable assets, but she had no information about how to make them profitable. She anticipated selling off some of her allotments but was unable to find buyers for her plots. She refused to "beg" Courtright for relief, and she relied on her small per capita payments and store credit to keep her from "starving to death." Tribal wealth did nothing to improve Mrs. Hecocta's life on the reservation, let alone help her navigate the complexities of the postwar American economy.[7]

George DuFault, who worked in Portland's Kaiser shipyard during the war and had not lived on the Klamath Reservation for many years, testified that such dependency only recently reached such depths. In past decades, the Klamath Reservation was a "hospitable community" where most people could earn a small living and use their per capita payments as supplemental income. Residents' credit was good, and they paid their bills promptly when they sold their cattle. DuFault believed that the longer the BIA involved itself in tribal and personal affairs, the more firmly a helpless "ward of the government" identity took hold. Tribal members became less consistent in paying their bills, lost their credit, and relied more heavily on their per capita payments and those of their children. He agreed with Mrs. Hecocta that the reservation system encouraged poverty and dependence, but on the issue of government support the two parted ways: where Hecocta saw government as the source for new solutions, DuFault saw legions of bureaucrats who could only make Indian poverty more firmly entrenched.[8]

Palpable anxiety about the prospects for the next generation ran through every tribal member's testimony. This common thread was most visible in statement after statement about the failure of the schools to prepare Klamath students for economic independence or participation in the American mainstream. Many went so far as to say that time spent in the classroom actually *hindered* families' efforts to free their children of their dependence on government. Although military discipline had been phased out of Indian schools, such "instructional activities" as cleaning chicken houses, chopping wood, doing laundry, and hoeing the garden remained central to the curriculum. Students dutifully performed their work, knowing all the while they did not have the language, business, and social studies training to succeed in the labor market.[9]

This deep, systemic alienation set off vicious cycles of "delinquent behavior" and frequent brushes with the law, which only reinforced Klamath youth's sense of frustration, hopelessness, and inferiority. While this predicament worsened, Courtright boasted to federal officials and the Klamath Falls community of the reservation's 250 high school graduates, six college attendees, and one college graduate. He never challenged government claims that Klamath's 17 percent high school graduation rate was comparable to that of any American community, and that at Klamath "the school situation certainly is O.K." He must certainly have known that schools in surrounding communities would never accept such abysmal graduation rates—particularly in the postwar era, when all educational efforts were directed toward forming the next generation of the well-adjusted suburban middle class.[10]

D. L. Miller, principal of Chiloquin High School, testified that Klamaths' education was far from "O.K." During the 1945–46 school year, eight of the twenty-five enrolled students had dropped out, and school officials were "unable to get them back into school, or did not try" because Klamath students were "educationally unprofitable." Most of the dropouts had trouble completing schoolwork, which bred frustration at their teachers' disinterest in their development and eventually humiliation. Native students were no more likely to present disciplinary problems than white students, but they were expelled at far greater rates under the rationale that "the school would be better off without them." No Klamath students graduated in 1946. Klamath educational problems became so dire that, according to the BIA's fiscal year-end report, Courtright received orders from Washington to give reservation parents a say in the school's hiring and firing decisions as a last-ditch attempt to get parents and children to stop complaining about teachers, get serious about studies, and—most importantly—boost the community's embarrassingly low graduation rates.[11]

Young Klamaths would not be the only ones for whom liquidation posed significant risks. Older tribal members were as vulnerable as the young in the mainstream capitalist marketplace. Farmer and stockman Watson Tupper, age "about 72," saw liquidating the reservation and its assets as the road to financial ruin. The reservation had been self-supporting and had sustained the Klamath Tribes for many years, but it also kept them in the dark about the competitive nature of capitalist society. Tupper declared simply, "[W]e cannot—cannot compete with the white friends of ours and never will." He further advised Indians who believed liquidation was the road to power, respect, and equal citizenship to hold on to their land base and not to "let boneheads influence you to throw your reservation over." Tupper had adopted American lifeways long ago and did well with them, but he had no information or power to negotiate life outside the reservation, making concepts of "assimilation" and "competence" more complicated than legislative language suggested.[12]

Tribal council secretary Dorothy McAnulty added that even if every tribal member were ready to vacate the treaty and the reservation, it was clear that their fellow American citizens were far from ready to welcome them into mainstream society. McAnulty, who had lived both on and off the reservation, favored ending the relationship in which tribal members were "the robots the BIA controlled." She could not envision a better life in Klamath Falls, however, where she was constantly aware of being "different from [other] citizens" and where "an Indian does not receive a fair deal." Klamath youth were not welcomed into any of Klamath Falls's social or recreational activities, and groups of Native people (especially interracial couples) were routinely refused service in restaurants and bars. The only place in town where they were allowed to congregate was along Klamath Avenue (known as "Indian Avenue"), which segregated them from the rest of the town with nothing to do but "loiter." McAnulty testified that the criminalization of Klamaths' limited social activity subjected them to incarceration. And while Indians had the right to a fair trial on paper, a 1948 government report noted that Klamath County judges took little care with cases involving Indian defendants.[13]

Proponents of liquidation turned a blind eye to these problems, portraying the Klamath Tribes as living lavishly at public expense in a cozy socialist cocoon. Will Vernon, a local rancher who leased tribal grazing lands, offered testimony on behalf of the Lake County Chamber of Commerce. The chamber of commerce had protested for decades the county's inability to tax Klamath land, and Vernon took advantage of the political climate of the moment to heighten the chamber's "freeloader" rhetoric with strenuous objections to the "communistic set-up" of the reservation. Vernon cast the BIA in the role of commissar, echoing McAnulty's criticism that the BIA made robots of Klamath Indians. Vernon's concern, however, was the emancipation not of Indian people, but of reservation resources. Wade and Ida Crawford added to charges of Communism in criticizing the BIA's "Stalin-like" control over tribal politics. The Crawfords testified that reservation agents interfered in elections, repressed anti-BIA ideas, and engaged in other "un-American activities." To substantiate their claims, the Crawfords produced a "power of attorney" signed by 180 tribal members declaring that their pro-emancipation views had been silenced by BIA officials in tribal council meetings. Mrs. Crawford recalled her disbelief at being silenced in a 1945 meeting because "we were in a war for freedom and democracy . . . and communism is what I found in that council."[14]

Interestingly, Mrs. Crawford's conclusion sheds light on the single point of consensus in the hearings — that "[t]he Klamath have been treated as children for too long and are not ready for adult life in modern competitive society." The testimony revealed the fundamental problem the government's inverse utopias created. Residents were hampered by social controls that placed obstacles on the path to assimilation, and they were in need of supports that would help them achieve greater independence. When this situation exasperated the War Relocation Authority, Topaz's "children" were simply abandoned by the federal agencies that made them dependent. Like the internees, Klamath tribal members who were unprepared for life outside the reservation were suddenly getting the message to simply "grow up fast," because no other program had worked thus far. Government officials seemed to believe that if the Japanese could adjust, so could the Indians. This view, however, failed to account for the vastly different historical experiences that shaped Japanese Americans' ability to assimilate after three years' internment versus the isolation, deprivation, and confusion after a century in the reservation system.[15]

Reactionary Rapid Assimilationism Redux

The 1948 Klamath Emancipation bill failed, but the push toward termination proceeded apace. The BIA stepped up efforts to help tribes mature by requiring each agency to submit a self-management plan to begin weaning their reservations from "federal dependence." The Klamath Agency drafted a policy whereby "the Klamath Indians and their property could be released from Federal Supervision at an early date." This initiative was hardly a new one, but it heightened anti-Communist sentiment, while a depressed regional timber supply placed Indian welfare among the secondary issues in reservation policy debates. By the end of the 1940s, even the BIA was bending toward getting rid of its expensive state-sponsored, segregated communities.[16]

Senator Watkins hailed again the emancipation of the Klamaths, while Oregon's Democratic senator Richard Neuberger blasted Watkins and Oregon Republican Douglas McKay for their transparent scheme to save the treasury the $150 million per year required to fulfill treaty obligations. According to Neuberger, "it made good political propaganda, along orthodox Republican lines, to be shutting down so expensive an undertaking," although he agreed that the reservation system failed to bring the Klamath Tribes to "the American standard." Congress showed its true social agenda by sliding in a last-minute provision to allow Klamaths to withdraw voluntarily and collect their share of assets immediately, which would also mean surrendering all further claims to tribal property. Neuberger denounced Congress for acting in the interest of the timber industry by dangling fifty thousand dollar payments in front of impoverished Indians who had no education in financial management or protections to replace those that had kept Indians ignorant of financial practices throughout the reservation era.[17]

Termination gathered steam in 1950, when Dillon Myer was appointed commissioner of the Bureau of Indian Affairs. Myer was still gathering laurels for having successfully "assimilated" the West Coast Japanese through the relocation program and for helping the Housing Authority dispose of war housing units when he arrived at the BIA. His aspirations for the Klamath Tribes were much like those he had for Topazians and Vanporters — a quick entry into the mainstream with an instant transformation to full self-sufficiency. He insisted that one of the foremost problems facing the government was to move Indians into the mainstream because reservation life "leads to a welfare type of state for the simple reason that there is not enough work available in many of the reservation areas. So poverty, problems of relocation, problems of education, problems of health and sanitation all go more or less hand in hand."[18] Neither Myer nor Congress stopped to consider that "problems of relocation" were government concerns. Indians, by and large, had no interest in leaving their homeland.

While federal officials contemplated how to do away with the reservations, veterans and defense workers returned in greater numbers than the BIA anticipated or wished. About 85 to 90 percent of Indians in defense industries returned to their reservations, straining economic resources. Myer quickly implemented his nationwide relocation program, which he had used to permanently dissolve Japanese communities at the end of the internment. As with the resettlement program at Topaz, federal funds and other forms of assistance would be used to move Indians off the reservations into industrial jobs in scattered urban areas. The BIA would provide transportation, housing, counseling, and some basic provisions for relocatees to get started.[19]

Despite the BIA's assistance packages, relocation failed to attract many Klamaths. The term *relocation* frightened many Indians because it sounded a lot like what *removal* had been in the nineteenth century, so the program was renamed "Employment Assistance." The name change—when added to an expanded benefits package that included clothing, furniture, tuition for job training, insurance, and matching-fund grants for the down payment on a house—drew a few more Klamath residents to the program, but not the numbers the BIA sought. Despite the BIA's generous provisions, between 24 and 32 percent of relocatees returned to their reservations each year. Few returnees made significant economic gains, and many were traumatized by the overwhelming foreignness of urban life. A few younger participants took advantage of the program to make short pleasure trips to distant cities by signing on and bailing out of the program, much to the consternation of the BIA.[20]

The relocation director at the Klamath Reservation had an especially hard time because Klamath peoples had almost no interest in leaving their homeland and community. His greatest triumph came in May 1957, when he received ninety-one inquiries about available training and services. The agency was dismayed to discover that most of these inquiries were from tribal members who had already established themselves outside the reservation. Single mothers showed the greatest interest in the program, but relocation officers held out "hope laced with pessimism" for their success and did not take great care with their cases. Faith Wright Mayhew's mother was one of many women who eagerly signed up for relocation. The relocation agent determined she should work as a dry cleaner and put her through an extensive training program. She paid her tuition and passed the training course with flying colors but was barred from working as a dry cleaner because she did not meet the five-foot height requirement.[21]

If nothing else, the relocation program was a strong indicator that separating the Klamath people from their reservation was an ill-fated prospect. Nevertheless, Congress passed the Klamath Termination Act in August 1954 without the consent of any recognized officials or delegates of Klamath Tribes. This occurred, in part, because federal officials declared, in spite of all evidence to the contrary, that the Klamath Tribes were fully prepared to enter the mainstream. The act required the Klamath Reservation be sold and proceeds distributed to all tribal members on the final enrollment. The Klamath Indians would be reclassified as "legal non-Indians," a sort of white-yet-not-white manufactured ethnicity, much like the popular conception of the Japanese American "non-alien enemy" that emerged in 1942.[22]

Forced to accept the changed status of their homeland and of themselves as people, tribal members were presented with two options. They could choose to withdraw from the tribe completely, taking their share in cash after a team of management specialists from Stanford University sold off sufficient acreage to pay withdrawing members. Those choosing to remain part of an informal tribal entity could join the tribal trust, which was operated by a private trustee who would manage each remaining member's assets, taking the place of the agency. In addition to liquidating tribal assets and establishing the trust, the management specialists would implement education programs as needed to prepare the Indians to assume "first-class citizenship" in time to meet the deadline on August 13, 1961. The agency had attempted to do this for a century, but to prepare for termination the BIA assembled new systems and institutions for rapid, rather than gradual, assimilation.[23]

The arrival of the management specialists sparked immediate controversy. In addition to arranging timber and land sales, they were charged with judging which tribal members could manage their own affairs and which would remain wards. Finally, they had to determine which non-federal entity would play the paternalist role when the Klamath Agency was dissolved. The Klamath General Council, angered that termination seemed to be bringing increased government intrusion, issued a resolution condemning the specialists for making too many critical decisions about personal and tribal affairs without consulting the council or even taking the time to get to know the Klamath people. A special committee of three tribal leaders was formed to "consult" with the management specialists, but they did not have decision-making power. Such familiar BIA maneuvers did little to inspire confidence or bring clarity to the purposes and processes of the Termination Act.[24]

The problem of planning for termination became more complicated for the management specialists the more they delved into the realities of social conditions on the reservation. Once the termination laws were in effect, the BIA and the management specialists began making inquiries into the competence of tribal members to manage their own affairs. They were astounded that 48.9 percent were deemed incompetent, a percentage due to the disproportionate number of minors and the number of Klamaths who were aged, suffered from untreated alcoholism, or had been officially declared non compos mentis. As preparation for termination moved forward, the specialists concluded that the premises underpinning the act were based on false information. They found that while Klamath household incomes were slightly higher than those of other Oregon reservations, they were "considerably lower" than the average incomes of non-Indians. And while farming, livestock, and wage labor represented a substantial percentage of family income, most individuals were dependent on per capita payments to raise household income above the subsistence level. Klamath people could live reasonably well on such incomes, but the medically indigent depended upon the tribally funded reservation hospital for all their health care. Public health officials worried that the most seriously ill among the Klamaths would simply be left to die.[25]

The management specialists also discovered that Klamath residents generally had very little experience with the American political system. Participation in the general council and other political bodies was also very low because people generally knew that the BIA ultimately determined all the outcomes of the political process. The specialists seemed surprised to find that the BIA was involved with every decision, either by presenting policy to the general council to rubber stamp, or by approving and vetoing general council decisions. In addition, there had never been anything resembling tribal unanimity, so most of the proceedings were hampered by factional maneuvering. Among the elderly, 3 percent spoke no English at all, which severely limited their understanding of American politics. Contrary to the image of the Klamath Tribes as fully versed in business and administrative matters, only fifteen of seventy employees of the Klamath Agency were tribal members, and none of these held administrative or finance positions.[26]

While a number of Klamath residents had solid employment histories, over two-thirds of the 270 men between eighteen and sixty-three deemed capable of working found only sporadic employment if they could find work at all, living from one per capita payment to the next. The Oregon State Employment Service informed the management specialists that, "almost without exception the employers in the Klamath Basin will not hire a Klamath Indian if they can possibly avoid doing so." The state attributed these attitudes to residents' long-standing belief that the Klamath Tribes were unskilled and unable to conform to regular work routines, making them unprofitable employees. Indian unemployment was reflected in an average annual unemployment rate of 16 percent for Indian and non-Indian workers in the area. Dutiful allotees who followed the dictates of the Allotment Act fared no better. The Oregon State University Extension Service reported that Klamath farmers and homemakers were under-skilled and would need intensive training if they were to maintain their property without the assistance of extension agents. In the end, all the premises for Klamath "emancipation" proved more illusory than substantive, yet neither Congress nor the BIA would reverse the course of termination when the bill was enacted.[27]

In this climate of uncertainty, confusion, and doubt about the wisdom of termination, tribal members were obligated to declare for themselves and their minor children whether to withdraw from the tribe and have their shares paid directly to them or to remain in the tribe under an as yet undefined management plan. Putting economic and political considerations ahead of the tribe's well being, the act imposed a firm deadline for the election, which was to be held immediately after the appraisal of tribal property. Tribal members were, for good reason, quite panicky at having to choose the course of their future as well as that of their descendants. When the executive committee of the tribal council polled the Klamath Tribes to see how many members intended to remain in the tribal entity, it prefaced the questionnaire with language heralding a grave crisis instead of long-awaited freedom: "Before long we must make the final decision according to what our thinking dictates, if we have not already done so. It is a vested right, which is proper for us to recognize, and of which the individual could not and should not be deprived."[28]

Klamaths' lack of faith in the process extended to the tribal government, whose ability to alter the course of termination was nil. It became harder to get a quorum in the general council as tribal members grew annoyed at the farcical proceedings at meetings. One tribal member recalled that when he and his mother would arrive at the council hall, a leader from "our faction" would tell them how to vote or instruct them to leave the hall before a vote was taken on a measure to prevent it being passed. The informant found the whole incident embarrassing and made a point of leaving before others received the same instructions. The exodus was, he noted, "something to see." Other tribal members saw older people being bused to the council hall, where they were told how to vote before being left in the back of the room. There they "chant[ed] away in Klamath and stamp[ed] their canes on the floor," showing no sign of understanding what was being said.[29]

The final vote shocked everyone. More than 70 percent of the tribe elected to receive a lump sum for their share of tribal assets and withdraw from the Klamath trust. Congress sprung to action to slow termination, not because there was potential harm to mass numbers of Klamath Indians, but because selling off so much timber would flood the market. Senators Richard Neuberger and Fred Seaton proposed legislation in which the federal government would acquire parts of the Klamath Marsh and the forestland would be held as public land and cut on a measured basis. This would make it possible to pay the claims on a longer timeline.

The senators also added language to the bill providing funds for extended education programs. The original bill left termination expenses to the tribal council to pay. Klamaths were angry enough at having to pay for their own dispossession, and Congress imagined a three-year extension would avoid a political firestorm on the reservation by allowing both Indians and timber companies enough time to prepare for the change. While timber dealers had adequate time to calculate profitable measured harvests, Klamaths would have three years to become worthy competitors in the market economy.[30]

The forest amendments most certainly spared everyone in the region economic disaster, but they also revealed a contradiction in termination policy. When the timber industry was imperiled, amendments to alter the course of termination passed. When advocates for the Klamaths warned Congress and the BIA of the coming disaster for the Klamath people, they were told termination was on an unstoppable legislative track. The Senate Committee on Indian Affairs was willing to hear testimony on the wisdom of termination but was selective about whom they listened to, and for how long. When general council chairman Seldon Kirk described termination as an old-fashioned land grab in a new guise and the management specialists as "puppets of the Indian Bureau," the presiding senator cut him off with a dismissive "thank you, Chief." Kirk conceded the floor with, "I have lots to say but you have squelched the thoughts that ran in my mind, so there you are."[31]

Back at the Klamath Reservation, in a sort of replay of early reservation planning, the BIA hurriedly created new federal institutions on the reservation to prepare the Klamath Tribes for rapid assimilation. Rather than building an Indian boarding school, it established a comprehensive Klamath Indian Education Program through the Oregon Department of Education and the Oregon State Extension Service to teach tribal members everything from job skills and banking and money management to how to understand the termination process. The head of the project, Hiroto Zakoji, was an anthropologist of Japanese descent who had studied the Klamath tribe as a graduate student at the University of Oregon. Prior to that, he had been confined to the Minidoka and Tule Lake relocation centers. The degree to which his experiences in the WRA camps informed his work with the Klamath Tribes is uncertain. Given that his 1956 dissertation, "Klamath Culture Change," remains a widely cited work, it is clear that his academic credentials and his longstanding concern for the Klamath people made him the ideal candidate for the position.[32]

Zakoji began the work of the Education Program with an assessment of the tribe's general preparedness to live without the benefit of their treaty rights. His findings fit the management specialists' portrayal of the state of reservation society. Klamaths had tremendous obstacles in their path to prosperous lives as equal American citizens, including delinquency, drinking, violence, intertribal conflict, negative responses to education and mainstreaming programs, and few prospects on the job market—conditions that developed and took root under BIA supervision. According to Zakoji, the rest of the staff came to the Klamath Reservation in much the same way Dillon Myer had arrived at the BIA: "without any knowledge of the Klamath Indian culture, or for that matter, without even knowing what a Klamath Indian looked like." The BIA saw the young staff's middle-class values and "missionary spirit" as their best qualifications, as they had been for reformers since the earliest days of the reservation system.[33]

To help non-Indian educators work with their new students, Zakoji's staff presented "psychological guides" to explain the general characteristics of the average Klamath personality. The guide identified six notable characteristics. Klamaths were suspicious of the motives of the federal government, of strangers, and even of members of their own tribe. They were reticent in expressing themselves and had trouble making long-range plans. Tribal members lacked confidence in their own abilities and expressed a pervasive sense of futility in improving their lot. Finally, Klamaths had a "persecution complex" and a distrust of federal authorities, which were expressed as "[d]eeply ingrained feelings of hostility over what the whites have and are doing to the Indian people." While Zakoji deemed the Klamaths' perceptions unreal, he noted that they were real to Klamaths and should be treated "as if" they were serious. By couching the failures of BIA-directed community building in terms of the Klamaths' "psychological problems," the agency could shift some of the blame for failed policies onto the Indians as it approached the point of abandoning them.[34]

Zakoji faced a more concrete obstacle to progress in Klamaths' education levels. While government statistics showed Klamaths' educational attainment to be average or somewhat better among Indian tribes, they were dismal in comparison to those of non-Indians. Klamath students had been in the public school system since 1928, and nearly one-fifth of graduates were advanced just to push them through. Little had changed at the high school level since 1947, when Principal Miller testified to elevated Klamath dropout rates. Klamath County schools were in such poor condition and had such a substandard curriculum that the BIA got the superintendent to "change the teachers that the Indians did not like to try to get the cooperation of the Indians on our program."[35]

Graduates of Chemawa Indian School, on the whole, did not fare much better than public school students. One young man, on the eve of his graduation, wrote with sadness that he was neither literate nor trained for gainful employment. Somehow, the BIA believed a crash course in good citizenship would make social, educational, and economic disadvantage irrelevant. These tactics had not worked for Klamaths in a century of reservation programming and had done little to help the Japanese leaving Topaz, yet federal planners forged ahead with the same reformatory scheme on the same speedy time frame.

The task would be impossible because Anglos had changed less than reservation Indians in the last hundred years. Their limited contact with Indians as trading partners after per capita payments were delivered, as laborers, as obstacles to reservation timber, as the criminal element, or as amusing and hapless primitives continued over decades. There had been no formal segregation in Klamath Falls, but there was a distinct low-rent area where the town's "undesirables" — poor whites, blacks, and especially Indians — could live. As in larger cities, realtors held the red line, renting to Indians with only the greatest reluctance, which they attributed not to race but to a tendency on the part of Klamath Indians to neglect their homes. When informal ghettoization failed, landlords put pressure on the government to firm up zoning restrictions to prevent termination from causing a drop in their property values. Tribal members who had lived away from the reservation long enough to have made inroads into the mainstream were of little help. Many of them refused to assist newly arrived tribal members, fearing their homes would become "Indian relocation centers for other Klamath[s]."[36]

Dispossession as Independence: The Empire for Liberty in Cold War America

The realities of their economic and social vulnerability in the mainstream were perfectly evident to the Klamath Tribes, if not to BIA officials. To many Klamaths, all roads ahead seemed to lead nowhere, and no special seminar or missionary pep talk could change that perception. Tribal members' powerlessness to change the course of their lives brought increased antisocial and self-destructive behavior at the worst possible moment. Indian Education Program workers often met indifference and occasionally violence from angry young Indian men. Zakoji's home visits sometimes interrupted drinking parties, which ignited the old furor about intrusive government paternalism. Even in less historically charged situations, angry, desperate Klamaths threatened staff members. In one instance, a tribal member demanded that an education staff member *really* listen to him by holding a knife at the worker's throat. Although there is no record of what they discussed, the two talked into the night until the Klamath man felt he had had his say. Clearly, the official report attributed the incident to the fact that interacting with "such groups of people" more frequently increased the likelihood of conflict and danger. There was no word for *resistance* in the lexicon of termination. Every act and word of protest from a tribal member made him or her yet another case for educational specialists.[37]

The hardest problems to solve were those that stemmed from economic policies on the reservation, in which the paternal figures of Congress and the superintendent had separated Klamath individuals from their economic resources and from most decisions determining how they gained, saved, and used those resources. The Klamath business committee had been involved in small tribal matters, such as petitioning Congress for tribal expenses, managing the Tribal Loan Fund, and consulting on issues of timber sales, but individuals had been isolated from mainstream economic life. The BIA had negotiated, drafted, and administered lease agreements; guaranteed credit; served as a collection agent; and acted on behalf of the Indians in every personal financial transaction. The per capita system exacerbated Indians' misunderstanding of mainstream economic life by positioning the BIA as sole provider to each person, separating economic gain from employment and investment. This arrangement was perhaps the strongest bond of dependency and the most dangerous to break suddenly.[38]

The program published a reservation-wide newspaper in 1956 called the *Klamath Tribune*, which provided news of termination and taught Klamaths the basics of American economic life. It featured numerous photographs for those unable to read and included ample space for tribal members' questions. Regular question-and-answer columns presented useful information for making wills, participating in elections, and understanding the roles of various government officials. The questions, however, were shockingly elementary for someone who would need to be fully functional in legal, political, and economic life. People were uncertain if they could make wills without approval from the secretary of the interior. Others wondered why wills were made at all. Still others asked how the sheriff was chosen, what his duties were, who was eligible to vote, and whether there were towns other than Klamath Falls in which one could register to vote. The last question is especially telling, given that three towns—Chiloquin, Beatty, and Fort Klamath—had registrars and were within the reservation boundary.[39]

Alongside the *Tribune*'s straight talk on American citizenship were mixed messages about young Klamaths' potential as "first-class citizens." Klamath youths who already had some cultural capital in the mainstream were able to use the educational opportunities Zakoji's program offered to great advantage. Several were successful in vocational and professional programs at nearby community colleges and universities, in fields ranging from gunsmithing to nursing, commercial illustration to accounting. These young people were placed at the vanguard of Klamaths' entry into the economic mainstream, even forming a Klamath Reservation Junior

Chamber of Commerce. Although they were to be an important segment of the post-termination Klamath community, they were encouraged to stay away from their families and the reservation so as to "stick to the grindstone" and avoid the "personal problems which reflect into family relationships." The Indian Education Program's policy seems to indicate that Klamaths had such serious impediments to being fully functioning "first-class citizens" that they could taint those who had a better chance of leading a successful American life.[40]

The inner pages of the *Klamath Tribune* showed a very different picture. Images of broken Klamath youth lying unconscious in drunk-driving accidents or gazing through the bars of a jail cell appeared in every issue. The captions reminded parents that "their future is in your hands" and instructed them not to let minors drink and to limit their own consumption as well. Other ads described Klamath children as "lonely and in trouble" and in need of parents to teach them "respect for the law, respect for property, respect for other people and respect for [themselves]" by setting an example.[41] For many Klamath parents, the reservation system and rapid termination made that all but impossible, and being saddled with the responsibility for problems caused by poorly conceived federal policies did not help.

Following the assessment of reservation land and the announcement that each tribal member would receive forty-eight thousand dollars, it became clear that some provision for minors and unprepared ("incompetent") members would have to be implemented. A trust was established for remaining tribal members at the U.S. Bank of Oregon. The bank knew nothing about the Klamath Tribes, but they offered the lowest bid for services. They opened a Chiloquin branch, and bank employees acted as trust officers, approving or disapproving transactions for every personal expense of the remaining Klamaths, just as reservation agents had done. Individual Klamaths could not access their funds directly and found that the stream of questions that came with requests for things like drugstore items were all the more humiliating because the interrogation took place in front of the wider population that scorned them, instead of just fellow Klamaths. Often, the trust officer treated the Klamaths with suspicion, as if they were begging for handouts or pulling a scam. In reality, the Termination Act had not made the remaining tribal members free, self-determining citizens at all. The government had simply privatized agency functions, which made terminated tribes more subservient to more institutions than ever before.[42]

The loss of treaty protections and services made the trustees vulnerable to lawyers and guardians who were purely corrupt, as opposed to the BIA, which was often confused, conflicted, and prone to convenience but not always malevolent. An investigation in the mid-1960s found that attorneys hired to act as guardians for remaining members charged a special "Indian guardianship rate" that was three times the prescribed rate set by the Oregon Bar Association. There were no agents to intervene in the scam, and the guardians would have to agree to allow aggrieved Klamath trustees to withdraw the necessary funds from their own accounts to file suit. When the tribe voted to terminate the trust, they had no idea the bank would attempt to sell the remaining 135,000 acres to distribute tribal assets in cash, rather than acreage. The federal government retained the land, forming the Winema National Forest instead of a restored Klamath homeland.[43]

Severing the federal government's relationship to the Klamaths saved $148 million in BIA services, gained $250 million in timber sales on former reservation lands, and decreased America's Indian population by revoking the Klamaths' tribal designation. A majority of tribal members opposed rapid termination because this policy, like the creation of the treaty, dispossessed them. One council member's lament echoes those of the treaty signers: "[W]e thought we would have a homeland . . . for all time not knowing laws and things that could be altered and changed and shifted around." As the management specialists warned, the isolation of the reservation and its false institutions had left the tribe woefully unprepared to fend for itself in the wider community.[44]

Their report was accurate. Most members, on receiving their share of liquidated tribal assets, which amounted to about forty-eight thousand dollars per person, fell prey to unscrupulous businessmen or to the guardians assigned to them by the BIA. Curiosity about what the Indians would do with such enormous lump sums was great enough for the *New York Times* to send a reporter to Klamath Falls. Stores and auto dealers swelled their inventories, while mutual fund and insurance salesmen planned their first visits to reservation homes. Interestingly, the *Times* portrayed Klamaths as being generally very prudent with their share of tribal assets. Other accounts played up their spending sprees, featuring auto sales to Indians who paid in cash with big bills carried in paper bags or stuffed in their pockets. After that, the Klamath Tribes disappeared from public view, from congressional responsibility, and from the public consciousness in the Klamath Falls area, where most tried to forge a life for themselves despite numerous handicaps.[45]

Although forty-eight thousand dollars seemed like an enormous amount of money, it was enough to buy a house and a car, with little left over. Not having been told this, Klamaths treated it as any other per capita payment (only much bigger) and used it to "assimilate" themselves by purchasing the consumer goods that were emblems of the American standard of living, such as cars, furniture, appliances, vacations, and clothing. Their standard of living plummeted, however, from extravagant to worse than ever within a matter of months. Klamaths' new possessions were repossessed or lost through their inability to pay property taxes or lack of information in home finance and other financial matters.

The loss of a land base, community, and legally recognized Indian identity bred deep despair that manifested itself in state statistics on alcoholism, suicide, violent crime, delinquency rates, and family disintegration among the Klamaths. The BIA knew that Klamaths were struggling, but it refused to abolish termination policy until 1986, when it restored the Klamaths' tribal status. The restoration of federal recognition gave the tribes some benefits but no land base. With that, Klamaths were left to fend for themselves, and the odds looked worse than ever as a generation of young Klamaths fell prey to poverty, chemical dependency, violence, and suicide. Klamaths were informed they were no longer Indians, yet they were clearly not full American citizens either. In an interview for a 1991 documentary film, one tribal member said of the Klamaths' status, "We had no home, no name, no identity. We were just a bunch of people with nothing."[46]

The Issei bachelors in Chicago and the Vanport flood victims may well have said the same thing. Only Los Alamosans, who held status in the American mainstream, were able to retain anything through the war and reenter American life when their federal community experience was over. White Vanporters with politically moderate views had an easier time as well, because they could eventually "pass" as Portlanders. For racial minorities and outspoken radicals at Klamath, Topaz, and Vanport, however, inverse-utopian life only reinforced their prewar Otherness. No matter how many resources the federal government put toward engineering postwar assimilation, its efforts only widened the gulf between the worlds inside and outside the perimeters of each enclave. Although rapid assimilation seemed to be the last best hope for bringing outsiders into the citizenry, the result was tragic for the thousands of Americans who fell into the breach.

Termination did not make the Klamath people or their ties to the land disappear. Nearly 60 percent of all tribal members remained near Klamath Falls, with an additional 30 percent living elsewhere in Oregon. Of the four federal community groups in this study, the Klamath Tribes were hit hardest by the loss of their federal reservation. In addition to losing critical federal protections and supports, Klamaths lost their homeland. For most tribal members, however, the most devastating blow dealt by termination was their redesignation as "legal non-Indians." The nonsensical label situated Klamaths outside the Indian community as well as the general American citizenry. Younger tribal members' attempts to reconfigure their social identity according to the label resulted in unending confusion and rejection from all corners of society.

The long, slow process of de-Indianizing the Klamath Tribes culminated in 1974, when the government purchased the last 9,693 acres of tribal lands and subsequently put them up for sale to the highest bidder. The sale was U.S. Bank's answer to the remaining Klamath members' petition to free themselves from the U.S. Bank trust. Instead of finding a new trustee, the bank liquidated all remaining Klamath assets and distributed the proceeds to tribal members, bringing an end to any formal Klamath organization and repeating earlier errors in which large cash payments were quickly depleted. Having lost any ties to their ancestral lands and their last vestige of tribal organization, Klamath citizens were truly placeless.[47]

Members who elected to withdraw in 1954 assimilated fairly well because they generally had higher income levels and lived off the reservation well before termination. Yet a study conducted by an Oregon state task force found most Klamaths had a limited understanding of what they had voted for when they approved termination. Years later, even Klamaths who had a promising start suffered from the loss of treaty protections. The government did not help them reverse their high rates of unemployment, incarceration, and homelessness, or stem the staggering death rates from accidents, alcoholism and drug overdose, homicide, and suicide. Klamath County welfare services had hundreds of "legal non-Indians" in their caseloads, but a study of Klamath Falls child welfare cases revealed that judges continued to use the "drunken Indian" stereotype to terminate Klamath parental rights without cause. Foster care and trans-racial adoptions became Klamath children's post-termination program for assimilation. This radically invasive policy fragmented families and dashed the heart of tribal life, and it never fulfilled the promises put forth in every major policy statement since the Treaty of 1864. Federal bureaucrats never realized the goals of Native self-sufficiency, self-determination, and political efficacy. Progress toward freedom and independence are only being realized through the work of Native individuals who persist in the 140-year-long struggle to live as Klamath, Modoc, and Yahooskin peoples — as *maqlaqs* — and not as government wards.[48]

CHAPTER SEVEN

NO CAMPS FOR COMMIES

The Dual Legacies of Dissonance and Dissidents

In 1950, as federal bureaucrats and their former wards assessed the results of their inverse-utopian experiments, Senator Pat McCarran sounded a warning to the American people. In a speech reminiscent of President Franklin D. Roosevelt's post–Pearl Harbor fireside chat about the threat from "crafty and powerful bandits" in Japan, McCarran informed Americans that "unidentified, uncontrolled communists" were engaged in "guerilla warfare of ideas fought principally by infiltration into the body politic of those people whose political convictions and dogmas conflict with those of this democracy." Fearing that the very life of the nation was at risk from an invisible internal enemy, McCarran sponsored the Internal Security Act, which allowed preventative detention if there was "reasonable cause to believe a person could pose a security danger to the state" in the event of insurrection, invasion, or declaration of war.[1]

Like the Japanese following Pearl Harbor, Communist Party members were required to register with the FBI. Knowing that saboteurs were unlikely to identify themselves, the FBI and Department of Justice "accumulated . . . the names, identities, and activities of individuals found to be potentially dangerous to the internal security through investigation." The resulting index numbered more than twelve hundred people for whom habeas corpus would be suspended in the event of a national emergency. The accused would have the opportunity to make the case for their innocence before a hearing board, but the procedure would not be bound by rules of evidence. FBI director J. Edgar Hoover noted in a letter to one of President Harry S. Truman's advisors that "the plan does not distinguish between aliens and citizens and both are included in its purview" but that it was possible to apply it exclusively to aliens.[2]

In addition, the Department of Justice would keep six "concentration camps" at the ready to detain between 12,000 and 15,000 people who the government believed "probably will engage or probably will conspire with others to engage in acts of espionage and sabotage." Passage of the act did not fully address what the government perceived as a growing crisis: the FBI's list of "hard-core" Communist subversives had reached approximately 22,663, leaving the government several thousand beds short in its "commie camps."[3]

Communists were spared confinement to barbed-wire democracies, but only after the administration calculated the financial and political costs of building new camps. Soviet emissaries were quick to draw parallels between the new camps and the War Relocation Authority (WRA) camps, which had already been relegated to history as America's "worst wartime mistake." Military intelligence intercepted Soviet propaganda detailing the federal government's plan to detain "progressive elements" in the camps without due process whenever national security crises arose. When a Soviet delegate to the United Nations mentioned the Communist concentration camps in the *New York Times*, military intelligence feared Moscow propagandists had an item in its "chamber of horrors" as dangerous as its "germ warfare theme." As the planning-stage camps became an unaffordable political liability, the idea was scrapped in favor of a registration system.[4] The decision was probably fairly easy to make, given recent revelations that all the security measures at Los Alamos had failed to prevent Klaus Fuchs (and eventually David Greenglass and Ted Hall) from channeling information to the Soviets that would expedite their development of the bomb by an estimated twelve to eighteen months.[5]

There was also little chance the "commie camps" would have ended internal subversion because individuals who had violated the antisubversion statues in the Smith Act of 1940 had already been charged and imprisoned. This was the lesson the government learned from Indians like Keintpoos, who was imprisoned and executed at Fort Klamath for his resistance in the Modoc War. The FBI was quick to arrest Japanese community leaders in the days after Pearl Harbor, place African American workers and their white radical counterparts under RACON surveillance, and support the MED's decision to bar Leo Szilard from Los Alamos. Although there were very few saboteurs among this set of individuals, the important point is that they were investigated as individuals, not swept away as part of an indistinct, racially or politically specific mass.

If the McCarran Internal Security Act had been signed into law, there would have been camps full of people whose only crime was being perceived as having "disloyal tendencies." Meanwhile — if the recent past is any guide — actual traitors of the Fuchs-Hall variety, as real spies, would either defy detection entirely and never go to camp (such was the case of Harry Gold, Fuchs's and Hall's handler in New Mexico) or would continue to operate within the camp by staying under the radar. To avoid suspicion, neither Fuchs nor Hall, for instance, was a card-carrying Communist. They were obedient Los Alamosans throughout the project, so military security paid relatively little attention to their off-duty activities. One could expect the same from McCarran's Communist operatives; they would not be among the First-Amendment aficionados making a ruckus in the public square. The camp would be long on American leftists and short on Soviet agents.

Why would one congressional committee fight for new camps when other branches of government were working so hard to terminate "socialist" reservations and ineffective government communities? The combination of high security, extensive social welfare, and scaled-down democratic institutions in Oregon, California, and New Mexico (to some degree) offered swift and simple responses to an array of complex security challenges and palliated fears about who might be likely to commit a breach. Unable to readily identify such individuals, let alone subject them to the rigors of due process, the U.S. government and the American people created the "red subversive" profile just as they had the "Indian hostile," the "disloyal Jap" and the "race-riot radicals" in the past.

The McCarran Act would have soothed America's collective psyche by identifying names, faces, and serial numbers in an abstract "red menace." It could wrap the threat in barbed wire, move the threat to the desert, watch everything it did, and, most fantastically, transform it into something patriotic through participation in pantomime democracies, structured work programs, and citizenship education. Then, once the "threat" was neutralized, its constituent individuals could rejoin American society as "first-class citizens," thus creating an inclusive, harmonious American family. The appeal of such a flawed utopian scheme to an anxious society is clear: casting a wide net appeared to be a surefire way to put all internal enemies out of commission. But if the inverse-utopian experience offered any lesson at all to legislators considering the McCarran Act, it was that the government's inverse utopias did far more to divide the nation along ethnic and political lines than it did to keep them safe and peaceful.

The McCarran Act stood to do more harm than good to the strength of the nation. Like earlier preventative detention measures, the act presumed that everyone who fits a particular profile is not innocent until proven guilty but has "dangerous tendencies" that warrant isolation, detention, and curtailed civil liberties. "Communists," like "foreigners" and "subversives" at Klamath, Topaz, Vanport, and Los Alamos, were suspected not because of what they did but because of who they were—an affront to American notions of social equality and the rule of law. Although officials were quick to admit that these groups consisted of mostly innocent people, confining them en masse sent a conflicting message. These were populations that could not be entirely trusted, so the government drew clear lines between them and the rest of the nation. Segregation has never been a tool of acceptance or a way to honor peoples' positive (or potentially positive) qualities. It draws lines in the sand that place the rejected group on the defensive against the institutions that put them there.

The government's problems started the minute it began housing its populations with "hostile tendencies" because its own officials had, in all four cases, already assumed a hostile stance and created a hostile environment. Residents of inverse utopias quickly realized that the soldiers at Fort Klamath were there to police them, that barbed wire surrounded Topaz to detain them, that agents patrolled Vanport to curb their political activity, and that the listening posts and armed guards monitored Los Alamos scientists, not necessarily saboteurs. It was also immediately clear to residents that their protection was a secondary consideration. The head counts, censored letters, confiscated books, closed perimeters, plainclothes agents, and armed guards only widened the gap between "real" Americans and suspect ones, curtailing the freedoms of individuals who had neither committed a crime nor conspired to do so. Set against government rhetoric that it was offering extra-special care through "protective custody" or a "worker's utopia," many residents began to see these "little Americas" as a grand hypocrisy.

The disjuncture between rhetoric and reality only grew through the communities' political, economic, and educational institutions. Government experts' structuring of community government to limit residents' decision-making power communicated their distrust of residents. One of the clearest signs was the way in which project directors bestowed legitimacy on "appropriate" community leaders and set their legislative parameters only wide enough to fulfill the federal government's agendas. As Vine Deloria Jr. points out in his discussion of reservation governments, restricted power precludes self-determination. While systems of restricted self-governance are preferable to more autocratic alternatives, they are not democratic, and they do not invest community members with significant political power. Far from regenerating democracy and individual initiative in the new western settlements, life in wartime federal communities either bred a political apathy born of learned helplessness, sowed seeds of distrust in the federal government, or stoked the flames of lifelong political activism. These were not the hopeful outcomes the government had anticipated in its plans for any of its barbed-wire democracies.[6]

Economic policies in all four communities only increased the dissonance in the government's messages about how to be a true American citizen. If property ownership and free enterprise were the cornerstones of American independence, how would people unable to engage in either prove their fitness to enter the democratic arena of free-market capitalism?

Even the Klamath Tribes, who did own property, had little control over what they did with their resources, ultimately rendering self-sufficient peoples government dependents. While Klamaths heard repeatedly that economic independence was one of the markers of the "maturity" needed for citizenship, it remained elusive to all but a few. Termination arguably fostered independence of a sort, but for Klamaths, Modocs, and Yahooskins who had experienced generations of wardship, their "emancipation" meant abandonment by a government looking for the ultimate way out of the insolvable "Indian question."

While Topazians, Vanporters, and Los Alamosans had a wider range of postwar alternatives, they, too, were left to deal independently with the property loss, dislocation, stigmatization, chronic health problems, and other impediments to economic self-sufficiency. One of the worst ironies of all was that, for all the discussion of "Americanization," the managed economies in inverse utopias made dependents of people with no history of accepting charity or public assistance. Native Americans had thriving precontact economies, which they maintained until the United States enacted its removal policies from the 1830s to the 1870s. Japanese Americans had the lowest rates of access to social services and welfare agencies, even during the Great Depression. Many Vanporters had availed themselves of New Deal programs during the war, but most had long employment histories and valued their independence. ("Rosie the Riveters" were an exception, though they, too, sought unprecedented economic independence by crossing the gendered frontier.) Los Alamosans also tended to be relatively affluent and steadily employed, as faculty positions and graduate assistantships tend to be less vulnerable to the forces of economic downturns.[7]

Labor, ordinarily the means by which poorer Americans ascend the ladder of affluence and social respectability, was tied more closely to social control than the accumulation of wealth in the Klamath Indian Reservation and the three wartime communities. With the exception of Los Alamosans and Vanporters who left before the flood, the closing of federal communities left all too many people with little to show for their labor and impeded their access to good jobs outside the community. One can only wonder what role such structured work routines might have played in the Americanization of interned Communists, given their attunement to the political dynamic between labor, capital, and the state.

Although it seems unlikely that children would have been sent to McCarran's camps, it is important to consider that the dissonances about freedom and citizenship rang loudly in the ears of school children as well as adults. Attending schools in an inverse utopia was, to quote Thomas James's study of WRA schools, "a tangle of opportunity and oppression." Some students found greater opportunities in Topaz; attending an all-Japanese school, they were not barred from activities like cheerleading and student council. But they also knew that they were falling behind their peers academically. Several students had to pursue remedial education before applying to college, and those with intact academic credentials were taught that well-educated Americans would reject them on the basis of their ethnic difference. Yet when they were sent from their government enclaves into the mainstream, they were bombarded with assurances that race and class had no bearing on their ability to succeed alongside their white counterparts.[8]

Young people experienced confusing gaps between rhetoric and reality that left many unprepared to face the challenges outside their enclosed community. In this way, the government's Americanization program hampered the promise of self-sufficiency by making it harder for the next generation to envision themselves as full and equal Americans. The government's inverse utopias did not fulfill the American promise that government would provide an even playing field for individuals to participate in political and economic life. They did not offer the education for social mobility that Americans since Horace Mann had considered both a birthright and an essential function of government. They did not promote integration but exacerbated marginalization.

As security structures, the inverse utopias functioned no better. Indian tribes had mostly been friendly to traders and settlers until whites threatened their lands and their lives. The Japanese American community did not participate in the Pearl Harbor bombing, and the FBI found no evidence that they engaged in sabotage in the interim period between Pearl Harbor and their removal. Vanporters were mostly patriotic war workers and families trying to pull out of the Depression. Los Alamosans were predominantly scientists devoted to freedom and to the advancement of knowledge, but the few who were disloyal were undeterred by the security and surveillance systems. The cost to loyal individuals and the integrity of American civil liberties was tremendous, and the gains toward national security negligible.

The federal government was not alone in struggling to assess the significance of its utopian experiments. Most federal community residents spent years recovering from the effects of being uprooted and isolated and considering whether they ought to make a public response. Most evaluated their time in federal communities in terms of the tradeoffs they had to make. The Klamath Reservation allowed the tribes to live on or near their ancestral homelands in a period when distant removal and extinction had been the government's approach to Indian people during the "inevitable" course of white settlement, resource exploitation, and economic development. Topazians were kept at a safe distance from California vigilantes who might have done them harm, and care was given to preserve as many of their freedoms and as much of their normal lives as the WRA could afford within budgetary and security restrictions. The living conditions of many Vanporters improved greatly following the years of economic depression. And Los Alamos scientists found their "Hollywood," an ideal community in which the great lights of their profession gathered to accomplish an important scientific mission. Better still, the army allowed families on the project in spite of its budgetary and security concerns. For many, the government made a mess of things, but it did not intend deliberate harm.

Others had a harder time putting their experiences to rest because the injustices were hard to articulate. Filmmaker Emiko Omori's statement that the internment was hard to talk about not because it was so bad but because "it wasn't that bad" applies as readily to Klamaths, Vanporters, and Los Alamosans as it does to Topazians. Former WRA internees are quick to distance the internment from Hitler's program of mass extermination, but it then becomes difficult to describe the intangible devastation of their own forced confinement. Black Vanporters echo similar uncertainties. The more evident horrors of lynching in the South made it difficult to convey what it meant to experience less overt forms of discrimination in the North and to lose in the Vanport flood whatever they had gained. Not only were the Klamath Tribes spared the extermination campaigns that wiped out numerous California tribes, they enjoyed a higher standard of living than many other reservation communities. While Klamaths suffered clear injustices in termination policy, they shared Topazians' and Vanporters' difficulty in fully assessing the damages from living in federal communities.[9]

Much of the difficulty in naming the problem stemmed from the fact that the federal government did not build fascist dystopias; it built inverse utopias, where all the key features of American life were in place but geared to work backwards. Representative government furthered government autocracy, economic participation fostered economic dependency, public education promoted second-class citizenship, and admission to the mainstream left many on the margins of American life. In no sense were these communities death camps, torture centers, or prisons in the strict sense. This left residents quite grateful but still confused about what, in fact, these communities actually *were*. Without the language to adequately describe Klamath, Topaz, Vanport, and Los Alamos, former residents were hard-pressed to voice their complaints or to make specific demands for redress.

Over the years, however, victims of this dissonance sorted through the rhetoric and realities of their experiences and became true dissidents. No matter how they were viewed by others or how they self-identified before war broke out, the war turned the people in all four communities into both insiders and outsiders. They were insiders in so far as they were expected to cooperate with the great American cause: the expansion of Thomas Jefferson's Empire for Liberty. Yet they were outsiders to the extent that they were viewed as dangerously "Other." Residents' fluctuating insider-outsider status initially carried many people down in confusion, but over time they used it as a unique position from which to argue authoritatively.

Political and legal challenges continued long after the protested built environments were gone, and they continued to intensify over the course of several decades. Although many of the campaigns by former wards were responses to their postwar circumstances, resistance had been a part of life since the opening day at each inverse utopia. The impressive roster of dissenters includes Keintpoos (Captain Jack), Jesse Kirk, Fred Korematsu, Miné Okubo, Sam Markson, Laura Kellar, Eleanor Jette, and Bences Gonzales. One of the great ironies of McCarran's call for "commie camps" is that Indians, Japanese American civil rights advocates, Vanport activists, and former Manhattan Project staff critical of the postwar nuclear program would most certainly be among the Americans housed there.

In fact, the House Un-American Activities Committee's hunt for "reds" in the West led it immediately back to Vanport and Topaz. After the Vanport Citizens' Emergency Disaster Committee disbanded, some members channeled their energies into the American Veterans Committee and the Progressive Party campaign to elect Henry Wallace as president in 1948. The activists were reunited in June 1954, when the House Un-American Activities Committee held hearings in Portland. The witnesses included Vanport Citizens' Emergency Disaster Committee members Spencer Gill and Thomas Moore (who led the caravan to the capitol), Robert Cannon, Homer Owen (who wrote the confrontational telegram to Governor John Hall), and Sam Markson (the worker arrested at Vanport for fraternizing with his black neighbors). Nels Peterson, who co-organized the caravan to the capitol with Gill, served as counsel to several of the accused. None of the witnesses mentioned Vanport by name (nearly everyone invoked the Fifth Amendment), yet the fact that so many Vanporters were called to testify suggests a link between challenging the federal government's policies and being cast as having questionable national loyalties.[10]

Four years after writing a series of newspaper articles criticizing the federal government for abandoning the victims of the Vanport flood, journalist Julia Ruuttila was called before the House Un-American Activities Committee (HUAC) to explain why she endorsed the Communist Party's plan for comprehensive flood relief. When she explained how she had been pleased that *someone* had finally come up with a plan, the HUAC spotlighted her dismissal from the Oregon Public Welfare Commission in 1948 for misusing agency files to write an exposé on the commission's refusal to assist homeless Vanporters. The publicity that followed might have discouraged any journalist from taking on the government, but even after being publicly branded a "red," Ruuttila went on to expose provisions of the McCarran Internal Security Act that would have placed suspected communists behind barbed wire.[11] While they savored the triumph of termination and managed the emerging threats of the atomic age, government officials were exasperated by an advocate for Vanport flood victims who reminded the public of the WRA camps. After all, Vanport was built to unify disparate citizens in a time of national crisis, not to serve as a symbol of social division and government malfeasance. Nevertheless, dissent has remained one of the most persistent unintended legacies of the government's utopian quest for social order.

Even the Japanese, America's postwar "model minority," whose representation in civil rights and radical political organizations was notably small, became suspect in California in a sort of postwar permutation of anti-Japanese agitation. As Topazians prepared to return to California, the state government published a report linking American Communists with Japanese Americans. The logic was this: American Communists kept close ties with the Soviets. Stalin had quickly reestablished friendly relations with Japan. Japanese Americans, though U.S. citizens, had blood ties to Emperor Hirohito (a view that largely went by the wayside during and after the U.S. occupation of Japan), which made them politically beholden to Stalin. This thin, fantastical tie to Stalin firmly bound the returnees from the relocation centers to the Communist infiltrators the nation had grown to fear.

The report continued to advise loyal Californians that the Communists cared little about social justice and only feigned outrage over the internment in order to turn the Japanese communities against the United States and lure them to Communism (ignoring the fact that the Party supported the evacuation in 1942). The state of California embellished this theory by suggesting that the Japanese American Citizens League (JACL), the Japanese American Committee for Democracy, and the American Civil Liberties Union were part of an elaborate network of Communist front organizations poised to conduct subversive operations in California. The HUAC did not find many Communists among Klamaths, Topazians, Vanporters, or Los Alamosans, but they did locate activists who sought justice and accountability for the decisions that the government made for them as *parens patriae*.[12]

This political trend is most pronounced among Klamaths, whose very identification as tribal members instead of as "legal non-Indians" was an act of resistance. Before joining the leadership of the American Indian Movement (or AIM, founded in 1968), Russell Means was a regular at an Indian bar in San Francisco called Warren's, which was owned by a Klamath family who purchased it with their share of liquidated tribal assets. Means recalls in his autobiography that he had not heard much about termination and, like Native people across the country, did not understand why any tribal group would vote to "sell off" their reservation "at 1850 prices." After several conversations with Klamaths at Warren's and some reflection on how tribal governance worked on all reservations, he concluded that "[t]ermination happened because the Tribal Council was an extension of the BIA, rubberstamping everything, and the BIA relentlessly bombards them with propaganda and promises of great benefits. If the tribe says yes, the payment's okay—if no, Termination happens anyway, but the payment is less." In Means's view, termination was the federal government's way of saying, "Here's a little money for everything we've done to you, for everything we're doing to you now, and for everything we're going to take away from you—and to hell with your heritage, to hell with your children, to hell with your future."[13]

Many Topazians, Vanporters, and Los Alamosans made similar charges that their government, in its function *parens patriae*, treated their futures dismissively, particularly when it was under pressure to move them into or out of their reservations. After Axis propagandists made hay with the WRA camps, Portlanders decried Vanport as the seed of a future slum, and New Mexicans learned they had a city of scientists and a center of intrigue and espionage, each community was forced to disappear or, in the case of Los Alamos, refashion itself into the democracy it never was. Despite the discussion of "restoring independence," Washington was primarily interested in removing these clusters of "undesirables" from both the physical and social landscapes.

Much to Washington's consternation, neither the emerging Red Power movement of the late 1960s nor the Klamath Tribes would allow the

Treaty of 1864 to disappear amidst the rush to termination. Once tribes across the nation realized, like Russell Means, that Klamaths did not "sell out" their reservation, the Red Power leadership added reversing the termination laws, reclaiming lost lands, and restoring tribal sovereignty and federal recognition for terminated tribes to its burgeoning agenda. National activists brought termination back into the national discourse in 1972, when more than five hundred travelers on the Trail of Broken Treaties presented their Twenty-Point Plan to President Richard Nixon calling for, among other things, repeal of the Klamath Termination Act, restoration of tribal land bases, and an end to federal authorities using threats of termination to coerce tribes with intact reservations into compliance. The plan also confronted the "widely known" practice of federal agents appointing reservation leadership. Tribal councils and other leadership positions had been created by federal agencies "desirous of having an Indian front group to work behind," as had been the case at Klamath with the appointment of leaders like Allen David and Wade Crawford.[14]

Meanwhile, back at what had been the Klamath Reservation, World War II veteran Edison Chiloquin waged his own war against the termination proceedings. Known mostly for his aimlessness and public drunkenness after the war, Chiloquin single-handedly thwarted plans to complete termination by refusing his forty-eight thousand dollar check for his share of tribal assets. When the federal government offered him $103,000 to surrender his allotment, Chiloquin again refused, explaining that the land was sacred and tradition was not a commodity. The U.S. Forest Service held the check in his name, assuming Chiloquin's "stubbornness" would wear out.

Instead, Chiloquin and his family built a village called Arrowhead, where the culture, traditions, and birthright of all Klamath people would be preserved. Younger Indians were especially encouraged to receive instruction in traditional lifeways at Arrowhead. Chiloquin and his supporters wanted to prepare a generation of young leaders in the hope that the Klamath Tribes would regain federal recognition, their lost lands, and the right to an independent tribal government. Arrowhead was the last connection younger Klamaths had to the tribal community, and because children born after termination were not on tribal enrollments, the village helped ensure that large numbers of the "lost generation" could be located easily and added to the official tribal membership.[15]

In the meantime, villagers built teepees from donated canvas for on-site housing and began to raise money for the village. They shared labor and resources, living independently of federal, state, and local government. Chiloquin and the Committee to Save the Remaining Klamath Indian Lands filed suit against U.S. Bank in 1972. The suit charged the bank with abuse of its position as trustee, particularly when it liquidated tribal lands in response to the tribes' decision to change its trusteeship arrangements. Although the suit did not reverse the final liquidation, it became the basis for passage of HR 7960 in 1980, which placed former reservation land managed by the U.S. Forest Service in Chiloquin's custody on the condition that it be used solely for "traditional Indian purposes." If Chiloquin and his heirs used the land for anything else, it would revert immediately to the Forest Service. In this small way, Chiloquin revived the relationship between the federal government and the Klamath Tribes, if only to secure conditional protection of Indian land-use rights. Chiloquin started a sacred fire in the spring of 1976, which Arrowhead residents vowed to keep burning until the Forest Service ceded Chiloquin's land to him completely.[16]

The Klamath Tribes scored a victory in 1986, when Congress voted to restore Klamaths' tribal status and to make all the 1,988 members on the final enrollment eligible for benefits as enumerated in statutes and the Treaty of 1864. The bill was written in recognition of the Arrowhead villagers and other Klamath activists in the area. Of these, a number adopted the Klamath Constitution of 1954 as the charter for a tribal political entity and fought successfully for the lost hunting, fishing, and water rights that were supposed to remain in place after termination. The Restoration Act went beyond merely conferring federal recognition on Klamaths; it acknowledged government wrongdoing in implementing the Klamath Termination Act. Instead of requiring Klamaths to achieve "economic self-sufficiency," a new BIA directive implemented a program of "economic self-development" as the next phase of the Klamaths' road to independence. The change in policy followed a review of the legislative history of the Klamath Termination Act, which revealed that "tribal members were never asked whether or not they were in favor of the bill."[17]

Public Law 99-398 included some subtle but significant changes. It ordered the secretary of the interior to conduct a special election for tribal government officers, but only on written request of the Klamath Tribes. Each phase of the Klamath Tribes Economic Self Sufficiency Plan would be subject to approval of the tribes, in addition to congressional review. The Restoration Act did not give Klamaths their land base, and activists continue to focus their energies on regaining their greatest loss. Klamath leaders assert that recovering their land base is essential to repairing the damage done to their community and their lives as individuals.

Arrowhead was a powerful force in Klamath politics for another reason. For the first time since the signing of the 1864 treaty, Klamath people were living on Klamath lands as builders of their own communities and agents of their own destiny. The teepees and sacred areas sprung up among numerous geographic features named after the Applegates, the trailblazing family of Klamath Indian agents. The Klamath presence continues to grow stronger in southern Oregon. Barbara Alatorre, historian and researcher for the Klamath Self-Development Plan, works through thousands of government and tribal documents archived in cardboard boxes in the kitchen of her small, brilliant-blue southeast Portland house. Persistent and determined, she is preparing to take on the National Park Service with a book about Crater Lake that recasts its significance from simply being the deepest lake in the United States to being the most sacred place in Klamath cosmology. Of perhaps greater significance to the government, however, is the fact that the Klamath Tribes have a historical claim to the property, which was included in the original treaty but excised and "forgotten" by surveyors in the official draft.[18] The status of Klamath Basin land and water as well as the prospects for reconstituting the reservation remain at play. Native activists point to the Treaty of 1864 to determine land and water rights, while activists opposed to recognizing Indian land rights cite Wade Crawford's request for termination as evidence that termination suited the entire community. The reservation may be gone, but Klamath Basin politics have changed little in either tenor or substance in over 150 years, the one great exception being that the Klamath people are now truly representing themselves in these contests.[19] Their efforts are aided by their longtime ally, Hiroto Zakoji. In a 2006 article in the *Eugene Weekly* titled "Forced Journeys: Local Native Americans and Japanese Americans discover kinship in a common history," Zakoji is identified as both a "former internee at Tule Lake" and "Director of the Klamath Adult Indian Education and Training program."[20]

Topazians, and all former Japanese internees, had a wider range of experiences with resettlement than the Klamaths did after termination, and while they seemed to disappear for several decades, they persisted in a decades-long campaign for government accountability and reparations for their internment. Unlike Oregon's "legal non-Indians," Japanese Americans had a wide range of post-reservation experiences. Many younger Topazians extricated themselves from the educational "web" of WRA schools to finish college and reestablish themselves in the Bay Area as part of a regenerative Japanese community. At the other end of the spectrum, however, were the older immigrant Issei, who were barred from citizenship until 1952. As twice-uprooted noncitizens, they fell between the cracks once the government's need to detain them at Topaz subsided. Both old and young kept silent about the experience, effectively creating a new form of invisibility. In a painful irony, many understood the internment as a government injustice, yet they viewed their victimization as a mark of personal shame. Ernest and Chizu Iiyama subconsciously tried to protect their daughter from insidious racism by giving her an English name. When asked why, they realized that "one of the dreams that happened was that we didn't want our children to go through . . . the difficulties of having a Japanese name."[21]

President Truman, in praising the 442nd Regimental Combat Team, declared a double victory for the Nisei seeking freedom at home by heroically defending freedom abroad. Through their exemplary service, the 442nd "fought against prejudice . . . and won," yet their struggles were far from over. One of the veterans' early rewards was passage of the Japanese American Evacuation Claims Act in 1948. The act allowed evacuees to file for reimbursement of property and assets lost as a consequence of their relocation. The payments were woefully inadequate, with only $38 million allocated to cover 23,000 claims worth $131 million. Nevertheless, the payments replaced some losses and, more importantly, stood as acknowledgement that the government committed civil rights violations. Over time, even the symbolic meaning of the act was tarnished by its ineffectiveness. Payment procedures lasted in some cases until 1965. This was often because the wheels of Washington bureaucracy turned slowly, but in many other instances it was due to the government challenging individual claims. It settled 378 by paying only a small percentage of the original claim. These delays were hard on Topazians who had returned to California, where real estate prices had soared to several times what they had been when internees lost their land. Without economic assistance, many returning Japanese were unable to start again on a new plot of land or compete in the wider marketplace.[22] The Japanese American Evacuation Claims Act did not change the direction of inverse utopianism; instead, it was an extension of the internment itself.

Demands for Redress

Japanese American activists, including many Topazians, pursued legislation, litigation, and grassroots mobilization to push the federal government to deliver the fair play and full equality promised them for their wartime sacrifices. The early campaigns centered on repealing discriminatory laws and race-based "emergency ordinances" enacted during the war. Initially, their victories were small, like the lifting of bans on Japanese nationals fishing and holding civil service jobs. A bigger victory came in 1952, when the McCarran-Walter Immigration and Nationality Act gave Japanese immigrants the right to apply for naturalization. Though separate from the McCarran Internal Security Act, the new immigration bill grew out of the same anti-Communist impulses. Its sponsors favored it as a declaration that Communist China had replaced Japan as America's Asian enemy, and that Japanese Americans were not prone to Communist subversion to the degree that Finns, Italians, African Americans, and other American ethnic groups were believed to be. In perhaps the most radical departure from previous anti-Japanese policy, the McCarran-Walter Act invalidated the Alien Land Laws, lifting all legal constraints on Japanese landownership for the first time in the twentieth century.[23]

Once Japanese Americans were on firmer political footing, Japanese American civil rights activists saw redress measures as concrete political possibilities. The climate for redress became increasingly favorable with the election of Senator Daniel Inouye, a veteran of the 442nd Regimental Combat Team, in 1959. The civil rights movement set the stage for presenting numerous hidden histories of racism in America. Although most Japanese Americans eschewed the confrontational politics of the black civil rights movement, it inspired many young third-generation Japanese with no direct memory of the camps to support redress efforts at the grassroots level. They found committed allies among African American civil rights organizations, which were among the non–Japanese American organizations to denounce the internment and the government's inadequate postwar response to it. The FBI's wartime concern that Bay Area African and Japanese Americans would form a united front came true in the postwar era, and some Japanese American individuals and organizations were placed under surveillance. For these activists as well as their African American counterparts, surveillance was nothing new and not a deterrent to pursuing their political goals.[24]

The redress movement gained visibility in the 1970s, as numerous memoirists joined Miné Okubo in publishing their camp experiences, and Japanese Americans continued to win seats in Congress. A 1974 survey of Japanese American attitudes toward redress showed dramatically increased interest, but there were varied opinions about the best route to take. Some strongly favored legislative action, while others saw the courts as the appropriate venue for addressing constitutional breaches. The JACL passed a resolution at its 1978 convention to work for monetary reparations through federal legislation, and the National Council for Japanese American Redress (NCJAR) prepared its 1983 suit in U.S. District Court on behalf of twenty-five plaintiffs seeking $27.5 billion, which amounted to $220,000 for each of the 120,000 internees. The moment was opportune for both actions, as President Gerald Ford had just formally rescinded Executive Order 9066 and lauded Japanese Americans for their loyalty, affirming the "unhyphenated American promise that we have learned from the tragedy of that long ago experience—forever to treasure liberty and justice for each individual American and resolve that this kind of error shall never be made again."[25]

The legislative campaign for redress began with the passage of a bill forming the Commission on Wartime Relocation and Internment of Civilians (CWRIC) to hold a series of eight hearings around the country in 1981. Comprised of seventeen appointees—only one of whom was Japanese—they spent several years conducting interviews with former internees, army supervisors, and WRA officials to determine the nature of the wrongs done the internees. They also conducted extensive studies of the extent of property losses and the degree to which Japanese Americans had been set back by their years in camp. For many Japanese Americans, their CWRIC testimony was the first time they had spoken publicly about their experiences in camp. Their courage brought results: the CWRIC's 1983 report *Personal Justice Denied* called on Congress to provide twenty-thousand-dollar payments for each surviving internee and declared that the internment resulted from "race prejudice, war hysteria and a failure of political leadership." While the twenty thousand dollars hardly compensated the former internees for their wartime losses, activists found that the statement by the committee on race hysteria changed the way the media and the public viewed both the internment and the redress movement. It was no longer viewed as a necessary—if regrettable—wartime measure, but a mistake to be rectified.[26]

Meanwhile, the district court's ruling in the NCJAR case showed the limits of the government's change in attitude toward redress. Although the judge found that relocation was not a military necessity and that the government had concealed information substantiating this point, he ruled that the statute of limitations had run out, and that the government had broad discretion to protect the nation in wartime and had not violated the plaintiffs' statutory, civil, or constitutional rights. The case was victorious on appeal, but it was a small victory, at least on the surface. The court ruled that the few internees who received no compensation from the Japanese American Evacuation Claims Act must be awarded damages for their losses. The important part of the decision was that its destabilization of the "military necessity" argument and high-dollar demand for damages made HR 442, the bill on the floor to put the CWRIC recommendations into effect, look moderate by comparison. President Ronald Reagan signed HR 442 — renamed the Civil Liberties Act of 1988 — into law after a years-long campaign headed by Japanese American activists, non-Japanese allies, and the Japanese American members of Congress — Daniel Inouye, Robert Matsui, Spark Matsunaga, and Norman Mineta. In 1990 President George H. W. Bush issued the government's formal apology, and the checks began to go out.[27]

Most accounts of the internment characterize former internees as apolitical by nature and as people who quietly endured the internment until they could repair their lives fully. While a small percentage of Topazians took to the streets to protest the injustices done to them, they exercised a politics deeply marked by their years in camp. Lee Suyemoto's parents were still so angry about the internment that they refused to become citizens after the McCarran-Walter Act. Both his mother and father were resident aliens until their death, despite their heartfelt loyalty to the United States as "their country," in which they encouraged their two sons to volunteer for military service. Another Topazian who worked with the elderly recalled that the Issei always asked about the progress toward official redress. They explained that they could do without the money but wanted to hear the president apologize for the internment so they could die peacefully.[28]

Other Topazians took their expanded political consciousness to the public sphere, participating in movements and community projects that were not directly related to internment but had strong underlying parallels. Nobu Hibino joined the civil rights movement of the 1960s and developed an interest in public housing issues. She helped run community action programs for low-income families for many years. Hibino was also active in the League of Women Voters. She believed the internment resulted from the lack of interaction between whites and Japanese before the war. As a Girl Scout leader, League of Women Voters director, and a community activist, Hibino sought to "show by personal example that we Japanese Americans are not that bad." Her husband Yosh, who never forgot his experience of powerlessness at Topaz, had always wished to do volunteer legal work in his retirement. He thus enrolled in the law school at the University of Connecticut, completed his degree, and provided forty-five hours' service per week representing illegal aliens involved in amnesty cases.[29]

The evacuation had been swift and confusing, and for many Topazians, contacts with African American and white civil rights activists helped put the political ramifications into perspective. Chizu Iiyama gained a fuller understanding of her experiences at Topaz after taking a class on the history of the Hopi Indians. Comparing the Japanese internment to the Hopi experience, she wrote in 1993 that "our civil rights were totally disregarded" and that both histories show how "racism is part of America's history, and we need to combat it wherever it appears." Midori Shimanouchi, who grew bored with her leisurely lifestyle in the 1970s, became a tireless activist on behalf of refugees from Cambodia who were struggling to settle in New York. Donald Nahakata also saw clear parallels between his family's relocation experience and that of Cambodian refugees, with whom he identifies because "we were the first American boat people." Like Shimanouchi and other Topazians, he provided aid and advocacy to the new wave of Asian refugees. Non-Japanese observers assumed racial co-identification was the reason, but that was only part of Japanese Americans' interest in Cambodian newcomers; placelessness, too, was an experience with which they could identify and sympathize.[30]

The moral dilemmas surrounding the war in Vietnam awakened bad memories of the loyalty issue at Topaz. Tom Kawaguchi served two tours of duty in Vietnam and returned when he became disillusioned by the government's failure to employ coherent policies. His new perspective on the war changed his views on civil disobedience. Earlier, Kawaguchi had frowned on draft resistance and other forms of civil disobedience at Topaz, but after having served he came to see them as a legitimate expression of patriotic feeling. He saw that both accommodationists and dissenters made tremendous personal sacrifices in their expressions of patriotism. Kawaguchi still admired the Topazians who served in the 442nd, but after Vietnam he added the dissidents to his list of camp heroes.[31]

Fred Korematsu was sixty-three when *Personal Justice Denied* was published. He had been working as a draftsman in Oakland for many years, living in the shadow of his 1942 conviction for ignoring the evacuation orders. For nearly forty years, Korematsu lived without hope of clearing his record. The government's cooperation with the redress movement created a favorable climate for revisiting his case, and he filed a writ of *error coram novis* in a California federal court in 1983. The Department of Justice presented the old argument of wartime necessity, with the added statement that the internment was "an unfortunate episode in our nation's history" that was "best put behind us." Korematsu's attorneys presented new evidence uncovered by a political scientist, which included memoranda from FBI director J. Edgar Hoover reporting that the agency had uncovered absolutely no evidence to suggest that any Nikkei had signaled or provided any assistance to the Japanese army, at Pearl Harbor or anywhere else.[32]

The judge threw out Korematsu's 1942 conviction, citing both the racist underpinnings of the laws and the recent discovery that prosecutors presented false evidence in the original trial. Korematsu received the Presidential Medal of Freedom in 1998 for having persevered for over fifty years in his fight for justice. Korematsu's victories, though widely celebrated, had a limited impact on Asian Americans' civil rights. The decision did not overturn the Supreme Court's ruling legitimating racially based detention, leaving available legal precedent that would support future internments if the government were ever inclined to target another racial group during a national emergency.[33]

None of the Nikkei victories in Washington or in the realm of public opinion brought an end to anti-Japanese racism in the West. The last push for redress in the 1980s was met with a wave of anti-Asian violence concentrated in California. Although the United States was not at war with an Asian nation, Japan's expanded economic influence renewed anxieties about the "Japanization" of the United States. The escalating hostility culminated in the murder of Vincent Chin in 1982. Chin, a young Chinese American draftsman, was attending his bachelor party in Detroit when he was accosted by two white men—a laid-off autoworker and his stepson—who beat him to death with a baseball bat. Reading Chin as

"Japanese American" and conflating Japanese nationals with Americans of Japanese ancestry, the autoworker yelled, "It's because of you little motherfuckers that we're out of work!" The number of successful Asian students in American universities and the prominence of Asian enclaves in California like Monterey Park garnered Asians grudging approval as a "model minority," yet it also rekindled Caucasians' fears of an alien takeover aided and abetted by U.S. citizens.[34]

All of a sudden, the rhetoric, imagery, and violence of the earlier half of the century reappeared on the American scene, with no reflection on the "lessons learned" from the internment. Senator Daniel Inouye, a decorated veteran of the 442nd, received racist hate mail while serving as chair of the Iran-Contra hearings. Inouye's defenders commented less on his participation in the hearings and more on his years of "loyal citizenship." In the same time period, Colorado police discovered the decomposed body of a Japanese American woman in the town of Clear Creek. The police could identify no motive or suspects but noted that she disappeared on December 7, 1985, which coincided with the date of the Pearl Harbor bombing. Forty years after the internment, fierce prejudice against "eternal foreigners" lay dormant in the American political imagination, making Japanese Americans' vigilant defense of fundamental civil liberties as important today as at any other point in history.[35] It is hardly surprising that Japanese American activists would be the first responders to the outbreaks of anti-Arab and anti-Muslim sentiments in the wake of the terrorist attacks of September 11, 2001. When public opinion polls showed that more than 30 percent of Americans said they would approve measures to register and detain the people who fit the profile of "terrorist threat," former internees and their descendants tried to remind the American public of where such measures would lead.[36]

Vanporters had less success in their quest for redress, receiving neither a payment nor an apology, yet they were no less politicized. Vanporters filed over three thousand individual claims at different venues, but like the plaintiffs in *Clark v. United States*, they found that the federal government never assumed liability for damages sustained in its inverse utopias. The hardest part of these decisions was the implication that Vanporters should have realized that the bowl-shaped lay of the land

and its proximity to two major rivers were obvious signs of flood risk. They had had difficulty enough being segregated, marginalized, and economically leveled, without being saddled with blame for answering the call of the War Manpower Commission.

The ruling against the seven hundred Vanporters was, in a sense, the formal termination of their relationship with the federal government. It was undoubtedly disappointing to residents that their shipbuilding experience ended with the Federal Public Housing Authority denying its special relationship to its tenant-wards. The plaintiffs filed appeals in the Ninth Circuit, where Judge James Alger Fee's rulings were upheld and the government's view of its responsibility to Vanporters was reaffirmed. Even if the *Clark* case had been successful, there were some Vanporters whose losses could never be compensated. Morian Ritchey, for example, lost her father in the flood, even though he was counted among the survivors. The realization that nothing he had worked for could be salvaged "broke my dad pretty much—his spirit . . . It was like he was heartbroken." Mr. Ritchey left the family to live as a recluse in a remote mountain cabin, moving from place to place each year.[37]

Vanporters who survived the flood were, like Klamaths and the poorly compensated Nikkei, "just these people with nothing." This was especially true for Japanese Vanporters, who received generous support from the Japanese American Citizens League and Portland's Japanese-owned businesses. Sadly, two of the flood deaths were Japanese women who had been relocated to Vanport by the War Relocation Authority. Portland's Japanese community also lost the printing press from the old Japantown newspaper in the flood. The publisher had retrieved the press after the internment in the hope of restoring this pillar of the prewar Nihonmachi. Instead, the Portland Nikkei who resettled in Vanport suffered another devastating obstacle to resuming their pre-internment lives: the Vanport flood abruptly uprooted them for the third time since 1942.[38]

Individual flood victims received almost no government compensation for their losses. The luckier ones, who tended to be better-off whites, were able to leave the Portland area or start again in inexpensive housing nearby. Caucasians were generally able to recover more quickly from the flood. They had the enormous advantages of being able to move into any affordable neighborhood and finding acceptance as Portlanders after a few years' residence. Black Vanporters, by contrast, generally did not have the means to leave and had difficulty finding housing within the confines of the Albina neighborhood. The deluge of African American flood victims seeking rental housing did nothing to bend the real estate agents' red lines. Outraged at the blatant housing discrimination, the new Portland chapter of the Urban League gained momentum by challenging discriminatory practices toward black Vanporters, who were now part of Portland's African American community.[39]

The political aftermath of the flood gave rise to broad-based progressive coalitions that included civil rights organizations and labor radicals. The Vanport Citizen's Emergency Disaster Committee branched into electoral politics as a sponsoring organization for the petition drive to put Henry Wallace on the 1948 presidential ballot. Portland's expanding progressive coalition encountered reinvigorated surveillance by Portland's Red Squad, which became especially alarmed when Paul Robeson came to Portland to campaign for Wallace. His frequent references to Nikkei internees and Vanport flood victims as Americans who "had no justice" spurred the Red Squad to warn Mayor Dorothy McCullough Lee that radicals and civil rights activists could wreak havoc in the community. A 1949 memo named former Vanporters Frank Patterson, Andrew Johnson, Estes Curry, and Sam Markson as leaders of a "pressure group" that intended to forcibly desegregate Portland's restaurants, theaters, and hotels. In the end, national attitudes against segregation paved the way for peaceful change. Even the American Federation of Labor, which supported the Boilermakers' segregation of black workers in auxiliary unions, sponsored a float in the 1953 Rose Parade with six little princesses representing "our three major racial groups" — two white, two Asian, and two black.[40]

But these civil rights victories are not Vanport's most evident legacy. The Housing Authority's dishonesty about its segregatory practices fostered lasting distrust between black and white residents. The flood shook all Vanporters' faith in their government. Residents continue to question why Vanport was built on a site that the Army Corps of Engineers knew was prone to flooding. Others wonder why a gravel railroad fill doubled as a dike and why the Housing Authority of Portland failed to warn flood victims as promised when water had been seeping through for at least a day. The *Clark* decision solidified many residents' resentments. Years after the judgment against the Vanporters was rendered, Grail Jarvi's family continued to believe that an insurance company or a government agent would send even a token settlement, but it never came. Their faith in the inherent fairness of the U.S. government was replaced with the perception that the government deliberately ignored Vanporters' needs because they were no longer needed in the shipyard.[41]

Fifty years after the flood, one former Vanporter wrote a letter to the Portland Community College Oral History Project challenging its statement that "miraculously, only 15 people died." The writer contended that "the subject of Vanport has been kept so quiet" and counted the government's response to the flood among a number of cover-ups. She included the Tuskegee syphilis experiments, the "forced internment of Japanese *Americans* during WWII," and the presence of nuclear fallout in the West. She stated plainly in her letter, "I don't feel the Federal Government met its responsibility in the Vanport flood disaster." While she did not believe there was any way to change the situation, she asked that the historical record reflect the fact that "we will *never* know how many lives were lost, but we . . . acknowledge there were an *unknown* number of lives lost."[42]

Enduring Legacies

How many Vanporters died in the flood and what government officials should have done to protect them remain open questions for many. For years, rumors abounded about hundreds of bodies being housed in cold storage facilities, bodies being shipped to Japan to fill the coffins of soldiers who were truly missing in action, and the government hoping the project would flood to prevent relocation throughout the Portland area. These theories have few adherents, but the core of the story concerning the government's intent to harm continues to resonate in many circles. Residents question why HAP issued a memo advising residents to stay and why the government would build on the flood plain to begin with. Even after Vanport faded from younger generations' historical memory, a lingering strain of distrust of government power persists in the grassroots political culture of both the left and the right.[43]

Los Alamos remains emblazoned in the New Mexican landscape and the nation's collective memory. The science town has evolved to a thriving community, though traces of its inverse-utopian past remain. To many, Los Alamos stands as a symbol of government secrecy; like Vanport, the mesa remains the flash point for local anxieties about a government that deceived them in the 1940s and, they fear, continues to mislead them about nuclear hazards and national security measures in the present. Activist movements for government accountability are part of the fabric of New Mexico politics, and they originated directly in Los Alamos's Tech Area, as early as the Hiroshima and Nagasaki bombings. As the affluent heroes who ended the Second World War, Los Alamosans were spared the social and economic hardships that Klamaths, Topazians, and Vanporters endured. There were, however, casualties within the relatively privileged enclave. Enrico Fermi became a scientific casualty in 1954, when he died of cancer related to his work with radioactive materials in primitive conditions. J. Robert Oppenheimer became the Hill's greatest political casualty in 1958, when the Atomic Energy Commission stripped the "father of the atomic bomb" of his security clearance based on shaky evidence that he was aiding the Soviets.[44]

Fifty years later, Los Alamosans, surrounding communities, and government agents continue to negotiate the terms of their now-permanent relationship. The questions involve new faces and new issues, but they still center around the fundamental problem of which rights and privileges citizens on special projects must surrender for the sake of national security, and what the government owes them in return. As with the reservation system, the internment camps, and war housing communities, policy makers at Los Alamos placed security goals ahead of civil and human rights. The fear of a German bomb made it acceptable for the government to make extensive intrusions into scientists' private lives, while exposing Los Alamosans and surrounding communities to radioactive materials without sufficient knowledge of their health consequences.

During the Manhattan Project, access to information was tied to power and prestige within the project. Compartmentalization was a military necessity, but it also defined hierarchical relationships up the scientific chain, between the young scientists and Oppenheimer's inner circle, the laboratory and the nonscientists at Los Alamos, and Los Alamosans and New Mexican outsiders. This social and informational configuration remained in place through the Cold War, and its traces are discernible today, despite demands by residents inside, outside, and around the laboratory for government transparency and accountability for the damaging effects of the nuclear program. Hispano villagers and Pueblo communities did not expect to know anything about the bomb, but José Gonzales wished that he had known what plutonium was when the army brought it into the area. His father lost the family homestead on a nearby mesa in 1942 when "the FBI" (probably military intelligence) gave him thirty days to move to El Rancho. His father took a new job in a strange new laboratory, working with unknown materials. Convoys would pass through his new neighborhood, always at one o'clock in the morning, offering no clues as to what was inside. One New Mexico rancher described the experience of the local populations as living in a state of "national insecurity" in which there was no way to know whether the water or air was contaminated. And neither the government nor the environmental advocates who flocked to the area represented their interests, with local voices rarely part of the dialogue.[45] Fifty years later, residents like Gonzales wonder what the full consequences of plutonium will be for their environment.[46] For years, locals unable to prosper in the post–Cold War economy scavenged for scrap metal and other usable items from the laboratory dump, unaware that they were handling hazardous items that had been placed out of harm's way—of Los Alamosans. When Pueblo communities pointed to increased numbers of cancer deaths in the postwar era, the Department of Energy dismissed their concerns.[47]

Instead of accepting the role of the information outsider, dependent on the government for essential knowledge, community leaders reminded the Department of Energy about the contributions their people had made to the American nuclear enterprise. With that declaration came their demand, as members of the scientific team, that the government fully disclose the amount and type of nuclear waste in their areas and the threat it posed to human health and the environment. They went further, pointing to the difference between the schools that the Department of Energy provided for children of laboratory workers at Los Alamos as compared to the education provided them by the state of New Mexico and the Bureau of Indian Affairs. Despite the fact that most of the people on the Los Alamos National Laboratory (LANL) payroll came from the villages and pueblos, only the white, middle-class children of scientists had access to the top-quality education provided especially to "the employees of Los Alamos." The government's lack of serious response maintained the divide between Los Alamos and the communities below; it also reinforced the racial hierarchy that formed the core of nineteenth-century expansionist rhetoric. Los Alamos was an outpost in the Empire for Liberty, and its subjects were brought into the "civilized" world of science—but not far enough to gain control of the technology or their colonized lands. Pueblo governors' reminders that they ceded their rights on a duration-only basis have been all but ignored, with all attention centered on the march to scientific frontiers as rich with possibilities as the geographic one had been in John O'Sullivan's day.[48]

The end of the Cold War brought a wave of political activity within the LANL as well. The Hispanic Roundtable called attention to the disproportionate number of both Caucasians in the top scientific positions and local New Mexicans (mostly of color) as lower-level scientists, technicians, and other low-paid positions. A new generation of New Mexicans who were raised near the lab did not see it as a miracle atop a mountain but as the leading local employer. This attitude changed for many in 1995, when the LANL announced the first massive layoffs in the history of Los Alamos. Most of the pink slips went to the same area locals who had come to see the laboratory as a permanent, positive economic change. Instead of passively accepting the change, they organized Citizens for LANL Employee Rights (CLER), whose first action was to sue the Department of Energy for the illegal layoffs of older employees, native New Mexicans, and critics of laboratory policy.

CLER went even farther by launching a campaign against New Mexico's automatic renewal of the University of California's contract to operate the laboratory at Los Alamos, calling for local control. In a letter to Secretary of Energy Hazel O'Leary, CLER and nine nongovernmental organizations cited "arrogance, secrecy, and privilege" that created a "corporate culture rooted firmly in denial." This culture bred distrust between scientists and management as well as between New Mexicans and the LANL. Their appeal to the government to "treat people fairly, pursue the 'best science,' respect the environment, and embrace meaningful contract reform" may not have been fully realized, but some changes did result. Renewal of University of California contracts became contingent on the university establishing a means to address the local community's concerns, and field offices in towns off the mesa are now in operation. The Department of Labor found in favor of CLER's complaints, ordering the LANL to rehire about half of the 102 workers laid off illegally and to pay approximately $3 million in damages. Although this kind of public critique of laboratory power structures was new, it did little to alter the racial order or the security regime at Los Alamos, even in peacetime.[49]

The ethical questions surrounding the exposure of Los Alamos laboratory workers, their families, surrounding communities, and the general public to dangerous radioactive materials remains the subject of much reflection and debate. Interestingly, many Los Alamosans were so unafraid of radiation (and angered by public "hysteria" over its dangers) that they volunteered their young children for experiments involving ingestion of radioactive substances. Further, a group of contaminated Los Alamosans like Bill Gibson, who was dismissed from working with radioactive materials after plutonium entered a cut in his hand, formed the elite "UPPU" Club ("pu" being the symbol for plutonium on the periodic table). Workers who received excessive doses of radioactive material in the 1940s were required to participate in a lifelong study by Los Alamos medical teams to determine the effects of plutonium on the body. The wartime experimentation on non-Los Alamosans who were injected with plutonium without their consent has been one of the most troubling problems for federal agencies. The Department of Energy was forced to face the issue publicly when the *Albuquerque Journal* revealed the identities of the subjects, wrote moving stories of their lives since the experiments, and drew analogies between the Los Alamos study and Nazi medical experiments.[50]

Energy Secretary Hazel O'Leary convened an advisory committee in 1993 to investigate the history of Los Alamos's medical research protocols. Their report refuted claims that Los Alamos employed Nazi methods, noting that any anticipated harm to human subjects was minimal. Nevertheless, the committee held government officials and medical investigators responsible for failing to "protect the rights and interests of human subjects." The committee also found that the government's secrecy surrounding plutonium research deprived subjects of their right to present evidence of harm, which blocked them from successful pursuit of compensatory damages. In the end, the report brought a long-awaited apology and justified financial compensation for the victims. The catch was that the funds for damages would require congressional approval, which was never granted.[51]

Even today, exposure to toxic levels of radioactive substances remains an ever-present hazard. The LANL and the Department of Energy continue to downplay the risks in the greater interest of national security. A group of Santa Fe activists released findings indicating an unusually high incidence of brain tumors among people who had played near Los Alamos's contaminated Acid Canyon as children and also found elevated cancer rates among long-term Los Alamos–area residents. The Los Alamos National Laboratory responded by forming the Working Group to Address Los Alamos Community Health Concerns, which spearheaded a study in conjunction with the federal government's Agency for Toxic Substances and Disease Registry. The agency found the contaminants in Acid Canyon posed no health risks, and it invited the public to hike the canyon with radiation monitors, which revealed no "hot spots." The federal government labeled skeptical activists as "nuclear hysterics," along with the plutonium subjects, local Indian tribes, and political agitators demanding accountability for the disposition of nuclear materials.[52]

Los Alamos's culture of secrecy has created a climate of suspicion across what has become known as "the atomic West." In the remote Southwest, the Defense Department and the Department of Energy continue to conduct top-secret experiments—a fact that leads to much speculation among the locals. Leading scientists and military officers at Kirtland Air Force Base, a gigantic self-contained federal community on the outskirts of Albuquerque, where Los Alamos's Z Division was relocated after the war, are rumored to be holding a number of space aliens on site. Although the public is allowed to enter the base to visit the National Museum of Nuclear Energy and Industry, some New Mexicans note that the army escorts visitors on and off base, never allowing outsiders to wander or enter for any other purpose, lest the public expose the army's secret. UFO watchers monitor government activity around Area 51, where a number of sightings have been reported since 1952.[53]

Area 51, like Los Alamos, is designed for top-secret defense projects and flies workers to a job site that has never been seen by outsiders. Although Area 51 is generally understood to be a high-security military research and development operation, New Mexicans maintain they have been fooled before and have learned from Los Alamos to try to look through the smoke screen, lest they suffer another shock like the Alamagordo test. So while federal communities succeeded in their immediate tasks, their political, economic, social, and security mechanisms did not mold all the residents into the citizens they had hoped. Suspiciousness toward government spread across the Southwest as the atomic energy program established new research and testing facilities in Nevada, Utah, and Colorado. "Downwinders," or westerners who have been exposed to radiation from government installations, keep watch over the government's handling of nuclear material, ever mindful that Los Alamos's secret was kept at the expense of the health of nearby residents, the land, and even their most gifted scientists.[54]

Even cases in which there is proof that government actions resulted in material harm to residents of federally run communities have not punctured the barriers of national security privilege and the government's right of sovereign immunity. In May 2000 the U.S. Forest Service set what was supposed to be a controlled burn of underbrush at the bottom of the mesa but which became a 47,000-acre blaze as a direct result of failed communication and bureaucratic bungling. Dozens of families lost homes and property in the White Rock area, and still more suffered more minor property losses of cars and other items. More than eighteen thousand people evacuated Los Alamos for shelters in Santa Fe or friends' homes in nearby communities. Their despair over their losses sounds much like that of Vanport flood victims. One resident described to a reporter his agony at waiting to hear whether he would have a house to return to, and another recalled how older children were visibly traumatized at the sight of their own houses burning to the ground.[55]

Like the victims of the Vanport flood, Los Alamosans ran up against the federal government's right of sovereign immunity: federal agencies admonished residents not to sue and reminded them that most of the structures lost were government housing, to which residents have no legitimate legal claim. The Internal Revenue Service offered residents settlements on uninsured and underinsured property and businesses with the stipulation that residents waive the right to sue under the Federal Tort Claims Act, which meant the only damages the government would pay were those not covered by residents' insurance carriers. In this way, the federal government accepted the minimum responsibility, both financially and morally. This may have been enough to help residents recover some of what they lost, but it did nothing to repair the injured relationship between the citizen of a federal community and his or her errant paternalist government.[56]

In the end, the government issued its findings of fact, which explained that the prescribed fire burned forty-seven thousand acres in northern New Mexico, destroying two hundred homes in Los Alamos and the nearby Santa Clara and San Ildefonso pueblos, resulting in a presidential declaration of disaster. Nowhere did the federal government hold its agencies responsible. Residents' assessments of their losses, however, echo the experience of Vanporter Marian Craig, who cried at the loss of her pinking shears. While such an item might appear insignificant, even the smallest belongings can hold great meaning in the wake of devastating tragedy. As Kim Holowell told a Santa Fe reporter covering the Cerro Grande fire, "It's not the computer for us. It's not the VCR . . . it's the family pictures."[57]

The espionage case against Los Alamos scientist Wen Ho Lee in 1999 represents one of the clearest repetitions of the pattern of enmification and preventative detention, especially in the public mind. Lee's arrest, detention, and subsequent exoneration reinvigorated the unresolved anxiety and anger from both the Manhattan Project era and, because Lee was a naturalized citizen born in Taiwan, the historical legacies of Asian exclusion, including the Japanese American internment. The FBI placed Lee under intense surveillance for four years to investigate whether he was spying for the Chinese government. The results of the investigation led to Lee's arrest in December 1999 and a subsequent six-month period of solitary confinement. The government dropped most of the fifty-nine charges against Lee after he admitted to one security violation that fell under the purview of espionage.[58]

While some government officials attributed the dismissal of the Lee case to weaknesses in nuclear security policy, the Asian American community linked the decision to the same practice of racial profiling that "justified" the wartime internment of the Japanese. Their suspicions were confirmed when Lee's daughter gave a description of the FBI raid on her father's Los Alamos home, which echoed the Nihonmachi raids of 1942. Agents seized a collection of short stories by Guy de Maupassant because Lee had scrawled notes in Chinese along the margins, with the same air of suspicion agents had when they gathered Japanese books from Nikkei households after Pearl Harbor. To many, the government's practice of racial profiling was confirmed when an investigator for the Department of Energy stated plainly, "Ethnic Chinese should not be allowed to work on classified projects." He stated further that the U.S. Attorney's Office was granted a search warrant on the basis of Lee's ethnicity, which was a criterion by which the FBI pursued espionage suspects.[59]

Op-ed pieces in the Asian American press on the Lee case could as easily have been written in 1942. One editor noted that no matter how "accomplished" or "prosperous" Asian Americans may become in America, they are still widely perceived as foreigners who cannot be completely trusted in sensitive positions. Novelist Gish Jen expressed the exasperation of Asian Americans past and present: "We are sick of being seen as not quite American, of being viewed, generation after generation, as guests to be welcomed—or not."[60] The general sense that Asian scientists are undervalued at the nation's weapons laboratories, including Los Alamos, has been cited as a factor in the dramatic rise in their attrition rates from 2.7 percent in 1996 to 4.1 percent in 1999. The case also created a cohort of "reluctant activists" who took messages such as "Wen Ho Lee should be supported (by the neck), cut down, drawn, and quartered" as the catalyst to resist being cast as "high-tech coolies" subject to marginalization, exploitation, and racial violence.[61]

For many Americans, the Wen Ho Lee case reinscribed in the post–Cold War period longstanding anxieties about race, loyalty, and the need for failsafe security. His status as an "American"—like that of nuclear scientists and "suspect" minorities before him—was scrutinized and revised constantly in public dialogue, based largely on how the Department of Justice, the FBI, and the Departments of Energy and Defense perceived him at any given point. One of the government's great fears is technology transfer; it imagined the Asians as great imitators who, though incapable of invention, were gifted imitators who would use western-style weapons to colonize the West Coast (just as the United States had colonized Hawaii and the Philippines to reach the great commercial frontier, China). Communists, too, were thought to be foreign parasites incapable of inventing their own atomic bomb, but they were ruthless enough to endanger the world by stealing plans from the laboratory. The worst of it was that the project depended on the expertise of potential disloyals. All these anxiety narratives came together again in the initial public impression of Wen Ho Lee as atomic scientist and Asian-born immigrant, with all the historical associations built into those categories.[62]

Asian Americans' resentment at the federal government's continued failure to protect their civil rights was reinforced in the midst of the Lee case, when the U.S. Census Bureau revealed that it had aided the army in 1942 by releasing block data to quickly locate Japanese families for interrogation and removal. Although confidentiality laws were enacted in the 1950s, the Asian American press had to dissuade readers from withholding information on their 2000 census forms as decades-old fears quickly resurfaced.[63]

Far from instilling faith, trust, and partnership between the citizens and government, the dynamics of race, citizenship, and security generated enduring currents of distrust. These trends are especially pronounced in the West, where federal communities have most significantly altered the region's demographic composition. The same dynamics between race, political conviction, and home front security arise in times of national crisis, which throughout the twentieth century played themselves out in the wide-open spaces of the western frontier.

If there is anything to be understood about American public opinion and federal security measures in periods of national emergency, it is that policies based on fear gravely compromise the rights of citizens and resident aliens who are fully loyal to the United States. Enclosing populations Americans feared in the isolated, wide-open expanses of the West gave a traumatized public an immediate, concrete reassurance that the government was able to act in defense of its safety. The injustices that federal community populations endured lasted far longer than the emergency at hand, creating barriers to enjoying their full rights and privileges as loyal American citizens. This ultimately undermined the fabric of American ideals, principles, and lifeways and, given the cases of Ted Hall and Klaus Fuchs at Los Alamos, failed to protect the American public from the threat the government feared most.

The enduring outcome of America's great experiment in demographic management was a crisis of faith in the federal government and its adherence to the principles of democracy, social equality, and due process. Depending on one's view of dissenters in American politics, this could be a positive or negative outcome. To some, these former wards' quests for government accountability can be read as polarizing, disrespectful of government authority, and in some cases, even as hostile to America. Others undoubtedly view their activism as the sort of mature patriotism that defends the principles of American freedom under any and all circumstances, even if it requires dutiful citizens to challenge their leadership. In any case, such distrust and hostility toward the federal government was not Washington's intended outcome. In attempting to purify the body politic and reunite the national family, the government reaped what it sowed—suspicion, hostility, and conflict. Yet these new activists did, in a way, fulfill the hopeful aims of the wra staff member who believed that life behind barbed wire could make better citizens who were more realistically democratic in principle, in thought, and in effect, "tempered . . . to carry forward the living principles of democracy."[64] In their attempts to awaken the conscience of the nation, these former wards admonish their fellow citizens to break the pattern of enmification and inverse utopianism and to challenge their leaders to govern according to what they know, instead of what they fear.

Notes

ABBREVIATIONS

ALSC   Allen Library Special Collections, University of Washington

NARAPAR   National Archives and Records Administration,
           Pacific Alaska Region

OHSRL   Oregon Historical Society Research Library

RHAP   Records of the Housing Authority of Portland

SPARC   Stanley Parr Archives and Records Center

TOHP   Topaz Oral History Project, University of Utah Marriott Library

INTRODUCTION

1. Historian Roger Daniels has reassessed the terminology scholars use to describe these facilities, arguing that the relocation centers were literally "concentration camps"—a term that government officials also used prior to revelations of the Nazi death camps. While it would be a gross distortion to equate the apparatus of the Final Solution with the mass incarceration of Japanese from the West Coast, the "relocation centers" were, in fact, structures for concentrating this ethnic group. I have nonetheless elected to use the term "relocation center" to preserve the terminology of the era and the familiar "internees" to refer to the inmates in the camps. See Daniels, "Incarceration of the Japanese Americans," 297–310.

2. Adorno, *Negative Dialectics*, 162–63; Hong, "Something Forgotten Which Should Have Been Remembered," 291–310; *Encyclopedia of Philosophy Online*, s.v. "Adorno, Theodor" (by Lambert Zuidervaart), http://plato.stanford.edu/entries/adorno/ (Accessed August 15, 2008). Curators Mari Carmen Ramirez and Hector Olea's preface to the exhibition catalogue *Inverted Utopias* demonstrates the benefits of a constellatory reading of disparate entities. Their rejection of traditional chronological, artist-, or movement-centered arrangements created an "open-flexible, and porous site of tensions" that revealed "a host of previously unnoticed links and unsuspected nexus between avant-garde manifestations." Their exhibition design was instrumental in helping me think through the structure of this project. I discovered their work by happenstance, while searching for other uses of the term "inverse utopias," which I use to describe the communities in this study. See Ramirez and Olea, *Inverted Utopias*.

3. Stember, "Reactions to Anti-Semitic Appeals," 119, 128–29.

4. "Judge Grants Bail to Wen Ho Lee," *Asian Reporter*, August 29, 2000; "Clinton 'Troubled' By Los Alamos Case," *New York Times*, September 15, 2000; "Lee Remains

Enigma at Center of a Storm," *Washington Post*, October 8, 2000; Freeh, *The Federal Bureau of Investigation*; Gish Jen, "For Wen Ho Lee, a Tarnished Freedom," *New York Times*, September 15, 2000; Lawler, "Silent No Longer," 1072–73.

5. "Rogue River Citizen," letter to the editor, *Oregonian*, November 27, 1855, from scrapbook compiled by Elwood Evans, "The Indian War, 1855–56," in Research Publications, Western Americana, reel 179, no. 1872.

6. "Rogue River Citizen," letter to the editor, from Evans, "The Indian War, 1855–56," in Research Publications, Western Americana, reel 179, no. 1872.

7. Trennert, *Alternative to Extinction*.

8. Department of the Interior, *Indian Affairs*, 2:865–68; Prucha, *The Great Father*, 317.

9. Stern, *The Klamath Tribe*; Prucha, *The Great Father*; Daniels, *American Concentration Camps*; Taylor, *Jewel of the Desert*; MacColl, *The Growth of a City*; Abbott, *Portland*; Maben, *Vanport*; Kunetka, *City of Fire*; Hales, *Atomic Spaces*.

10. Rieber and Kelley, "Substance and Shadow," 14.

11. Thomas Jefferson to James Madison, April 27, 1809, in Lipscomb and Bergh, eds., *The Writings of Thomas Jefferson*, 277; Smith, *Virgin Land*, 254–56.

12. John O'Sullivan, "The Great Nation of Futurity," *American Democratic Review* 6, no. 23 (November 1839): 430.

13. Morton, *Crania Americana*, 7.

14. Morton, *Crania Americana*, 2.

15. Morton, *Crania Americana*, 47.

16. Morton, *Crania Americana*, 6.

17. Horsman, *Race and Manifest Destiny*, 18, 125–28; Takaki, *A Different Mirror*, 176–77, 191.

18. Morton, *Crania Americana*, 3, 20.

19. Morton, *Crania Americana*, 18–19, 79.

20. Morton, *Crania Americana*, 4, 81.

21. Morton, *Crania Americana*, 7, 87.

22. Morton, *Crania Americana*, 88.

23. Morton, *Crania Americana*, 7.

24. O'Sullivan, "The Great Nation of Futurity," 427.

25. Franklin, *War Stars*, 39–45; Sharp, *Savage Perils*, 107–12.

26. Sayers and Kahn, *Sabotage!*, 68; Jacobson, *Barbarian Virtues*, 125.

27. Foucault, *Discipline and Punish*, 146–47.

28. *Portland Oregonian*, August 13, 1915, quoted in Mangun, "As Citizens of Portland We Must Protest," 379–80.

29. For the history of African Americans in prewar Portland and an overview of black migration to Western defense industries, see McLagan, *A Peculiar Paradise*, 24–27; Nash, *The American West Transformed*, 88–106; and Pearson, "A Menace to the Neighborhood," 158–79.

30. Federal Bureau of Investigation, J. *Robert Oppenheimer Security Files*, Memorandum, March 28, 1941, File #116-2717; Bernstein, "Oppenheimer Loyalty-Security Case," 1391; Fried, *Nightmare in Red*, 51.

31. Gould, "Morton's Rankings of Races by Cranial Capacity," 503–9.

32. Ford, *The International Jew*, 1:22, 1:16.

33. Ford, *The International Jew*, 1:39–40, 1:44, 2:44.

34. Ford, *The International Jew*, 1:10.

35. Ford, *The International Jew*, 1:22, 2:41.

36. Ford, *The International Jew*, 1:235.

37. Werner Sombart qtd. in Ford, *The International Jew*, 1:11.

38. Ford, *The International Jew*, 1:67, 1:41, and 1:16.

39. Stember, "Reactions to Anti-Semitic Appeals," 119; Lanouette and Silard, *Genius in the Shadows*, 248–52; Rhodes, *The Making of the Atomic Bomb*, 506–8.

40. The Bureau of Indian Affairs estimates that 394,000 Native Americans lived on reservations; the remaining 280,000 represent the combined population of the internment camps, civilian installations like Vanport, and the three Manhattan Project towns. See Table Ag 700–703 — Population on Reservations — Bureau of Indian Affairs and Census estimates: 1860–1995, in *Historical Statistics of the United States Online*, Cambridge University Press.

41. War Relocation Authority, *The Impounded People* (1946), 48.

42. Oregon Public Broadcasting, *Your Land, My Land*, VHS, directed by Reagan Ramsey.

43. Myer and Krug, *The WRA*, 184.

44. War Relocation Authority, *The Impounded People* (1946), 42.

45. Jefferson to James Madison, April 27, 1809, in Lipscomb and Bergh, eds., *The Writings of Thomas Jefferson*, 277; Smith, *Virgin Land*, 254–56.

46. O'Sullivan, "The Great Nation of Futurity," 426–30.

47. Turner, *Significance of the Frontier*, 2–3; Limerick, *Legacy of Conquest*, 163; White, "It's Your Misfortune," 58.

48. Nash, *Federal Landscape*; Lotchin, *Fortress California*; Abbott, "The Federal Presence," 469–99.

49. Franklin Delano Roosevelt, "Report on the Home Front," October 12, 1942, Franklin Delano Presidential Library Digital Archives, http://www.fdrlibrary.marist .edu/10142.html (accessed May 30, 2006).

50. *Nikkei* is an inclusive term that refers to all people of Japanese ancestry. The Issei, as immigrants from Japan, were ineligible for naturalization until passage of the McCarran-Walter Immigration and Nationality Act of 1952. The Nisei, as children of the Issei, were U.S. citizens by birthright. The Kibei were the members of this generation of American citizens who were educated in Japan.

51. Martha Calhoon, "Forced Journeys: Local Native Americans and Japanese Americans Discover Kinship in a Common History," *Eugene (OR) Weekly*, November 16, 2006.

I. BEWARE OF CRAFTY BANDITS

1. Franklin D. Roosevelt, "On the Declaration of War with Japan," December 9, 1941, Fireside Chats, Franklin D. Roosevelt Presidential Library Digital Archives, http://www .fdrlibrary.marist.edu/120941.html (accessed June 6, 2006).

2. Jones and Rakestraw, *Prologue to Manifest Destiny*, 155; Pomeroy, *The Pacific Slope*, 24–33; Schwantes, *The Pacific Northwest*, 110–21.

3. Thomas Hart Benton, "On the Bill for Occupation of the Columbia River," in *Selections of Editorial Articles from the St. Louis Enquirer on the Subject of Oregon and Texas, as Originally Published in That Paper in the Years 1818–19 and Written By the Hon. Thomas H. Benton* (St. Louis: Missourian Office, 1844), in Research Publications, Western Americana, reel 50, no. 475.

4. Rakestraw, *For Honor or Destiny*, 167.

5. Loewenberg, "New Evidence, Old Categories," 366–67.

6. Kelley, "A General Circular," 76.

7. Jones and Rakestraw, *Prologue to Manifest Destiny*, 167.

8. Kelley, "A General Circular," 77; Powell, *Hall J. Kelley on Oregon*, xv.

9. Gray, *A History of Oregon*, 194–95; Robbins, *Landscapes of Promise*, 75–87.

10. "President Polk's Message," *Oregon Spectator*, June 11, 1846, 1.

11. Jones and Rakestraw, *Prologue to Manifest Destiny*, 3.

12. Rakestraw, *For Honor or Destiny*, 124.

13. Jones and Rakestraw, *Prologue to Manifest Destiny*, 3.

14. "Philadelphia Citizens, Great Oregon Meeting, on Monday evening, the 12th inst. several thousands of the citizens and voters of the city and country of Philadelphia . . . assembled together in public meeting, to take into consideration the situation of the country in respect to the Oregon question" (Philadelphia: s.m., 1846), in Research Publications, Western Americana, reel 420, no. 4256.

15. Jessett, "Christian Missions to the Indians of Oregon," 147–56.

16. Pomeroy, *The Pacific Slope*, 25–33; Schwantes, *The Pacific Northwest*, 83–90.

17. Prucha, *The Great Father*, 396–97.

18. Culver, "Report to the Secretary of the Interior, July 20, 1854," 500–501.

19. Hines, *Touching Incidents*, 124.

20. Lindsay Applegate, "Recollections," *Portland Telegram*, August 13, 1904.

21. Robbins, *Landscapes of Promise*, 87; Applegate Family, Genealogy Vertical Files, Oregon Historical Society Genealogy Vertical Files; Milner, "National Initiatives," 171; Glassley, *Pacific Northwest Indian Wars*, 152–53; Riddle, *Indian History of the Modoc War*, 29–31.

22. Jackson and Spence, *The Expeditions of John Charles Frémont*, 2:120; "President Polk's Message," *Oregon Spectator*, June 11, 1846.

23. "President Polk's Message," *Oregon Spectator*, June 11, 1846.

24. Robbins, *Landscapes of Promise*, 87; Applegate Family, Genealogy Vertical Files, OHSRL; Milner, "National Initiatives," 171; Glassley, *Pacific Northwest Indian Wars*, 152–53; Riddle, *Indian History of the Modoc War*, 29–31. Riddle's version of the Wright incident indicates that Wright's men fired on forty Modocs as they approached to negotiate peace.

25. Coan, "Adoption of the Reservation Policy," 3–6.

26. Huntington, "Report of the Oregon Superintendency," 102.

27. Huntington, "Report of the Oregon Superintendency," 103.

28. Stern, *The Klamath Tribe*, 48; Good, *History of Klamath County*, 45–46; Applegate Family, Genealogy Vertical Files, Oregon Historical Society Research Library.

29. Cornwall, "Oliver Cromwell Applegate," 17–18.

30. Gatschet, *Klamath Indians of Southern Oregon*, 10; Stern, "The Klamath Indians and the Treaty of 1864," 229–65.

31. Department of the Interior, *Indian Affairs*, 2:865–68.

32. Martin, "'Neither Fish, Flesh, Fowl,'" 51–55.

33. Jacobson, *Barbarian Virtues*, 35.

34. Franklin D. Roosevelt, Address to Congress Requesting a Declaration of War Against Japan, December 8, 1942, Franklin D. Roosevelt Presidential Library Digital Archives, http://www.fdrlibrary.marist.edu/tmirhdee.html (accessed May 30, 2006); Dower, *War Without Mercy*, 29, 36–37.

35. Tom K. Ritchie, interview by Harry Behn, January or February 1942, in American Folklife Center, *After the Day of Infamy*.

36. Jacobson, *Barbarian Virtues*, 34–35.

37. Franklin, *War Stars*, 39–45; Sharp, *Savage Perils*, 107–12.

38. Office of War Information, *Our Enemy: The Japanese*.

39. Sharp, *Savage Perils*, 99–106.

40. Franklin D. Roosevelt, Address to Congress Requesting a Declaration of War Against Japan, December 8, 1942, Franklin D. Roosevelt Presidential Library Digital Archives, http://www.fdrlibrary.marist.edu/10142.html (accessed May 30, 2006); War Relocation Authority, *Wartime Exile*, 99; "Public Schools Hold First Air Raid Drill—a Success," *San Francisco Chronicle*, January 15, 1942, 20.

41. Daniels, "Incarceration of Japanese Americans," 300.

42. House Committee on Un-American Activities, *Investigation of Un-American Propaganda Activities*; "Gen. John De Witt Comes from a Famous Family of American Fighting Men," *Washington Daily News*, October 18, 1943.

43. Dower, *War Without Mercy* 177, 182–86.

44. War Relocation Authority, *Wartime Exile*, 51.

45. Sharp, *Savage Perils*, 109–10.

46. House Committee on Un-American Activities, *Investigation of Un-American Propaganda Activities*; O'Neill, *A Democracy at War*, 235.

47. Robinson, *By Order of the President*, 75; Grodzins, *Americans Betrayed*, 133–36.

48. Letters to the Editor, *San Francisco Chronicle*, December 8, 1941–January 20, 1942; "The Question of Loyalty is Personal," *San Francisco Chronicle*, January 20, 1942; "Japs Poised to Invade Singapore," *San Francisco Chronicle*, January 29, 1942.

49. Arthur Caylor, "Behind the News," *San Francisco News*, March 2, 1942, 4; Fuji, interview, TOHP; Iiyama, interview, TOHP, 9–10; Raineri, *The Red Angel*, 182, 205; Isserman, *Which Side Were You On?*, 143–45.

50. Kikuchi, *The Kikuchi Diary*, 42; Thomas, *The Salvage*, 248.

51. War Relocation Authority, *The Impounded People*, 14; House, Select Committee Investigating National Defense Migration, *Final Report*, 10966–68, 11128; House, House Report No. 2124, *Fourth Interim Report*, 1–2.

52. House, *House Naval Affairs Subcommittee*, pt. 3, 739–40; "Counties Rap Proposal to Accept Japs," *Salt Lake City Tribune*, March 17, 1942, 9; Hosokawa, *JACL in Quest of Justice*, 162.

53. Robinson, *By Order of the President*, 99–101; Taylor, "Our Stakes in the Japanese Exodus," 423; War Relocation Authority, *Wartime Exile*, 70.

54. tenBroek, Barnhardt, and Matson, *Prejudice, War, and the Constitution*, 235–38.

55. tenBroek, Barnhardt, and Matson, *Prejudice, War, and the Constitution*, 251–52; Tateishi, *And Justice for All*, 60–61. The Supreme Court ruled in *Takao Ozawa v. United States*, 260 U.S. 178 (1922), that Japanese were ineligible for citizenship because they could not be classified as "white" or "black."

56. House, Select Committee Investigating National Defense Migration, *Final Report*, 11012.

57. House, Report No. 2124, *Fourth Interim Report*, 1; War Relocation Authority, *The Impounded People*, 14; "SF Clear of All But 6 Sick Japs," *San Francisco Chronicle*, May 21, 1942, 1; Kikuchi, *The Kikuchi Diary*, 49–51; "Tea Garden Won't Stay Japanese but It'll Be Oriental," *San Francisco Chronicle*, March 14, 1942, 8.

58. Ben Takeshita in Tateishi, *And Justice for All*, 244; Okubo, *Citizen 13660*, 26–32; Verdoia, *Topaz*, VHS; Daniels, *Prisoners Without Trial*, 55; Yoshino, "Barbed Wire and Beyond," 34.

59. War Relocation Authority, *Questions and Answers for Evacuees*, n.p.; Okubo, *Citizen 13660*, 79, 87.

60. Myer and Krug, *The WRA*, 20; Arrington, *The Price of Prejudice*, 12–13.

61. Tolbert, interview, TOHP; Myer and Krug, *The WRA*, 20; Arrington, *The Price of Prejudice*, 12–13.

62. Johnson, *The Second Gold Rush*, 30; Fryer, "Pioneers All," 62–68.

63. "Fred" to Faith Terasawa, September 11, 1942, Terasawa Papers, University of Utah Marriott Library.

64. DeNevi, *West Coast Goes to War*; House, Special Committee to Investigate Communist Activities in the United States, *Hearings Before a Special Committee*; MacColl, *Growth of a City*, 468.

65. MacColl, *Growth of a City*, 468; Lane, *Ships for Victory*, 202; War Relocation Authority, *The Evacuated People*, 48–49; Bureau of Municipal Research, University of Oregon, Ordinance 22-412, "War Code of the City of Portland, Oregon" (Portland: WPA Project 165-1-94-33), Oregon Collection, Multnomah County Public Library; "Texas Cool to Gypsy Bands: Jail Awaits Caravan," *Oregon Journal*, January 6, 1945.

66. "Kaiser Brought 2500 New Yorkers," *Oregonian*, July 11, 1943; U.S. Department of Commerce, Bureau of the Census, *Wartime Changes in Population*, 1–2; Abbott, *Portland*, 109.

67. War Manpower Commission, "A Survey of Shipyard Operations," 12, 51.

68. Beecroft and Janow, "Toward a National Policy for Migration," 488.

69. Department of Commerce, Bureau of the Census, *Wartime Changes in Population*, 1–2; War Manpower Commission, "A Survey of Shipyard Operations," 53. For a history of housing segregation in Portland, see Pearson, "A Menace to the Neighborhood," 158–79; and McElderry, "Building a West Coast Ghetto," 137–48.

70. U.S. Committee for Congested Production Areas, "Report on Conditions in Portland, Oregon," February–May 1942, Wartime Housing Vertical Files, Loeb Design Library, Harvard University; Hill, *The FBI's RACON*, iii–xi, 382–83; Raineri, *The Red Angel*, 182, 205–7; and Isserman, *Which Side Were You On?*, 141–42, 167–69.

71. Smith and Taylor, "Racial Discrimination," 35–54.

72. Smith and Taylor, "Racial Discrimination," 46–50; Hill, *FBI's RACON*, 384; Records of Portland Police Bureau Red Squad, July–August 1942, SPARC.

73. War Manpower Commission, "A Survey of Shipyard Operations," September 1943, 2:51.

74. Little and Weiss, *Blacks in Oregon*, 58; "Third Kaiser Train Arrives," *Oregonian*, October 3, 1942; "New Negro Migrants Worry City," *Oregonian*, September 23, 1942; "Court Action Voted to Block Housing Plan for Negroes," *Oregonian*, September 30, 1942; "Negro House Plan Brings Albina Fight," *Oregon Journal*, September 30, 1942.

75. Colean, *Housing for Defense*, 114–17.

76. Klutznick, *Angles of Vision*, 125–27.

77. Garner, *The Model Company Town*, 9–10.

78. Garner, *The Model Company Town*, 54.

79. The federal government was very explicit about its restrictions on constructing war housing in flood-prone areas. See Housing Authority of Portland, "History of the Construction of Vanport City."

80. Maben, *Vanport*, 32–35.

81. Grandy, *Leo Szilard*, 68–73; and Lanouette and Szilard, *Genius in the Shadows*, 184–93.

82. Albert Einstein to Franklin D. Roosevelt, August 2, 1939, Franklin D. Roosevelt Presidential Library Digital Archives, http://www.fdrlibrary.marist.edu/psf/box5/ab4a01.html (accessed June 5, 2006); Kunetka, *City of Fire*, 23–24; Lawren, *General and the Bomb*, 137.

83. Schwartz, *Atomic Audit*, 437. For the development of the Manhattan Engineer District and the bomb project, see Gosling, *The Manhattan Project*.

84. Groves, *Now It Can Be Told*, 140–43.

85. Segrè, *A Mind Always in Motion*, 173.

86. Fermi, *Atoms in the Family*, 163–68; Segrè, *Enrico Fermi*, 122.

87. Quoted from "Memorandum for the Officer in Charge," 201 file (Szilard), U.S. Army Intelligence and Security Command, Fort George C. Meade, Maryland 1940, in Grandy, *Leo Szilard*, 87. The text of the unsigned letter, dated October 28, 1942, reads: "Dear Mr. Attorney General, The United States will be forced without delay to dispense with the services of Leo Szilard of Chicago, who is working on one of the most secret War Department projects. It is considered essential to the prosecution of the war that Mr. Szilard, who is an enemy alien, be interned for the duration of the war. It is requested that an order of internment be issued against Mr. Szilard and that he be apprehended and turned over to [the War Department] for internment." See Lanouette and Szilard, *Genius in the Shadows*, 240; Grandy, *Leo Szilard*, 158.

88. Federal Bureau of Investigation, *J. Robert Oppenheimer Security Files*, File #116-2717. See document series one (1939–41) for numerous reports on Lomanitz and his relationship to Oppenheimer and other key Rad Lab scientists as well as Steve Nelson and the California Communist Party.

89. Federal Bureau of Investigation, *J. Robert Oppenheimer Security Files*, Memorandum, March 28, 1941, File #116-2717.

90. U.S. Atomic Energy Commission, *In the Matter of J. Robert Oppenheimer*, 35–36; Larsen, *Oppenheimer and the Atomic Bomb*; Memorandum, March 28, 1941, File #116-2717, in Federal Bureau of Investigation, *J. Robert Oppenheimer Security Files*.

91. Hilgartner, Bell, and O'Connor, *Nukespeak*, 25; Federal Bureau of Investigation, *J. Robert Oppenheimer Security Files*, pt. 3, 1943; Davis, *Lawrence and Oppenheimer*, 150; Groves, *Now It Can Be Told*, 63.

92. Federal Bureau of Investigation, *J. Robert Oppenheimer Security Files*, pt. 1, 1940–41. Morrison, Hawkins, and Frank Oppenheimer later testified before Congress that they had been members of the Communist Party in the 1930s but turned away from radical politics after Stalin signed the pact with Hitler and Soviet scientists recounted the purges. See Stern, *The Oppenheimer Case*, 42.

93. Michelson, *The Swift Years*, 84.

94. Rothman, *On Rims and Ridges*, 214, 221–22; Smith and Weiner, *Robert Oppenheimer*, 239; "Personalities Around the Hill: Bences Gonzales," *Los Alamos Times*, December 6, 1946. New Mexico was also considered more hospitable because the number of New Mexican servicemen who had been victims of the Bataan Death March heightened the state's support for any retaliatory effort against the Axis powers. See Chambers, "Technically Sweet Los Alamos," 30.

95. Carl Peter interviewed by Lansing Lamont (July 6, 1963), 3. Lansing Lamont Papers box 1, Harry S. Truman Presidential Library; Jette, *Inside Box 1663*, 33; Hilgartner, Bell, and O'Connor, *Nukespeak*, 30; Smith and Weiner, *Robert Oppenheimer*, 256.

96. Hunner, *Inventing Los Alamos*, 41–42; Serber, *Peace and War*, 79.

97. Jane Wilson quoted in Wilson and Serber, *Standing By and Making Do*, 51; Fisher, *Los Alamos Experience*, 39; Los Alamos Historical Society, prod., *Remembering Los Alamos*, VHS.

98. Kunetka, *City of Fire*, 46; Truslow, *Manhattan District History*, 24; Hales, *Atomic Spaces*, 75.

99. Gosling, *The Manhattan Project*, 37–39.

100. Gosling, *The Manhattan Project*, 39. The army never held the scientists to their military commitment because it was more important that they work long hours than be bugled out of bed on a regular schedule. Davis, *Lawrence and Oppenheimer*, 165.

101. Groves, *Now It Can Be Told*, 142–43, 164; Segrè, *A Mind Always in Motion*, 183.

102. Franklin Delano Roosevelt, "Report on the Home Front," October 12, 1942, Fireside Chats, Franklin Delano Presidential Library Digital Archives, http://www.fdrlibrary.marist.edu/10142.html (accessed January 30, 2005).

2. THE GREAT CITIZENSHIP PANTOMIME

1. War Relocation Authority, *The Impounded People*, 48; Taylor, *Jewel of the Desert*, 112; Netz, *Barbed Wire*, 128–30.

2. War Relocation Authority, *Legal and Constitutional Phases*, 1.

3. War Relocation Authority, *Legal and Constitutional Phases*, 25. *Black's Law Dictionary* defines *parens patriae* as "parent of his/her country"; the state, as sovereign, may invoke its capacity to provide care, protection, or guardianship to citizens unable to act on their own behalf. It also refers to the doctrine allowing the state to sue on behalf of its citizens, in rare instances. *Black's Law Dictionary*, 7th ed., s.v. "parents patriae," 1137.

4. Spicer et al., *The Impounded People*, 81. (Originally published by the U.S. Government Printing Office in 1946 under the corporate authorship of the War Relocation Authority.)

5. War Relocation Authority, *Legal and Constitutional Phases*, 1, 25.

6. Colonel George Curry of Fort Klamath to Fort Vancouver, September 20, 1865, O. C. Applegate Papers, University of Oregon Libraries, Special Collections and University Archives.

7. Meacham, *Wigwam and Warpath*, 248; "Klamaths and Modocs," *New York Times*, July 14, 1873.

8. Stern, *The Klamath Tribe*, 77–78; Good, *Klamath County History*, 53; Cornwall, "Oliver Cromwell Applegate," 18.

9. Stern, *The Klamath Tribe*, 80–81.

10. Otis, *The Allotment Act*, 25–26.

11. Meacham, *Wigwam and Warpath*, 270.

12. Meacham, *Wigwam and Warpath*, 418; Riddle, *Indian History of the Modoc War*, 20–27.

13. Meacham, *Wigwam and Warpath*, 418–19.

14. "SAVAGES. Letter of Mr. Meacham Detailing the Brutal Treachery of Modoc Jack — Latest from the Front," *New York Times*, April 29, 1873.

15. Quinn, *Hell With the Fire Out*, 96–129; "David Allen on Captain Jack and the Modocs," *New York Times*, July 14, 1873; "Captain Jack's Duplicity," *New York Times*, August 11, 1873.

16. Colonel George Curry of Fort Klamath to Fort Vancouver, September 20, 1865, O. C. Applegate Papers, University of Oregon Libraries, Special Collections and University Archives.

17. "Modoc Lands," *New York Times*, July 2, 1873, 4; Bancroft, *History of Oregon*, 636.

18. Frantz, *Indian Reservations in the United States*, 15–20; *An illustrated history of central Oregon, embracing Wasco, Sherman, Gilliam, Wheeler, Crook, Lake and Klamath counties, state of Oregon* (Spokane WA: Western Historical Publishing Company, 1905), quoted in Good, *History of Klamath County*, 24.

19. Britten, *American Indians in World War I*, 21.

20. Britten, *American Indians in World War I*, 21–22; Stern, *The Klamath Tribe*, 90–93.

21. Dyar, "Annual Report to the Commissioner of Indian Affairs, Klamath Agency," 324; Good, *History of Klamath County*, 24; Stern, *The Klamath Tribe*, 90; Barker, "American Indian Tribal Police," 51–54; "Law and Order Correspondence, 1879," Records Relating to Law Enforcement 1879–1954, Records of the Klamath Indian Agency (RG 75.19.51), NARAPAR; Britten, *American Indians in World War I*, 20–21.

22. Barlow, "Minorities Policing Minorities," 141–63.

23. Stern, *The Klamath Tribe*, 92.

24. Jackson, *A Century of Dishonor*, 337.

25. Copp, *The American Settler's Guide*, 97.

26. The Homestead Act was conceived as a measure for national security and economic stability. Stephen C. Foster made a clear statement of this in his 1880 speech before the House of Representatives, "Republican Land Policy: Homes for the Million: Give the Public Lands to the People, and You settle the Slavery Question, obliterate the Frontiers, dispense with a Standing Army, and extinguish Mormonism" (Washington DC: Republican Congressional Committee, 1880). In a few cases, Indians were granted homesteads on similar terms as non-Indian homesteaders, but they had to renounce all tribal ties and have the land held in trust for twenty-five years. See U.S. Supreme Court, *United States v. Jackson*, 280 U.S. 183 (1930).

27. Hoxie, *A Final Promise*, 53.

28. Fey and McNickle, *Indians and Other Americans*, 83–85; Trennert, *Alternative to Extinction*, vi–vii; Hoxie, *A Final Promise*, 70; Martin, "'Neither Fish, Flesh, Fowl,'" 51–55.

29. Stern, *The Klamath Tribe*, 58.

30. Stern, *The Klamath Tribe*, 131–33; Otis, *The Allotment Act*, 89; Oliver Applegate, Report to the Indian Bureau, November 1888, O. C. Applegate Papers, University of Oregon Libraries, Special Collections and University Archives.

31. Minutes of the Klamath Tribal Council, September 5, 1908, Records of Tribal Councils and Committees, 1895–1960, Records of Klamath Indian Agency (RG 75.19.51), NARAPAR.

32. Minutes of the Klamath Tribal Council, September 5, 1908, Records of Tribal Councils and Committees, 1895–1960, Records of Klamath Indian Agency (RG 75.19.51), NARAPAR.

33. Minutes of the Klamath Tribal Council, June 13, 1909, Records of Tribal Councils and Committees, 1895–1960, Records of Klamath Indian Agency (RG 75.19.51), NARAPAR.

34. Minutes of the Klamath Tribal Council, June 13, 1909, Records of Tribal Councils and Committees, 1895–1960, Records of Klamath Indian Agency (RG 75.19.51), NARAPAR.

35. Frather, "Fourth of July at Klamath Reservation," 116–23.

36. Myer and Krug, *The WRA*, 6.

37. War Relocation Authority, *The Japanese Relocation*; War Relocation Authority, *The Impounded People* (1946), 87; War Relocation Authority, *Community Government*, 6.

38. E. R. Fryer to Solon Kimball, 1942, quoted in War Relocation Authority, *Community Government*, 17; Myer and Krug, *The Impounded People*, 83.

39. Okubo, *Citizen 13660*, 15; War Relocation Authority, *The Japanese Relocation*.

40. Takahashi, interview, TOHP; Okubo, *Citizen 13660*, 35–41; Oshita, interview, TOHP.

41. Girdner and Loftis, *The Great Betrayal*, 179–83.

42. House Committee on Un-American Activities, *Investigation of Un-American Propaganda Activities*, 9468–9973. The Japanese American Citizens for Democracy (JACD) membership included numerous high-profile people whom the FBI found suspect, including atomic scientists Albert Einstein and Harold Urey; anthropologist Franz Boas; National Congress of American Indians leader Oliver LaFarge; Congressman Adam Clayton Powell; and civil libertarians Carey McWilliams, Galen Fisher, Pearl Buck, and Katherine Terrill. In 1948 Topazian Chizu Iiyama was named national chair. The group remained on the FBI's list of front organizations until well after the war, and western police bureaus were instructed to monitor the committee's activities. See Records of the Portland Police Bureau Red Squad, SPARC; Chang, *Morning Glory, Evening Shadow*, 100–115, 124.

43. John F. Embree, "Community Analysis Report No. 1: Dealing with Japanese Americans" (unpublished typescript, October 1942), 4–7, Records of the War Relocation Authority Central Utah Relocation Project (WRA CURP), ALSC.

44. WRA Administrative Notice #130, "Relocation Plans for Unattached Children," July 28, 1944, Japanese American Internment Collection, University of Utah Marriott Library; Kobi, interview, TOHP; War Relocation Authority, "Excerpts from Administrative Manual," Section 30.31, July 14, 1944, Terasawa Papers, University of Utah Marriott Library.

45. War Relocation Authority, *Questions and Answers for Evacuees*; War Relocation Authority, "Welcome to Topaz" (unpublished pamphlet, ca. 1943, acc. 56), 12, ALSC; Tom Kawaguchi, "Topaz, 442nd Regimental Combat Team, France, Italy," in Tateishi, *And Justice for All*, 180.

46. Evelyn Kimura, "To the Women," *Topaz Times*, September 25, 1943, 4; Kobi, interview, TOHP; Taylor, *Jewel of the Desert*, 112.

47. Uchida, *Desert Exile*, 109; Okubo, "Artist Statement," 107–9; "Words," *Topaz Times*, September 17, 1942.

48. Verdoia, *Topaz*, VHS; Suyemoto, interview, TOHP; Katayama, interview, TOHP.

49. James, *Exile Within*, 91.

50. War Relocation Authority, *The Relocation Program*, 28; Oshita, interview, TOHP.

51. "Headquarters, Western Defense Command and Fourth Army, Presidio of San Francisco, California, September 17, 1942 Circular No. 19: Policies Pertaining to Use of Military Police at War Relocation Centers," in U.S. Department of War, Fourth Army, *Final Report*, 527–29; Senate Committee on Military Affairs, *Report of the Subcommittee on Japanese War Relocation Centers*, 262; War Relocation Authority, *Community Government in the Relocation Centers*, 6–7.

52. War Relocation Authority, *Supplemental Policy Statement*, 12.

53. War Relocation Authority, *Community Government in the Relocation Centers*, 3–5; Fuji, interview, TOHP; Katayama, interview, TOHP.

54. War Relocation Authority, "Welcome to Topaz," ALSC; Iyama, interview, TOHP; Katayama, interview, TOHP; Fuji, interview, TOHP.

55. Lewis, "Annual Report," 1–2; Barlow, "Minorities Policing Minorities," 141–63; Roy Ikeda to Charles Ernst, September 10, 1943, addendum to interview with Sandra Taylor, TOHP.

56. Shimamoto, interview, TOHP; War Relocation Authority, *Administrative Highlights*, 58.

57. Housing Authority of Portland (HAP), "Vanport Tenant's Handbook" (Portland: HAP, 1943), RHAP, OHSRL; Gray and Robinson, interview, Oregon Historical Society Research Library.

58. Vanport Public Schools, *6,000 Kids from 48 States*, 12.

59. "Those Newcomer Votes," *Oregon Journal*, September 17, 1942; "Agreement Between the United States and the City of Portland," December 10, 1941, Riley Papers, OHSRL.

60. Charter of the City of Portland, 1942, sec. 3-118, Multnomah County Public Library; State of Oregon, *Oregon Laws Enacted and Joint Resolutions Adopted by the 44th Regular Session of the Legislative Assembly*, chapter 329, 468–69.

61. "Trailer Leases Merely a Snare and a Delusion," *The East Side Post* (Portland OR), July 14, 1948; Maben, *Vanport*, 32–35; HAP, "Vanport Residents Handbook," 3, RHAP, OHSRL.

62. Minutes of the Board of Commissioners, HAP, February 8, 1943, RHAP, SPARC.

63. John A. Jessup, "Facilities and Personnel for Project Services" (unpublished speech ca. 1943), Jessup Papers, Harry S. Truman Presidential Library.

64. Minutes of the Board of Commissioners, HAP, May 10, 1943, RHAP, SPARC.

65. HAP urged Franzen to distribute fliers "carefully worded so as to indicate that it is a plan to be worked out by the people of Vanport City, for their own benefit." Minutes of the Board of HAP, June 7, 1943, RHAP, SPARC.

66. Minutes of the Board of Commissioners, HAP, August, 4, 1943, and August 17, 1944, RHAP, SPARC; Vern Marshall, interview by author, Portland OR, June 18, 2001.

67. Minutes of the Board of Commissioners, HAP, July 12, 1943, and May 18, 1944, RHAP, SPARC; Fuji, interview, TOHP.

68. Minutes of the Board of Commissioners, HAP, June 1, 1944, RHAP, SPARC.

69. Minutes of the Board of Commissioners, HAP, August 17, 1944, RHAP, SPARC; Barlow, "Minorities Policing Minorities," 141–63; Barker, "American Indian Tribal Police," 51–54.

70. Hewlett and Anderson, *The New World*, 235; FBI Report, April 17, 1950, in Espionage Files, Szasz Papers, Mss 552, University of New Mexico Center for Southwest Research.

71. Hewlett and Anderson, *The New World*, 238; Davis, *Lawrence and Oppenheimer*, 186; Sykes, *No Ordinary Genius*, 49.

72. Jette, *Inside Box 1663*, 17; Rhodes, *The Making of the Atomic Bomb*, 565; Charlotte Serber in Wilson and Serber, *Standing By and Making Do*, 61; Hales, *Atomic Spaces*, 120.

73. "Second Memorandum on Los Alamos Project" (n.d.), Froman Papers, Los Alamos Historical Museum Archives.

74. Chambers, "Technically Sweet Los Alamos," 213.

75. Chambers, "Technically Sweet Los Alamos," 213.

76. Smith and Weiner, *Robert Oppenheimer*, 87; Los Alamos Community Bulletin, December 24, 1943, and April 7, 1944, Froman Papers, Los Alamos Historical Museum Archives.

77. McMillan, *The Atom and Eve*, 33–34; Smith and Weiner, *Robert Oppenheimer*, 84; Chambers, "Technically Sweet Los Alamos," 132.

78. McMillan, *The Atom and Eve*, 34.

79. Chambers, "Technically Sweet Los Alamos," 135.

80. Jette, *Inside Box 1663*, 52; Jones, *Manhattan, the Army, and the Bomb*, 355–62.

81. Chambers, "Technically Sweet Los Alamos," 114; Jette, *Inside Box 1663*, 52.

82. Jette, *Inside Box 1663*, 57–59.

83. Jette, *Inside Box 1663*, 98.

84. Ruth Marshak in Wilson and Serber, *Standing By and Making Do*, 16; Alice Kimball Smith in Wilson and Serber, *Standing By and Making Do*, 73; McMillan, *The Atom and Eve*, 35.

85. Minutes of the Los Alamos Town Council, July 9, 1943, Los Alamos Town Council Records, Los Alamos Historical Museum Archives. For the issue of jukeboxes at Vanport, see Minutes of the Board of Commissioners, HAP, September 16, 1943, and December 6, 1944, RHAP, SPARC.

86. Brode, *Tales of Los Alamos*, 11.

3. CULTIVATING DEPENDENCY

1. Cullen, *The American Dream*; White House Press Release, "Expanding Home Ownership For All Americans," March 15, 2004, http://www.whitehouse.gov/news/releases/2004/03/20040315-3.html (accessed March 8, 2007).

2. Studebaker, *Plain Talk*, 17.

3. Department of the Interior, Division of Subsistence Homesteads, "A Homestead and a Hope"; Miller, "An Initial Report"; Deverell, "To Loosen the Safety Valve," 270–71.

4. Reese, *America's Public Schools*, 27–29.

5. Foster, "Republican Land Policy," 7.

6. Deverell, "To Loosen the Safety Valve," 269. The federal government offered homesteads to Indians who "abandoned the habits of tribal life." The Interior Department retained its powers to "protect the rights of the Indian homesteader" by retaining control over the disposition and use of homesteads granted to off-reservation Native people. See U.S. Supreme Court, *United States v. Jackson*, 280 U.S. 183 (1930).

7. Foster, "Republican Land Policy," 3.

8. Department of the Interior, *Indian Affairs*, 2:865–68.

9. Stern, *The Klamath Tribe*, 63. For an overview of outwork programs for girls in domestic service, see Margaret Jacobs, "Working on the Domestic Frontier," 165–99.

10. Stern, *The Klamath Tribe*, 60.

11. Department of the Interior, Office of Indian Affairs, *Annual Report*, 74–75.

12. While such arrangements were common on reservations, Oliver Applegate played multiple roles in the Klamath economic system. In addition to reservation agent, he was the founder of the *Klamath Republican*, where he published his view on reservation issues, placed ads for bids on reservation commodities, and negotiated with vendors who were also his customers. By 1925 the *Republican* made regular announcements of pending disbursements so that non-Native vendors could be prepared to sell to Klamath

customers. See Trumbull, *A History of Oregon Newspapers*, 403; and "Indians Will Receive Big Payment," *Klamath Republican*, September 16, 1925.

13. Prucha, *The Great Father*, 527–33.

14. Prucha, *The Great Father*, 70–71.

15. Cornwall, "Oliver Cromwell Applegate," 27–28; Prucha, *The Great Father*, 190; Stern, *The Klamath Tribe*, 159–61.

16. Reyhner and Eder, *American Indian Education*, 67–74; Szasz, *Education and the American Indian*, 9–10.

17. U.S. Board of Indian Commissioners, *What the Government and the Churches Are Doing for the Indians*, 17; Stern, *The Klamath Tribe*, 48, 105–10.

18. Hoxie, *A Final Promise*, 67–68; Stern, *The Klamath Tribe*, 105–10.

19. Livingston, "Klamath Indians in Two Non-Reservation Communities," 95; Reyhner and Eder, *American Indian Education*, 72–78.

20. Reese, *America's Public Schools*, 103–7.

21. Stern, *The Klamath Tribe*, 107; Livingston, "Klamath Indians in Two Non-Reservation Communities," 97.

22. Livingston, "Klamath Indians in Two Non-Reservation Communities," 96.

23. John Albert to Eva Emery Dye, June 1, 1886, Dye Papers, OHSRL. John Albert's letter to Eva Emery Dye opens with, "I thought I would write a letter to you this time, for the reason that one of our Schoolmates died day before yesterday named Nancy Amos from Idaho Territory. . . . The rest of the scholars are well except as you know James George, is getting very low spirit at this time he has been sick since early in the spring. And some boys and girls having mumps, not as worse as him. I believe, he going to die pretty soon."

24. Lorenz, *The Time of My Life*, 108–11; Dippie, *The Vanishing American*, 26; Fey and McNickle, *Indians and Other Americans*, 125–41; John Albert to Eva Emery Dye, June 1, 1886, Dye Papers, OHSRL.

25. Cornwall, "Oliver Cromwell Applegate," 27–28; Prucha, *The Great Father*, 190; Stern, *The Klamath Tribe*, 159–61.

26. Stern, *The Klamath Tribe*, 163.

27. Stern, *The Klamath Tribe*, 167–69.

28. Stern, *The Klamath Tribe*, 173–74.

29. Stern, *The Klamath Tribe*, 175.

30. Stern, *The Klamath Tribe*, 172–77.

31. Stern, *The Klamath Tribe*, 177.

32. Department of the Interior, Division of Subsistence Homesteads, "A Homestead and a Hope," 21; Miller, "An Initial Report," 28. Congress authorized the creation of the Division of Subsistence Homesteads as a branch of the Resettlement Administration (NRA), which was itself part of the National Industrial Recovery Act (NIRA). The division was transferred to the Farm Security Administration, which was housed within the

Department of the Interior and supervised by Harold Ickes in 1937 after the Supreme Court ruled that NIRA operated outside constitutional bounds.

33. Miller, "An Initial Report," 5. Daniel Rodgers also notes that the Resettlement Administration's critics denounced the enclaves as vessels for the "foreign ideas" of European progressives, including Communism, making restrictions on "un-American" activities like collective farming absolutely imperative. See Rodgers, *Atlantic Crossings*, 468–69.

34. Department of the Interior, Division of Subsistence Homesteads, "A Homestead and a Hope," 6.

35. Department of the Interior, Division of Subsistence Homesteads, "A Homestead and a Hope," 6.

36. Department of the Interior, Division of Subsistence Homesteads, "A Homestead and a Hope," 4, 19.

37. U.S. Department of Agriculture, "Planning a Subsistence Homestead," 4; U.S. Department of the Interior, *Homestead Houses*, 1–3.

38. Rodgers, *Atlantic Crossings*, 346–49, 350–52. Asian immigrants were barred from the settler communities. See Rodgers, *Atlantic Crossings*, 350.

39. Miller, "An Initial Report," 9.

40. Miller, "An Initial Report," 9.

41. Department of the Interior, Division of Subsistence Homesteads, "A Homestead and a Hope," 10; Reese, *America's Public Schools*, 141–43; Dewey and Dewey, "Democracy and Education," 257–58.

42. Miller, "An Initial Report," 10.

43. Franklin D. Roosevelt, "Annual Message to Congress, January 6, 1941," Franklin D. Roosevelt Presidential Library Digital Archives, http://www.fdrlibrary.marist.edu/4free.html (accessed August 3, 2005).

44. Rodgers, *Atlantic Crossings*, 448.

45. Miller, "An Initial Report," 27.

46. Lippard, *The Lure of the Local*, 64.

47. Takahashi, interview, TOHP; Roy Ikeda to Ernst, addendum to interview, TOHP; Arrington, *The Price of Prejudice*, 18.

48. War Relocation Authority, *The Relocation Program*, 9–12; "Community Analysis Report No. 10," in War Relocation Authority, *Community Analysis Reports* no. 1–18, 7–8, 21; Lasker, "Friends or Enemies?" 279.

49. War Relocation Authority, *The Relocation Program*, 5. The WRA supplemented evacuee wages with a monthly clothing allowance, but this benefit looked so much like welfare that few Topazians would take it. An internee social worker had to go from barrack to barrack, explaining the odd economics of the camp and reframing the allowance as compensation for aiding in Pacific Coast security. Katayama, interview, TOHP.

50. James F. Hughes, Assistant Project Director, "Annual Report: Central Utah Relocation Center" (unpublished report), January 1, 1944; John F. Embree, "Community Analysis Report No. 2: Causes of Unrest at Relocation Centers," (unpublished typescript, ca. 1944), Records of the WRA CURP, ALSC.

51. Nagata-Aikawa, interview, TOHP.

52. Uchida, Desert Exile, 110–11; War Relocation Authority, Administrative Highlights, 58; Nakagawa, Ijima, and Kariya, interview, TOHP.

53. Embree, "Community Analysis Report No. 1," 6, Records of the WRA CURP, ALSC. The WRA dropped food costs from 43.2 cents per person per day to 31 cents (substantially less than the 55 cents per day to feed members of the armed services), while quelling unrest with better-quality meals. Food production reached $100,000 in value. Roscoe Bell, Assistant Project Director in Charge of Operations, Central Utah Relocation Center, annual report (unpublished typescript), 1. Records of the WRA CURP, ALSC; Verdoia, Topaz, VHS.

54. Central Utah Relocation Center, Historical Reports Division, "Organization and Development of the Topaz Consumer Cooperative Enterprises," (unpublished typescript, n.d.), 8, Records of the WRA CURP, ALSC.

55. Central Utah Relocation Center, Historical Reports Division, "Organization and Development of the Topaz Consumer Cooperative Enterprises," 4, Records of the WRA CURP, ALSC.

56. Okubo, Citizen 13660, 153–54; "Women's Mirror," Topaz Times January 23, 1943, and April 24, 1943; Marii Kyogoku, "A La Mode," Trek (December 1942), 27–28; Takahashi, interview, TOHP, 62; Kitano, interview, 6–7, TOHP.

57. Fujita, interview, TOHP.

58. Central Utah Relocation Center, Historical Reports Division, "Organization and Development of the Topaz Consumer Cooperative Enterprises," 5, Records of the WRA CURP, ALSC; Samuel, Pledging Allegiance, 104–6; Bell, "Relocation Center Life, Topaz, Utah, 1942–1945" (unpublished typescript, 1982), 36, Japanese-American Internment Collection, University of Utah Marriott Library.

59. "Community Analysis Report #5: Reactions to Lifting of Exclusions and Closing of Centers," January 15–21, 1945, 6, Records of the WRA CURP, ALSC; Department of the Interior, War Agency Liquidation Unit, People in Motion, 52–55.

60. War Relocation Authority, Semi-Annual Report, July 1–December 31, 1943, in War Relocation Authority Reports, 67; Department of the Interior, War Agency Liquidation Unit, People in Motion, 52–55.

61. War Relocation Authority, Education Program in the Evacuation Centers, 4.

62. James, Exile Within, 29–30, 37.

63. James, Exile Within, 59.

64. Nagata-Aikawa, interview, TOHP; Uchida, Desert Exile, 118; Suyemoto, interview, TOHP.

65. One Topazian noted that at her old high school, white students held all the leadership positions, but at Topaz High, she could be involved in any activity she wanted. See James, *Exile Within*, 45; Kiyota, *Beyond Loyalty*, 77–81.

66. War Relocation Authority, *Education Program in the Evacuation Centers*, 9. The Parents' Advisory Council, weary of "advising" the WRA, held a mass meeting to pressure the Education Department into both providing the necessary curriculum so that students would not have to repeat grades after the war and stopping the automatic promotion of under-achieving students on the grounds that conditions prohibited remedial interventions. See James, *Exile Within*, 72 and Verdoia, *Topaz*, VHS.

67. Department of the Interior, War Agency Liquidation Unit, *People in Motion*, 50; Embree, "Community Analysis Report No. 1," 2, Records of the WRA CURP, ALSC.

68. Minutes of the Board of Commissioners, HAP, January 29, 1943, RHAP, SPARC; HAP, "Vanport Tenant's Handbook," RHAP, OHSRL.

69. "Vanport Grows," *Business Week*, December 11, 1943, 74. To be considered for a lease, HAP had to determine that "in the operation and management of Project Ore. 35053 [Vanport] . . . it is necessary that commercial facilities [proposed by the applicant] be established." See Minutes of the Board of HAP, January 29, 1943, RHAP, SPARC.

70. Minutes of the Board of Commissioners, HAP, August 18, 1943, and May 18, 1944, RHAP, SPARC.

71. "Facilities and Personnel for Project Services," Jessup Papers, Harry S. Truman Presidential Library; Vanport Public Schools, "Bulletin of General Information," 2, RHAP, OHSRL. For more on childcare for defense workers, see Kesselman, *Fleeting Opportunities*, 65–89; and Skold, "Women Workers and Childcare during World War II."

72. U.S. War Manpower Commission, *A Survey of Shipyards in the Portland, Oregon Metropolitan Area*, 53; Novak, interview, Pacific Northwest Oral History Project, OHSRL; Vanport Public Schools, *6,000 Kids from 48 States*, 5.

73. Kaiser Shipbuilding Company, "General Information Sheet on Kaiser Childcare Centers," n.d., Skold Collection, OHSRL; Oregon Shipbuilding Company, *Child Service Centers: An Experiment in Services for Employees*, 1945, 5, Kaiser Shipbuilding Company Records, Mss 2978, OHSRL.

74. *New York Times*, August 15, 1944; Althans, "Reclaiming Place," 31.

75. Kaiser Shipbuilding Company, "General Information Sheet," Skold Collection, OHSRL; Vanport Public Schools, "Bulletin of General Information," RHAP, OHSRL.

76. Vanport Public Schools, *6,000 Kids from 48 States*, 4, 48–49.

77. Vanport Public Schools, *6,000 Kids from 48 States*, 48.

78. Vanport Public Schools, *6,000 Kids from 48 States*, 5.

79. Minutes of the Board of Commissioners, HAP, July 20, 1944, RHAP, SPARC.

80. Vanport Public Schools, *6,000 Kids from 48 States*, 7.

81. Vanport Public Schools, *6,000 Kids from 48 States*, 62–63.

82. Vanport Public Schools, *6,000 Kids from 48 States*, 63; Althans, "Reclaiming Place," 103.

83. Gosling, "The Manhattan Project," 137–39; Davis, *Lawrence and Oppenheimer*, 165; Segrè, *Atoms, Bombs and Eskimo Kisses*, 183.

84. Smith Oral History, Radcliffe College Archives, Schlesinger Library, Radcliffe Institute, Harvard University; Charlotte Serber in Wilson and Serber, *Standing By and Making Do*, 67.

85. Davis, *Lawrence and Oppenheimer*, 186; Hales, *Atomic Spaces*, 211–21.

86. Lydia Martinez, head maid in Los Alamos Historical Society, prod., *Remembering Los Alamos*, VHS; Hales, *Atomic Spaces*, 206–8, 211–21; Hunner, *Inventing Los Alamos*, 63–65.

87. Fisher, *Los Alamos Experience*, 89. For prewar San Ildefonso, see Linton, *Acculturation in Seven American Indian Tribes*, 390–459.

88. "Personalities Around the Hill," *Los Alamos Times*, July 3, 1946.

89. Agoyo, "LANL 2000" (unpublished typescript, August 1993), supplied to the author by the Los Alamos Study Group, Santa Fe, New Mexico. Linton, *Acculturation in Seven American Indian Tribes*, 390–450; "Personalities Around the Hill," *Los Alamos Times*, July 3, 1946; "San Ildefonoso Pueblo Watched Secret City Grow," *Albuquerque Journal*, November 29, 1970.

90. Davis, *Lawrence and Oppenheimer*, 186.

91. Hales, *Atomic Spaces*, 211.

92. Hales, *Atomic Spaces*, 211.

93. Hunner, *Inventing Los Alamos*, 51–53.

94. Emilio Segrè, *Enrico Fermi*, 190.

95. Charlotte Serber in Wilson and Serber, *Standing By and Making Do*, 57; Bernice Brode to Evangeline, November 2, 1943, Brode Papers, Los Alamos Historical Museum Archives.

96. Jette, *Inside Box 1663*, 29–30.

97. Hales, *Atomic Spaces*, 216.

98. Hewlett and Anderson, *The New World*, 311; Jones, *Manhattan*, 350–62; Sauer, "The Forgotten SG," Los Alamos Historical Museum Archives; Bell, *Los Alamos WAACs*, 41, 21–13; Roensch, *Life Within Limits*.

99. Miller, "An Initial Report," 10.

4. TRAGIC IRONIES

1. Oliver Applegate to Miss Horner, March 28, 1913, O. C. Applegate Papers, University of Oregon Libraries, Special Collections and University Archives; Salyer, "Baptism by Fire," 848–49.

2.Britten, *American Indians in World War I*, 21, 131.

3.Superintendent's Memo on Indian Participation in Red Cross Activities, May 18, 1925, and American Red Cross, Indian School Letter No. 13, April 1925, from "Indians in World War I," RG 75.19.51, NARAPAR; Britten, *American Indians in World War I*, 133.

4.Oregon Secretary of State, *Oregon Blue Book, 1925–26*, 158.

5.Britten, *American Indians in World War I*, 178–80; Crain Sconchin to Supt. L. D. Arnold, May 21, 1926, Records of Klamath Indian Agency (RG 75.19.51), NARAPAR.

6."Famous for Murders," *Oregonian Sunday Magazine*, March 6, 1928, 6. For an example of Natives' postwar invisibility, see Klamath County Historical Society, *The History of Klamath County, Oregon*, 17–19.

7.Institute for Government Research, *The Problems of Indian Administration*, 42–43.

8.Philp, *John Collier's Crusade*, 228–29.

9.Rusco, *A Fateful Time*, 128–30, 165; Subcommittee of the Senate Committee on Indian Affairs, *A Resolution Directing the Committee on Indian Affairs*.

10.The Klamath General Council voted against the IRA by a margin of 408 to 56, which represents an overwhelming rejection given the difficulty of assembling a quorum and the practice of counting abstentions as "yes" votes. See Collier's statement in the appendix to House Committee on Indian Affairs, *Dismissal of Superintendent Wade Crawford*, July 1–8, 1937, 339; and O'Brien, *American Indian Tribal Governments*, 82.

11.Tyler, *A History of Indian Policy*, 128. Theodore Stern attributes the Klamath and Umatilla tribes' rejection of the IRA to their absorption of Oregon's rural anti-Communism. Crawford's reasons for withdrawing support are unclear, though general council minutes reveal concern about how the IRA laws would interact with other established laws and privileges. In congressional testimony, Crawford roundly criticized the act for failing to establish true self-government on the reservations in favor of diverting power over Indian affairs from Congress to the Interior Department. Crawford and Senator Burton K. Wheeler, an original sponsor of the bill, were also hostile to Collier. Crawford accused him of pressuring Klamaths to vote for the IRA, and Wheeler of crafting a communist policy. See Stern, *The Klamath Tribe*, 259–60; House Committee on Indian Affairs, *Dismissal of Superintendent Wade Crawford*, 145, 206, 337–44.

12."Chief," *Oregon Journal*, June 2, 1933; "Klamath Tribe Votes: Delegates at Washington Are Recalled," *Oregonian*, February 17, 1930; John Collier to Ethel Copeland, May 29, 1933, and June 18, 1933, in Collier, John Collier Papers; Collier to Crawford, June 10, 1933, "Correspondence 1926–60," RG 75.19.51, NARAPAR.

13.Deloria and Lytle, *The Nations Within*, 48–54; "Second Indian Cases Ended" and "Reservation Problem a Serious One," *Klamath News*, July 12, 1932; "Single Officer Preserves Order on Reservation," *Klamath News*, July 29, 1932, 1.

14.Collier to Crawford, May 29, 1934, "Correspondence 1926–60," Records of Klamath Indian Agency (RG 75.19.51), NARAPAR; Barbara Alatorre, interview by the author, March 10, 2000.

15. "Klamath Indians Would Oust Collier," *Oregon Journal*, May 30, 1934; Collier to Crawford, May 29, 1934, "Correspondence 1931–35," RG 75-16a, NARAPAR; House Committee on Indian Affairs, *Dismissal of Superintendent Wade Crawford*.

16. "Klamath Indians Would Oust Collier," *Oregon Journal*, May 30, 1934, 5; Stern, *The Klamath Tribe*, 249; Collier to Crawford, May 29, 1934, "Correspondence 1926–60," Records of Klamath Indian Agency (RG 75.19.51), NARAPAR; Wade Crawford to F. A. Goss, Superintendent, Fort Hall Agency, April 19, 1935, "Forms of Government, Indian Judges, etc.," Records of Klamath Indian Agency (RG 75.19.51), NARAPAR.

17. "Ousting of Indian Agent Requested," *Oregonian*, February 16, 1935.

18. "Supt. Crawford of Klamath Indian Agency Ousted by Secretary Ickes," *Oregon Journal*, April 30, 1937. Three weeks later, Senator Charles McNary of Oregon asked Ickes to reinstate Crawford so he could "resign with a clean record." See "McNary Asks Clear Record for Crawford," *Oregon Journal*, May 21, 1937; Crawford to Collier, May 30, 1937, Collier, John Collier Papers; Senate Committee on Indian Affairs, *Dismissal of Superintendent Wade Crawford*.

19. "Indian to Oppose Pierce at Polls," *Oregonian*, December 29, 1937.

20. Cohen, *Handbook of Federal Indian Law*, 128.

21. BIA Circular 3439, January 29, 1943, "Reservation Programs, General 1943–44," Records of the Portland OR Area Office (RG 75.16.10), NARAPAR; Courtright to Collier, January 14, 1941, "Indians in World War 1940–50," Records of Klamath Indian Agency (RG 75.19.51), NARAPAR.

22. For the tribes' approval of the conscientious objectors' camp, see Minutes of the Klamath General Council, July 16, 1942, Records of Tribal Councils and Committees, Records of Klamath Indian Agency (RG 75.19.51), NARAPAR; Fred Heilbronner, Klamath County Draft Board to Joseph S. Monks, Klamath Agency, December 10, 1942, "Correspondence, 1926–60," Records of Klamath Indian Agency (RG 75.19.51), NARAPAR.

23. BIA Circular 3439, January 29, 1943, Klamath Indian Reservation, "Indians in World War 1940–50," Records of Klamath Indian Agency (RG 75.19.51), NARAPAR.

24. Sheriff Low to Superintendent John Arkell, July 14, 1943, November 10, 1943, November 18, 1943, and January 5, 1944, Records Relating to Law Enforcement, Records of Klamath Indian Agency (RG 75.19.51), NARAPAR.

25. Courtright to Louis Mueller Chief Special Officer for the BIA, Denver, June 14, 1943, Records Relating to Law Enforcement, Records of Klamath Indian Agency (RG 75.19.51), NARAPAR; Fred Daiker, BIA, Washington, to Superintendent Raymond Bitney, January 10, 1950, "Correspondence, 1926–60," Records of Klamath Indian Agency (RG 75.19.51), NARAPAR; Courtright to Collier, n.d., "Deputy Special Officers Commissions 1944–54," Records Relating to Law Enforcement, Records of Klamath Indian Agency (RG 75.19.51), NARAPAR; Carl Donaugh, U.S. Attorney to Courtright and

Arkell, October 27, 1941, "Correspondence, 1926–60," "Law and Order Correspondence, 1940–49," Records of Klamath Indian Agency (RG 75.19.51), NARAPAR.

26. House Committee on Indian Affairs, *An Act Relating to Marriage and Divorce*; B. G. Courtright, Klamath Agency Press Release, May 18, 1945, "Marriage and Divorce Records," RG 75-16, NARAPAR.

27. Courtright to Robert. M. Elder, Jackson County Juvenile Officer, November 19, 1946, "Delinquent Juveniles," Records of Klamath Indian Agency (RG 75.19.51), NARAPAR.

28. Bernstein, *Indians in World War II*; Townsend, *World War II and the American Indian*; Parman, *Indians and the American West*, 110–11.

29. Courtright to John G. Rockwell, Sacramento Agency, January 2, 1942, "Superintendents' Correspondence," Records of Klamath Indian Agency (RG 75.19.51), NARAPAR; Victoria Schwartz to Courtright, August 27, 1945, "Klamath Report," "Superintendents' Correspondence," Records of Klamath Indian Agency (RG 75.19.51), NARAPAR.

30. Courtright to Mr. Charles Mack, Klamath Falls Chamber of Commerce, April 11, 1945, "Publicity 1941–50," Records of Klamath Indian Agency (RG 75.19.51), NARAPAR.

31. "V-E Day Sees 2 Launchings: Negroes, Indians, Aid Ceremonies," *Oregonian*, May 9, 1945.

32. Courtright to 20th Century Fox News, August 25, 1945, "Publicity 1941–50," Records of Klamath Indian Agency (RG 75.19.51), NARAPAR; printed program for Klamoya dedication, n.d., "Indians in World War 1940–50," Records of Klamath Indian Agency (RG 75.19.51), NARAPAR.

33. "Canyon Passage Comes to Oregon," *Oregon Journal Pacific Parade Magazine*, July 7, 1946, 1–2.

34. Nipo Strongheart to Courtright, n.d., "Publicity 1941–50," Superintendent's Correspondence, Records of Klamath Indian Agency (RG 75.19.51), NARAPAR.

35. Klamath Agency Memo, December 12, 1941, "Indians in World War 1940–50," Records of Klamath Indian Agency (RG 75.19.51), NARAPAR.

36. Barbara Alatorre, interview by author, March 10, 2000; Hood, *Return of the Raven*, VHS; Vern Marshall, interview by author, Portland OR, June 18, 2000.

37. "Civic Betterment Group Named to Uplift Morale," *Topaz Times*, June 5, 1943; "A Lotta Chatter By the Sports Editor," *Topaz Times*, June 5, 1943; Kawaguchi, interview, TOHP; War Relocation Authority, San Francisco Office, *Pertinent Facts About Relocation Centers*, n.p.; R. A. Bankson, "Spring Festival at Topaz," April 1943, Records of the WRA CURP, ALSC.

38. House Committee on Un-American Activities, "Hearings before a Special Committee on Un-American Activities, House of Representatives, Seventy-fifth Congress, third session–Seventy-eighth Congress, second session, on H. Res. 282, to investigate (1) the extent, character, and objects of un-American propaganda activities in the United

States, (2) the diffusion within the United States of subversive and un-American propaganda that is instigated from foreign countries or of a domestic origin and attacks the principle of the form of government as guaranteed by our Constitution, and (3) all other questions in relation thereto that would aid Congress in any necessary remedial legislation, vol. 15, July 1943," 9108, 9686–89.

39. Myer, *Uprooted Americans*, 157–58; Kitano, interview, TOHP; Tom Kawaguchi, "Topaz, 44nd Regimental Combat Team. France, Italy," in Tateishi, *And Justice for All*, 180.

40. "The Wrong Ancestors," *Oregonian*, February 14, 1943. Myer's exact words of assurance were, "The prime objective is dispersal. The colonists are not being released in batches. There will be no case of '50 Japs heading for Chicago.'" See Dillon S. Myer, Transcript of Press Conference, May 14, 1943, Washington DC. Reported by Office for Emergency Management Division of Central Administrative Services Minutes and Reports Section, 29, Myer Papers, Harry S. Truman Presidential Library.

41. New York Branch NAACP to Mayor Fiorello LaGuardia, April 27, 1944, and Press Release, Minorities Workshop, May 12, 1944, in "White Supremacy," NAACP Special Subject Files, part 18, section C.

42. Dillon S. Myer, "Remarks for the *March of Time*," June 24, 1943, Myer Papers, Harry S. Truman Presidential Library.

43. "Community Analysis Report No. 6: Nisei Assimilation," in War Relocation Authority, *Community Analysis Reports no. 1–18*.

44. Salyer, "Baptism by Fire," 847–76; Duus, *Unlikely Liberators*, 58; Weglyn, *Years of Infamy*, 140; Embree, Project Analysis Series Report No. 1, "Registration at Central Utah," February 1943, 5–7.

45. Some Nisei were allowed to continue as translators for military intelligence, but most were immediately discharged. See Duus, *Unlikely Liberators*, 57.

46. Weglyn, *Years of Infamy*, 141.

47. Question 28 read: "Will you swear unqualified allegiance to the United States of America and faithfully defend the United States from any or all attack by foreign or domestic forces, and foreswear any form of allegiance or obedience to the Japanese emperor, any foreign government, power or organization?"

48. Morgan Yamanaka in Tateishi, *And Justice for All*, 113; Akiya, interview, TOHP; Embree, Project Analysis Series Report No. 1, "Registration at Central Utah," February 1943, 5–6.

49. Morton Grodzins noted in 1955 that internees in all ten centers who answered "no" to Questions 27 and 28 were not asserting loyalty to Japan, but to their families, their block, their ideals, or their own strategies for self-preservation. See Grodzins, "Making Un-Americans," 572, 582.

50. Nearly 1,500 Topazians were sent to Tule Lake for answering "No" to Questions 27 and 28. Of these, 876 were men and 583 were women. Of the men, 240 were Japanese

nationals and 636 were U.S. citizens; of the women, 150 were Japanese nationals and 433 were citizens. See War Relocation Authority, *The Evacuated People*, 115; Embree, Project Analysis Series Report No. 3, "Registration at Central Utah," February 1943, 1; Verdoia, *Topaz*, VHS; Shimanouchi Lederer, interview, TOHP. Section Three of the Espionage Act (1917) provides a twenty-year prison sentence and/or a ten thousand dollar fine for citizens or aliens who "utter, print, write, or publish any disloyal, profane, scurrilous, or abusive language about the form of government of the United States [or] urge, incite, or advocate any curtailment of production in this country of any thing or things . . . necessary or essential to the prosecution of the war." U.S. Congress, *Statutes at Large*, 40:553.

51. Duus, *Unlikely Liberators*, 58; Weglyn, *Years of Infamy*, 140; Embree, Project Analysis Series Report No. 1, "Registration at Central Utah," February 1943, 8–10; "Registration Proceeds," *Topaz Times*, February 15, 1943; "The Segregation Program," forward by Dillon S. Myer (unpublished statement for appointed personnel), Records of the WRA CURP, ALSC.

52. Bankson, "The Wakasa Incident," Records of the WRA CURP, ALSC; and Taylor, *Jewel of the Desert*, 137–38; "Resident Killed" and "Administration Statement," *Topaz Times*, April 12, 1943.

53. Verdoia, *Topaz*, VHS; Bell, "Relocation Center Life," n.p., Japanese American Internment Collection, University of Utah Marriott Library.

54. Taylor, *Jewel of the Desert*, 138; Bell, "Relocation Center Life," n.p., Japanese American Internment Collection, University of Utah Marriott Library.

55. "Committee Asks No Stoppage of Work," *Topaz Times*, April 17, 1943; Bankson, "The Wakasa Incident," 7–11, Records of the WRA CURP, ALSC; Myer and Krug, *The WRA*, 19; "Shooting of Evacuee Recalled at Central Utah Relocation Center," *Pacific Citizen* (Salt Lake City UT), February 12, 1944, 2; Oshita, interview, TOHP.

56. Taylor, *Jewel of the Desert*, 139–40; Bankson, "The Wakasa Incident," 13, Records of the WRA CURP, ALSC.

57. Bankson, "Crisis in the Topaz Community Council," December 24, 1943, 5, Records of the WRA CURP, ALSC.

58. Bankson, "Crisis in the Topaz Community Council," December 24, 1943, 6–10, 14, Records of the WRA CURP, ALSC.

59. "Community Analysis Report No. 10," in War Relocation Authority, *Community Analysis Reports no. 1–18*, 9–17.

60. "Community Analysis Report No. 10," in War Relocation Authority, *Community Analysis Reports no. 1–18*, 15–18.

61. "Community Analysis Report No. 10," in War Relocation Authority, *Community Analysis Reports no. 1–18*, 16–17.

62. Minutes of the Board of Commissioners, HAP, July 20, 1944, RHAP, SPARC. The National Housing Authority announced in October 1944 that it would cut off start-up

funding for any new war housing in the Portland area "except fifty houses for colored families." See HAP Minutes, October 19, 1944.

63. Vern Marshall, a Caucasian boy who had a paper route on Cottonwood, noted this pattern each time he went to collect, stating emphatically that while he may not remember all the facts, figures, and dates concerning Vanport, "I remember this—there was segregation!" Vern Marshall, interview by author, June 18, 2000; "Worker Arrested for Fraternizing," *Portland Observer*, July 16, 1943; "Lift Ev'ry Voice," *Portland Observer*, August 18, 1943.

64. Minutes of the Board of Commissioners, HAP, September 16, 1943, December 6, 1944, and December 13, 1944, RHAP, SPARC.

65. Minutes of the Board of Commissioners, HAP, September 16, 1943, RHAP, SPARC.

66. Minutes of the Board of Commissioners, HAP, September 16, 1943, RHAP, SPARC.

67. Kilbourn and Lantis, "Elements of Tenant Instability," 63; "Lift Ev'ry Voice," *Portland Observer*, August 18, 1943; *Portland Observer*, August 18, 1943; Maben, *Vanport*, 88–91.

68. Hill, The FBI's RACON, 656; "Worker Arrested for Fraternizing," *Portland Observer*, July 16, 1943.

69. *Portland Observer*, August 31, 1943.

70. *The Pacific Citizen*, March 24, 1945; *Oregonian*, December 10, 1944.

71. War Relocation Authority, *Legal and Constitutional Phases*, 57–58; War Relocation Authority, "Final Report," 21, 25.

72. Novak, interview, OHSRL; War Relocation Authority, "Resettlement Bulletin," 21. A publicity photograph in *6,000 Kids from 46 States* shows four students reading the full text of the speech and smiling, under the title "Strength for Democracy." The four children were white, black, or Asian, projecting the ideals behind industrial democracy.

73. Minutes of the Board of HAP, September 12, 1944, RHAP, SPARC.

74. Hales, *Atomic Spaces*, 76; Truslow, *Manhattan District History*, 3–22.

75. Jette, *Inside Box 1663*, 16.

76. Smith Oral History, Radcliffe College Archives, Schlesinger Library, Radcliffe Institute, Harvard University; Charlotte Serber in Wilson and Serber, *Standing By and Making Do*, 67.

77. Bernice Brode to Evangeline, December 18, 1943, Brode Papers, Los Alamos Historical Museum Archives; Jane Wilson in Wilson and Serber, *Standing By and Making Do*, 5.

78. Jette, *Inside Box 1663*, 24, 26; Wilson and Serber, *Standing By and Making Do*, 7. Rather than excise or obliterate text, the censors would mark objectionable passages and send them to the letter-writer for revision. Outgoing mail would not be marked

with censors' stamps, but incoming would. See "Project Security" (n.d.), Froman Papers, Mss 33, Los Alamos Historical Museum Archives.

79. Segrè, *A Mind Always in Motion*, 182; Jette, *Inside Box 1663*, 25.

80. Jungk, *Brighter Than a Thousand Suns*, 115–16.

81. Segrè, *A Mind Always in Motion*, 183; Hales, *Atomic Spaces*, 28–29, 117–19.

82. "Project Security" (n.d.), Froman Papers, Mss 33, Los Alamos Historical Museum Archives.

83. See Jones, *Manhattan*, 282. Laura Fermi was disturbed by persistent rumors that her husband was having an affair with his bodyguard, John Baudino, but understood the confusion, given that the man slept in Fermi's room when he traveled. See Fermi, *Atoms in the Family*, 215.

84. Sherwin, *A World Destroyed*, 62; Lang, "The Tip Top Secret," 52–53; Hilgartner, Bell, and O'Connor, *Nukespeak*, 26.

85. Los Alamos Historical Society, prod., *Remembering Los Alamos*, VHS.

86. Jones, *Manhattan*, 262–63; Jennings, *Los Alamos*, 82; Sherwin, *A World Destroyed*, 62; Los Alamos Historical Society, prod., *Remembering Los Alamos*, VHS.

87. Jane Wilson in Wilson and Serber, *Standing By and Making Do*, 46; Fermi, *Atoms in the Family*, 201; Blumberg and Owin, *Energy and Conflict*, 133–34; Segrè, *Atoms, Bombs and Eskimo Kisses*, 39; Fisher, *Los Alamos Experience*, 39.

88. Brode, *Tales of Los Alamos*, 13.

89. Jette, *Inside Box 1663*, 38–39.

90. Smith Oral History, Radcliffe College Archives, Schlesinger Library, Radcliffe Institute, Harvard University, 74.

91. Rhodes, *The Making of the Atomic Bomb*, 569; Hales, *Atomic Spaces*, 282–83

92. Inkret and Miller, "On the Front Lines," 128–32; Shroyer, *Secret Mesa*, 93.

93. Inkret and Miller, "On the Front Lines," 132, 148.

94. Inkret and Miller, "On the Front Lines," 126, 148.

95. In August 1944 Oppenheimer and Groves approved a research project to measure how quickly the body rid itself of plutonium. Starting in April 1945, sixteen hospital patients with terminal diagnoses were injected with one microgram (the recommended limit of plutonium intake was five micrograms during the Manhattan Project era) without patients' fully informed consent. The word "plutonium" was classified, as were references to radioactive materials generally, though some patients were possibly told they were aiding the war effort. Several patients lived decades longer than expected but suffered mysterious, painful chronic illnesses. The information gathered at such economic and human cost did nothing for Bill Gibson and his coworkers, who were exposed and had no available remedy once the damage was done. See Welsome, *The Plutonium Files*.

96. Segrè, *Atoms, Bombs and Eskimo Kisses*, 45.

97. Segrè, *Atoms, Bombs and Eskimo Kisses*, 45; Roensch, *Life Within Limits*, 23; Fermi, *Atoms in the Family*, 223.

5. FROM BARBED WIRE TO BOOTSTRAPS

1. "Issei, Nisei, Kibei," *Fortune*, April 1944, quoted in Adams, *Born Free and Equal*, 103.

2. For an overview of the Student Relocation Program, see Austin, *From Concentration Camp to Campus*.

3. James, *Exile Within*, 7; Shimanouchi Lederer, interview, TOHP; Nakagawa, Ijima, and Kariya, interview, TOHP.

4. "1942: A Calendar Record of Evacuation, Relocation," *Pacific Citizen* (Salt Lake City), December 31, 1942; Mitsuye Endo, "Topaz," in Tateishi, *And Justice for All*, 60.

5. Okubo, *Citizen 13660*, 175.

6. "Relocation Movies to Be Presented Soon," *Topaz Times*, September 9, 1943, 3; Oshita, interview, TOHP; Okubo, *Citizen 13660*, 205–7; "Questions About Relocation," *Topaz Times*, May 15, 1943.

7. Verdoia, *Topaz*, VHS; "Nisei Platoon Goes on 'suicide Mission' — Eleven Return," *Topaz Times*, February 22, 1944; Kawaguchi, interview, TOHP.

8. Their pictorial, *Nisei in Uniform*, promoted the Nisei in much the same fashion as the BIA's pictorial *Indians in World War II* promoted Indians, emphasizing the Nisei's "[f]earless courage and excellent morale" and making them America's best bet against the Japanese at Attu or in India (although most Nisei units were sent to Europe). See War Relocation Authority, *Nisei in Uniform*.

9. Anonymous to Charles Ernst, n.d., Records of the WRA CURP, ALSC.

10. Anonymous to Charles Ernst, February 19, 1944, Records of the WRA CURP, ALSC.

11. Toshio Mori, "Housing Problem at Topaz," unpublished memorandum, July 9, 1943, Records of the WRA CURP, ALSC.

12. Evacuees were issued purchase offers with ten days to respond before personal property ("idle farm machinery") was requisitioned. The WRA reported that at the end of December 1943 "only" thirty-eight such requisitions had been made. See War Relocation Authority, Semi-Annual Report, July 1–December 31, 1943, in *War Relocation Authority Reports*, 67–68. "Relocation Procedures," *Topaz Times*, May 11, 1943, 5; "Community Analysis Report #5: Reactions to Lifting of Exclusions and Closing of Centers," January 15–21, 1945, in War Relocation Authority, *Community Analysis Reports no. 1–18*; Department of the Interior, War Agency Liquidation Unit, *People in Motion*, 52–55.

13. Confidential Memo, "Reports Round Table #23," January 15, 1945, Records of the WRA CURP, ALSC; Senate Committee on Military Affairs, *Report of the Subcommittee on Japanese War Relocation Centers*, 98; "New Slum Area: SF Nihonmachi," *Topaz Times*, June 15, 1943.

14. War Relocation Authority, Semi-Annual Report, January 1 to June 30, 1945, in *War Relocation Authority Reports*, n.p.; "Topaz Community Council Opposes Closing of Center," *Topaz Times*, July 20, 1945; Taylor, *Jewel of the Desert*, 217–20; War Relocation Authority, *The Evacuated People*, 149.

15. Brooks, "In the Twilight Zone," 1662–64.

16. Brooks, "In the Twilight Zone," 1676–78; "Chicago's Issei Bachelors," *Pacific Citizen*, December 25, 1948.

17. "Navajo Indian Chief Protests Hiring of Japanese American," *Pacific Citizen*, October 9, 1943; "Nevada to Bar Nisei Teachers in Indian Schools," *Pacific Citizen*, January 29, 1944.

18. Anonymous to Charles Ernst, August 30, 1943; anonymous to Ernst, n.d., 1943; and Anonymous to Ernst, March 1944, R. A. Bankson, Incoming Correspondence File, Records of the WRA CURP, ALSC; Embree, Project Analysis Series Report No. 1, "Registration at Central Utah," February 1943, 4.

19. Hugo Black's majority opinion clearly separates military decision making and racism: "All legal restrictions which curtail the civil rights of a single racial group are immediately suspect. That is not to say that all such restrictions are unconstitutional. . . . Pressing public necessity may sometimes justify the existence of such restrictions; racial antagonism never can." *Korematsu v. United States* 65 S Ct 193 (December 13, 1944), 194. Peter Irons argues that the Court gave a contrary decision a year after Korematsu in *Duncan v. Kahanamoku*, concerning the imposition of martial law in Hawaii. In this case, the Court emphasized that in the territories, loyal citizens are to be ruled by civilian governors only, and that the military is still subject to judicial review when it assumes any power or function of civil authorities. See U.S. Commission on the Wartime Relocation and Internment of Civilians, *Personal Justice Denied*, 238.

20. Department of the Interior, War Agency Liquidation Unit, *People in Motion*, 8; "Escort Incident from Topaz" (unpublished typescript, November 27, 1943), 2–6, Records of the WRA CURP, ALSC.

21. "Thunder in Congress on Evacuee Problem," and "Rep. Johnson Has 'Solution' for U.S. Japanese Americans," *Pacific Citizen*, October 30, 1943. The state of California warned that the ACLU and the Japanese American Committee for Democracy were "controlled by the Communist Party." See State of California, *California's Future* (Sacramento: California State Printing Office, 1944), Race Relations Files, Administrative Records of Governor John Hall, Oregon State Archives.

22. Gorham, "Negroes and Japanese Evacuees," 314. Although most Topazians surveyed stated that they did not anticipate conflict with their black neighbors, the WRA maintained that Japanese were susceptible to white influence and would likely develop racial animosity. WRA Community Analysis Report, "San Francisco City and County: Economic Base of Population," 9, Records of the WRA CURP, ALSC.

23. War Relocation Authority, *The Relocation Program*, 86.

24. War Relocation Authority, *The Evacuated People*, 10; Dillon S. Myer, "Annual Report of the Director of the War Relocation Authority to the Secretary of the Department of the Interior, Fiscal Year End June 30, 1945," Myer Papers, Harry S. Truman Presidential Library.

25. Myer, "An Autobiography of Dillon S. Myer," 230–37; Maben, *Vanport*, 106.

26. Althans, "Reclaiming Place," 116.

27. Portland State University Department of Urban Studies, *History of the Albina Plan Area*, 33; Oregon State System of Higher Education, "Progress Report," 1; Maben, *Vanport*, 74–75; Housing Authority of Portland, *Voice of Vanport*, May 25, 1946; Urban League of Portland, "First Annual Report," 8, Urban League Pamphlet Collection, Multnomah County Library.

28. Out of the college's first-quarter enrollment of 1,410 students, 90 percent were veterans, and there were 19 women, 8 African Americans, 8 Japanese Americans, and 7 Chinese Americans. In May 1948 there were 4,135 white families living in Vanport, 1,021 black families, and 182 families "of other races, mostly Japanese." Approximately half the black and white families included veterans, who were either attending Vanport College or pursuing vocational training. See Oregon State System of Higher Education, "Progress Report", 1.

29. Helen Haslett, "Voice of Vanport," n.p.

30. "The Vanport Feud" *Oregonian*, September 1, 1947.

31. *Voice of Vanport*, May 25, 1946.

32. *Oregonian*, April 18, 1946; Maben, *Vanport*, 70.

33. Communist Party of Oregon, Press Release, n.d., Records of the Portland Police Bureau Red Squad, SPARC.

34. Philip Klutznick to Dillon Myer, July 31, 1946, and Senator Robert A. Taft to Don Tobin, Executive Secretary Ohio Savings, Myer Papers, Harry S. Truman Presidential Library; Myer, "Autobiography," 230–37.

35. The memo read, "The dikes are safe at present. You will be warned if necessary. You will have time to leave. Don't get excited." "Memorandum to Vanport Residents," May 30, 1948, RHAP, OHSRL.

36. "Evacuees Find Life in Trailers Far from Utopia of Vacation Ads," *Oregonian Magazine*, July 16, 1948, 16; "Former Vanport Residents Barred in Trailer Sale," *Oregon Journal*, August 13, 1948. By 1950 90 percent of householders in Albina were black, and the district had the lowest income levels in Portland. See City of Portland, *A History of Portland's African-American Community*, 56.

37. *Oregon Journal*, June 22, 1948.

38. "Demonstration Halts Hearing of Flood Group," *Oregon Journal*, June 30, 1948; Minutes of the Board of HAP, July 1, 1948. Portland police records indicate that the Red Squad first placed Todd under surveillance when he was named editor of a radical labor publication in the 1930s. See Records of the Portland Police Bureau Red Squad, SPARC.

39. VECDC to Governor John Hall, June 28, 1948, Administrative Records of Governor John Hall, Oregon State Archives.

40. Brummett, "The Vanport Flood", 58–60.

41. Brummett, "The Vanport Flood," 68–69; "U.S. Cleared in Vanport Tragedy; Judge Voids $6.5 Million Claims," *Oregon Journal*, October 24, 1952.

42. Truman posed a security threat when, as head of the Senate Investigating Committee on Military Expenditures, he asked Groves about federal funds in a secret budget. An MED official promised he would be the first to see the mysterious defense project if he held his silence for the duration of the war. See Lawren, *General and the Bomb*, 26, 56–60, 170; Tolan, interview, Oral History Collection, Harry S. Truman Presidential Library.

43. *Los Alamos Bulletin*, August 18, 1945; Ethel Froman Scrapbook, Froman Papers, Los Alamos Historical Museum Archives, 61.

44. "Council Raps Use of Commissary Cards," *Los Alamos Times*, August 26, 1946.

45. War Department press release, n.d., Froman Papers, Los Alamos Historical Museum Archives; *Los Alamos Times*, May 10, 1946.

46. McWilliams, "Shangri-La of the Atom," 639–40; University of New Mexico Bureau of Business Research, "Los Alamos," 5.

47. Hewlett and Anderson, *The New World*, 626.

48. Gosling, "The Manhattan Project," 57.

49. "ALAS Hits at Army's Tight Atomic Control," *Los Alamos Times*, March 29, 1946.

50. Lilienthal, *Change, Hope and the Bomb*, 115.

51. Hunner, "Family Secrets," 186.

52. Hunner, "Family Secrets," 186; Hewlett and Anderson, *The New World*, 638.

53. McKee, *The Zia Company*, 3–10.

54. "Los Alamos," *Saturday Evening Post*, January 21, 1951.

55. Lindberg, *One Body, One Spirit*, 10–12; Shinedling, *History of the Los Alamos Jewish Center*, 35.

56. Gerold Tenney to the Los Alamos Town Council, September 16, 1946, Town Council Minutes, August 1946, and Addendum to the Minutes of the Los Alamos Town Council, September 16, 1946, Mss 69, Los Alamos Historical Museum Archives.

57. The Buck Act authorized the state of New Mexico to levy sales, income, gasoline, and use taxes against Los Alamos residents despite the federal government's exclusive jurisdiction and Los Alamosans' lack of state voting rights. E. J. Demson, assistant project director and counsel to the town council, found legal precedent supporting Los Alamosans' status as both tax-paying and nonvoting citizens (but that states with similar reservations tended to extend voting rights) and advised the matter would have to be settled in federal court. "Demson Finds State Vote Refusal Legal; Tax Decision Pending," *Los Alamos Times*, April 26, 1946; Town Council, September 1946, Los Alamos Historical Museum Archives; "Suit Evokes Doubt Over Jurisdiction" *Los Alamos Times*, December 19, 1947.

58. "Local History of the Los Alamos League 1947–1981," Los Alamos League of Women Voters Papers, Los Alamos Historical Museum Archives.

59. "Hill Streets Named as Contest Closes," *Los Alamos Times*, December 6, 1946.

60. Holmes, *Science Town*, 17–18.

61. "Local History of the Los Alamos League 1947–1981," Los Alamos League of Women Voters Papers, Los Alamos Historical Museum Archives.

62. Chambers, *The Battle for Civil Rights*, 12.

63. Chambers, *The Battle for Civil Rights*, 16–19.

64. Rothman, *On Rims and Ridges*, 241–42.

65. Moore, "Federal Enclaves," 117.

66. McWilliams, "Shangri-La of the Atom," 639–40; "Atomic Cities Boom," *Business Week* (December 18, 1948): 65–66.

67. "Los Alamos' Monopoly Pains," *Business Week* (August 20, 1949): 74.

68. "Analysis of Retail Merchandising in Los Alamos," August 4, 1959, Los Alamos Historical Museum Archives; McKee, *The Zia Company*, 18. *Business Week* augmented merchants' complaints in declaring, "Few businessmen would expect that they could operate on a successful free-enterprise basis in the midst of socialism. But that is just what one unique group of small businessmen are doing right in the U.S." "Atomic Cities Boom," *Business Week*, (December 18 1948): 65–66. The concession system remained in place until the 1960s.

69. Chambers, "Technically Sweet Los Alamos," 205–6.

70. McWilliams, "Shangri-La of the Atom," 639–40.

71. Cotter and Smith, "An American Paradox," 20–21. A third Los Alamos spy, nineteen-year-old physicist Ted Hall, was discovered through the Venona intercepts in the 1990s. The Soviets documented Hall passing information on the Manhattan Project (code word "ENORMOZ") with specifics on Los Alamos ("CAMP 2"). Hall has never confessed to the allegation, and the U.S. government opted against bringing formal charges to protect the highly sensitive decrypted Soviet intelligence documents. For the Department of Energy's view of the Hall matter, see U.S. Department of Energy, Office of History and Heritage Resources, "Espionage and the Manhattan Project, 1940–1945," http://www.cfo.doe.gov/me70/manhattan/espionage.htm.

72. U.S. Atomic Energy Commission, *In the Matter of J. Robert Oppenheimer*; Federal Bureau of Investigation, J. Robert Oppenheimer Security Files, File #1100-17828; Rothman, *On Rims and Ridges*, 243.

73. Welsome, *The Plutonium Files*, 183.

74. Letter to the Editor, *Los Alamos Times*, August 6, 1947.

75. Moore, "Federal Enclaves," 36; "The Hairline of Democracy," *Time* 151 (December 18, 1950): 22.

76. Hewlett and Duncan, *Atomic Shield*, 451.

77. Hunner, "Family Secrets," 314.

6. TERMINATION OF THE KLAMATH RESERVATION

1. The agency certified and recorded all reservation marriages until March 7, 1958. See volume 3 of the Klamath Agency Marriage Records (RG 75.19.51), NARAPAR.

2. When the Allotment Act allowed Indians to live as citizens outside the reservation, Klamath residents with the means to move established residences just outside the reservation border to remain part of the community but free of agency controls. Technically, 10 percent of Klamath tribal members lived off the reservation in 1900, but most of them occupied homes on the perimeter. The trend continued, and in 1955, when the number of urban Klamaths peaked, 40 percent of the off-reservation population lived on the reservation border. See Stern, *The Klamath Tribe*, 185.

3. Stern, *The Klamath Tribe*, 239, 246–47.

4. Senate Interior and Insular Affairs Committee, Subcommittee on Public Lands, Hearings on S 1222, *A Bill to Remove Restrictions*. (Hereafter referred to as "S 1222.")

5. Fixico, *Termination and Relocation*, 32–47.

6. S 1222, 390–91.

7. S 1222, 392–93.

8. S 1222, 408; S 1222, 398.

9. S 1222, 226.

10. Livingston, "Klamath Indians in Two Non-Reservation Communities"; S 1222, 226.

11. Bureau of Indian Affairs, 1948 Fiscal Year Report: "Education—Oregon/Washington Narrative Reports," Brophy Papers, Harry S. Truman Presidential Library.

12. S 1222, 412–13.

13. S 1222, 383–84; Livingston, "Klamath Indians in Two Non-Reservation Communities," 18–19.

14. S 1222, 370, 28–29, 326, 550–52.

15. S 1222, 29–30. The WRA similarly cast resettlement as a mark of "maturity," stating, "[D]ispersal means that the Nisei—and it was because of the rude shock of evacuation—grew up within a few short months. The dutiful son became a responsible adult. The Nisei became an individual; a mature self-confident, tax-paying man who depended upon his own decisions. It is demonstrably true that the engineering graduate moved from the produce bench in California to a relocation center in Arkansas to a drafting table in Boston.'" See Department of the Interior, War Agency Liquidation Unit, *People in Motion*, 31.

16. Superintendent Raymond Bitney to Morgan Pryse, Portland Regional Director, August 11, 1948, "Competency of Indians" file, Records of the Portland Area Office (RG 75.16.10), NARAPAR.

17. Neuberger, "How Oregon Rescued a Forest," 49.

18. Myer, "Autobiography,"290.

19. Hesse, "Termination and Assimilation," 131.

20. Tyler, *A History of Indian Policy*, 153–55; Peter Nabokov, *Native American Testimony*, 336; Fixico, *Termination and Relocation*, 149–54.

21. Fey and McNickle, *Indians and Other Americans*, 185–93; Parman, *Indians and the American West*, 132–35; Leonard G. Allen to Don Foster, BIA Portland Area Office, and Charles Miller, Chief Branch of Relocation Services, February 8, 1957, "Relocation Program," RG 75-16, NARAPAR; Klamath Agency Relocation Officer to Don Foster, Portland Area Office of the Bureau of Indian Affairs, May 31, 1957, "Relocation Program," Records of the Portland OR Area Office (RG 75.16.10), NARAPAR; Nichols, *Images of Oregon Women*, 54.

22. Oregon Public Broadcasting, *Your Land, My Land*, VHS, directed by Reagan Ramsey; Barbara Alatorre, interview by author, September 25, 1999; Stern, *The Klamath Tribe*, 254.

23. Parman, *Indians and the American West*, 139–42. Congress reported that of the reservation's 900,000 acres, 856,593.20 acres were in tribal ownership and the remainder was federally owned and managed.

24. "Recommendation of Advisory Committee Regarding Welfare Committee," June 16, 1955, Records of the Klamath Tribal Council, University of Oregon Libraries, Special Collections and University Archives.

25. U.S. Department of Health, Education, and Welfare, *Indians on Federal Reservations*, pt. 1, June 1958, 13; "Some of the Social Implications of Public Law 587," n.d., Records of the Klamath Management Specialists, University of Oregon Libraries, Special Collections and University Archives.

26. "Recommendation of Advisory Committee Regarding Welfare Committee," June 16, 1955, Records of the Klamath Tribal Council, University of Oregon Libraries, Special Collections and University Archives.

27. Draft of Memorandum of Agreement Between the Bureau of Indian Affairs and the Extension Service of Oregon State College (n.d.), Records of the Oregon State University Extension Service, Oregon State University Archives.

28. Minutes of the Klamath Executive Committee, June 16, 1955, Records of the Klamath Tribal Council, University of Oregon Libraries, Special Collections and University Archives.

29. Livingston, "Klamath Indians in Two Non-Reservation Communities," 160.

30. House Committee on Indian Affairs, *Authorizing the United States*.

31. Senate Committee on Interior and Insular Affairs, Subcommittee on Indian Affairs, *Klamath Indian Tribe*, 119. Kirk had reason to question management specialists' loyalties: Favell came from Wisconsin, where Menominees were also being terminated and their forest land sold. Philips had worked for Senator McKay, who was Secretary of the Interior when PL 587 passed in 1954. Watters, as a former businessman and mayor of Klamath Falls, sympathized with the chamber of commerce.

32. Proceedings of the Third Annual Historical Forum, "A New Status for the American Indian," OHSRL; Zakoji, *Klamath Indian Education Program*, 16; Calhoon, "Forced Journeys," 1.

33. Proceedings of the Third Annual Historical Forum, "A New Status for the American Indian," OHSRL; Zakoji, *Klamath Indian Education Program*, 16.

34. Zakoji, *Klamath Indian Education Program*, 18. Termination changed social scientists' designation of Klamaths from ethnographic or anthropological subjects to psychological ones. A later study of Klamath responses to Rorschach tests drew the same profile as Zakoji's assessment of Klamath personalities, but without considering the stresses of termination. From this angle, the trauma of termination was a sort of racial characteristic, rather than a psychological consequence of careless policymaking. See Clifton and Levine, *Klamath Personalities*.

35. Bureau of Indian Affairs, 1948 Fiscal Year Report "Education—Oregon/Washington Narrative Reports on Education," Brophy Papers, Harry S. Truman Presidential Library.

36. Zimmerman and Aberle, *The Indian*, 138–41; Livingston, "Klamath Indians in Two Non-Reservation Communities," 9, 19.

37. Zakoji, *Klamath Indian Education Program*, 13.

38. Trulove and Bunting, "Economic Impact of Federal Indian Policy," 6–7, Oregon State University Special Collections.

39. "County Government Services: County Electorate and County Court," *Klamath Tribune*, April 1957; "Questions and Answers: Wills and Closing Estates," *Klamath Tribune*, May 1957.

40. Report of Allen P. Jeffries, Klamath Adult Education Program, Minutes of the Klamath Executive Committee, January 17, 1956, Records of the Klamath Tribal Council, University of Oregon Libraries, Special Collections and University Archives.

41. "Will Your Child Be Next?" *Klamath Tribune*, December 1959; "He's Lonely and In Trouble," *Klamath Tribune*, January 1960.

42. Task Force Ten, "American Indian Policy Review Commission"; Oregon Public Broadcasting, *Your Land, My Land*, VHS; Barbara Alatorre, interview by author, September 25, 1999.

43. Trulove and Bunting, "Economic Impact of Federal Indian Policy," 15–16, Oregon State University Special Collections; Brown, "Identification of Selected Problems," 27–28; Oregon Public Broadcasting, *Your Land, My Land*, VHS.

44. "An Account of the Termination of the Klamath Reservation from the Tribes' Point of View," *Klamath Falls Herald and News*, October 1999; Minutes of Klamath Tribal Executive Meeting, October 29, 1956, Records of the Klamath Tribal Council, University of Oregon Libraries, Special Collections and University Archives.

45. "Klamath Indians Wary With Funds," *New York Times*, July 2, 1961; Oregon Public Broadcasting, *Your Land, My Land*, VHS.

46. Ramona Rank, interview by author, Portland OR, August 18, 2001; Oregon Public Broadcasting, *Your Land, My Land*, VHS.

47. "Proud Indian Tribe Ends Long Struggle to Keep Timberland," *Oregonian*, December 7, 1974, C5.

48. "Proud Indian Tribe," *Oregonian*, December 7, 1974; Task Force Ten, "American Indian Policy Review Commission"; Red Bird and Melendy, "Indian Child Welfare in Oregon," 44–45.

7. NO CAMPS FOR COMMIES

1. Cotter and Smith, "An American Paradox," 20–21.

2. Hoover to Souers, July 7, 1950, in Keane and Warner, *Foreign Relations*, 18–19.

3. Cotter and Smith, "An American Paradox," 20–21; Pat McCarran quoted in Shanks, *Immigration*, 129.

4. Memo to Dr. Wilson Compton, Chairman, Psychological Operations Coordinating Committee, from Charles R. Norberg, July 28, 1952, SMOF, Psychological Strategy Board Files, Truman Papers, Harry S. Truman Presidential Library; Wallace Irwing Jr. to Mallory Browne, June 17, 1952, Staff Member and Office Files (SMOF), Psychological Strategy Board Files, Truman Papers, Harry S. Truman Presidential Library.

5. Rostow, "Our Worst Wartime Mistake," 193–201; Morgan, *Reds*, 281–91; Austin, "Loyalty and Concentration Camps," 253–70.

6. Deloria and Lytle, *The Nations Within*, 123–25.

7. The WRA notes Japanese Americans' minimal reliance on public assistance in Department of the Interior, War Agency Liquidation Unit, *People in Motion*, 50; Embree, "Community Analysis Report No. 1," 2, Records of the WRA CURP, ALSC.

8. James, *Exile Within*, 7.

9. Omori, *Rabbit in the Moon*, VHS.

10. House Un-American Activities Committee, *Investigation of Communist Activities*.

11. House Un-American Activities Committee, *Communist Political Subversion*, 7028–35.

12. State of California, *Senate Report on Un-American Activities*," 23–25.

13. Means, *Where White Men Fear to Tread*, 96.

14. American Indian Movement, *Trail of Broken Treaties*, 77, 88; Calloway, *First Peoples*, 418.

15. Hood, *Return of the Raven*, VHS.

16. House Committee on Interior and Insular Affairs, Report 99-1406, "Providing for the Setting Aside"; Native American Solidarity Committee, Portland Chapter, "Arrowhead."

17. House Committee on Interior and Insular Affairs, HR 99-630, "Providing for the Restoration."

18. The Applegate family and its contributions to Oregon's development remain central to the state's historical memory. In 1968 Jesse Applegate — great-great-grandson of the first Jesse Applegate — kicked off a commemorative ceremony with a mock Indian raid at the festival grounds. The Applegates did not report unprovoked Indian attacks, but the reenactment accurately portrayed settler anxieties and captured their sense of triumph. See "Jesse Applegate to Ride Trail," *Eugene (OR) Register-Guard*, August 2, 1968.

19. For the current state of the debate, see the Klamath Tribes' statements on land and water rights at the Klamath Tribes' official Web site, *http://www.klamathtribes.org/water-rights.htm*, and those of Klamath Basin ranchers, miners, loggers, and fishermen at "Klamath Basin Crisis: the Voice of Irrigators and Their Communities," http://www.klamathbasincrisis.org/op2toc.htm.

20. Calhoon, "Forced Journeys."

21. "Postwar and the Nisei," *Pacific Citizen*, December 22, 1945, 1; Iiyama, interview, TOHP.

22. Daniels, *Prisoners Without Trial*, 86–91; Iiyama, interview, TOHP.

23. Shanks, *Immigration*, 123–37.

24. Maki, Kitano, and Berthold, *Achieving the Impossible Dream*, 55–59.

25. Maki, Kitano, and Berthold, *Achieving the Impossible Dream*, 71–75, 125–26.

26. U.S. Commission on Wartime Relocation and Internment of Civilians, *Personal Justice Denied*, 18.

27. Maki, Kitano, and Berthold, *Achieving the Impossible Dream*, 126–18, 214.

28. Suyemoto, interview, TOHP; Kitashima, interview, TOHP.

29. Hibino, interview, TOHP.

30. Iiyama, interview, TOHP; Shimanouchi Lederer, interview, TOHP; Nakahata, interview, TOHP.

31. Kawaguchi, interview, TOHP.

32. U.S. Commission on Wartime Relocation, *Personal Justice Denied*; "Bad Landmark: Righting a Racial Wrong," *Time*, November 12, 1983, 151; Tateishi, "The Japanese American Citizens League," 190–95.

33. "Once a Fugitive, Now a Hero," *AsianWeek* (January 15, 1998): 1.

34. "Racial Violence Against Asian Americans," *Harvard Law Review* 106 (June 1993): 1927–29, 1931–33.

35. House Committee on the Judiciary, Subcommittee on Civil and Constitutional Rights, "Anti-Asian Violence," 21–22.

36. MSNBC News, Questions and Answers, "The Legacy of Internment Camps," www.msnbc.com/news/644274 (accessed October 10, 2001); "A Deliberate Strategy of Disruption: Massive, Secretive Detention Effort Aimed Mainly at Preventing More Terror," *Washington Post*, November 4, 2001.

37. Brummett, "The Vanport Flood," 58–60; "U.S. Cleared in Vanport Tragedy; Judge Voids $6.5 Million Claims," *Oregon Journal*, October 24, 1952; Ritchey, interview, OHSRL.

38. June Schumann, Director of the Oregon Nikkei Legacy Center, telephone interview by author, August 9, 2001. HAP reported that over one hundred Japanese families were displaced by the flood. See "Vanport Victims Mostly Veterans, Children," *Oregonian*, June 2, 1948.

39. Marilynn Johnson and Quintard Taylor have located the origins of the Bay Area and Seattle civil rights movements in the demographic shifts of defense migration, and this pattern is clearly apparent in Portland as well. See Johnson, *The Second Gold Rush*, 209–33; and Taylor, *Forging a Black Community*, 175–89.

40. "Wallace Party Files Petitions, Calls Convention," *Oregonian*, July 14, 1948; W. B. Odall, Portland Police Bureau, to Mayor Dorothy McCullough Lee, January 6, 1949, Records of the Portland Police Bureau Red Squad, SPARC.

41. Jarvi, interview, OHSRL.

42. Janet Christopherson Madson to Linda Elegant, August 19, 1997, in Elegant, "The Vanport Flood," n.p.

43. McElderry, "Vanport Conspiracy Rumors," 134–63.

44. U.S. Atomic Energy Commission, *In the Matter of J. Robert Oppenheimer*; Federal Bureau of Investigation, *J. Robert Oppenheimer Security Files*, File #1100-17828; Bird and Sherwin, *American Prometheus*, 546–60.

45. Masco, *The Nuclear Borderlands*, 207.

46. Inkret and Miller, "On the Front Lines," 135.

47. Masco, *The Nuclear Borderlands*, 193–96, 203;

48. Masco, *The Nuclear Borderlands*, 208.

49. Masco, *The Nuclear Borderlands*, 210–12.

50. Petersen, "Child Volunteers," 266–67; Yesley, "'Ethical Harm,'" 271–73.

51. Welsome, *The Plutonium Files*, 478–80. For more on the government's use of human subjects in radiation experiments, see the Department of Energy, "DOE Openness: Human Radiation Experiments," http://www.eh.doe.gov/ohre/index.html.

52. Moore, "Federal Enclaves," 111–12.

53. Loy Lawhon, "UFOs/Aliens Kirtland AFB Sightings and Area 51," http://ufos .miningco.com (accessed June 5, 2000).

54. Downwinders Web site, http://www.downwinders.org/Aboutus.html; Department of Energy, Radiation Claims Compensation Act, http://www.usdoj.gov/civil/torts/ const/reca/about.htm (accessed July 10, 2003).

55. "Los Alamos Burns, Thousands More Flee Today," *Santa Fe New Mexican*, May 11, 2000.

56. "Los Alamos Burns," *Santa Fe New Mexican*, May 11, 2000; Internal Revenue Service Memorandum #200111056, "Federal Emergency Management Agency Payments—Cerro Grande Fire," February 15, 2001.

57. Marian Craig, Interview, OHSRL; Internal Revenue Service, "Federal Emergency Management," 2; "Families Cope With Losing Their Homes," *Santa Fe New Mexican*, May 11, 2000.

58. Theodore Hsien Wang, "Wen Ho Lee: Helping to Empower Asian Americans," Chinese for Affirmative Action, July 2000, http://www.caasf.org (accessed May 20, 2003); "Judge Grants Bail to Wen Ho Lee," *Asian Reporter*, August 29, 2000; Gish Jen, "For Wen Ho Lee, a Tarnished Freedom," *New York Times*, September 15, 2000; "Clinton 'Troubled' By Los Alamos Case, " *New York Times*, September 14, 2000; "Lee Remains Enigma at Center of a Storm," *Washington Post*, October 8, 2000; Freeh, *The Federal Bureau of Investigation*, 8.

59. Wang, "Wen Ho Lee"; "Judge Grants Bail to Wen Ho Lee," *Asian Reporter*, August 29, 2001; "Clinton 'Troubled,'" *New York Times*, September 15, 2000; "Lee Remains Enigma," *Washington Post*, October 8, 2000.

60. Wang, "Wen Ho Lee," Chinese for Affirmative Action, July 2000, http://www.caasf .org; Jen, "For Wen Ho Lee," *New York Times*, September 15, 2000; "Clinton 'Troubled,'" *New York Times*, September 15, 2000; "Lee Remains Enigma," *Washington Post*, October 8, 2000; Freeh, *The Federal Bureau of Investigation*, 8.

61. Lawler, "Silent No Longer," 1072–73.

62. Jacobson, *Barbarian Virtues*, 49–57; Franklin, *War Stars*, 41–42; Sharp, *Savage Perils*, 221–22.

63. "Census Data Used to Foist Wartime Japanese Internment," *Asian Reporter*, March 28, 2000.

64. Spicer et al., *The Impounded People*, 81.

Bibliography

PRIMARY SOURCES

Allen Library Special Collections (ALSC), University of Washington
War Relocation Authority. Records of the War Relocation Authority Central Utah
    Relocation Project. Accn 0056-001.

Harry S. Truman Presidential Library, Independence MO
William F. Brophy Papers.
Tom C. Clark Papers.
John A. Jessup Papers.
Lansing Lamont Papers.
Dillon S. Myer Papers.
John H. Tolan Interview by James R. Fuchs. San Francisco, March 5–10, 1983. Oral
    History Collection.
Harry S. Truman Presidential Papers.

Harvard University
Alice Kimball Smith Oral History. 1987. Radcliffe College Archives, Schlesinger
    Library, Radcliffe Institute.
U.S. Congress. House. House Naval Affairs Subcommittee to Investigate Congested
    Production Areas, part 3. 78th Cong., 1st sess., April 13, 1943. In President's
    Committee for Congested Production Areas, Final and Miscellaneous Reports,
    1943–44. Vertical File, Loeb Design Library.
Wartime Housing Vertical Files, Loeb Design Library.

Los Alamos Historical Museum Archives
"Analysis of Retail Merchandising in Los Alamos," August 4, 1959. Mss 1984-852-1-1.
Bernice Brode Papers. Mss 1992.04.
Ethel Froman and Darol K. Froman, Papers. Mss 1994-049.
Los Alamos League of Women Voters. Records. Mss M1991-19-1-28.
Los Alamos Town Council, Records. Mss 69.
Bert Sauer. "The Forgotten SG." Unpublished manuscript, n.d. Mss 1950-58-1-2.

Multnomah County Library, Portland OR
Bureau of Municipal Research, University of Oregon. Ordinance 22-412 (1942), "War Code of the City of Portland, Oregon, WPA Official Project No. 164-1-94-33." Portland: Dept. of Public Safety, 1950. Oregon Collection.
Charter of the City of Portland. 1942. Sec. 3-118.
Urban League of Portland. "First Annual Report." 1945. Urban League Pamphlet Collection.

National Archives and Records Administration, Pacific
Alaska Region (NARAPAR), Seattle WA
Records of the Bureau of Indian Affairs. Records of Klamath Indian Agency. RG 75.19.51.
Records of the Bureau of Indian Affairs. Records of the Portland OR Area Office. RG 75.16.10.
Records of Tribal Councils and Committees, 1895–1960. Records of Klamath Indian Agency. RG 75.19.51.

Oregon Historical Society Research Library (OHSRL), Portland
Applegate Family. Genealogy Vertical Files.
Luther Avery. Interview by Linda Elegant. Portland OR, August 14, 1997. SR 11001.5.
Eva Emery Dye Papers. Mss 1089.
Dallas Gray and Priscilla H. Robinson. Interview by Linda Elegant. Portland OR, July 8, 1999. SR 11001.1.
Grail Jarvi. Interview by Linda Elegant. Portland OR, June 24, 1997. SR 11001.4.
Kaiser Shipbuilding Company. Records. Mss 2978.
Cornella Novak. Interview by Karen Beck Skold. Pacific Northwest Oral History Project Inventory 1686.
Proceedings of the Third Annual Historical Forum, "A New Status for the American Indian: Can He Achieve It?" March 23, 1957. Mss 779.
Records of the Housing Authority of Portland (RHAP). Mss 1413.
Robert Earl Riley Papers. Mss 1123.
Morian Ritchey. Interview by Linda Elegant. Portland OR, July 2, 1999. SR 11001.8.
Karen Beck Skold. "Women in the Shipyards" Research Notes. SR 1674.1.

Oregon State Archives, Salem
John Hall. Administrative Correspondence, 1947–49. Governor John Hall Papers.

Oregon State University Archives, Corvallis
Records of the Oregon State University Extension Service. RG III.

Oregon State University Special Collections, Corvallis
W. T. Trulove and David Bunting. "The Economic Impact of Federal Indian Policy: Incentives and Responses of the Klamath Indians." Proceedings of the 46th Conference of Western Economic Association, Simon Fraser University, Burnaby, British Columbia, Canada, June 30, 1971.

University of New Mexico Center for Southwest Research, Albuquerque
Ferenc M. Szasz Papers. Mss 522 BC.

University of Oregon Libraries, Special Collections and University Archives, Eugene
O. C. Applegate Papers, 1845–1938. Mss Ax5.
Klamath Management Specialists. Records. Mss Bx 125.
Klamath Tribal Council. Records. Mss Bx 51/2.

University of Utah Marriott Library, Salt Lake City
Japanese American Internment Collection. Mss 0114.
Grace Oshita. Interview by Leslie Kelan. February 20, 1985. "Interviews with Japanese in Utah." Accn 1209.
Faith Terasawa Papers. Accn 1473.
Sherman Tolbert. Interview by Georgy Henrich. Spring 1983. Accn 1002.

Topaz Oral History Project (TOHP), *Accn 1002*
Kenji Fuji. Interview by Sandra Taylor. November 5, 1987.
Tad Hayashi. Interview by Sandra Taylor. October 28, 1987.
Nobu Kumekawa Hibino. Interview by Sandra Taylor. June 12 and June 20, 1988.
Chizu Iiyama and Ernest Iiyama. Interview by Sandra Taylor. May 13, 1988.
Hiromoto Katayama. Interview by Sandra Fuller. October 27, 1987.
Tom Kawaguchi. Interview by Sandra Taylor. November 5, 1987.
Tsuyako Kitashima ("Sox"). Interview by Sandra Taylor. November 6, 1987.
Michi Kobi. Interview by Sandra Taylor. October 6, 1987.
Maya Nagata-Aikawa. Interview by Sandra Taylor. November 4, 1987.
Kitty Nakagawa, Mari Ijima, and Jean Kariya. Interview by Sandra Taylor. June 14, 1988.
Don Nakahata and Alice Nakahata. Interview by Sandra Taylor. May 12, 1988.
Lee Suyemoto. Interview by Sandra Taylor. Newton MA, June 12, 1988.
Midori Shimanouchi Lederer. Interview by Sandra Taylor. June 17, 1988.
Tomoye Takahashi. Interview by Sandra Taylor. October 29, 1987.

Stanley Parr Archives and Records Center, Portland OR
Records of the Housing Authority of Portland. Mss 0605-02.
Records of the Portland Police Bureau Red Squad. Mss 8090-03.

Abbott, Carl. "The Federal Presence." In Milner, O'Connor, and Sandweiss, *Oxford History of the American West*, 469–99.

———. *The Metropolitan Frontier: Cities in the Modern American West*. Tucson: University of Arizona Press, 1993.

———. *Portland: Politics, Planning, and Growth in a Twentieth-Century City*. Lincoln: University of Nebraska Press, 1983.

Adams, Ansel. *Born Free and Equal: Photographs of the Loyal Japanese-Americans at Manzanar Relocation Center Inyo County, California*. New York: U.S. Camera, 1944.

Adorno, Theodor. *Negative Dialectics*. Translated by E. B. Ashton. New York: Seabury Press, 1973.

Agoyo, Herman. "LANL 2000—the Role of the National Laboratory in the 21st Century." Unpublished typescript. Santa Fe NM: Los Alamos Study Group, 1993.

Althans, Tracey. "Reclaiming Place: Wartime Housing and the Memory of Vanport." Master's thesis, University of Oregon, 2000.

American Folklife Center. *After the Day of Infamy: "Man on the Street" Interviews Following the Attack on Pearl Harbor*. Washington DC: Library of Congress, 2003. http://memory.loc.gov/ammem/afcphhtml/afcphhome.html (accessed August 10, 2006).

American Indian Movement. *Trail of Broken Treaties: BIA I'm Not Your Indian Anymore*. Rooseveltown NY: Akwesasne Notes, 1976.

Anderson, Andy. *Me, Melvin 'n Andy*. Bend OR: Maverick Publishing Company, 1997.

Arrington, Leonard J. *The Price of Prejudice: The Japanese-American Relocation Center in Utah during World War II*. Logan: Utah State University, 1962.

Austin, Allan Wesley. *From Concentration Camp to Campus: Japanese American Students and World War II*. Urbana: University of Illinois Press, 2004.

———. "Loyalty and Concentration Camps in America: The Japanese American Precedent and the Internal Security Act of 1950." In *Last Witnesses: Reflections on the Wartime Internment of Japanese Americans*, edited by Erica Harth, 253–70. New York: Palgrave MacMillan, 2001.

Bancroft, Hubert Howe. *History of Oregon*. Vol. 2. San Francisco: The History Company, 1888.

Barker, Michael. "American Indian Tribal Police: An Overview and Case Study." PhD diss., SUNY Albany, 1994.

Barlow, David E. "Minorities Policing Minorities as a Strategy of Social Control: A Historical Analysis of Tribal Police in the United States." *Criminal Justice History* 15 (1994): 141–63.

Beecroft, Eric, and Seymour Janow. "Toward a National Policy for Migration." *Social Forces* 16 (May 1938): 486–92.

Bell, Iris. *Los Alamos WAACs/WACS: World War II 1943–1946.* Edited by Charlie Briggs. Sarasota FL: Coastal Printing Company, 1993.

Bell, Leland V. *In Hitler's Shadow: The Anatomy of American Nazism.* Port Washington NY: Kennikat Press, 1973.

Berkhofer, Robert F., Jr. *The White Man's Indian: Images of the American Indian from Columbus to the Present.* New York: Knopf, 1978.

Bernstein, Alison. *Indians In World War II: Toward a New Era In Indian Affairs.* Norman: University of Oklahoma Press, 1991.

Bernstein, Barton J. "The Oppenheimer Loyalty-Security Case Reconsidered." *Stanford Law Review* 42 (July 1990): 1383–1484.

Bird, Kai, and Martin J. Sherwin. *American Prometheus: The Triumph and Tragedy of J. Robert Oppenheimer.* New York: Knopf, 2005.

Blumberg, Stanley A., and Gwin Owens. *Energy and Conflict: The Life and Times of Edward Teller.* New York: G. P. Putnam's Sons, 1976.

Bristow, Nancy K. *Making Men Moral: Social Engineering During the Great War.* New York: New York University Press, 1996.

Britten, Thomas. *American Indians in World War I: At Home and At War.* Albuquerque: University of New Mexico Press, 1997.

Brode, Bernice. *Tales of Los Alamos: Life on the Mesa, 1943–1945.* Los Alamos: Los Alamos Historical Society, 1997.

Brooks, Charlotte. "In the Twilight Zone Between Black and White: Japanese American Resettlement and Community in Chicago, 1942–45." *Journal of American History* 86 (March 2000): 1655–98.

Brown, Charles Crane. "Identification of Selected Problems of Indians Residing in Klamath County, Oregon: An Examination of Data Generated since Termination of the Klamath Indian Reservation." Ph.D. diss., University of Oregon, 1973.

Brummett, Franklin. "The Vanport Flood: *Clark v. United States.*" *Litigation* 25 (Spring 1999): 55–73.

California State Board of Control. *California and the Oriental: Japanese, Chinese and Hindus.* Report of the California State Board of Control to Governor William Stephens, June 19, 1920. Sacramento CA: California State Printing Office, 1922.

Calloway, Colin G. *First Peoples: A Documentary Survey of American Indian History.* Boston: Bedford St. Martin's Press, 2004.

Chambers, Marjorie Bell. *The Battle for Civil Rights, or How Los Alamos Became a County.* Los Alamos NM: Los Alamos Historical Society, 1999.

———. "Technically Sweet Los Alamos." PhD diss., University of New Mexico, 1974.

Chang, Gordon, ed. *Morning Glory, Evening Shadow: Yamato Ichihashi and His Internment Writings, 1942–1945.* Stanford: Stanford University Press, 1997.

City of Portland. *History of Portland's African American Community (1805–present)*. Portland: Portland Bureau of Planning, 1993.

Clifton, James A., and David Levine. *Klamath Personalities: Ten Rorschach Case Studies*. Lawrence KS: Sociology Department, University of Kansas, 1963.

Coan, C. F. "The Adoption of the Reservation Policy in Pacific Northwest, 1853–55." *Oregon Historical Quarterly* 23 (March 1922): 1–38.

Cohen, Felix S. *Handbook of Federal Indian Law: With Reference Tables and Index*. Washington DC: U.S. Government Printing Office, 1942.

Cole, Olen, Jr. *The African-American Experience in the Civilian Conservation Corps*. Gainesville: University Press of Florida, 1999.

Colean, Miles L. *Housing for Defense: A Review of the Role of Housing in Relation to America's Defense and a Program for Action*. New York: Twentieth Century Fund, 1940.

Collier, John. *John Collier Papers, 1922–1968*. Stanford NC: Microfilming Corporation of America, 1970.

Copp, Henry N. *The American Settler's Guide: A Popular Exposition of the Public Land System of the United States of America*, 3rd edition. Washington DC: Henry N. Copp, 1882.

Cornwall, Robert. "Oliver Cromwell Applegate: Paternalistic Friend to the Indians." *Journal of the Shaw Historical Society* 6 (1992): 17–36.

Cotter, Cornelius P., and J. Malcolm Smith. "An American Paradox: The Emergency Detention Act of 1950." *Journal of Politics* 19 (February 1957): 20–33.

Cullen, Jim. *The American Dream: A Short History of an Idea That Shaped a Nation*. New York: Oxford University Press, 2003.

Culver, Samuel L. "Report to the Secretary of the Interior, July 20, 1854." In *Annual Report of the Commissioner of Indian Affairs*, 292–97. Washington DC: Office of the Commissioner of Indian Affairs, 1855.

Daniels, Roger, ed. *American Concentration Camps*. New York: Garland Press, 1989.

———. "Incarceration of the Japanese Americans: A Sixty Year Perspective." *The History Teacher* 35, no. 3 (May 2002): 297–310.

———. *Prisoners Without Trial: Japanese Americans in World War II*. New York: Hill and Wang, 1993.

Davis, Nuel Pharr. *Lawrence and Oppenheimer*. New York: Simon and Schuster, 1968.

Deloria, Vine, Jr., and Clifford M. Lytle. *The Nations Within: The Past and Future of American Indian Sovereignty*. Austin: University of Texas Press, 1998.

Denevi, Donald. *The West Coast Goes to War*. Missoula MT: Pictorial Histories Publishing Company, 1998.

Deverell, William. "To Loosen the Safety Valve: Eastern Workers and Western Lands." *Western Historical Quarterly* 19 (August 1988): 269–85.

Dewey, John, and Evelyn Dewey. "Democracy and Education." In *Social History of American Education vol. II: 1860 to the Present*, edited by Rena L. Vassar, 257–60. Chicago: Rand McNally, 1965.

Dippie, Brian W. *The Vanishing American: White Attitudes and U.S. Indian Policy.*
Middletown CT: Wesleyan University Press, 1982.

Dower, John W. *War Without Mercy: Race and Power in the Pacific.* New York: Pantheon Books, 1986.

Drinnon, Richard. *Facing West: The Metaphysics of Indian-Hating and Empire-Building.* New York: Schocken Books, 1990.

———. *Keeper of Concentration Camps: Dillon S. Myer and American Racism.* Berkeley: University of California Press, 1987.

Duus, Masayo Umezawa. *Unlikely Liberators: The Men of the 100th and 442nd.* Honolulu: University of Hawaii Press, 1987.

Dyar, L. S. "Annual Report to the Commissioner of Indian Affairs, Klamath Agency." In *Annual Report of the Commissioner of Indian Affairs to the Secretary of the Interior for the Year 1873,* 323–24. Washington DC: U.S. Government Printing Office, 1873.

Elegant, Linda. "The Vanport Flood and Its Impact on the African American Community of Portland." Proceedings of the Jackson Forum Symposium. Portland: Portland Community College, 1998.

Embree, John F. WRA Community Analysis Section, Topaz, Project Analysis Series Report No. 1, "Registration at Central Utah," February 1943. War Relocation Authority Project Analysis Series. Washington DC: War Relocation Authority, 1943.

Fermi, Laura. *Atoms in the Family: My Life with Enrico Fermi.* Chicago: American Institute of Physics Press, 1987.

Fey, Harold E., and D'Arcy McNickle. *Indians and Other Americans: Two Ways of Life Meet.* New York: Harper and Row, 1958.

Fisher, Phyllis K. *Los Alamos Experience.* Tokyo: Japan Publications, 1985.

Fixico, Donald. *Termination and Relocation: Federal Indian Policy, 1945–1960.* Albuquerque: University of New Mexico Press, 1986.

Foner, Eric. *The Story of American Freedom.* New York: Norton, 1998.

Ford, Henry. *The International Jew: The World's Foremost Problem.* Vols. 1 and 2. Dearborn: The Dearborn Publishing Company, 1920.

Foster, Mark S. *Henry J. Kaiser: Builder in the Modern American West.* Austin: University of Texas Press, 1989.

Foster, Stephen C. "Republican Land Policy: Homes for the Million: Give the Public Lands to the People, and You settle the Slavery Question, obliterate the Frontiers, dispense with a Standing Army, and extinguish Mormonism." Washington DC: Republican Congressional Committee, 1880.

Foucault, Michel. *Discipline and Punish: The Birth of the Prison.* Translated by Alan Sheridan. New York: Vintage Books, 1995.

Franco, Jere Bishop. *Crossing the Pond: The Native American Effort in World War II.* Denton: University of North Texas Press, 1999.

Franklin, H. Bruce. *War Stars: The Superweapon and the American Imagination*. New York: Oxford University Press, 1988.

Frantz, Klaus. *Indian Reservations in the United States: Territory, Sovereignty, and Socioeconomic Change*. Chicago: University of Chicago Press, 1999.

Frather, Julia E. A. "The Fourth of July at Klamath Reservation." *Overland Monthly* 42 (July–December 1903): 116–23.

Freeh, Louis B. *The Federal Bureau of Investigation: Ensuring Public Safety and National Security Under the Rule of Law*. Washington DC: Department of Justice, Federal Bureau of Investigation, 1999.

Fried, Richard M. *Nightmare in Red: The McCarthy Era in Perspective*. New York: Oxford University Press, 1990.

Fryer, Heather. "Into the Prefab West: Federal Communities and Migration during World War II." In *Moving Stories: Migration and the American West, 1850–2000*, edited by Scott E. Casper and Lucinda M. Long, 213–48. Reno: University of Nevada Press, 2001.

———. "Pioneers All: Civic Symbolism and Social Change in World War II Portland." *Journal of the West* 39 (Spring 2000): 62–68.

Garner, John S. *The Model Company Town: Urban Design Through Private Enterprise in Nineteenth-Century New England*. Amherst: University of Massachusetts Press, 1984.

Gatschet, Albert Samuel. *The Klamath Indians of Southwestern Oregon*. Washington DC: U.S. Government Printing Office, 1890.

Girdner, Audrie, and Anne Loftis. *The Great Betrayal: The Evacuation of the Japanese-Americans during World War II*. London: Macmillan, 1969.

Glassley, Ray H. *Indian Wars of the Pacific Northwest*. Portland: Binfords and Mort, 1972.

Good, Rachel Applegate. *History of Klamath County, Oregon: Its Resources and its People Illustrated*. Klamath Falls OR: Klamath County Historical Society, 1941.

Gorham, Thelma Thurston. "Negroes and Japanese Evacuees." *The Crisis* 52 (November 1945): 314–16, 330–31.

Gosling, F. G. *The Manhattan Project: Making the Atomic Bomb*. Washington DC: U.S. Department of Energy, 1999.

Gould, Stephen Jay. "Morton's Rankings of Races by Cranial Capacity." *Science*, n.s., 4341 (May 5, 1978): 503–9.

Grandy, David A. *Leo Szilard: Science as a Mode of Being*. New York: University Press of America, 1996.

Gray, W. H. *A History of Oregon 1792–1849*. Portland: Harris and Holman, 1880.

Grodzins, Morton. *Americans Betrayed: Politics and the Japanese Evacuation*. Chicago: University of Chicago Press, 1949.

———. "Making Un-Americans." *American Journal of Sociology* 60 (May 1955): 570–82.

Groves, Leslie R. *Now It Can Be Told: The Story of the Manhattan Project*. New York: Harper and Row, 1962.

Hales, Peter Bacon. *Atomic Spaces: Living on the Manhattan Project*. Urbana: University of Illinois Press, 1997.

Haslett, Helen. "Voice of Vanport." In Proceedings of the Jackson Forum Symposium. Portland: Portland Community College, 1998. Portland Community College Library, Cascade Campus.

Hesse, Larry. "Termination and Assimilation: Federal Indian Policy, 1943 to 1961." PhD diss., Washington State University, 1974.

Hewlett, Richard G., and Oscar E. Anderson. *Atomic Shield, 1947–1952*. University Park: Pennsylvania State University Press, 1969.

———. *The New World: A History of the United States Atomic Energy Commission*. Washington: USAEC, 1972.

Hilgartner, Stephen, Richard C. Bell, and Rory O'Connor. *Nukespeak: Nuclear Language, Visions, and Mindset*. San Francisco: Sierra Club Books, 1982.

Hill, Robert A., ed. *The FBI's RACON: Racial Conditions in the United States during World War II*. Boston: Northeastern University Press, 1995.

Hines, Joseph Wilkinson. *Touching Incidents in the Life and Labors of a Pioneer on the Pacific Coast since 1853*. San Jose CA: Eaton and Co. Printers, 1911.

Holmes, Jack E. *Science Town in the Politics of New Mexico*. Albuquerque: Department of Political Science, University of New Mexico, 1967.

Hong, Grace Kyungwon. "Something Forgotten Which Should Have Been Remembered: Private Property and Cross-Racial Solidarity in the Work of Hisaye Yamamoto." *American Literature* 71 (June 1999): 291–310.

Hood, Barry, dir. *Return of the Raven: The Edison Chiloquin Story*. VHS. Eugene OR: Barry Hood Films, 1984.

Hoover, J. Edgar. J. Edgar Hoover to Admiral Sidney William Souers, July 7, 1950. In *Foreign Relations of the United States: The Intelligence Community, 1950–1955*, ed. Douglas Keane and Michael Warner. Washington DC: U.S. Government Printing Office, 2007.

Horsman, Reginald. *Race and Manifest Destiny: The Origins of American Racial Anglo-Saxonism*. Cambridge: Harvard University Press, 1981.

Hosokawa, Bill. *JACL in Quest of Justice*. New York: William Morrow and Company, 1982.

Housing Authority of Portland. "A History of the Construction of Vanport City, Federal Housing Project Number Oregon 35053." Portland: Housing Authority of Portland, 1943.

Hoxie, Frederick E. *A Final Promise: The Campaign to Assimilate the Indians 1880–1920*. Lincoln: University of Nebraska Press, 1984.

Hughes, James F. "Annual Report of the Deputy Director, Central Utah Relocation

Center." In Records of the War Relocation Authority, 1942–46, reel 7, Project Reports. Alexandria VA: Chadwyck-Healey Inc., 1991.

Hunner, Jon. "Family Secrets: The Growth of Community at Los Alamos, New Mexico." PhD diss., University of New Mexico, 1996.

———. Inventing Los Alamos: The Growth of an Atomic Community. Norman: University of Oklahoma Press, 2004.

Huntington, J. W. Perit. "Report of the Oregon Superintendency No. 11, December 10, 1864." In Report of the Commissioner of Indian Affairs for the Year 1865. Washington DC: U.S. Government Printing Office, 1865.

Inkret, William C. T., and Guthrie Miller. "On the Front Lines: Plutonium Workers Past and Present Share Their Experiences" (roundtable). Los Alamos Science 23 (1995): 125–61.

Institute for Government Research. The Problems of Indian Administration. Baltimore: Johns Hopkins University Press, 1928.

Isserman, Maurice. Which Side Were You On? The American Communist Party During The Second World War. Middletown CT: Wesleyan University Press, 1982.

Jackson, Donald, and Mary Lee Spence. The Expeditions of John Charles Frémont. Vol. 2. Urbana: University of Illinois Press, 1973.

Jackson, Helen Hunt. A Century of Dishonor: A Sketch of Some of the United States Government's Dealings With the Indian Tribes. New York: Harper and Brothers, 1881.

Jacobs, Margaret. "Working on the Domestic Frontier: American Indian Domestic Servants in White Women's Households in the San Francisco Bay Area, 1920–1940." Frontiers: A Journal of Women Studies 28 (Winter 2007): 165–99.

Jacobson, Matthew Frye. Barbarian Virtues: The United States Encounters Foreign Peoples at Home and Abroad 1876–1917. New York: Hill and Wang, 2000.

James, Thomas. Exile Within: The Schooling of Japanese Americans, 1942–1945. Cambridge: Harvard University Press, 1987.

Jennings, Sandy. Los Alamos Pioneers. Los Alamos NM: Los Alamos Relief Society. 1997.

Jessett, Thomas. "Christian Missions to the Indians of Oregon." Church History 28 (June 1959): 147–56.

Jette, Eleanor. Inside Box 1663. Los Alamos: Los Alamos Historical Society, 1977.

Johnson, Marilynn S. The Second Gold Rush: Oakland and the East Bay in World War II. Berkeley: University of California Press, 1993.

Jones, Howard, and Donald A. Rakestraw. Prologue to Manifest Destiny: Anglo-American Relations in the 1840s. Woodbridge CT: Scholarly Resources, 1997.

Jones, Vincent C. Manhattan, the Army, and the Bomb. Washington DC: Center of Military History, U.S. Government Printing Office, 1985.

Jungk, Robert. Brighter Than a Thousand Suns: A Personal History of the Atomic Scientists. Translated by James Cleugh. New York: Harcourt Brace, 1958.

Kelley, Hall J. "A General Circular to All Persons of Good Character Who Wish to Emigrate to the Oregon Territory, Embracing Some Account of the Character and Advantages of the Country: The Right and the Means and Operations By Which It Is to Be Settled;—and All Necessary Directions for Becoming An Emigrant." In Powell, Hall J. Kelley on Oregon, 69–92.

Kesselman, Amy. Fleeting Opportunities: Women Shipyard Workers in Portland and Vancouver During World War II and Reconversion. Albany: State University of New York Press, 1990.

Kikuchi, Charles. The Kikuchi Diary: Chronicle from an American Concentration Camp. Edited by John Modell. Urbana: University of Illinois Press, 1973.

Kilbourn, Charlotte Lee, and Margaret Lantis. "Elements of Tenant Instability in a War Housing Project." American Sociological Review 11 (February 1946): 57–66.

Kiyota, Minoru. Beyond Loyalty: The Story of a Kibei. Translated by Linda Klepinger Keenan. Honolulu: University of Hawaii Press, 1997.

Klamath County Historical Society. The History of Klamath Country, Oregon. Klamath Falls OR: Klamath County Historical Society, 1984.

Klutznick, Philip. Angles of Vision: A Memoir of My Lives. Chicago: Ivan R. Dee, 1991.

Kunetka, James. City of Fire: Los Alamos and the Birth of the Atomic Age, 1943–1945. Englewood Cliffs NJ: Prentice-Hall, 1978.

Lane, Frederic C. Ships for Victory: A History of Shipbuilding Under the United States Maritime Commission in World War II. Baltimore: Johns Hopkins University Press, 1951.

Lang, Daniel. "The Tip Top Secret." The New Yorker, October 27, 1945, 54.

Lanouette, William, and Bela Silard. Genius in the Shadows: A Biography of Leo Szilard. New York: Charles and Scribners Sons, 1992.

Larsen, Rebecca. Oppenheimer and the Atomic Bomb. New York: Franklin Watts, 1988.

Lasker, Loula. "Friends or Enemies?" Survey Graphic 31 (June 1942): 277–79.

Lawler, Andrew. "Silent No Longer: 'Model Minority' Mobilizes." Science 290 (November 10, 2000): 1072–77.

Lawren, William. The General and the Bomb: A Biography of General Leslie R. Groves, Director of the Manhattan Project. New York: Dodd, Mead and Co., 1988.

Lewis, Theodore. "Annual Report on Internal Security at Topaz." In Records of the War Relocation Authority, 1942–46, reel 7, Project Reports. Alexandria VA: Chadwyck-Healey, Inc., 1991.

Lilienthal, David. Change, Hope and the Bomb. Princeton NJ: Princeton University Press, 1963.

Limerick, Patricia Nelson. The Legacy of Conquest: The Unbroken Past of the American West. New York: Norton, 1987.

Linfield, Michael. U.S. Civil Liberties in Times of War. Boston: South End Press, 1990.

Linton, Ralph. *Acculturation in Seven American Indian Tribes.* Gloucester MA: Peter Smith Publishing, 1963.

Lippard, Lucy. *The Lure of the Local: Senses of Place in a Multicentered Society.* New York: The New Press, 1997.

Lipscomb, Andrew A., and Albert Ellery Bergh. *The Writings of Thomas Jefferson.* Vol. 12. Washington DC: Thomas Jefferson Memorial Association, 1903.

Little, William A., and James E. Weiss, eds. *Blacks in Oregon: A Statistical and Historical Report.* Portland: Black Studies Research Center and the Center for Population Research, Portland State University, 1978.

Livingston, Marilyn Gerber. "Klamath Indians in Two Non-Reservation Communities: Klamath Falls and Eugene-Springfield." PhD diss., University of Oregon, 1959.

Los Alamos Historical Museum. *Remembering Los Alamos, World War II.* VHS. Los Alamos: Los Alamos Historical Society. 1993.

Lotchin, Roger. *Fortress California, 1910–1961: From Warfare to Welfare.* New York: Oxford University Press, 1992.

Maben, Manley. *Vanport.* Portland: Oregon Historical Society Press, 1987.

MacColl, E. Kimbark. *The Growth of a City: Power and Politics in Portland, Oregon, 1915–1950.* Portland: Georgian Press, 1979.

Maki, Mitchell T., Harry H.L. Kitano, and S. Megan Berthold. *Achieving the Impossible Dream: How Japanese Americans Achieved Redress.* Urbana: University of Illinois Press, 1999.

Mangun, Kimberly. "As Citizens of Portland We Must Protest: Beatrice Morrow Cannady and the African American Response to D. W. Griffith's 'Masterpiece.'" *Oregon Historical Quarterly* 107 (Fall 2006): 372–99.

Martin, Jill E. "'Neither Fish, Flesh, Fowl, nor Good Red Herring': The Citizenship Status of American Indians, 1830–1924." In *American Indians and U.S. Politics,* edited by John M. Meyer, 51–72. Westport CT: Praeger Publishing, 2002.

Masco, Joseph. *The Nuclear Borderlands: The Manhattan Project in Post-Cold War New Mexico.* Princeton NJ: Princeton University Press, 2006.

McElderry, Stuart. "Vanport Conspiracy Rumors and Social Relations in Portland, 1940–1950." *Oregon Historical Quarterly* 99 (Summer 1998): 134–63.

McKee, Robert. *The Zia Company in Los Alamos: A History.* El Paso TX: Carol Herzog, 1950.

McLagan, Elizabeth. *A Peculiar Paradise: A History of Blacks in Oregon, 1788–1940.* Portland: The Georgian Press, 1980.

McMillan, Elsie. *The Atom and Eve.* New York: Vantage Press, 1995.

McWilliams, Carey. "Shangri-La of the Atom." *The Nation* 176 (December 31, 1949): 639–40.

Meacham, A. B. *Wigwam and Warpath, or the Royal Chief in Chains*. Boston: John P. Dale, 1875.

Means, Russell. *Where White Men Fear to Tread: The Autobiography of Russell Means*. New York: St. Martin's Press, 1995.

Michelmore, Peter. *The Swift Years: The Robert Oppenheimer Story*. New York: Dodd, Mead and Company, 1969.

Miller, E. Lynn. "An Initial Report: The Subsistence Homestead Communities of the Franklin D. Roosevelt Administration." Unpublished manuscript, Michigan State University Library, 1978.

Milner, Clyde A. "National Initiatives." In Milner, O'Connor, and Sandweiss, *Oxford History of the American West*, 155–94.

Moore, Patrick Kerry. "Federal Enclaves: The Community Culture at Department of Energy Cities; Livermore, Los Alamos, and Oak Ridge." PhD diss., Arizona State University, 1997.

Morgan, Ted. *Reds: McCarthyism in Twentieth-Century America*. New York: Random House, 2003.

Morton, Samuel. *Crania Americana*. Philadelphia: Dobson, 1839.

Mullner, Ross. *Deadly Glow: The Radium Dial Worker Tragedy*. Washington DC: American Public Health Association, 1999.

Myer, Dillon S. "An Autobiography of Dillon S. Myer." University of California at Berkeley Regional Oral History Office, Bancroft Library, 1970.

———. *Uprooted Americans: The Japanese Americans and the War Relocation Authority During World War II*. Tempe: University of Arizona Press, 1971.

Myer, Dillon S., and Julius Krug. *The WRA: A Story of Human Conservation*. Washington DC: U.S. Government Printing Office. 1946.

Lindberg, Janet. *One Body, One Spirit: The Ecumenical Experience at the Church on the Hill*. Albuquerque: Academy Press, 1997.

Loewenberg, Robert J. "New Evidence, Old Categories: Jason Lee as Zealot." *Pacific Historical Review* 47 (August 1978): 366–67.

Lorenz, Claudia Spink. *The Time of My Life*. Klamath Falls OR: Klamath County Museum, 1969.

Nabokov, Peter, ed. *Native American Testimony: A Chronicle of Indian-White Relations from Prophecy to the Present, 1492–1992*. New York: Penguin Books, 1991.

Native American Solidarity Committee, Portland Chapter. "Arrowhead: Reclaiming Klamath Land, Rebuilding Klamath Culture." Portland: Native American Solidarity Committee, ca. 1976.

NAACP Special Subject Files, part 18 section C, 1944–1958. Frederick MD: University Publications of America, 1982.

Nash, Gerald D. *The American West Transformed: The Impact of the Second World War*. Bloomington: Indiana University Press, 1985.

———. The Federal Landscape: An Economic History of the Twentieth-Century West. Tucson: University of Arizona Press, 1999.

Netz, Reviel. *Barbed Wire: An Ecology of Modernity.* Middletown CT: Wesleyan University Press, 2004.

Neuberger, Richard. "How Oregon Rescued a Forest." *Harper's* 218 (April 1959): 48–52.

Nichols, Eileen. *Images of Oregon Women.* Salem OR: Madison Press, 1983.

O'Brien, Sharon. *American Indian Tribal Governments.* Norman: University of Oklahoma Press, 1989.

Okubo, Miné. "Artist Statement." In *Beyond Words: Images from America's Concentration Camps,* edited by Deborah Gesensway and Mindy Roseman, 66–74. Ithaca NY: Cornell University Press, 1987.

———. *Citizen 13660.* New York: Columbia University Press, 1946.

Omori, Emiko. *Rabbit in the Moon.* VHS. Written and produced by Emiko Omori. New York: Wabi-Sabi Productions, 1999.

O'Neill, William L. *A Democracy at War: America's Fight at Home and Abroad in World War II.* New York: The Free Press, 1993.

Oregon Public Broadcasting. *Your Land, My Land.* VHS. Directed by Reagan Ramsey. Portland: Oregon Public Broadcasting. 1991.

Oregon Secretary of State. *Oregon Blue Book, 1925–26.* Salem: State Printing Office, 1925.

Oregon State System of Higher Education. "Progress Report on University of Oregon Extension Center at Vanport City, July 22, 1946." Eugene: University of Oregon, 1946.

O'Sullivan, John. "The Great Nation of Futurity." *United States Democratic Review* 6, no. 23 (November 1839): 426–30.

Otis, D. S. *The Dawes Act and the Allotment of Indian Lands.* Edited and with an introduction by Francis Paul Prucha. Norman: University of Oklahoma Press, 1973.

Parman, Donald L. *Indians and the American West in the Twentieth Century.* Bloomington IN: Indiana University Press, 1994.

Pearson, Rudy. "A Menace to the Neighborhood: Housing and African Americans in Portland, 1941–1945." *Oregon Historical Quarterly* 102 (Summer 2001): 158–79.

Petersen, Don. "Child Volunteers: One Dad Tells the Story." *Los Alamos Science* 23 (1995): 266–68.

Philp, Kenneth. *John Collier's Crusade for Indian Reform, 1920–1954.* Tucson: University of Arizona Press, 1977.

Pomeroy, Earl. *The Pacific Slope: A History of California, Oregon, Washington, Idaho, Utah, and Nevada.* New York: Knopf, 1965.

Portland State University Department of Urban Studies. *History of the Albina Plan Area.* Portland: Portland State University, 1990.

Powell, Fred Wilbur, ed. *Hall J. Kelley on Oregon.* Princeton NJ: Princeton University Press, 1932.

Prucha, Francis Paul. *The Great Father: The United States Government and the American Indians.* Lincoln: University of Nebraska Press, 1984.

Quinn, Arthur. *Hell With the Fire Out: A History of the Modoc War.* Boston: Faber and Faber, 1997.

"Racial Violence Against Asian Americans." *Harvard Law Review* 106 (June 1993): 1926–43.

Rakestraw, Donald A. *For Honor or Destiny: The Anglo-American Crisis Over the Oregon Territory.* New York: Peter Lang, 1995.

Ramirez, Mari Carmen, and Héctor Olea, eds. *Inverted Utopias: Avant-Garde Art in Latin America.* Houston: Museum of Fine Arts Houston, 2004.

Raineri, Vivian McGuckin, ed. *The Red Angel: The Life and Times of Elaine Black Yoneda.* New York: International Publishers, 1991.

Red Bird, Aileen, and Patrick Melendy. "Indian Child Welfare in Oregon." In *The Destruction of American Indian Families,* edited by Stephen Unger, 43–46. New York: Association on American Indian Affairs, 1977.

Reese, William J. *America's Public Schools, From the Common School to "No Child Left Behind."* Baltimore: Johns Hopkins University Press, 2005.

Research Publications. *Western Americana: Frontier History of the Trans-Mississippi West, 1550–1900.* Woodbridge CT: Research Publications, 1975.

Reyhner, John, and Jeanne Eder. *American Indian Education: A History.* Norman: University of Oklahoma Press, 2004.

Riddle, Jefferson C. Davis. *The Indian History of the Modoc War.* Mechanicsburg PA: Stackpole Books, 2004.

Rieber, Robert W., and Robert Kelley. "Substance and Shadow: Images of the Enemy." In *The Psychology of War and Peace: The Image of the Enemy,* edited by Robert Rieber, 3–39. New York: Plenum Publishing Corporation, 1991.

Rhodes, Richard. *The Making of the Atomic Bomb.* New York: Simon and Schuster, 1986.

Robbins, William. *Landscapes of Promise: The Oregon Story, 1800–1940.* Seattle: University of Washington Press, 1997.

Robinson, Greg. *By Order of the President: FDR and the Internment of Japanese Americans.* Cambridge MA: Harvard University Press, 2001.

Rodgers, Daniel T. *Atlantic Crossings: Social Politics in a Progressive Age.* Cambridge MA: Harvard University Press, 1998.

Roensch, Eleanor Stone. *Life Within Limits: Glimpses of Everyday Life at Los Alamos, New*

Mexico, Seen Through the Eyes of a Young Female Soldier While on Military Service There, May 1944 to April 1946. Los Alamos NM: Los Alamos Historical Society, 1993.

Rostow, Eugene V. "Our Worst Wartime Mistake." *Harper's Magazine* 191 (September 1945): 193–201.

Rothman, Hal K. *On Rims and Ridges: The Los Alamos Area since 1880*. Lincoln: University of Nebraska Press, 1992.

Rousch, Donald C. "The Development and Organization of Student Government in Canyon Elementary School, Los Alamos, New Mexico." PhD diss., Drake University, 1951.

Rusco, Elmer R. *A Fateful Time: The Background and Legislative History of the Indian Reorganization Act*. Reno: University of Nevada Press, 2000.

Salyer, Lucy. "Baptism by Fire: Race, Service and U.S. Citizenship Policy, 1918–1935." *Journal of American History* 91 (December 2004): 847–76.

Samuel, Lawrence R. *Pledging Allegiance: American Identity and the Bond Drive of World War II*. Washington DC: Smithsonian Institution Press, 1997.

Sayers, Michael, and Albert E. Kahn. *Sabotage! The Secret War Against America*. New York: Harper Brothers, 1942.

Schwantes, Carlos. *The Pacific Northwest: An Interpretive History*. Lincoln: University of Nebraska Press, 1996.

Schwartz, Stephen I., ed. *Atomic Audit: The Costs and Consequences of U.S. Nuclear Weapons since 1940*. Washington DC: Brookings Institution Press, 1998.

Sears, Paul. *Los Alamos: Boom Town Under Control*. Albuquerque: Bureau of Business Research, University of New Mexico, 1953.

Segrè, Claudio. *Atoms, Bombs, and Eskimo Kisses: A Memoir of Father and Son*. New York: Viking Press, 1995.

Segrè, Emilio. *Enrico Fermi: Physicist*. Chicago: University of Chicago Press, 1970.

———. *A Mind Always in Motion: The Autobiography of Emilio Segrè*. Berkeley: University of California Press, 1993.

Serber, Robert. *Peace and War: Reminiscences of a Life on the Frontiers of Science*. New York: Columbia University Press, 1998.

Shanks, Cheryl. *Immigration and the Politics of American Sovereignty, 1890–1990*. University of Michigan Press, 2001.

Sharp, Patrick B. *Savage Perils: Racial Frontiers and Nuclear Apocalypse in American Culture*. Norman: University of Oklahoma Press.

Sherwin, Martin J. *A World Destroyed: The Atomic Bomb and the Grand Alliance*. New York: Knopf, 1975.

Shinedling, Abram I. *History of the Los Alamos Jewish Center 1944–1957*. Albuquerque: Valliant Print Co., 1958.

Shroyer, Joann. *Secret Mesa: Inside Los Alamos National Laboratory*. New York: John Wiley and Sons, 1997.

Skold, Karen Beck. "Women Workers and Childcare during World War II: A Case Study of Portland, Oregon Shipyards." Ph.D. diss., University of Oregon, 1981.

Smith, Alice Kimball, and Charles Weiner, eds. *Robert Oppenheimer, Letters and Recollections*. Cambridge MA: Harvard University Press, 1980.

Smith, Alonzo, and Quintard Taylor. "Racial Discrimination in the Workplace: a Study of Two West Coast Cities During the 1940s." *Journal of Ethnic Studies* 8 (Spring 1980): 35–54.

Smith, Henry Nash. *Virgin Land: The American West as Symbol and Myth*. Cambridge MA: Harvard University Press, 1950.

Spicer, Edward, Asael T. Hansen, Katherine Loumala, and Marvin K. Opler. *The Impounded People: the Japanese Americans in Relocation Centers*. Tempe: University of Arizona Press, 1969.

Starobin, Joseph R. *American Communism in Crisis, 1943–1957*. Cambridge MA: Harvard University Press, 1972.

State of California. *Senate Report on Un-American Activities Having Special Reference to Japanese Problems in California*. Sacramento: California Printing Office, April 1945.

State of Oregon. *Oregon Laws Enacted and Joint Resolutions Adopted by the 44th Regular Session of the Legislative Assembly*. Salem: Oregon State Printing Department, 1947.

Stember, Charles. "Reactions to Anti-Semitic Appeals Before and After the War." In *Jews in the Mind of America*, edited by George Salomon, 110–35. New York: Basic Books, 1966.

Stern, Philip M. *The Oppenheimer Case: Security on Trial*. New York: Harper and Row, 1969.

Stern, Theodore. "The Klamath Indians and the Treaty of 1864." *Oregon Historical Quarterly* 57 (September 1956): 229–65.

———. *The Klamath Tribe: A People and Their Reservation*. Seattle: University of Washington Press, 1965.

Studebaker, John. *Plain Talk*. Washington: National Home Library Foundation, 1936.

Sykes, Christopher, ed. *No Ordinary Genius: The Illustrated Richard Feynman*. New York: Norton, 1994.

Szasz, Margaret Connell. *Education and the American Indian: The Road to Self-Determination Since 1928*. Albuquerque NM: University of New Mexico Press, 1999.

Takaki, Ronald. *A Different Mirror: A History of Multicultural America*. Boston: Little, Brown, 1993.

Task Force Ten. "Final Report to the American Indian Policy Review Commission: Report on Terminated and Nonfederally Recognized Tribes." Washington DC: U.S. Government Printing Office, 1976.

Tateishi, John, ed. *And Justice for All: The Story of the Japanese Detention Camps*. New York: Random House, 1984.

———. "The Japanese American Citizens League and the Struggle for Redress." In

The Japanese Americans: From Relocation to Redress, edited by Roger Daniels, Sandra Taylor, and Harry H. L. Kitano, 191–95. Seattle: University of Washington Press, 1991.

Taylor, Paul S. "Our Stakes in the Japanese Exodus." *Survey Graphic* 31 (September 1942): 372–78.

Taylor, Quintard. *Forging a Black Community: Seattle's Central District, from 1870 through the Civil Rights Era*. Seattle: University of Washington Press, 1994.

Taylor, Sandra C. *Jewel of the Desert: Japanese-American Internment at Topaz*. Berkeley: University of California Press, 1993.

tenBroek, Jacobus, Edward N. Barnhart, and Floyd W. Matson. *Prejudice, War, and the Constitution*. Berkeley: University of California Press, 1954.

Thomas, Dorothy Swaine. *The Salvage*. Berkeley: University of California Press, 1952.

Townsend, Kenneth William. *World War II and the American Indian*. Albuquerque: University of New Mexico Press, 2000.

Trennert, Robert A., Jr. *Alternative to Extinction: Federal Indian Policy and the Beginnings of the Reservation System, 1846–51*. Philadelphia: Temple University Press, 1975.

Trumbull, George S. *A History of Oregon Newspapers*. Portland: Binfords and Mort, 1939.

Truslow, Edith. *Manhattan District History: Nonscientific Aspects of Los Alamos Project Y 1942–1946*. Edited by Kasha V. Thayer. Los Alamos NM: Los Alamos Historical Society, 1997.

Turner, Frederick Jackson. *The Significance of the Frontier in American History*. Huntington NY: Robert E. Kreiger Publishing, 1976.

Tyler, S. Lyman. *A History of Indian Policy*. Washington: United States Bureau of Indian Affairs, 1973.

Uchida, Yoshiko. *Desert Exile: The Uprooting of a Japanese-American Family*. Seattle: University of Washington Press, 1982.

U.S. Atomic Energy Commission. *In the Matter of J. Robert Oppenheimer: Transcript of Hearing Before Personnel Security Board and Texts of Principal Documents and Letters*. Cambridge MA: MIT Press, 1971.

U.S. Board of Indian Commissioners. *What the Government and the Churches Are Doing for the Indians*. Washington DC: U.S. Government Printing Office, 1874.

U.S. Commission on Wartime Relocation and Internment of Civilians. *Personal Justice Denied: Report of the Commission on Wartime Relocation and Internment of Civilians*. Washington DC: U.S. Government Printing Office, 1983.

U.S. Congress. *Statutes at Large*. Vol. 40. Washington DC: U.S. Government Printing Office, 1918.

U.S. Congress. House. Committee on Indian Affairs. *Authorizing the United States to Defray the Cost of Assisting the Klamath Tribe of Indians to Prepare for Termination of*

Federal Supervision, and to Defer Such Termination for a Period of 18 Months. 85th Cong., 1st sess., February 19, 1957.

———. An Act Relating to Marriage and Divorce Among Members of the Klamath and Modoc Tribes and Yahooskin Band of Snake Indians. 78th Cong., 2nd sess., January 1, 1945.

U.S. Congress. House. Committee on Interior and Insular Affairs. HR 99-630, Providing for the Restoration of the Federal Trust Relationship with the Klamath Indians. 99th Cong., 2nd sess., June 11, 1986.

———. Report 99-1406, Providing for the Setting Aside in Special Trust Lands and Interests Within the Winema National Forest to Edison Chiloquin. 96th Cong., 2nd sess., September 26, 1980.

U.S. Congress. House. Committee on the Judiciary. Subcommittee on Civil and Constitutional Rights. Anti-Asian Violence: Oversight Hearing before the Subcommittee on Civil and Constitutional Rights of the Committee on the Judiciary, House of Representatives. 100th Cong., 1st sess., November 10, 1987. Washington DC: U.S. Government Printing Office, 1988.

U.S. Congress. House. Committee on Un-American Activities. "Hearings before a Special Committee on Un-American Activities . . ." 75 Cong., 3rd sess., through 78 Cong., 2nd sess. Washington DC: U.S. Government Printing Office, 1943.

———. Investigation of Un-American Propaganda Activities in the United States. 77th Cong., 1st sess., 1942. Washington DC: U.S. Government Printing Office, 1943.

U.S. Congress. House. Select Committee Investigating National Defense Migration. Part 29, San Francisco Hearings: "Problems of Evacuation of Enemy Aliens and Others from Prohibited Military Zones." 77th Cong., 2nd sess., February 21, 1942. H. Doc. 68, serial 10966. Washington DC: U.S. Government Printing Office, 1943.

———. Report No. 2124, Fourth Interim Report of the Select Committee Investigating National Defense Migration, . . . Pursuant to H. Res. 113, a Resolution to Inquire Further into the Interstate Migration of Citizens, Emphasizing the Present and Potential Consequences of the Migration Caused by the National Defense Program. 77th Cong., 2nd sess., May 13, 1942. Washington DC: U.S. Government Printing Office, 1942.

U.S. Congress. House. Special Committee to Investigate Communist Activities in the United States. Hearings Before a Special Committee to Investigate Communist Activities, in the U.S. Pursuant to H. Res. 220, Providing for an Investigation of Communist Propaganda in the U.S. 71st Cong., 2nd sess., 1930. Washington DC: U.S. Government Printing Office, 1931.

U.S. Congress. House. Un-American Activities Committee. Communist Political Subversion; the Campaign to Destroy the Security Programs of the United States Government. 84th Cong., 2nd sess., November 12–December 14, 1956. Washington DC: U.S. Government Printing Office, 1957.

———. Investigation of Communist Activities in the Pacific Northwest Area. 83rd Cong.,

2nd sess., June 18, 1954. Washington DC: U.S. Government Printing Office, 1954.

U.S. Congress. Senate. Committee on Indian Affairs. *Dismissal of Superintendent Wade Crawford.* 75th Cong., 1st sess., July 1–8, 1937.

U.S. Congress. Senate. Committee on Interior and Insular Affairs, Subcommittee on Public Lands. Hearings, *A Bill to Remove Restrictions on the Property and Moneys Belonging to the Individual Enrolled Members of the Klamath Indian Reservation in Oregon, to Provide for the Liquidation of Tribal Property and Distribution of the Proceeds Thereof, and to Confer Complete Citizenship upon Such Indians, and for Other Purposes.* S 1222. 80th Cong., 1st sess., March 13–28 and August 18–21, 1947. Washington DC: U.S. Government Printing Office, 1948.

U.S. Congress. Senate. Committee on Military Affairs. *Report of the Subcommittee on Japanese War Relocation Centers to the Committee on Military Affairs, United States Senate on S. 444 Providing for the Transfer of Certain Functions of the War Relocation Authority to the War Department.* 78th Cong., 1st sess., May 7, 1943. Washington DC: U.S. Government Printing Office, 1943.

U.S. Congress. Senate. Subcommittee of the Senate Committee on Indian Affairs. *A Resolution Directing the Committee on Indian Affairs to Make a General Survey of the Condition of the Indians of the United States (pursuant to SR 79),* part 1. 70th Cong., 2nd sess., November 16, 1928.

U.S. Department of Agriculture. "Planning a Subsistence Homestead." *Farmer's Bulletin 1773.* Washington: U.S. Government Printing Office, 1934.

U.S. Department of Commerce. Bureau of the Census. *Wartime Changes in Population and Family Characteristics in Congested Production Areas: Portland Vancouver, May 1944.* Washington: U.S. Government Printing Office, 1944.

U.S. Department of Health, Education, and Welfare. *Indians on Federal Reservations in the United States: A Digest.* Vol. 1. Washington DC: U.S. Dept. of Health, Education, and Welfare, Public Health Service, Division of Indian Health, Program Analysis and Special Studies Branch, 1958.

U.S. Department of the Interior. Division of Subsistence Homesteads. "A Homestead and a Hope: Bulletin Number One." Washington DC: U.S. Government Printing Office, 1935.

————. *Homestead Houses: A Collection of Plans and Perspectives Issued by the Division of Subsistence Homesteads of the United States Department of the Interior.* Washington DC: Department of the Interior, 1934.

————. *Indian Affairs: Laws and Treaties.* Vol. 2. Edited by Charles J. Kappler. Washington DC: U.S. Government Printing Office, 1904.

————. Office of Indian Affairs. *Annual Report of the Commissioner of Indian Affairs to the Secretary of the Interior for the Year 1874.* Washington DC: U.S. Government Printing Office, 1874.

————. War Agency Liquidation Unit. *People in Motion: The Postwar Adjustment of the*

Evacuated Japanese Americans. Washington DC: U.S. Government Printing Office, 1947.

U.S. Department of War, Fourth Army. *Final Report: Japanese Evacuation from the West Coast.* Washington DC: U.S. Government Printing Office, 1942.

U.S. Federal Bureau of Investigation. *J. Robert Oppenheimer Security Files.* Wilmington DE: Scholarly Resources, Inc., 1978.

U.S. Internal Revenue Service. Memorandum #200111056, "Federal Emergency Management Agency Payments: Cerro Grande Fire Property Loss." February 15, 2001 (released March 16, 2001).

U.S. Office of War Information, Bureau of Motion Pictures. *Our Enemy: The Japanese.* 1943. From Prelinger Archives Online. MPEG, http://www.archive.org/details/OurEnemy1943 (accessed September 15, 2007).

U.S. Secretary of the Interior. "Extract from the report of the Secretary of the Interior relative to the report of the Commissioner of Indian Affairs." In *Report of the Commissioner of Indian Affairs for the Year 1865.* Washington DC: U.S. Government Printing Office, 1865.

U.S. War Manpower Commission. *A Survey of Shipyard Operations in the Portland, Oregon, Metropolitan Area.* Portland: WMC, 1943.

U.S. War Relocation Authority. *Administrative Highlights of the WRA Program.* Washington: U.S. Government Printing Office, 1946.

———. *Community Analysis Reports no. 1–18.* Washington DC: U.S. Government Printing Office, 1947.

———. *Community Government in the Relocation Centers.* Washington: U.S. Government Printing Office, 1946.

———. *Education Program in the Evacuation Centers.* Washington: U.S. Government Printing Office, 1945.

———. *The Evacuated People: A Quantitative Description.* Washington DC: U.S. Government Printing Office, 1946.

———. "Final Report of the Activities of the Portland District Office" (1946). In Final Reports of the War Relocation Authority. Selected Correspondence, Publications, and Issuances: Records of the War Relocation Authority. RG 210, reel 10. Washington DC: National Archives and Records Service, 1955.

———. *The Impounded People: The Japanese-Americans in the Relocation Centers.* Washington DC: U.S. Government Printing Office, 1946.

———. *The Japanese Relocation.* VHS. Produced by the United States Office of War Information, 1942. Washington DC: National Audiovisual Center, 1982.

———. *Legal and Constitutional Phases of the WRA Program.* Washington DC: U.S. Government Printing Office, 1946.

———. *Nisei in Uniform.* Washington DC: U.S. Government Printing Office, 1944.

———. *Questions and Answers for Evacuees: Information Regarding the Relocation Program.* Washington DC: U.S. Government Printing Office, ca. 1942.

———. *Records of the War Relocation Authority, 1942–46.* Alexandria: Chadwyck-Healey, Inc., 1991.

———. *Relocation of Japanese-Americans.* Washington DC: U.S. Government Printing Office, May 1943.

———. *The Relocation Program: A Guidebook for Residents of Relocation Centers.* Washington DC: U.S. Government Printing Office, 1943.

———. *The Relocation Program.* Washington DC: U.S. Government Printing Office, 1946.

———. *Resettlement Bulletin.* Washington DC: U.S. Government Printing Office, 1945.

———. San Francisco Office. *Pertinent Facts About Relocation Centers and Americans of Japanese Ancestry.* San Francisco: Interior Department, 1944.

———. *Supplemental Policy Statement on Project Government.* Washington DC: U.S. Government Printing Office, July 20, 1942.

———. *A Voice that Must Be Heard.* Washington: U.S. Government Printing Office, 1943.

———. *Wartime Exile: The Exclusion of the Japanese-Americans from the West Coast.* Washington: U.S. Government Printing Office, 1946.

Vanport Public Schools. *6,000 Kids from 46 States.* Portland: Vanport Public Schools, 1946.

Verdoia, Ken. *Topaz.* VHS. Salt Lake City: KUED Public Broadcasting, 1987.

Weglyn, Michi Nishiura. *Years of Infamy: The Untold Story of America's Concentration Camps.* Seattle: University of Washington Press, 1996.

Welsome, Eileen. *The Plutonium Files: America's Secret Medical Experiments in the Cold War.* New York: Dial Press, 1999.

White, Richard. *"It's Your Misfortune and None of My Own": A History of the American West.* Norman: University of Oklahoma Press, 1991.

Wilson, Jane S., and Charlotte Serber, eds. *Standing By and Making Do: Women of Wartime Los Alamos.* Los Alamos: Los Alamos Historical Society, 1988.

Yesley, Michael S. "'Ethical Harm' and the Plutonium Injection Experiments." *Los Alamos Science* 23 (1995): 280–83.

Yoshino, Ronald W. "Barbed Wire and Beyond: a Sojourn Through the Internment—a Personal Recollection." *Journal of the West* 35 (January 1996): 34–43.

Zakoji, Hiroto. *Termination and the Klamath Indian Education Program, 1955–1961.* Salem: Oregon State Department of Education, 1961.

Zimmerman, William, and Sophie D. Aberle. *The Indian: America's Unfinished Business.* Norman: University of Oklahoma Press, 1966.

Index

American Red Cross. *See* Red Cross
American Veterans Committee, 227, 285
Angelenos, 61
annuity payments. *See* treaty payments
anthropological racism. *See* racism: in
  anthropology
anti-Asian racism, 6, 297; called "Jap
  Crow," 223
anti-Asian violence, 297–98; threatened,
  309–10
anti-Communism, 21, 250; Indian
  Reorganization Act and, 332n11;
  Klamath Indian Reservation, 179,
  258–59; Los Alamos and, 208,
  236–37, 248; McCarran-Walter
  Immigration and Nationality Act
  and, 292; Portland and, 63–64. *See
  also* Internal Security Act (proposed);
  red-baiting; Red Squads
antidiscrimination laws, 155
antidiscrimination policies, 67, 198
anti-Semitism, 18. *See also* fear of Jews
apathy, 154, 240, 280
apologies, 295, 306
Applegate, Elisha, 44, 47
Applegate, Ivan, 44, 47
Applegate, Jesse, 348n18
Applegate, Jesse (1811–88), 44
Applegate, Lindsay, 43, 44, 47, 48, 85–
  87; as Klamath tribal court arbiter,
  87; use of commodities as disciplinary tool, 134
Applegate, Lucian, 44, 47
Applegate, Oliver Cromwell, 44, 47,
  85, 99, 138, 140–41, 171; Allotment
  Act and, 96; *Klamath Republican* and,
  326n12; La-Lakes and, 86; as tribal
  court justice selection, 92
Applegate family, 43–44, 45, 47, 48, 90,
  91, 103, 290, 348n18

architectural homogeneity, 110, 146
Area 51, 307
Arizona, 57
Arkell, John, 182
arms race, 246, 277
Army Corps of Engineers. *See* U.S. Army
  Corps of Engineers
army post exchanges. *See* post exchanges
Arrowhead (Klamath village), 288–89,
  290
Arthurdale WV, 144
Asians, 49; Samuel Morton and, 11, 12.
  See also Cambodian refugees; Chinese
  Americans; Japanese; Japanese
  Americans; Taiwanese American
  scientists
assimilation: Allotment Act and, 97;
  Indians and, 15, 130, 172, 186–87,
  251; Japanese Americans and, 189,
  190, 191; Jews and, 17; Klamath
  Tribes and, 43, 47, 48, 141, 180, 183,
  253, 262, 266, 273, 275; Los Alamos
  and, 164; Wade Crawford and, 179,
  180. *See also* Indian schools
Association of Los Alamos Scientists
  (ALAS), 236
Astoria OR, 36–37
Atchison, David Rice, 39
atomic bomb, 16, 73, 79, 81; Trinity
  Test, July 1945, 211, 307. *See also*
  Hiroshima and Nagasaki bombings,
  1945
Atomic Energy Act, 236
Atomic Energy Commission (AEC), 8,
  235–48
attorneys. *See* lawyers
automobile mechanics, 197–98
automobile searches, 123

Bacher, Robert, 81

Chavez, Dennis, 122

Chemawa Indian School, 137–38, 184, 268

Chicago, 219–21

Chiloquin, Edison, 187, 288–89

Chiloquin High School, 257

childcare centers, 157–60

children: accepted in Los Alamos, 166; assaulted, 245; boarded at schools (and abused), 136–37, 138; employed as servants and laborers, 31–32; exposed to health hazards, 306; forced to work in fields, 153; given English name to protect from racism, 291; killed in Modoc War, 45; labeled "retarded," 162; placed in foster care by WRA, 103; registered by first name only, 80; shot at, 105; volunteered as medical guinea pigs, 305. See also Indian children; Indians: treated as children; public education

Chin, Vincent, 297–98

China, 51, 292, 309

Chinese Americans, 297–98

Chinook language, 47

Christian missionaries, 37–38, 41, 42–43; Klamath schools and, 136

Christians: Los Alamos, 238–39

Citizens for LANL Employee Rights (CLER), 304–5

citizenship: African Americans and, 48–49, 173; children of subsistence homesteaders and, 144; Homestead Act and, 95; Indians and, 48–49, 96, 135, 136, 172, 174, 184, 262; Japanese resident aliens and, 59, 192, 295, 318n55; New Mexican, 242; public education and, 128; refusal of, 295; renunciation of, 192, 193; second-class, 128, 169, 201, 224, 284; seen

as undeserved, 62; Vanport and, 111, 161; WRA internment camps and, 101, 103, 192, 193. See also Indian Citizenship Act; Japanese citizenship

civil defense workers, 180, 181, 183, 184

Civilian Conservation Corps, 99

Civil Liberties Act of 1988, 295

civil rights movement, 293, 295, 349n39

Clark v. United States, 231–32, 298–99, 301

class. See social class

class-action lawsuits, 231–32, 293, 294–95

classism, 160

CLER. See Citizens for LANL Employee Rights (CLER)

clothing, 150, 328n49

coal miners, 144

Cold War, 213–14, 245–46, 248, 303

collectivism, 142, 214

colleges and universities, 270, 301; Japanese American students, 214–15; Vanport, 226, 341n28. See also graduate students; University of California (UC)

Collier, John, 58, 68, 100, 106–7, 146, 175–81, 249, 253

colonies, farming. See farming colonies

colonization, 13, 37

Colorado, 57

Colorado River Relocation Center, 100

The Coming Conflict of Nations (Fitzpatrick), 51

commissaries, 121, 124, 163, 233–34, 240, 243

Commission on Wartime Relocation and Internment of Civilians (CWRIC), 294, 295

Committee for Congested Production Areas, 65

Committee to Save the Remaining Klamath Indian Lands, 289

commodities, 47, 48; controls on, 133; as disciplinary tool, 134

common school movement, 127, 144

Communism: Indian reservations and, 213, 258–59; Japanese Americans and, 286. *See also* anti-Communism; fear of Communists and Communism

Communist internment (proposed), 276–79, 282

Communist Party USA, 13, 320n92; African Americans and, 66, 67; Berkeley CA, 76; FBI registration and, 276, 277; Japanese Americans and, 55–56, 66, 286; Vanport, 228; Vanport flood and, 230, 285. *See also* Daily Worker

community centers, 127, 143, 144 ; so-called, 243

community government, 83–84; Klamath Indian Reservation, 84–99; Los Alamos, 116–24; Vanport, 113–15; WRA internment camps, 100–109, 148, 194, 195–96, 198. *See also* town councils; tribal councils; tribal courts

community policing, 69, 115–16; Klamath Indian Reservation, 91–92; Topaz, 108–9; Vanport schools, 161

companion animals. *See* pets

company towns, 69–70; Los Alamos and, 74, 117, 237, 238, 244

compartmentalization of information. *See* information compartmentalization

concentration camps. *See* internment camps

"concentration camps" (term), 313n1

concessionaires. *See* vendors

condemnation of real estate, 79

Confederated Tribes of the Grande Ronde, 32

confidentiality rules, 156

confiscation of land. *See* land seizure

confiscation of personal property. *See* seizure of personal property

conformity, 20, 24, 128

congressional redistricting. *See* redistricting

conscientious objectors, 181

conscription deferments. *See* military draft deferments

Constitution. *See* U.S. Constitution

consumer cooperatives, 149–51

controlled markets, 133, 155–56, 163, 243–44. *See also* post exchanges

cooperatives, 143. *See also* consumer cooperatives

Cordon, Guy, 255

corruption, 177, 272

counterintelligence agents, 207

courts. *See* New Mexico: Supreme Court; traffic courts; tribal courts; U.S. Supreme Court

Courtright, Bert, 181–86, 254, 257

cover-ups, 301

Craig, Morian, 308

Crania Americana (Morton), 11–13

Crater Lake, 290

Crawford, Ida, 254, 259

Crawford, Wade, 175, 176–79, 251, 254, 259, 332n11

Crawford, William, 139

crime: Los Alamos, 208–9. *See also* murder; rape

criminal justice: Klamath Indian Reservation, 86–88, 91–93; Los Alamos, 245

criminalization: of Indian customs, 87, 92; of Klamath social activity, 258
Culver, Samuel L., 42, 46
curfews, 199
Curry, Estes, 300

Daily Worker, 236–37
Daniels, Roger, 313n1
David, Allen, 86, 179
Davis, Elmer, 191
Dawes Act. *See* General Allotment Act of 1887
day-care services, 157–60
decolonization, 37
defense workers: housing, 68; race and, 63; San Francisco, 223. *See also* Indian defense workers; shipyard workers
"de-Indianization," 136–37, 274
Deloria, Vine, Jr., 280
democracy, limited, 83–84; Klamath Indian Reservation, 84–99; Los Alamos, 116–24; Topaz, 106–9; Vanport, 113–15
demonstrations, 124, 140–41, 228, 230, 240. *See also* sit-ins; walkouts
Demson, E. J., 342n57
Department of Labor. *See* U.S. Department of Labor
Department of the Interior. *See* U.S. Department of the Interior
Department of Veterans Affairs. *See* Veterans Administration (VA)
Department of War. *See* U.S. Department of War
deportation, 63, 64
depression, 166, 167, 168, 273
Depression era. *See* Great Depression
detention of dissidents (proposed), 276–79

detention of Germans, 56
detention of Italians, 56
detention of Japanese Americans. *See* Japanese Americans: arrest and detention
detribalization, 22, 250–51, 272. *See also* "de-Indianization"
Dewey, John, 144
DeWitt, John, 53
disinformation campaigns, 79
"disloyals" (label), 192, 197, 278; "dangerous disloyal," 67
disloyalty, 189, 192
dissidents, 284, 285–86, 311; proposed detention of, 276–79. *See also* draft resisters and draft resistance
Division of Subsistence Homesteads, 141–42
dormitories, 67, 68, 204; lock-ins, 137; searches of, 123
"downwinders," 307
draft deferments, 181
draft registration, 183
draft resisters and draft resistance, 182, 296
Dred Scott v. Sanford, 48
dress. *See* clothing
driver's licenses, 79
dropouts, 257
due process, 54, 119, 203, 277, 278
DuFault, George, 255–56
Duncan v. Kahanamoku, 340n19

economic aspects of federally run enclaves, 21, 26, 127, 169–70, 280–81; Klamath Indian Reservation, 91, 96, 97, 130–35, 140–41, 251–75; Los Alamos, 163–69, 234, 243–44, 304–5; Topaz, 61, 101–2, 146–48, 149–52, 218–19, 328n49; Vanport, 155–57

fear of Indians, 43, 116
fear of Jews, 5–6, 17–18, 72
fear of juvenile delinquency, 161
fear of leftists and radicals, 63, 72, 74, 76
fear of race riots, 190, 201
fear of racism, 159, 291
fear of technology transfer, 310
Federal Bureau of Investigation. See FBI
Federal Public Housing Authority (FPHA), 8; community government and, 113; Vanport and, 16, 67–68, 70–71, 113–16, 157–58, 198, 226–29, 231–32
Federal Tort Claims Act, 231, 308
Fee, James Alger, 299
FEPC. See Fair Employment Practices Commission (FEPC)
Fermi, Enrico, 16, 72, 75, 76, 117, 118, 205; AEC and, 236; bodyguard of, 207, 338n83; cancer death of, 302; family pseudonym, 80; May-Johnson Bill and, 235
Fermi, Laura, 208, 338n83
Feynman, Richard, 118–19, 211
fingerprinting, 165, 205
Finns, 63, 292
firearm registration, 114
fires, 307–8
firings. See job terminations
Fisher, Galen, 323n42
Fisher, Phyllis, 165, 208
Fitzpatrick, Ernest H.: The Coming Conflict of Nations, 51
floods, 229–32, 285–86, 298–302, 319n79, 341n35, 349n38
flour, 47, 48
Food for Victory program, 147
food provisions, 88; at Indian boarding schools, 137; to Indians at Fort

Klamath, 47; Los Alamos commissary and, 124, 233; at Topaz, 101, 109, 149, 188; at Vanport child service centers, 160–61; withheld as punishment, 134; WRA expenditure on, 329n53
foods, ethnic. See ethnic foods
Ford, Gerald, 293
Ford, Henry, 17–18
forest fire lookouts, 181
forest management, 253–53, 265–66
Forest Service. See U.S. Forest Service
Fort Klamath, 8, 46, 47, 85
Fortune, 213, 215
Fort Vancouver, 38
Foster, Stephen C., 128–30, 322n26
foster care, 275
Fourteenth Amendment. See U.S. Constitution: Fourteenth Amendment
FPHA. See Federal Public Housing Authority (FPHA)
Franzen, James, 113, 158, 199, 203
freedom of movement, 111, 119, 193, 203, 208. See also travel restrictions
freedom of speech, 129; Los Alamos, 118–19, 203, 205–6, 208
Frémont, John, 44–45
"friendly aliens" (label), 193
Fryer, E. R., 100
Fuchs, Klaus, 118, 245–46, 277, 278
funerals, 194, 195

G-2, 75, 77, 205
Geisy, John Ulrich: All for His Country, 51, 53
General Allotment Act of 1887, 95, 101, 132, 135, 264, 344n2
general strikes, 197
Geneva Conventions, 101
German Americans, 56

House Committee on Indian Affairs. *See* U.S. House of Representatives: Committee on Indian Affairs

House Committee on Un-American Activities (HUAC), 102, 188, 285, 286, 334–35n38

housekeepers, 156, 165–66

housing, 99; de facto segregation in, 198–99; of defense workers nationwide, 68; of displaced coal miners, 144; of Japanese American evacuees and internees, 60–61, 101, 106, 148–49; of Los Alamos workers, 121–22, 203–4, 205, 207, 234, 237, 238; of migrant workers in Portland, 67, 68, 336–37n62; postwar boom, 252; searches of, 123, 207; of shipyard workers in Vanport, 110, 155, 198–99; unmentionable nature of, 206. *See also* barracks; dormitories; huts; redlining

Housing Authority of Portland (HAP), 71, 112–16, 155–56, 198–201, 225, 301

housing leases, 111–12

HR 442. *See* Civil Liberties Act of 1988

HR 7960, 289, 290

HUAC. *See* House Committee on Un-American Activities

humanitarian aid from Japan, 195

Hungary, 208

Hunters Point, 223

Huntington, J. W. Perit, 46–47

huts, 122

hydrogen bomb, 235, 245, 246

Ichihashi, Yamato, 102

Ickes, Harold, 145, 179, 328n32

identification cards, 233

identification numbers: Japanese Americans and, 60

Iijima, Mary, 215

Iiyama, Chizu, 291, 296, 323n42

Iiyama, Ernest, 55, 291

immigrant Europeans. *See* European immigrants

immigration laws, 192, 292–93

Indian actors, 186

Indian agents, 39, 42, 45, 47, 71, 87, 90, 326n12; as parental figures, 133–34

Indian agriculture, 96, 132, 172, 264

Indian Bureau. *See* Bureau of Indian Affairs (BIA); Office of Indian Affairs

Indian children, 135–39, 162, 172, 178, 183, 275, 289, 327n23

Indian Citizenship Act, 173, 184

Indian courts. *See* tribal courts

Indian defense workers, 180, 255, 261

Indian elections. *See* tribal elections

Indian languages: punishment for speaking, 137

Indian New Deal, 175

Indian Reorganization Act (IRA), 106, 175, 176, 179, 332n10–11

Indian reservations, 13, 41, 49, 129; arrest of Issei and, 54; compared to prisoner-of-war camps, 91; compared to Vanport, 69, 70, 71; as embarrassment to federal government, 93; liquidation of, 22, 213–14; as model for Los Alamos, 117; as model for WRA internment camps, 100, 102; as permanent homelands, 133; return of Indian defense workers to, 261; rhetorical foundation for, 42; seen as Communist enclaves, 213, 258–59; survey of conditions in, 174; termination of, 8, 22, 249, 250–75; WRA internment camps located on, 148. *See also* Klamath Indian Reservation; Navajo Reservation; Umatilla Indian Reservation

Indians, 13; Americanization and, 7, 8, 47, 90, 92, 135–36, 171; assimilation and, 15, 130, 172, 186–87, 251; Britain and, 36; California, 284; Christianization of, 37–38; citizenship, 48–49; delegations to Washington, 139; detribalization, 22, 250–51, 272; enmification, 37, 38, 41, 42, 45, 251; extermination campaigns and, 284; Helen Hunt Jackson on, 93–94; Homestead Act and, 322n26, 326n6; Japanese Americans and, 32, 147, 152, 189, 191, 196–97, 221, 224, 266–67, 291, 296; John Frémont and, 44–45; as laborers at Los Alamos, 164–66; Oregon, 6–8, 41–48; population, 315n40; resistance by, 38, 44–45, 54, 85, 88–91, 92, 136, 139; Samuel Morton and, 12; Stephen C. Foster on, 130; stereotyped as "drunken," 275; treated as children, 131, 133, 259. *See also* Cayuses; Hopis; Klamaths; Menominees; Modocs; Pueblos; Paiutes

Indian schools, 135–40

Indian soldiers, 171–72, 173, 187. *See also* Indian veterans

Indian treaty payments. *See* treaty payments

Indian tribal councils. *See* tribal councils

Indian veterans, 173–74, 187, 261

Indian women: as forest fire lookouts, 181; *Modoc Point* launching and, 185; per capita treaty payments and, 255

information compartmentalization, 118, 206, 209, 303. *See also* censorship

Inouye, Daniel, 293, 295, 298

INS. *See* U.S. Immigration and Naturalization Service

institutional racism, 6

integrated dances. *See* interracial dances

Internal Revenue Service, 308

Internal Security Act (proposed), 276–79, 282, 285, 286, 292

internment camp guards, 105, 153; James Wakasa killing by, 193–95

internment camps, 2, 8, 15, 58; attacked for their "luxuriousness," 188; community councils, 106–8, 115; deaths in, 103–4, 193–95; food costs, 329n53; Los Alamos and, 208; terminology, 313n1; Vanport and, 70. *See also* Colorado River Relocation Center; Manzanar Relocation Center; Topaz Relocation Center; Tule Lake Relocation Center

internment of Communists (proposed). *See* Communist internment (proposed)

interracial couples, 258

interracial dances, 199–200

interracial relations. *See* race relations

inter-tribal factionalism. *See* tribal factionalism

Inverted Utopias (Ramirez and Olea), 313n2

Iriki, Masanori, 196

Irons, Peter, 340n19

irradiated humans, 210–11

Issei, 54, 101, 192, 193, 295; resettlement and, 220–21, 250, 291

"Issei" (word), 315n50

Italians: in the U.S., 16, 56, 57, 75

Jackson, Boyd, 254

Jackson, Helen Hunt: *A Century of Dishonor*, 93–94
Jackson, Henry, 139
JACL. *See* Japanese American Citizens League (JACL)
James, Clyde, 185
James, Thomas, 282
"Jap" (label), 61, 100, 105, 154, 216, 217, 221, 222
Japan, 51, 55. *See also* Pearl Harbor: Japanese attack on
Japanese: enmification of, 14, 35, 50, 51–52; stereotyping of, 12, 38, 51–52, 56, 190, 191. *See also* fear of Japanese
Japanese American Art Memorial, 32
Japanese American Citizens League (JACL), 188, 190, 286, 293, 299
Japanese American Committee for Democracy, 102, 286, 323n42, 340n21
Japanese American Day of Remembrance, 32
Japanese American Evacuation Claims Act, 291
Japanese American legislators, 293, 295
Japanese Americans, 14; African Americans and, 219, 220, 223, 293, 295, 340n22; arrest and detention of, 54, 56, 62; assimilation and, 189, 190, 191; censuses and, 310; enmification, 52–56, 61; Chicago, 219–21; Communists and, 286; evacuation and internment, 2–3, 14, 53, 57–58, 60–62, 100–110, 147–55, 188–98, 283; FBI and, 14, 16, 54, 59, 154, 188, 195–96, 282, 293, 297, 309; Indians and, 32, 147, 152, 189, 191, 196–97, 221, 224, 266–67, 291, 296; military service and, 56, 191, 192, 202, 216–17; passing as "Chinese," 202;

potential vigilantism and, 283; property loss, 151–52, 218, 291–92, 294, 339n12; proposed dispersal to eastern cities, 189–90; redress, 291–95; rejection of Japanese heritage, 215, 291; resettlement, 190, 213–24, 222–23; 286, 291, 344n15; resettlement in Vanport, 201–2, 299, 349n38; rights, 292. *See also* Issei; Kibei; Nisei; Sansei
Japanese American soldiers, 191, 202, 216–17
Japanese American Student Relocation Council, 214
Japanese citizenship: renunciation of, 192
Japanese Hawaiians, 53
"Japanification" and "Japanization," 13, 297
Japantowns. *See* Nihonmachi
Jarvi, Grail, 301
Jefferson, Thomas: "Empire for Liberty" vision, 10–11, 24, 27, 51–52, 94, 126, 132, 284
Jen, Gish, 309
Jessup, John, 113
Jette, Eleanor, 168
Jewish Americans, 5
Jewish scientists, 18, 75
Jews: Los Alamos, 239; Samuel Morton and, 17. *See also* anti-Semitism; fear of Jews
job layoffs. *See* layoffs
job terminations: Japanese Americans and, 55, 59
Johnson, Andrew, 300
Johnson, Marilynn, 349n39
judges, tribal. *See* tribal judges
jukeboxes, 123–24, 199
jurisprudence. *See* criminal justice

juvenile delinquency, 256. *See also* fear of juvenile delinquency

Kaiser, Henry, 67
Kaiser Shipbuilding Company, 64–68, 70, 76, 255; childcare services and, 158; "Indian" and "Negro" launchings, 184–85
Kawaguchi, Tom, 104, 296
Keintpoos, 88, 89, 278
Kellar, Laura, 228
Kelley, Hall, 38
Kelley, Robert, 10
Kibei, 191, 192
"Kibei" (word), 315n50
Kikuchi, Charles, 56
Kimball, Solon, 100
Kirk, Clayton, 139
Kirk, Jesse, 93, 98, 139–40, 254
Kirk, Seldon, 266, 345n31
Kirtland Air Force Base, 306–7
Kitano, Harry, 150
Kiyota, Minoru, 153–54
Klamath Constitution of 1954, 289
Klamath County (Oregon), 179, 183; schools, 268
Klamath Court of Indian Offenses, 92
Klamath Falls OR, 258, 268, 274, 275, 345n31
Klamath Incorporation Bill, 175
Klamath Indian Education Program, 266–67, 269, 270–71
Klamath Indian Reservation, 6–8, 85–99, 171–87, 283; compared to Topaz, 224–25; Crawford administration, 176–79; creation of, 43, 46–48; economic aspects, 91, 96, 97, 130–35, 140–41, 172–74, 251–75, 281; "Emancipation Bill" (S. 1222), 254–56, 259; factionalism, 141, 176,
178, 183, 254, 264, 265; General Council, 97, 176, 177, 178, 181, 263–64, 265; incorporation, 175, 176; Indian Reorganization Act and, 176, 332n11; as inverse utopia, 27; as kindergarten for Americanization, 29; landholding reduction, 47–48, 140, 274; newspaper views of, 174; off-reservation residents, 344n2; population, 19; powerlessness of residents, 26, 269; schools, 136–39, 252, 256–57, 327n23; termination of, 22, 249, 250–75, 281, 287; termination reversal, 273, 288, 289; touted wealth of, 184, 185, 255, 258; tribal business council, 97–98, 175, 177, 184, 269–70; Tribal Loan Fund, 270
Klamath Marsh, 265
Klamath Republican, 326n12
Klamath Reservation Junior Chamber of Commerce, 270–71
Klamaths, 7, 21, 22; distrust and, 267; education, 136–39, 252, 256–57, 266–68, 270; employment and, 264, 270; enmification of, 42, 45; Japanese Americans and, 32; parental rights termination, 275; psychological testing, 267–68, 346n34; reclassification as "legal non-Indians," 262, 274, 275; resistance, 44–45, 287; restoration of tribal status (1986), 273; rivalry with Modocs, 87, 88; termination payment, 271–73; termination payment refusal, 288; treaties and, 47–48; Vanport, 187
Klamath Termination Act, 8, 22, 263, 272, 288; reversal of, 289–90
Klamath Tribes Economic Self Sufficiency Plan, 290
Klamath Tribune, 270–71

Cold War defense project, 232–48; economy of, 163–69, 304–5; fear of foreign scientists and, 16, 18; fires, 307–8; health hazards, 303–4, 305–6; housing, 121–22, 203–4, 205,207, 234, 237, 238; Indian labor, 164–66; as inverse utopia, 27; as kindergarten for Americanization, 29; legal standing of residents, 239–43; population, 19; powerlessness of residents, 20, 26; schools, 167, 168, 211, 234, 243, 304; secrecy and, 73–74, 79–80, 163, 165, 205, 207, 232; setting of, 7; termination and transition into "real American town," 8, 22, 244, 246–47, 248; as three-sector community, 238; town council, 119–22, 123, 124, 238, 239, 241; women residents, 124, 164–66; workforce, 164–69

Los Alamos Ranch School, 79, 164, 241

Los Alamos Times, 239

Los Angeles residents. *See* Angelenos

loss of personal property. *See* personal property loss

loyalty, 59; dependency and, 169; Indians and, 49, 85, 90, 165, 172, 251; Japanese Americans and, 59, 101, 106, 147, 151, 188, 190–91; scientists and, 77, 78, 118. *See also* disloyalty

loyalty oaths, 81, 215

loyalty tests, 191–92, 335n47, 335–36n50

Macmillan, Edward, 77

magazines, 123, 150, 151

maids. *See* housekeepers

mail censorship. *See* censorship: of mail

Manhattan Engineer District (MED), 73–80, 116, 120–24, 164–68, 207, 233–35; radioactive materials handling and, 210

Manhattan Project, 4–6, 16, 71–82; conversion into Cold War defense project, 232–48; Harry S. Truman and, 232–33; Jews and, 17; secrecy and, 73–74. *See also* Los Alamos NM

"manifest destiny," 7, 14, 25, 37, 49; fear of its reversal, 52

Manzanar Relocation Center, 56

markets, controlled. *See* controlled markets

Markson, Sam, 201, 285, 300

marriage, traditional Indian, 87, 177, 183

Marshak, Robert, 118

Marshall, Vern, 337n63

massacres, 41, 45–46

Maw, Herbert, 146–47

May-Johnson Bill, 235, 236

McAnulty, Dorothy, 258

McCarran, Pat, 276

McCarran Act (proposed). *See* Internal Security Act (proposed)

McCarran-Walter Immigration and Nationality Act, 292–93, 315n50

McKee Company, 237

McNary, Charles, 68, 175

McNickle, Darcy, 107

McWilliams, Carey, 189, 235, 323n42

Meacham, Alfred B., 89

Mead, Elwood, 143

Means, Russell, 287

measles, 41

MED. *See* Manhattan Engineer District (MED)

media. *See* magazines; newspapers; radio stations

medical examinations, 105

medical research, 306. *See also* nonconsensual medical experiments
medical services, 137, 209, 234, 263
Meek, Joseph, 41
Menominees, 345n31
"mental retardation" (label), 162
Meriam Report, 174
Mexico, 40
migrant workers, 64–65, 159; civil rights movement and, 349n39; Indians as, 186
military draft deferments. *See* draft deferments
military draft registration. *See* draft registration
military draft resisters. *See* draft resisters
military enlistment: Klamaths and, 183–84; attempts by Japanese Americans, 56
military induction, 180
military influence on Los Alamos, 117
military police (MPS), 197, 205, 208–9, 211, 233; deputization of (New Mexico), 244; killing of James Wakasa, 193–95; removal of from Topaz, 196
Miller, D. L., 257
missionaries, Christian. *See* Christian missionaries
Modoc Point (ship), 185
Modocs, 7, 32, 44, 45, 46, 173–74, 192, 275; as farmers, 132; rivalry with Klamaths, 87; ruled by U.S.-picked Klamath, 86; treaties and, 47
Modoc War, 88–90, 91, 171, 192
monopolies, 133
monotony, 110
Monroe, James, 36
Monroe Doctrine, 37
Moore, Thomas, 285

morale, 105, 114, 118, 122, 146, 189, 246; Nisei soldiers and, 217
More, Thomas, 24
Morrison, Philip, 77, 320n92
Morton, Samuel, 17, 51; *Crania Americana*, 11–13, 24
MPS. *See* military police (MPS)
Multnomah County (Oregon), 111; sheriffs, 114, 115
Mundt, Karl, 188–89
murder: of Indians, 46; of Asian Americans, 297–98
music, 188. *See also* jukeboxes
Myer, Dillon, 57–58, 107, 146, 149, 153, 224, 248–49; appointed commissioner of BIA, 248–49, 252, 267; appointed commissioner of FPHA, 228–29, 248–49; disaster housing and, 230; ignorance about Klamaths, 267; Japanese American resettlement and, 189, 190, 215; resignation demanded, 202

NAACP, 190
Nagasaki bombing, 1945. *See* Hiroshima and Nagasaki bombings, 1945
Nahakata, Donald, 296
names of streets. *See* street names
naming of children, 291
National Council for Japanese American Redress (NCJAR), 293
National Defense Research Committee, 73
National Industrial Recovery Act, 327n32
National Park Service. *See* U.S. National Park Service
Native Americans. *See* Indians
naturalization, 48, 95, 192
Naturalization Service. *See* U.S.

Potter, William, 115
Powell, Adam Clayton, 323n42
Pratt, Henry C., 135
Pratt, Martin, 114, 199, 200, 202
Presidential Medal of Freedom, 297
Prevost, James, 36–37
price regulation, 244
profiling by race. See racial profiling
profiling of foreign nationals, 54
profiling of radicals, 16, 54, 279
profiling of spies, 245–46
profiteering, 230, 272
propaganda, 55, 66, 287; Japanese, 191, 194; Soviet, 277
Progressive Party, 229, 285
protests. See demonstrations
pseudonyms, 80
pseudoscience, 11–13
public education, 127–28, 135, 160–62, 252, 268
public housing, 68–69
Public Housing Authority. See Federal Public Housing Authority
public land, 265, 272
Pueblos, 164–66, 303, 304. See also San Ildefonso Pueblo; Santa Clara Pueblo
punishment: commodity withholding as, 134; at Klamath Indian Reservation, 87, 137; May-Johnson Bill and, 235–36. See also execution of Indians
pxs. See post exchanges

Quapaw Agency, 90, 192

Rabi, Isador, 81, 236
race-baiting, 219, 223
race relations: Chicago, 219–20; Klamath Falls, 258, 268; Los Alamos, 165; Portland, 1, 63, 67–68; San

Francisco Bay Area, 223, 340n22; Topaz, 148, 153, 197; Vanport, 161, 162, 198–203, 225. See also interracial couples; interracial dances; segregation
race riots, 15, 65. See also fear of race riots
racetracks: used to house Japanese evacuees, 60–61, 101
racial classification, 318n55
"Racial Conditions Unit" (FBI). See RACON
racial profiling, 309
racism, 296; in anthropology, 11–13; in education, 153, 162; enmification and, 14–15; in fiction, 14, 51; in housing (alleged), 122; Klamath Falls, 258; Los Alamos, 247; in unions, 66–67; in voter registration, 173. See also anti-Asian racism; fear of racism; institutional racism; redlining
racist legislation, 15, 297
RACON, 65, 66, 67, 76
radiation exposure, 209; health hazards, 302, 306, 307
radicals: arrest and deportation, 63; Nisei, 102. See also dissidents; fear of leftists and radicals; profiling of radicals
radio stations, 123
railroads, 47
Ramirez, Mari Carmen, 313n2
rape, 245
Reagan, Ronald, 295
real estate condemnation. See condemnation of real estate
Reber, Robert, 10
"red" and "reds" (labels), 6, 278, 279, 286
red-baiting, 230, 244

sawmills, 131, 132

scab laborers, 101, 195

schools, 69, 79, 101, 282; Klamath Indian Reservation, 136–39, 252, 256–57; Los Alamos, 167, 168, 211, 234, 243, 304; Navajo Reservation, 221; subsistence homesteaders and, 144; Topaz, 61, 152–54, 330n65–66; Vanport, 160–62, 198, 202, 228. *See also* college and universities; public schools

scientific laboratories. *See* laboratories, scientific

scientists, 16, 72–82, 117–19, 238, 283; AEC and, 236; bodyguards of, 207, 208, 338n83; censorship of, 206; fatal accidents of, 246; health hazards and, 209–10, 246; military induction and, 80–81; postwar conversion of Los Alamos and, 235; self-censorship, 72. *See also* Association of Los Alamos Scientists (ALAS); Jewish scientists; wives of scientists

Seaborg, Glenn, 209–10, 236

search and seizure, 123, 183, 207. *See also* seizure of personal property

searches of automobiles. *See* automobile searches

Seaton, Fred, 265

Seattle WA, 349n39

secrecy: Area 51 and, 307; Los Alamos and, 73–74, 79–80, 163, 207, 302, 305, 306–7; Los Alamos Pueblo speakers and, 165; Los Alamos regulations and, 205; postwar Los Alamos and, 232, 240, 245. *See also* confidentiality rules

Segrè, Claudio, 208

Segrè, Elfriede, 167, 205

Segrè, Emilio, 16, 75, 117

segregation, 198–200, 221, 223, 225, 268, 279; in barbershops, 247; in jobs, 220; Portland, 300; in U.S. Army, 191, 217; Vanport, 199, 337n63

seizure of land. *See* land seizure

seizure of personal property, 151–52, 218, 339n12

self-censorship, 72

Sells, Cato, 172

Senate Committee on Indian Affairs. *See* U.S. Senate: Committee on Indian Affairs

Senate Committee on Public Lands and Surveys. *See* U.S. Senate: Committee on Public Lands and Surveys

September 11, 2001, terrorist attacks, 298

Serber, Charlotte, 167

Serber, Robert, 77

servants, 131

settlers: Homestead Act and, 94–95; Oregon, 7, 37, 38, 39, 42–48

sex crimes, 208–9

sexually transmitted disease, 65

shame, 60, 215, 291

Sherwin, Martin, 207

Shimamoto, George, 109

Shimanouchi, Midori, 296

Shipyard Negro Organization for Victory (SNOV), 67, 70, 116

shipyard workers, 1, 64, 67–71, 110–16, 155–62, 225; African American, 185, 201; compared to scientists, 117; Indian, 255

Singapore, 55

sirens: use of at Los Alamos, 119, 203

sit-ins, 124

skull size, 11–12

sleep deprivation, 153

Smith, Alice Kimball, 120–21, 163

Smith, Henry Nash, 24
Smith Act, 278
Smith College, 214
Snake Paiutes, Yahooskin. *See* Yahooskin Snake Paiutes
snakes: Japanese compared to, 50
Snell, Earl, 186
SNOV. *See* Shipyard Negro Organization for Victory (SNOV)
social class: Los Alamos, 238, 304. *See also* classism
"socialist" and "socialistic" (labels), 143, 238; "socialism" in Los Alamos, 248, 343n68
Socialist Party, 190, 229
soldiers: Indian, 171–72, 173, 187; Nisei, 191, 202, 216, 291, 339n8
Soviet Union, 76; Internal Security Act (proposed) and, 277; invoked regarding BIA, 258; invoked regarding John Collier, 179; invoked regarding Vanport childcare services, 159; J. Robert Oppenheimer and, 77, 246, 302
special education, 161–62
spies and spying, 118, 245–46, 343n71; alleged, 76, 246, 302, 308–10
Stalin, Joseph, 286, 320n92
Stanford University, 262
stereotyping: of African Americans, 65–66, 199; of Indians, 186, 275; of Japanese, 12, 38, 51–52, 56, 190, 191
Stern, Theodore, 332n11
stigmatization, 69, 128, 230, 281
Stimson, Henry L., 75, 193
Stone, William G., 247
street names, 104, 240–41
strikes, 101–2, 194, 195, 197. *See also* general strikes
Strongheart, Nipo, 186

Studebaker, John, 126
students: conformity and, 128; Klamath, 136–38, 256–57; as laborers, 153; monitored for absenteeism, 183; as scab laborers, 101; at Topaz, 105–6, 153–54. *See also* colleges and universities: Japanese American students; dropouts; graduate students
subsistence homesteads and homesteaders, 127, 141–46, 156, 169–70
suicide, 273, 275
Supreme Court. *See* New Mexico: Supreme Court; U.S. Supreme Court
surveillance: of Leo Szilard, 75; Los Alamos, 74, 117, 245, 309; Portland, 341n38; Topaz, 3, 105, 196; Vanport, 201, 225; at WRA assembly centers, 101
Szilard, Leo, 18, 72, 75–76, 81, 117, 320n87

Tafoya, Cleto, 166
Taiwanese American scientists, 6, 308–10
Takahashi, Tomoye, 147
Takao Ozawa v. United States, 318n55
Takeshita, Ben, 60
Taney, Roger B., 48, 95
Tanforan racetrack, 60, 101, 104
taxation, 111, 234, 239, 342n57
Taylor, Quintard, 349n39
Taylor, Sandra, 83
teachers, 153, 160, 167
tear gas, 194
technology transfer, fear of. *See* fear of technology transfer
telephone call censorship, 206
Teller, Mici, 124, 208
termination of Indian reservations. *See* Indian reservations: termination

Terrill, Katherine, 323n42

Texas: Roma people bussed to, 64

threat of blacklisting. See blacklisting (threatened)

timber industry, 131, 138, 140, 172, 177, 178, 179; Klamath business council and, 270; Klamath termination and, 252–53, 259, 260, 265–66, 272

Tobin, Thomas, 185

Todd, Victor, 230, 341n38

Tolan, John H., 233

Tolan Commission, 53, 48–49, 59–60, 65, 223

Tolbert, Sherman, 61, 165, 216

Topaz Relocation Center, 2–3, 61, 71, 100–110, 188–98; armed guards, 105; as "barbed-wire democracy," 83, 84, 106–8, 115; clothing and, 150; clothing allowance, 328n49; compared to Los Alamos, 80; consumer co-ops, 149–51, 155; factionalism, 193, 219; housing, 148–49; as inverse utopia, 27; killing of James Wakasa and, 193–95; as kindergarten for Americanization, 29; labor by internees, 147–48, 197; leaves for college students, 214–15; Nisei soldiers and, 216–18; official closing, 224; official opening, 104; population, 19; powerlessness of residents, 20, 26, 295; resettlement and, 213–16, 218–24; schools in, 152–54; setting of, 5

Topaz Times, 114, 150, 194, 219

Tort Claims Act. See Federal Tort Claims Act

town councils: Los Alamos, 119–22, 123, 124, 238, 239, 241

trade restrictions, 155–56

traditional Indian practices: criminalization of, 87, 92. See also marriage, traditional Indian

traffic courts, 120–21

Trail of Broken Treaties, 288

trans-racial adoption, 275

travel restrictions, 56, 75, 80, 215

treaties, 7–8, 22; British-American, 37, 39, 40–41; Indian, 47–48, 66, 88, 90, 129, 130, 134, 213, 251–52. See also Oregon Treaty; Trail of Broken Treaties; Treaty of 1864

Treaty of 1864, 47–48, 88, 98, 130–31, 253, 288, 290

treaty payments, 131–32, 134, 180, 255, 256, 263, 264, 270; children and, 178, 256

tribal councils, 97, 177–78, 265, 266

tribal courts, 86–88, 177

tribal elections, 265, 290, 332n10

tribal factionalism, 141, 176, 178, 183, 254, 264, 265

tribal judges, 86–87

tribal police, 91–92, 132, 177, 182; FBI training, 183

Trujillo, Henry, 241

Truman, Harry S., 232–33, 236, 252, 291, 342n42

Tuck, James, 119

Tule Lake Relocation Center, 32, 183, 192, 195, 197

Tupper, Watson, 257

Turner, Frederick Jackson, 28–29, 126

Tuskegee Victory (ship), 185

UC. See University of California (UC)

Uchida, Yoshiko, 214

UFO sightings, 307

Umatilla Indian Reservation, 332n11

unemployment: Klamaths and, 264

uniformity, 146, 150. See also conformity

unions, 66–67, 76, 300
universities. *See* colleges and universities
University of California (UC), 76, 77, 168, 232, 239, 304–5
uranium, 207, 209, 210
Uranium Advisory Committee, 73
Urban League, 300
Urey, Harold, 323n42
U.S. Army: Corps of Engineers, 233, 300; 442nd Regimental Combat Team, 191, 202, 216, 251, 291, 293, 339n8; Indian wars, 38, 39, 44; Los Alamos and, 122, 123, 168–69; Special Engineer Detachment, 122, 211, 245. *See also* G-2; post exchanges; soldiers; Women's Army Corps (WACS)
U.S. Bank, 271, 274, 289
U.S.-Britain relations, 36–41
U.S. Census Bureau, 310
U.S. citizenship. *See* citizenship
U.S. Constitution: Fourteenth Amendment, 48, 49
U.S. Department of Energy, 303–4, 305
U.S. Department of Labor, 143, 305
U.S. Department of the Interior, 14, 45, 57, 58, 328n32; community policing and, 115–16; state-sponsored settlements and, 143; WRA internment camps and, 106, 146, 152, 189
U.S. Department of Veterans Affairs. *See* Veterans Administration (VA)
U.S. Department of War: Indians and, 44, 45, 93; Japanese American internment and, 57; Manhattan Project and, 75–76; Vanport and, 71
U.S. Forest Service, 289, 307
U.S. House of Representatives: Committee on Indian Affairs, 179, 189, 213; as model for Klamath

tribal council, 97. *See also* House Committee on Un-American Activities (HUAC); HR 7960
U.S. Immigration and Naturalization Service, 173
U.S. Maritime Commission, 68, 158
U.S. National Park Service, 290
U.S. Office of War Information. *See* Office of War Information (OWI)
U.S. Senate: Committee on Indian Affairs, 213, 254, 260–61; Committee on Interior and Insular Affairs, Subcommittee on Indian Affairs, 266; Committee on Public Lands and Surveys, 254–55; Investigating Committee on Military Expenditures, 342n42
U.S.S.R. *See* Soviet Union
U.S. Supreme Court, 49, 59, 106, 215, 222, 297, 318n55, 340n19
Utah: American voluntary migration and, 57; farm labor by Topaz internees and, 146–47. *See also* Oak City UT; Topaz Relocation Center
utopia, inverse, 24–31

Vanishing Fleets (Norton), 51
Vanport Child Service Center, 159, 225, 227
Vanport Citizens' Emergency Disaster Committee (VCEDC), 229–30, 285, 300
Vanport College, 226, 341n28
Vanport Interracial Council, 201
Vanport OR, 1–2, 8, 16, 21, 68–71, 110–16, 225–32, 273–74; childcare services and schools, 157–62, 198, 202, 228; compared to Indian reservations, 69, 70, 71; compared to Los Alamos, 80, 237–38; demographics,

Working Group to Address Los Alamos
    Health Concerns, 306
World War I, 15, 83, 171–73, 184
World War I veterans, 143
Wright, Ben, 45–46, 317n24
Wright, Richard, 28–29
Wyoming, 57

xenophobia. *See* fear of foreigners

Yahooskin Snake Paiutes, 7, 46, 275; as

farmers, 132; ruled by U.S.-picked
    Klamath, 86; treaties and, 47
Yamanaka, Morgan, 192
Yoneda, Elaine, 55–56
Young Democrats, 55, 102, 192

Zakoji, Hiroto, 32, 266–68, 269, 291,
    346n34
Zia Company, 237–39, 240, 241, 247;
    price regulation and, 244
zoning restrictions, 268–69